The American Farmer in the Eighteenth Century

The American Farmer in the Eighteenth Century

A Social and Cultural History

Richard Lyman Bushman

Yale
UNIVERSITY PRESS
NEW HAVEN AND LONDON

Published with assistance from the Annie Burr Lewis Fund.
Published with assistance from the Louis Stern Memorial Fund.

Yale University Press books may be purchased in quantity for educational, business, or promotional use. For information, please e-mail sales.press@yale.edu (U.S. office) or sales@yaleup.co.uk (U.K. office).

Set in Fournier type by IDS Infotech, Ltd.
Printed in the United States of America.

Library of Congress Control Number: 2017942158
ISBN 978-0-300-22673-7 (hardcover: alk. paper)

A catalogue record for this book is available from the British Library.

This paper meets the requirements of ANSI/NISO Z39.48-1992 (Permanence of Paper).

10 9 8 7 6 5 4 3 2 1

For Claudia Bushman

Contents

Preface

Twenty years ago, my wife, Claudia Bushman, and I decided to work together on a farm book. To get a feeling for the life, we went to county fairs and struck up conversations about hogs and corn. We leapt at the chance to see tobacco sprouts put in the ground in North Carolina. We talked with rice and walnut farmers in California and cattle ranchers in Utah. We repeatedly visited farm museums like Old Sturbridge Village. Eventually, Claudia struck out on her own to write a book on John Walker, a pre–Civil War Virginia farmer whose diary she had discovered (*In Old Virginia: Slavery, Farming, and Society in the Journal of John Walker*, Johns Hopkins University Press, 2002). I labored on in hopes of constructing a broad outline of farm lives in Britain's North American colonies in the eighteenth century.

I cannot explain my fascination with agriculture. I have no farmers in my immediate background. One great-grandfather farmed forty acres in Utah County south of Salt Lake City in the late nineteenth century; another raised hay in Garfield County, Utah. Since then, no one in my family has farmed; both of my grandfathers found jobs in town. My experience as a twelve-year-old picking strawberries for six cents a pound on truck farms in the Columbia River Basin west of Portland did not inspire a desire to know more. Nor did I begin with a historiographical problem or a demanding question about how the agricultural economy worked. I was motivated only by a desire to understand farmers. I wanted to know how they thought, their strategies for getting on, the obstacles and dangers they faced, their fears and hopes. I aspired to write a social and cultural history of eighteenth-century farmers.

As I learned more, I was struck by the secure base that farming provided for British North American society in the eighteenth century. The tens of thousands of farms planted up and down the coast and spreading into the mountains formed a great productive system that yielded the bulk of what was needed to sustain life. When European population growth in the eighteenth century left the continent short of food, the American population, although expanding at a far faster rate, continued to supply its own needs and much of Europe's besides. Despite meteoric growth, starvation and shortages were never problems. Without any management or government directives, the population swarmed onto the land and went to work. No one had to prod farmers to produce food. Given the opportunity, they eagerly made the most of the continent's ample resources.

This simple fact, I realized, brought to light the most basic imperative of farm culture. Farmers strove to provide for themselves. They wanted land because it allowed them to grow and make what they required to live. As I looked more closely, it became clear that the most fundamental aim of all farmers in all regions and at all levels was self-provisioning. Even on southern plantations, nearly half of everything that was produced was consumed by the people who produced it, and on smaller farms the proportion was even higher. On every kind of farm, a basic subsistence economy underlay every other form of production. In North and South, small farmers and great planters grew corn and hogs, raised cattle and milked cows. They sheared wool from sheep and made leather from animal hides. They made soap and candles from ashes and fat. They obtained lumber and fuel from their woodlots and planted apple trees. They wove cloth or brought spinners and weavers into their households. Farmers of all kinds made a concerted effort to satisfy their own basic needs.

Moreover, others who would not be called farmers, such as merchants, ministers, and tradesmen, had the same goal. They acquired land to support animals, grow corn, and raise vegetables. The desire to secure a subsistence from the land motivated nearly everyone. This core domestic economy, driven by family needs, constituted the secure foundation on which all other forms of production and trade rested. Subsistence production was sorely missed in the 1930s when most of the population had no land to fall back on in a time of economic stress, forcing the nation to resort to other forms of social security.

Farmers' compulsion to provision their own families did not interfere with production for the market. Subsistence farming and commercial farming were once considered opposite ends of a spectrum. Small, poor farmers, so it was believed, provided only for themselves with little left over to trade; more prosperous farmers and great planters sent crops to market. It is now clear that all eighteenth-century farmers did both. All provisioned themselves, and all were avid traders. Large planters marketed tobacco, rice, and indigo through elaborate commercial networks, building up credit for purchasing fine cloth and stylish furniture. More modest farmers sold animal pelts, wool, barrels of meat, wheat, and firewood. With the returns, they purchased fabric, buttons, sugar, and rum for comfort and pleasure. Even the smallest farmers were eager to truck and barter. The market was not their enemy; it was a necessary component of their domestic economy. They pursued these exchanges for the same reason they produced food—to add to family well-being.

Family was foremost in their thinking. Farmers' accounts show no signs of seeking profits in the capitalist sense. When British agricultural reformers asked about the return on agricultural investment, farmers were at a loss. They accumulated land, tools, animals, and household comforts for their families and then went on to acquire luxuries such as snuff, rum, sugar, and fine cloth. Farmers did not measure their achievement by abstractions like profit. Their aim was to flourish. Most of the violence and struggle of eighteenth-century farmers—fights over titles, resistance to the Revolutionary War draft, protests against debt collection, demands for currency—occurred when events threatened their livelihood on the land. They fought for family.

The pursuit of family well-being formed the overarching framework of North American agriculture. The mingling of domestic production and trade constituted the basic strategy of all farmers. Within this framework, however, the variations were immense. New England farmers supported themselves on eighty-acre family farms. Carolina and Virginia planters raised rice and tobacco on plantations of five thousand acres or more. Small farmers barely survived; great planters acquired fabulous wealth. Going from North to South, the labor systems varied widely. Family labor predominated in New England, tenants and cottagers in the Middle Colonies, and slavery from Maryland south. Farms and plantations operated on different work calendars and cultivated different crops. New Englanders spent much of their summer haying; most southern farmers provided little fodder for their cattle, letting them forage for themselves in the winter. Climate led to sharply different agricultural regimens within the common framework of self-provisioning and trade.

When it came to telling the story of North American farming, the differences from section to section required more attention than the common practices. The similarities are summed up in my first and second chapters; most of the rest of the book describes the differences. Chapter 3, "The Nature of the South," analyzes the origins of South and North as distinct sections. Chapter 4, "Generation of Violence," pauses in the analysis of differences to describe the stress created by an expanding population in all sections as farmers strove to find land for their children. In the succeeding chapters, Connecticut, Pennsylvania, and Virginia represent New England, the Middle Colonies, and the South in a more fine-grained analysis of sectional variations. These three places also represent periods: Connecticut the first half of the century; Pennsylvania the pre-Revolutionary period; and Virginia the Revolution and after. Through them, I look at how farmers responded to the great national events that swept over them as the colonies became a nation. To conclude, I look ahead to the twentieth century.

Along the way, I try to recover farm culture. I note patterns of thought and characteristic forms of knowledge. What maps and schedules guided farmers' thinking? What facts mattered to them? These mentalities weave through the story of how farm families sustained themselves and sought to flourish three hundred years ago in British North America.

I cannot say that the book has taken twenty years to complete because of my lack of time. I have enjoyed yearlong fellowships at the Huntington Museum, the National Humanities Center, and the American Antiquarian Society. I have a particularly warm place in my heart for the generous and perceptive people who managed these centers of learning: Roy Ritchie at the Huntington, Kent Mullikin at the National Humanities Center, and Paul Erickson at the American Antiquarian Society. These great research centers are powerful engines of historical scholarship. The entire profession is in their debt. Claudia and I also enjoyed six heavenly weeks at the Rockefeller Foundation's Bellagio Center on Lake Como, reflecting on farmers and explaining our work to the assembled company.

In the final stages, I relied on friends in the profession to tell me whether I was making sense: Alan Taylor, Richard Brown, Daniel Howe, Jack Larkin, David Hall, Patricia M. Schaefer, Lucia Stanton, Jefferson Looney, and Barbara Oberg read chapters. Laurel Ulrich gathered graduate students to criticize a chapter on the South. Grant Wacker read every word and offered sage advice. Andrew Kimball, an extraordinarily talented and tactful editor, read the entire manuscript and showed me how to reduce its length while improving its coherence. At the end, Chris Rogers, about to retire as editor at Yale University Press, gave useful advice on how to position the book. His successor, Jean Thomson Black, took his place in shepherding the manuscript through production. Michael Deneen and Dan Heaton answered many technical questions. Dan judiciously edited the final text.

Talks at Clark University, the University of Connecticut, the USC-Huntington Early Modern Studies Institute, the University of California at Davis, Stanford University, the Agricultural History Society, and the American Antiquarian Society helped to bring my thoughts into focus. I benefited immensely from visits to farms, where we talked with Corbin Sharp in North Carolina about tobacco, with the friends of Dan and Elaine Jorgensen about ranching in Utah, and with Rebecca Williams's parents, Nancy and Terry Williams, about rice and walnut production in northern California.

My daughter Clarissa Bushman helped at key moments, and Claudia Bushman read every word. Because of her own studies of farmers, she could answer questions about farming that puzzled me. Claudia has worked on everything I have written, but on this book more than any. The dedication to her is long overdue.

PART ONE

Farm Thought

1. The Farm Idea

The Life Plans of Family Farmers

In the aftermath of the Revolution, Hector St. John de Crèvecoeur, the French immigrant turned British citizen, asked in his *Letters from an American Farmer:* What is an American? His answer: "Some few towns excepted, we are all tillers of the earth, from Nova Scotia to West Florida. We are a people of cultivators."[1] Economic historians estimate that three-quarters of the United States population in 1790 made their livings from farms. We can scarcely think about American society in the eighteenth century without imagining farmers. Farm culture was embodied everywhere, enacted in a thousand particulars. In my other works as an early American historian, farmers have stood in the background. This book puts them at center stage. What was their experience as farmers? How did they think?[2]

Agriculture in eighteenth-century North America was a vast, diverse, and fruitful industry. At the time of the Revolution, when the population was more than two million, there were perhaps 300,000 farms.[3] Besides feeding the entire colonial population, farmers filled the holds of the ships leaving colonial ports each year for destinations around the Atlantic.[4] According to custom records, 70 percent of the products flowing outward from the colonies to the Caribbean, Europe, and Great Britain came from farms. Only the fisheries came close to agriculture in contributing to the cargoes. Measured by value, four times as much beef and pork was exported as ship masts.[5] Agricultural production overshadowed all other sources of goods.

Beyond the three-quarters of the population counted as farmers by historians, many others farmed a little. In his diary for 1770, the eminent Dedham, Massachusetts, clergyman Jason Havens recorded the usual round of ministerial work, preaching, funerals, and trips to Boston, then casually added "Mr. Mullen bo't Two Cows of me," and a little later "killed 2 Pigs."[6] Havens would never be called a farmer, yet he owned cattle and land which he supervised himself. He included farming in his diary as naturally as the weather. In the Chesapeake, Lorena Walsh has found, "even professionals such as ministers, lawyers, physicians, and merchants as well as established artisans at a minimum produced most of the food that their families ate."[7] Crèvecoeur spoke of "Mèchanicks who are ½ farmers themselves."[8] Farming has been thought of as an exclusive vocational identity like lawyer or carpenter. But it was also an activity, like gardening, that could be combined with other work. Many who were identified with other occupations also farmed.

Farming infiltrated towns and cities. The town lots laid out by Andrew Hamilton in Lancaster, Pennsylvania, in 1730 reached back 245 feet to allow for gardens and outbuildings. In addition, Hamilton granted forty-five-acre lots on the outskirts for more serious farming, because "the people would not be satisfied without them."[9] Jackson Turner Main found more laborers than farmers in eighteenth-century Connecticut, suggesting the presence of a large working class and a minority of farmers, but many of these laborers were actually on the farm track. Very few bachelors younger than twenty-five owned land. They worked for wages and bided their time. By age forty, 60 percent of the adult male population had become primarily farmers; in addition, some who had entered the professional class or become artisans also owned farms. Landless men were often farmers by aspiration.[10] The author of *American Husbandry* noted in 1775 that "no mechanic or artisan—sailor—soldier—servant, &c. but what, if they get money, take land, and turn farmers."[11] Farming as an activity spread far and wide, thwarting any attempt at a precise definition of its outer limits. It drew people of all occupations to it, as if it were an essential component of a complete household economy.

Farming had less to do with scale than with an idea. In rudimentary form, the idea was that a family with land could provide most of what it needed for itself by its own labor using its own resources—something no other occupation could promise. Moreover, it could produce sufficient surplus to trade for the remainder of the essentials and a few luxuries. This desire for self-sufficiency applied to farms of all kinds. Large rice plantations worked by gangs of slaves in the Carolinas and small holders barely scraping by with family labor in Nova Scotia both sought to provision themselves. The principle applied to farmers who worked land they owned or land they leased, who employed slaves or relied solely on themselves and their children, who marketed immensely valuable staples or skimmed off a surplus from their family provisions. The variety was immense, but all farms, of every size, pursued basic self-provisioning.[12] The promise of self-sufficiency attracted people to farming in many forms. If a family had no land, it tried to get a tiny parcel for grazing a cow. If family members were artisans or merchants, they raised their own food on an acre or two. Artisans, professional men, and the poor became partial farmers in hopes of providing for themselves.

In conception, the farm idea promised security. In reality, disease, drought, falling prices, debt, illness, family disputes, and failed crops often defeated farm plans. People were forever losing their land, dropping into the ranks of the poor, succumbing to debt or their own imprudence. In virtually every community, a large proportion of the households were landless. Farmers felt cheated by merchants and greedy government officials. Taxes imposed an onerous burden. Merely to maintain a competence—that is, to supply the family's needs day by day and provide for the next generation—was an accomplishment to be envied.[13] No matter their success in years past, the next year could doom them. But sustaining farmers through all the adversity was the potential of the farm idea, the belief that with land and their own labor, the family could provide for themselves with a surplus to trade. No matter the repeated setbacks, the farm idea was strong enough to renew hope in each generation. From the first years of settlement to the end of the nineteenth century, the number of farms multiplied generation after generation, sustained by the elusive potential of a farm.

Farm Logic

The practical workings of the farm economy can be found in the account books where farmers recorded their obligations to trading partners and neighbors. Account books are surprising for their omissions as well as for their inclusions. For readers with modern expectations, the accounts leave out the very point of bookkeeping in other contexts, the calculation of profit. No one asked how much they had come out ahead, much less the return on capital. Farmers' accounts had another purpose. David Minor, a Stonington, Connecticut, farmer, assigned two pages to each of the neighbors with whom he exchanged work and goods. On one page, Minor listed the services he performed for the neighbor or the goods delivered; on the facing page, he noted what the neighbor did for him. For one neighbor, Minor built a wall, spent two and a half days digging potatoes, supplied a bushel and a half of turnips, and wove linen, each item specified with a date and a money value. In turn, the neighbor performed work, supplied goods, or paid in cash, which Minor recorded on the facing page. Every year or so, they would have a reckoning at which they balanced accounts. One entry noted: "Stonington, January 15th, 1767. Then Mr. William Denison and I Reckoned and Balanced all accounts from the Beginning of the world to this day." The moment of reckoning was not always recorded so dramatically. Usually Minor simply put a large X through the list of obligations, indicating they had been settled.[14] In each case, the object was to come out even, to be sure each party had met his obligations.

The object of accounting, like national accounts today, was not to calculate profits but to stay in balance. The United States government does not try to determine the profits made in the nation's trade with China; the point of national accounts is to see how far exports and imports are out of balance. Farmers thought basically the same way. The farm family's aim was to keep in balance with the world outside the household.[15]

Farmers showed no signs of thinking like capitalists who measure their success by the return on capital. The anonymous author of *American Husbandry*, apparently a capitalist-minded British agricultural reformer, tried to calculate the profitability of American farms. He assembled information about the costs of purchasing and opening farms in the colonies and compared it with the revenue to be expected in a few years. His aim was to estimate in capitalist fashion the rate of return on the original investment. In 1775 he published the results, specifying the rate of return colony by colony coming down the coast. No one in America showed any interest in the book, nor could American farmers calculate for themselves the return on their own investments. Their bookkeeping system did not record the required information. By capitalist standards, American farmers were irrational and showed no interest in changing their ways.[16]

The logic of their accounts imposed another discipline on farmers. Much like households today, they sought to increase income and reduce outgo. The higher the income and the lower the debts, the greater the likelihood of staying in balance. To increase income, farmers performed services like Minor's work for Denison, and to decrease outgo, they purchased as little as possible. They made things rather than incurring a debt by buying them. They spun their own flax, raised their own food, made their own shoes. From their woodlots, they obtained timber for their houses and fuel for their fireplaces. When it came to working wood, Crèvecoeur noted, farmers had tools and "most of us are skillful Enough to use them with some dexterity in mending & making whatever is wanted on the farm."[17] The reason for putting so much effort into family sustenance was the skein of debts in which the family was entangled. To stay out of trouble, farmers had to minimize their debts. Just as Britain sought to produce all of its vital needs within the Empire, farmers sought to make all they could within the household and thus keep debt at a minimum.

This was the reasoning behind the small farm operations set up by apparent nonfarmers—artisans, storekeepers, and professionals. People doing other kinds of work bought land, pastured a few cows, planted fruit trees, kept geese so they could meet their own needs and minimize purchases of essentials. They made no money from their efforts, but they kept down costs. All along the farming spectrum, the object of subsistence production was to keep in balance with the world.[18]

A better name for household production than "subsistence" is "self-provisioning." Subsistence farming implies the achievement of some minimal level of survival as the goal, as if the family could provide for itself and nothing more. "Self-provisioning" implies not the achievement of a bare minimum but the aim of producing as much as a family could for itself, however much went to market. In this sense, every eighteenth-century farmer in North America was a self-provisioning farmer. No matter how involved in production for the market or in exchanges with neighbors, all farms, large or small, partial or well balanced, relied on a core household economy to satisfy most of the family's wants.[19] Self-provisioning constituted the largest single component of the agricultural economy. Nearly half of everything produced in the British colonies—half of the GNP, as it were—was produced and consumed at home. Some historians estimate 75 percent.[20]

The alternative to self-provisioning was pure market farming, the predecessor of today's commercial farm. West Indian planters put their land in sugar and bought their food from North America, just as wheat farmers today buy packaged bread in the grocery store. The returns on sugar were too high to devote land and labor to corn and cattle. For a few decades, seventeenth-century Chesapeake tobacco planters inclined in the West Indian direction. They raised their food and gathered their own fuel, but imported cloth and leather. The returns on their tobacco paid for imported fabric. That was not to last. Over the course of the century, the reliance on imports declined. When tobacco prices fell near the end of the century, planters began to divert more of their resources to self-provisioning. They had their workers spin yarn and tan leather for shoes. The number of estate inventories with spinning wheels jumped from less than 15 percent before 1720 to more than 50 percent after 1740. Planters marketing thousands of pounds of tobacco each year became increasingly self-sufficient in rough cloth.[21] Because of their greater resources, the great planters became perhaps the most proficient self-provisioners. Everywhere, the production of market crops rested on the foundation of a self-provisioning domestic economy.

That was not all families consumed, of course. The great planters went far beyond household production in their consumption habits, and so did many lesser households. Families strove to raise the level of their living by purchasing tea and coffee, snuff, sugar, rum, imported cloth, and decorations like buttons and cuff links, tea cups, and mahogany furniture.[22] But striving for social improvement did not diminish production for household consumption. The high-living William Byrd rarely purchased any of the rudiments for basic sustenance. "I have no bills to pay," he boasted to an English acquaintance, "and a half-a-crown will rest undisturbed in my pockets for many moons together."[23] He made all the basics on his own plantation. He sent off many hogsheads of tobacco to British markets to purchase luxuries—fine furniture, books, ceramics, and silk—and still produced food for himself and his slaves.

The self-provisioning farm economy generated a work culture of a particular cast. Crèvecoeur said of his fellow farmers, each was "an universal Fabricator Like Crusoe."[24] The effort to be self-sufficient instilled a mentality something like the survival strategies of Daniel Defoe's fictional Robinson Crusoe after he was shipwrecked on a South Atlantic island. Like Crusoe, farmers tried to make do with whatever was at hand. Crusoe made his house, his food, his furniture. He was always on the lookout for whatever would serve his purposes. He used canvas and rope from his wrecked ship, adapted a cave as a house and fortress, domesticated wild goats, used trees to build a fence. To make a lamp, he derived tallow from wild goats, baked a small dish made of clay, and used oakum for a wick. Crusoe learned to make nearly everything he needed. "I found at last that I wanted nothing but I could have made it, especially if I had had tools." If he could not make an implement like a wheelbarrow, he fashioned a hod instead.[25]

Like Crusoe, farmers cobbled together land, tools, skills, and animal products to make all they could for themselves; each farmer was, as Crèvecoeur said, a "universal Fabricator." "Every man here understands to spin his own Yarn & to lie his own Ropes."[26] Farmers were constantly improvising, making do, getting by. They managed piecemeal. Bricolage, the assembly of a product from whatever tools and materials were at hand, was their method. The bricolage mentality showed up in estate inventories with their odd-lot collections of tools, utensils, animals, furniture. Each inventory was unique, each with strange gaps and incongruous combinations. Each farmer possessed the equipment that circumstances allowed him to accumulate. Bricolage was manifest at estate auctions where neighbors came to purchase a tool or a piece of furniture, adding to the assortment of goods they already owned. People put together what they could from the resources available. Bricolage is evident too in the imbalances of land and animals in tax appraisals. Farmers purchased property when they had the chance, but rarely assembled a perfect balance of tillage, pasture, meadow, and woodlots. The same spirit governed the work agendas that farmers put together each day. Farmers' diaries and account books show them dipping into this job and that, moving around the landscape to whatever site provided employment or an exchange of goods, fitting their efforts to the demands of their crops and animals. They were men of piecemeal minds, ever alert for opportunities to sell produce, rent out a skill, or lend a son's labor, adapting every day to small openings in the local economy.

Family Farming

The work, the planning, the adaptability recorded in the pages of the account books all originated in families. To imagine farm lives three centuries ago, we must return to a time when family life and the economy blended to a degree unknown today. Farm men and boys worked in their own barnyards and fields. Artisan shops were attached to the house or stood nearby. Women and girls cooked and preserved in the house and garden. People did not "go" to work. Work space, living space, and owned space coincided. The same blend carried over to authority. Work authority and family authority were one. In the eighteenth century, fathers and mothers were always the bosses. They governed during the workday and at night, in the house and in the fields. Children worked at whatever tasks their parents assigned them.

Plantations functioned in the same way. Slaves and servants were considered family, in the sense that father-planters took responsibility for treating their sicknesses and keeping them in line much as fathers cared for their free children. Plantation wives had production responsibilities with a slave workforce to carry them out. Sons of planters learned the business from their fathers and at death took over in their stead. The organization of large plantations followed family lines. The family farm was not just one type of farming in early America. The blending of family and the economy applied to virtually everyone.

The melding of family and economy affected nearly every aspect of life. On the family farm, gender relations and parent-child relationships were largely defined by work and ownership. The patriarchal father-husband owned the property and by right assigned the labor. A good husband was a good husbandman. The two roles intermingled, as did wife and huswife. A woman's role in marriage consisted of bearing children and doing her work in the household economy. Love was expressed by cooking meals, making butter, spinning, and gardening. For children, it was the same. They accepted the father's right to work them for no pay. The children obeyed because he was their father. Work bonds and family ties were interwoven. Some children went to school, but they learned the skills of husbandry and huswifery within the family. The system was highly efficient. Family, household production, and education for life were synonymous.[27]

The combination of home and workplace meant that thinking about the farm and thinking about the family were intertwined. Farm families did not farm to make a profit. They farmed to flourish as a family. As the historian Peter Laslett said of English farm families: "Working the land, managing, nurturing a 'family' were then one and the same thing, and could no more be 'rationalized' than the cherishing of a wife or the bringing up of children."[28] As Laslett suggests, family farmers did not manage their operations as strict capitalists would to improve profits. Farm parents could not fire incompetent workers when they fell down on the job; the workers were their children. They could not cut back on growing vegetables when grain was more profitable because the family ate the vegetables. Farmers could not comply with a rationality that hurt the family when sustaining the family was the purpose of farm life.[29]

To achieve well-being, families operated in two economies, the self-provisioning economy of the household and the exchange economy where they bartered and sold. In practice, production for the household and production for exchange blended imperceptibly; the same people did the work using the same tools and the same land. But the two economies functioned on different principles. One was a market economy; the other was not. Outside the household, buying and selling prevailed; everything was assigned a price. Within the household, there was no buying and selling, no setting of prices, no exchanges, no market. Nothing was a commodity; everything was for use.[30] Workers consumed what they produced. Food, fuel, building materials and clothing were made and used without having been bought or sold. Family production was subject to the whims of weather and disease but not to market vacillations. Food went from the hands of the parents to the mouths of children without a value ever being assigned.

Inside the household, there was no labor market. Children did not apply for jobs or bargain for wages. They always had work and never got paid. The same was true for slaves. No one applied for a job or was hired. There was no job market. No one received wages. Family workers were never fired, no matter how badly they performed. Children worked because they were children, and parents instructed the children until they learned how. Slaves worked because they were forced to. The core domestic farm economy, by far the largest single component of the North American economy, constituted a precapitalist, nonmarket family economy enclosed within the market economy beyond the household.[31]

This partial isolation from the market was one reason the farm was so secure. Self-provisioning, the supply of the essentials for life, carried on whatever the ups and downs in the encompassing market economy. The whims of nature affected home production but not the vagaries of the capitalist marketplace. This buffered domestic economy, encased within the market economy, enabled farmers to ride out whatever storms originated in European and continental markets, securing the basic welfare of the farm population against external disruptions. The shrinkage of this self-provisioning economy in the twentieth century required massive reorientations of government and society to sustain families who had lost this elemental safety net.

The ideology that sustained the social relations of family production was patriarchy, the unquestioned assumption that authority resided rightfully in the father, and all were obligated to follow him. Patriarchy did not have to be trumpeted or preached; it seemed completely natural. Fathers governed by right of having generated their children. According to a New England aphorism, "Disobedience to Parents is against the Lawes of Nature and Nations." The father, like the king, governed by divine right. The basis of chattel slavery could be questioned; the authority of fathers could not.[32] To patriarchy was added the imperative of survival. The brute facts of farming meant that the family had to work. Everyone knew their lives depended on it. Much as children may have resented their father's heavy hand, they knew that only constant toil kept them from hunger. Reality as well as ideology was on the father's side.

Matthew Patten and the Local Economy

This mixture of household and market economies on the eighteenth-century farm comes together in the account books and diaries of actual farmers. In their pages, the various household economies are made visible. Account books record transactions with neighbors, storekeepers, and artisans with whom the farmers had dealings. Farmers assigned a page to each account and recorded obligations and payments for each person. Diaries, as the name implies, were a day-by-day record of events and transactions. Diaries were the raw material for account books, with a few added details like the subject of the weekly sermon, the weather, and illness. Diaries contained a daily record of business transactions, which could be extracted and arranged into individual accounts for easy reckoning when farmers settled up with their trading partners.[33]

One of the best, the diary of Matthew Patten (1719–95) of Bedford, New Hampshire, reveals the world governed by the farm idea. Patten migrated with his parents from Ireland to New England in 1728 and settled in Bedford a decade later. In 1750 he married Elizabeth McMurphy. By the time of his marriage, he was already near the top of the community's wealth pyramid, as measured by taxes levied. From 1771 until his death, he was justice of the peace, then judge of probate, representative to the General Court, and member of the governor's council for a year. His extant diary picks up in June 1754 and continues until 1788, though it probably commenced earlier and continued longer. He and Elizabeth had eleven children, the first born seven months after their marriage. At least nine of the children grew to adulthood.[34]

Patten's diary from July 1754 through June 1755 averaged about eighteen entries a month, about one every other day. He faithfully recorded the scripture text of each Sabbath's sermon and briefly noted illness in the family. In March 1755, he recorded the death of his infant namesake. "Our youngest Child was Taken sick a little before night very bad he Continued till Thursday about the middle of the afternoon and then Departed this Life. He was thirteen months and 20 days old."[35] Mostly Patten briefly noted business dealings: work he did for others and they for him, items bought and sold, money lent and borrowed. The book is an account of obligations, his obligations to others and theirs to him.

On first sight, the center of Patten's economy is hard to locate. What was his occupation? The first entry notes "makeing sashes being 132 squares," a fairly large order of windows for someone's house. A few entries later, he made "a smoothing plain for John" and "a fore plain for Robt Walker." Soon after he delivered a cupboard and a table, later a frame for a looking glass. Throughout the year, he made gun stocks. This is not rough carpentry; Patten charged £3 for stocking a gun.[36] Such items required skill. He was somewhere between a carpenter and a joiner.

Then as winter approached, Patten went hunting and "Catched a sable."[37] All through the winter, he gathered raccoon and fox pelts. He borrowed traps, lent traps, and had them made. Some of the animals he trapped himself, other pelts he traded for. During the winter and spring, he accumulated fifty-three pelts, more than half of them sable, at an average price of less than £1 each. In April, he sold a bundle of pelts in Newbury for £71 and another batch of raccoon skins in Boston for £7. For this year at least, he was a fur trader. Besides all this, he surveyed property lines, drafted titles, and helped settle estates.[38] He was a man of many trades, an opportunist.

Yet behind this pastiche of many transactions can be seen a farmstead. Whatever else he did, Patten also grew crops and raised cattle. He mowed hay, broke up new ground, bought a scythe, killed a heifer, slaughtered a hog. The diary is filled with entries like: "Jerrett Rowan and his wife and Smith Kennedy Junr wife helping me reap rie."[39] Later he takes the rye to the miller to be ground into meal.[40] He was definitely farming in the background of his active trading life.

The point of the account book, however, was not to describe the farm. The domestic farm economy is largely invisible in the diary. Patten's wife is rarely mentioned during the year; Patten notes when she receives payment for a loan, or when the two of them go to visit her parents. Yet we know she was hard at work in the kitchen, garden, and barn. When his children got older, they would labor away at their chores without being mentioned in the diary. Patten's indentured servant Benjamin Linkfield appears occasionally, yet every day he was at work on the farm without note. No mention is made of him cutting firewood and feeding the livestock in winter. He turns up in the account book when he works for others.[41] Work on the farm itself is mentioned only when money values are involved—an obligation to hired workers or the value of a slaughtered animal. The father-farmer Patten is involved in every transaction in the account book. The other farm people, consisting of wives, children, servants, hired hands, and slaves—more than 80 percent of the farm population—rarely appear. They labored as diligently as the father-farmer yet rarely surface in the records.

The account book, then, is notable for its silences as well as for its voices. It implies the existence of an unrecorded household economy standing alongside an economy of record. One required accounts, the other did not. One assigned prices like all market exchanges, the other never did. Children received no compensation for their labor any more than they paid for their room and board. Yet work went on every day; the labors of the entire family were devoted constantly to production. The diary was as silent about this household economy as it was articulate about the exchange economy.

In reality, the two, rather than being isolated from one another, were interlaced. The account book was a record of points where the domestic and the exchange economies joined. Patten noted when he sold something produced by the family that was headed for outside markets, and he also traced the completion of products that were made for household consumption but had to be finished outside of the household. Much of household production could not be completed without engaging the town. The most obvious instance was Patten's trips to James Moor's mill to have his grain ground into meal.[42] The rye grown at home with family labor was useless to the family until it passed through Moor's mill. The toll paid to the miller was not an affront or a contradiction but a continuation of the self-provisioning economy. Growing and milling were parts of a single process.

To provision his household, Patten repeatedly called upon resources in Bedford and surrounding towns to supplement the family's efforts. Akin to grinding meal was the cutting of cherry and maple logs that he had sawed into planks at Major Goffe's mill for his joinery practice. Patten cut the trees himself, hauled the logs to Goffe's, had them sawed, then carried the planks home. Shoes came along in the same way. Hides were a by-product of the animals Patten slaughtered, but first they had to be taken to the tanner and currier and then to the shoemaker. Lieutenant Barron (who two weeks earlier had pulled Patten's tooth) tanned a nine-pound cowhide, which Patten then took to Chester to be curried. At the end of the year, he picked up the "remainder of my sole Leather and upper Leather and Carried it to Noah Thayers to Get a pair of shoes made for Cutting and John."[43] Patten managed the whole process. He began with the hide from his own barnyard, paid Barron to tan it, and ended with Thayer stitching the leather into shoes. All the while he moved effortlessly between his nonmarket family economy and the exchange economy in the town, integrating community resources into his family's domestic economy. Almost everything Patten did was woven into the communal economy.[44]

During the year, Patten dealt with 170 different persons in several hundred transactions.[45] His method was to produce as much as he could himself and then to deploy local resources to finish the job. Trade was not a single exchange between the farmer and the storekeeper. In 1754–55, the account book does not record a single occasion when Patten brought his harvest into the store to pay off the year's bill for imported goods. Patten went to stores to buy thread and buttons and sent others for sugar and salt, making payments in cash he had accumulated from other transactions, such as his pelt trade. He bought five pair of brass hinges, fourteen fishhooks, and a scythe.[46] But the store visits, critical as they were, are overshadowed by hundreds of other transactions in which Patten buys and sells, lends and borrows, works for others, and has them work for him. Farmers made use of land, tools, skills, and animals to make some things and barter for others. Trade at the store for imports was one node of a multifaceted communal exchange network.

Over the past half-century, historians have asked how this colonial economy made the transition to capitalism. Was the highly entrepreneurial Patten already a capitalist, or did farmers have to undergo an elemental alteration to function in a capitalist economy? How close was Patten to Adam Smith's vision? To make the transition to capitalism, farmers did not have to learn to trade.[47] Buying and selling came as naturally to Patten as planting and harvesting. What had to give way for capitalist farming to reach full flower was the elemental urge to provision the family by its own efforts. Change would come when the farm family wanted products its members could not make themselves, like carpets and stylish furniture or books and prints. In time, the family would come to believe that to flourish in a more genteel world, it would need items available only through purchase, and to get them, the family would have to increase its income. The family had to acquire the means to purchase desirables that were beyond its powers to manufacture, and improved income could be achieved only by specializing in crops that yielded the highest returns.

The transition from making to purchasing and from varied forms of production to specialization would lead farmers to see their communities differently. Everything about Patten's economy led to an intense localism. Markets in Boston and abroad were only vaguely represented in his accounts. He was much more fixed on people close by. Except for visits to Boston now and then, Patten worked within a small circle of towns around Bedford. His buying and selling in these places required him to concentrate on people and situations in his local sphere of activity. He had to know what people needed, what they were capable of, how he could use them. He was involved with many of them in ongoing obligations and credit relations. His thoughts were constantly on his neighbors.

In the transition to capitalism, the communal economy would be eroded. Farmers would stop seeing the towns in their immediate vicinity as markets and resources. They would give up on finding local help in making shoes, weaving cloth, and grinding grain. They would stop moving from skill to skill and from product to product in search of items for local exchange. To become proper participants in a capitalist system, farmers would turn their attention to distant places where the best prices could be obtained for their major crops. The rich, variegated, incessant transactions within the community would be curtailed in favor of commerce with faraway cities and markets. Instead of dealing close to home, families would sell to distant places and buy from distant manufacturers. Systems would be constructed for carrying their produce to the places where the best price was to be had and in bringing back items that farm families now could not make themselves. Impersonal forms of credit would be necessary to facilitate long-distance transactions. Within the community, friendships and neighborliness did not necessarily have to give way.[48] But the constant din of local exchanges found in Patten's account book would diminish. All that happened gradually over a century and a half as eighteenth-century farming underwent the transition to modern capitalist agriculture.

Imperial Families

Complex self-provisioning such as Patten's was the first pillar of eighteenth-century farm thinking. The second was provision for children as they entered adulthood. Families lived by an annual production calendar that sustained family members from day to day; at the same time, they followed a long plan that extended to the end of their lives. The long view aimed at the point when their offspring would break free to begin independent lives. Farm parents' long-term goal was to set up their children in their own households. As John Murrin summed up these intentions: "The most distinctive feature of settler households was the patriarch's goal. He hoped to pass on his status to all of his sons and to marry his daughters to young men of comparable status."[49]

Farmers hoped that the strain of providing for their children's futures would be eased by the natural rhythms of the family life cycle. As young couples set out, they could foresee the stages the family would pass through over the course of a lifetime.[50] They knew the early years would be the hardest. Children then presented the double burden of requiring additional clothing and food and of diverting the mother's labor. Families had to scrape by, calling on neighbors to help with planting and harvests, and renting out their own labor to supplement family production. Then as children matured, they turned from liabilities into assets. Probably by age ten, they could be put to work on simple tasks like churning and hoeing. By twelve or fourteen, a boy could drive an ox team and work long days in the field. Girls tended younger siblings, cooked, weeded kitchen gardens, spun, and dairied. From fifteen until marriage or until their mid-twenties, children were full-fledged members of the family workforce. With children laboring for the family, parents could manage more land, tend more animals, produce more butter, weave more cloth. For ten or so years, the sons' and daughters' labor doubled and tripled the family's capacity economy. During that time, the parents, at least theoretically, could accumulate more land or build up credit toward buying land. That spurt of economic power came just before the children departed to start new domestic economies of their own.[51] Knowing all this gave families reason to hope that they could help their children set up for themselves.

At a certain point—a time much debated and often contested within the family—a boy or a girl claimed his or her own labor, either to marry or to reap the benefit from that work. If they could, parents provided their sons and daughters with the resources to start families. Some fathers held on to the land until late in life, perhaps until death; others gave their sons and daughters land early on.[52] The tensions moved an almanac maker to print a small essay under the heading "Early Marriages." "From early Marriages proceeds the rivalry of parents and children. The son is eager to enjoy the world, before the father is willing to forsake it; and there is hardly room at once for two generations. The daughter begins to bloom, before the mother can be content to fade; and neither can forbear to wish for the absence of the other."[53] The tension was real but temporary. All understood that the parents would distribute the property in time. Everything parents had was intended for the children.[54]

This disposal of family property could be conceived as a right growing out of the children's unpaid labor during their late adolescence. It probably was so ingrained into the family's sense of the natural that no conception of right or repayment had to be invoked. The intestacy laws, which came into play in most deaths, encoded that assumption. The legal system defined the intricate degrees of relationship to be sure the nearest relatives had first claim, beginning with the children. Orphans' courts oversaw the stewardship of minors to be sure a greedy executor did not pillage their inheritances. Custom, justice, the legal system, and the life cycle all conspired to perpetuate families on their property. Family was interwoven into the institutional and cultural environment to the point of merger with the agricultural system, the legal system, and the society's cultural ethos.[55] Family was the instrument for reproducing society across the generations.

The reproduction of agricultural society depended on the safe transmittal of land. Without that crucial capital, the entire system would break down. Much as families send children to college today, families then strove to bestow land on their children. As now, not all families succeeded. The ideal life course was disrupted by sickness and death, crop failures, debt, or bad judgment. Probably most children had at best partial support from their families. Many dwelled in the parents' household for a few years, or rented land from families with a surplus. Resources could be stretched by moving to the frontier, where landless families occupied land without title before remote owners drove them off.[56] A 1721 petition to the Massachusetts General Court for outlying land sounded the common refrain: "being straitned for Accomodations for themselves and their posterity."[57] By one expedient or another, the pitfalls in the ideal life course could be worked around.

The need to amass resources for the next generation created immense pressure within the national domain. The early generations of American colonists took up unoccupied land within the counties or towns of their parents. Later they filled in the pockets of less desirable land that had been left untouched during the first years of settlement. By the end of the seventeenth century, the pressure on the outer limits of the early settlements began to build.[58] In the eighteenth century, families moved to northern New England and into Canada. In a 1764 essay written for Governor Wentworth of New Hampshire, Thomas Hutchinson, then chief justice of Massachusetts Bay, thought it "the ruling passion to be a freeholder." "Most men as soon as their sons grow up endeavor to procure tracts in some new township where all except the eldest go out one after another with a wife a yoke of oxen a horse a cow or two & maybe a few goats and husbandry tools."[59] There the letter breaks off, but the point was clear. People were moving out to find land for their children.

They moved across the Hudson into the interior of upstate New York. They pressed north into Vermont and Canada and west into western Pennsylvania and then down the Appalachian valleys into the backcountry of the southern colonies. In the South, they moved from the Tidewater to the Piedmont. Eventually people spilled over the mountains into the Ohio Valley. The propulsive forces were irresistible. The British government, in a vain attempt to keep order, temporarily forbade settlement beyond a line following the crest of the Appalachian Mountains, but settlers broke through the legal constraints.[60] These propulsive pressures underlay the unusually fluid and ever-expanding boundaries of the United States. Both the national boundaries and the outline of settlement were unlike any the world had ever known. For more than a century after Independence, the population bulged outward, spreading into every empty space as it crossed the continent like floodwaters rushing onto a plain. To accommodate the spread, the national government negotiated for one new territory after another, halting at the Mexican and Canadian borders but not without calls to fill out all of North America.

Ultimately, national acquisitions were driven by family need. It would have made little sense to bargain for one new territory after another had not the negotiators understood the potential of filling these new spaces with people. Jefferson enthusiastically purchased Louisiana, in contradiction of his constitutional principles, because he knew that vast territory would eventually fill up. By 1800 he had already seen farmers beating down the doors of the federal land offices to purchase western land. Battles for control of western lands by speculators and farmers had been waged over his entire political life. How the nation and the continent were to accommodate this pressing need absorbed the attention of Congress from its inception. The authors of land bills from 1785 to the Homestead Act of 1862 envisioned a carpet of small farms unrolling into the West. The authors believed this was the way of economy, society, and civilization.

These irrepressible forces pressed against the frontiers of settlement largely unconcerned about the havoc they wrought in the population already occupying the western territories. In the forests and clearings along the western edge of the colonies, Native American families had their own way of life to perpetuate. It usually involved small patches of land for beans, corn, and squash and large expanses of hunting land, plus movement from coasts and rivers to mountains and upland valleys to benefit from fish or berries harvested in their seasons. The contours of Indian family life are less easily delineated from the records than the Europeans', but Native American parents and children managed systems of production and consumption every bit as intricate as the family farms of Europeans. Their lands were guaranteed to individual families not by a court system but by village custom and traditional rights. The treaties and purchases that bit by bit ripped away tract after tract of hunting and planting grounds disrupted a family life that was as integrated with the land as were family farms in Connecticut and Virginia. As European settlers moved into regions that were once hunting grounds, one set of families essentially vanquished the other.

The same preoccupation with family perpetuation desensitized the European settlers to the toll exacted from captive laborers in the slave regions. White settlers refused to acknowledge marriage among their captive workers and broke up slave families whenever white interests required it. The disregard for the welfare of red and black populations grew in part from the barrier of race, but race only buttressed a sense of a right to prevail over other populations that Europeans had felt from the beginning. By suppressing and exploiting the labor and land of these others, the Europeans functioned as "imperial families." They possessed a sense that their family project must prevail over all others. Their presumption was as imperious as the British government's sense of its right to rule native peoples. In this presumed superiority of European families, the government concurred. No one questioned the rights of European white families to preserve and perpetuate themselves. The courts enforced their claim to property; colonial governments negotiated with native peoples for ever more extensive tracts; the militias drove back the Indians when they attempted to defend their lands; land companies purchased Indian lands, surveyed the new territories, and advertised the available tracts. From one perspective, the entire imperial structure served the needs of white families. Under the rubric of property, both right and might were on their side.

The farm family thus was at the heart of the European conquest of North America.[61] It was the compulsion to perpetuate family life—to fulfill the quintessential American dream of a competence for ordinary people—that ultimately displaced the native populations. The speculators and government agents who spearheaded the acquisition of native lands are often depicted as the villains of the piece, heartless and cruel minions of a blindly expansive capitalism. But backing the power institutions were families providing for their children. Their need for land and their willingness to go into debt to purchase it underlay the work of land speculators, government negotiators, and soldiers. The negotiators would not have practiced the chicanery they did were it not for the voracious market for land created by tens of thousands of farm families. The farm family's drive to reproduce itself in accord with the farm idea ultimately propelled American expansion.

We implicitly condemn farmers by speaking of land "hunger," as if it were an appetite they could not control. Having gotten some land, so the word "hunger" implies, they perpetually wanted more and so drove the Indians out of their forests to make way for themselves. But children, not land hunger, compelled them. The farmers took up onetime Indian lands, put themselves into the hands of speculators, mobbed government land offices, warred with those who contested their entry, all to provide for their offspring. By denigrating their motives, we make the displacement of the Indian population into a melodrama with villains and victims. But when we go back to the root impulses that drove expansion, we find not villainy but family survival. The displacement of one population by another was not melodrama but tragedy.

The family farmer was both the embodiment of the American dream and the leading actor in the displacement of the native peoples. Family farmers were ultimately responsible for the conquest of America and the subordination of its original inhabitants.[62] So long as soldiers, merchants, government officials, and missionaries predominated on the frontier, a tenuous modus vivendi with the Native American populations could be negotiated. A "middle ground" formed where all parties achieved their ends without one dominating the other. They bought and sold, entered into treaties, heard about, received, and rejected religion, set up hierarchies of government, and found a hundred ways to live and let live.

These tenuous middle-ground societies persisted for decades—until the farmers arrived. All the other parties to the agreements had reasons to negotiate with the native populations. They all had something to give and something to get. The farmers wanted nothing from the natives but their land. They did not need tenuous forms of mediation; they wanted the Indians removed and their planting fields and hunting grounds opened for European settlement. The farmers were inexorable, and they were numerous. The balance of power that defined the middle ground fell apart when hordes of farmer-soldiers came on the scene. They not only wanted land, they had the means to wrest it from the Indians. Their very numbers upset the middle-ground balance of power. The Indian's doom was sealed once the farmers with their insatiable demand for land moved in.[63]

Family farmers played an ambiguous role in American history. Although in its essence the farm idea was optimistic and filled with promise, it frequently was overcast with unintended consequences, struggles, and failure. Family farmers faltered when nature, debt, or the markets overcame them. Worse still, the success of farm families came at the expense of the native population. Farmers were, on the one hand, the embodiment of the American dream; on the other, they enacted the American nightmare—the decimation of one people by another.

2. A Note on Sources

How Documents Think

Farmers left their fingerprints all over colonial records. Newspaper ads, tax lists, town meeting minutes, legislative minutes and petitions, imperial correspondence, a few diaries and many account books, all yield information about farmers. Among the abundance of sources, court records, including wills and estate inventories, are the richest single trove. At court, young farmers received inheritances from their fathers and registered deeds to their first land purchases. At the end of life, their wills were probated in court and their estates inventoried. Along the way, they went to court to sue or be sued, to petition for mills or taverns, to have roads laid out and repaired, and to register cattle marks.

Ordinarily we mine this mountain of records for what we take to be the gold, such nuggets as average amount of property per person, the frequency of debts, the division of property among children, the value and types of objects in estate inventories. After arduous and ingenious refinement in the mills of the historians, these materials are then used to reconstruct rural society.

But in mining the ore and refining the gold, we may lose sight of the mountain from which the data were taken. The immense pile of legal texts stacked in the archives is filled with ideas. The documents record a cultural system, a set of routines, a vast map of social interactions and human purposes. Like all texts, judicial texts created specialized worlds, peopled with characters and specifying habits of living, actions, dangers, and rewards.

The farmers who came to court to conduct their business entered into those worlds and became actors in their plots. If we limit our research to the recovery of a few key facts embedded in the court record, we lose sight of the complex textual worlds that encompassed farmers as much as the physical world of fields, barns, and fences. Court texts constructed both farms and farmers in the largest sense of producing identities and formulating imagined worlds. The texts constitute a window on how farmers thought.

We may be slow to recognize that farms and farmers were constructed by words and ideas as well as by their physical beings. The farm planted in the earth seems so real, it is easy to forget that farms existed in people's minds as well as on the earth. A migrating farm family carried the essentials of a farm in their heads as they rolled along in their wagon. Family members already knew the routines of cutting, plowing, sowing, weeding, harvesting, slaughtering, gardening, preserving, cooking, dairying. They could imagine every step of farm construction before putting their feet on the soil. They bore the resolve to work the land and possessed bodies inured to hard labor. Their muscles held memories that enabled them to swing an axe or work a churn.[1]

Just as essential parts of a farm existed in the farmer's imagination, so the farm existed in court records. A farm took on a form in courthouse documents just as it existed on the earth. Courts made farms into texts. The representations of the farm in deeds, wills, inventories, and promissory notes affected its shape, size, and ownership as much as did fence lines or cleared fields. The documentary farm in the court records at times overruled the physical farm formed by labor on the land. An execution for debt could snatch away animals, tools, and acres; a paper description of a boundary could shift a property line between neighbors. Lines scrawled on plat maps in the courthouse preempted the farm laid out on the landscape. The court's job was to preserve, interpret, and enforce the documentary farm created in those papers.

The texts, brief and stilted as they might be, contained worlds. A deed, a promissory note, a will, a tax list, each constructed an imagined relationship, framed to suit the purposes of the court in the action of the case. Legal documents crystallized experience in a peculiarly intense and focused form. The document reduced the people and the society to a few essentials, the qualities required to transmit property or sue for repayment of a loan. For the purposes of the case, representation of physical reality and of personality was drastically simplified. But though specialized, truncated, and highly stylized, the texts represented a recognizable world where farmers lived out important fragments of their lives. Each type of document discloses one part of farm thinking, revealing segments of the farmer's mind that cannot be so clearly seen anywhere else.

Deeds, Promissory Notes, Wills, Estate Sales

The Deed and Space

The deed creates spaces within the farmer's imagination. Take, for example, the deed of J. Jonas Brown of Sutton in Worcester County, Massachusetts, in April 1756. Brown granted five acres of land to Sarah Grover of Grafton, "Spinstress and wife" of Benjamin Grover of Grafton, "Husbandman." The land lay in Grafton adjoining Sutton and is described as follows: "Abutted and bounded as follows: Viz Begining at the Gravel pitt; at a grey Oak Stubb, thence running Westerly to an Ash Tree on Sutton Line, thence turning and running Northerly on Said Sutton Line to a White Pine tree marked, Still on sd Line to a heap of Stones a Corner near quest Medow So Called; thence turning & Runing Easterly fourteen rods on Elisha Brigham's Land, to a heap of Stones at Corner, thence turning and runing Southerly on Said Brighams Land Sixty Rods to the bounds first Mentioned."[2]

Deeds described landscapes of a peculiarly desiccated kind. Many things that would be visible to anyone standing on the land are left out. The deed says very little about the natural topography of slopes, waterways, tree coverage, boulders and outcroppings, or the human additions of crops, fences, and animals. The personalities of the people who buy and sell are not mentioned; there is nothing about society. The deed is all about bounds, sizes, and owners. Natural objects such as the gravel pit, the oak stub, the ash tree, the white pine figure only as meeting places of nature and the artificial landscape of boundary lines.

This stylized landscape is made visible in a related document, the plat map. The work of a surveyor, the plat map provides a graphic representation of the meeting of natural and artificial features. The map represents a space created in the course of dividing the town lands to one of the legal proprietors in Worcester. Undivided lands in the original town grant were distributed over the years as town inhabitants needed land for themselves or their offspring. In 1718 Nathaniel Moor received seventy-five acres adjoining his thirty-acre house lot (fig. 2.1).

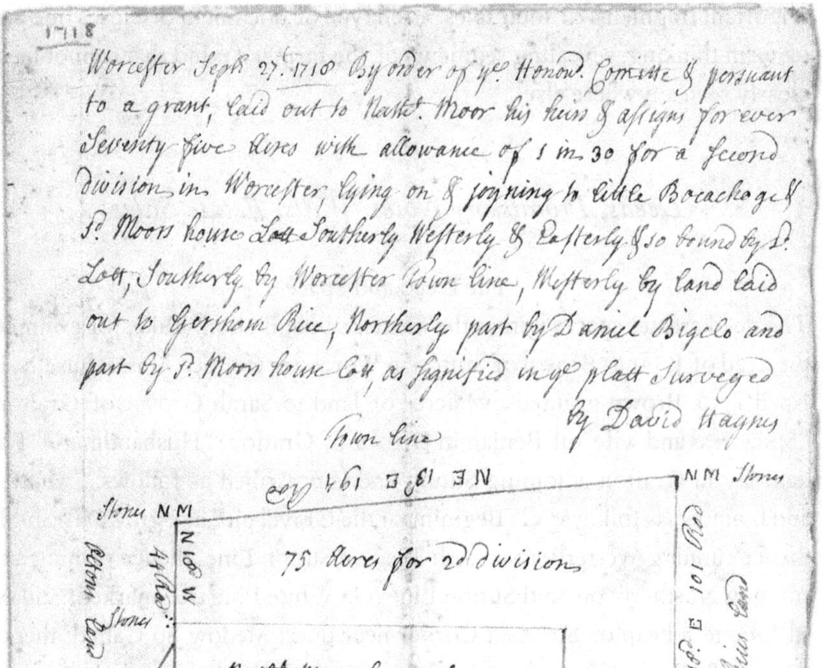
1718

Worcester Septr 27. 1718 By order of ye Honourd Comitte & persuant to a grant, laid out to Nathl. Moor his heirs & assigns for ever Seventy five Acres with allowance of 1 in 30 for a Second division in Worcester, lying on & joyning to Little Bocachoge & Sd Moors house Lott Southerly Westerly & Easterly & so bound by Sd Lott, Southerly by Worcester Town line, Westerly by land laid out to Gershom Rice, Northerly part by Daniel Biglo and part by Sd Moors house Lott, as signified in ye platt Surveyed by David Haynes

The above is a true Coppy of Seventy five Acres of Land laid out to Nathl. Moor for his second division in Worcester as returned p David Haynes. Entred in the Town book of Worcester fol 84 & Examined p Wm Jayne Clarke

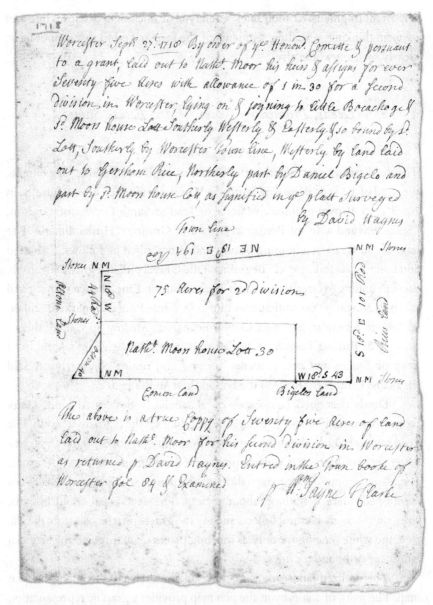

Figure 2.1 Map of seventy-five acres granted to Nathaniel Moor for his second division, Worcester, September 27, 1718. "Deeds and Maps, Auburn-Hardwick, 1665–1954," Worcester County, Mass., Records, box 5, folder 7. Courtesy American Antiquarian Society, Worcester, Massachusetts.

Here we see the artificial geometry that surveyors imposed on the natural contours of the land and that farmers held in their minds. Before settlement, the land had a natural form and texture composed of contours, vegetation, soils, outcroppings, and waterways. The settlers overlaid this natural landscape with a purely artificial, largely invisible, mathematical set of lines. Surveyed land has square corners and straight lines not to be seen in nature. On the land itself, the geometric configuration of the land would have been only partially visible along fence lines. Probably there were no fences on the fresh land granted to Moor. But in Moor's mind, the geometry of boundary lines running through woods was as evident and important as natural features such as a stream or a bluff. The regularities of the surveyed farm were as vital to him as the soils and vegetation of the visible farm. Many farmers patrolled their boundaries every year to be sure the markers were still in place and there was no room for disagreement. It required constant effort to hold the geometric farm in place on the ever-evolving natural landscape.

The creator of the deeded farm was the surveyor. With his compass and chains, he brought forth the plat map. The surveyor's compass with two slotted uprights attached enabled him to sight a line from one point to another following a mark on the compass. To fix the line on the landscape, the surveyor tied it to something visible like a gravel pit or an ash tree. Sometimes he extended a line a little beyond its specified length to reach a suitable marker. The lengths of the lines were measured by a chain, at its best a Gunter's chain, the invention of an English mathematician Edmund Gunter around 1607. A Gunter chain was sixty-six feet or twenty-two yards long and composed of one hundred links. It had the useful property of measuring an acre, 4,840 square yards exactly. Ten square chains—ten squares measuring one chain on each side—added up to an acre. A plot ten chains on a side measured ten acres.[3] Not all lands were accurately surveyed by compass and chain. Jonas Brown's deed granted "five acres be it more or less." Good surveyors were scarce and expensive. George Washington said he could make a doubloon a day, the equivalent of about $100 a week.[4] But he was worth it. A trusted surveyor was essential to fix and maintain the artificial landscape. Farmers everywhere had to depend on a neighbor's skill and honesty to effect the constant passage of land from person to person.

The surveyor's chains, as well as fixing the bounds of ownership, measured the farmer's space. Farmers left a huge footprint on the earth. By comparison, merchants and storekeepers required mere points, a cargo in a ship, a warehouse, a shop, a house, a wagon. Their spaces were measured in square feet. Farmers' spaces occupied acres, each acre containing 43,560 square feet. A modest farm could easily take up 4 million square feet. Wherever he went, a farmer had attached to him bulky tracts of forest and fields. Space stretched out in great sweeps around him.

These huge chunks of space gave him existence in the world of the deed. The central human activity in the deed is to possess and exchange property. The deed projects a future in which the land passes down through the generations of the possessor's family, keeping the owner and his property at the center of attention. Nonpossessors—the large population of women, children, servants, laborers, and slaves—are nearly invisible. Only occasionally are women possessors, and slightly more often children. The male possessors are the players in this world. Women and children are dimly visible as "heirs and Assigns," but they are always "his" heirs and assigns, extensions of the possessor's persona. They remain in the wings in the constant dance of landed property exchange and so are only bit players in the spatial episodes in farm thought.

The Promissory Note and Time

The landscape recedes from view in the promissory note, the document behind debt suits, the largest single category of county court cases. The action in the promissory note takes place over time rather than in space: "I promise to pay or cause to be paid unto John Amstead his Hairs or assigns the Just and full Sum of three hundred pounds current Money of North Carolina on or before the first Day of October next ensuing the date hereof for Value received as Witness my Hand and Seal this 11th Day of August 1792. Andrew Burke."[5]

Money is lent on one day, and the borrower promises to return the amount at a specific later time. The note controls an exchange of money now and in the future, as compared with the deed's exchange of property on the landscape at one moment in time. The parties again are owners, but the possession is money, not land, and the dimension is time, not space.[6] The note tries to regulate what will happen in the future when the borrower returns the money to the lender.

The futuristic quality of the note is in keeping with a common purpose for borrowing—to develop the farm or to provide for children. Farmers were projectors; they had to live in the time ahead. Crops were planted in the expectation of growth and harvested many months later after passing through all the havoc that weather, pests, and disease could wreak. Still farther into the future, the farmer foresaw the development of his land: forested acres cleared, fences built, swamps drained, parcels added, herds enlarged, buildings constructed. Advertisements for tracts of land sketched in the various uses to which the land could be put in time. Ads spoke of timber that could be harvested and milled into lumber. They referred to soils suitable for grain that could be turned into flour for the Philadelphia market. There were sites where gristmills or sawmills could be erected. The art of selling land was to evoke possible futures—what could be accomplished in time. Speculators knew that every farmer lived in the time ahead. His life depended on events hard to foretell and indifferently regulated, yet necessary for him to envision in order to sustain his family and carry on his work. The promissory note reveals the farmer in his futuristic orientation, in the critical act of promising, hoping, and trusting what the future will bring.

Unlike deeds, these promissory notes bound borrowers and lenders for a period of time and so created a little society of debtors and creditors within the larger society. Deeds had no time dimension. The sale of land occurred in the seconds when the signature was affixed; the link between the parties lasted only for the moment of transaction. The promissory note tied lender to borrower for months or years. The key act for both borrower and lender was the promise. The entire transaction rested on both parties' confidence in the borrower's ability to pay at a future date. Both parties trusted in the borrower's accurate prediction of what he would do months or years in advance.

For the period while the note was in effect, then, each had an interest in the other, the debtor had an obligation, and the creditor had expectations; probably both had fears. A lender could demand payment at an embarrassing time; a borrower could fail to pay. The notes said nothing of fear and anger, reducing the bond to purely financial and temporal terms—I will pay this much in this time—but promissory notes were necessarily touched with anxiety. The notes imply a community laced with such relationships, scores of them in even a small village, each one fraught with the apprehensions of borrowers and lenders.

The Estate Sale and Material Culture

The estate sale returns to the instant transaction of the deed, leaving behind the time dimension of the promissory note. But in place of the land or money, estate sale records emphasized things—hoes, chairs, clothing, bushels of corn—the farmer's material possessions. The sales dealt with a deceased person's movable estate, consisting of all the tools and furnishings in house and barn, the animals, slaves, and crops. Wills did not usually name the recipient of each item, and so to manage distribution among the heirs, the sales disposed of the goods and added the receipts to the cash balance of the estate. At the sale, the wife and children of the deceased purchased items against the inheritance they would soon receive. A clerk of the court oversaw the sale, recording each item sold, the purchaser, and the price, and prepared a list for inclusion in the probate file. People from outside the family attended and bought goods for cash. At the estate sale of Ephraim McCaleb in Orange County, North Carolina, in November 1770, five family members, including the widow, purchased goods, and thirty-three others bought from one to five items, the prices ranging from a few pennies to ten pounds.[7]

The old pots, chipped dishes, axes, and hoes that appeared on most of the lists can only be imagined as a ragged assemblage. In Orange County at midcentury, few farmers owned display objects. McCaleb, a fairly well-off tobacco planter, had only eight pewter plates to go with his wooden trenchers. Although he owned a walnut table and chest, no ceramic table dishes connected him with rising genteel styles. The rest of the list named only utilitarian items, a dough trough, a sidesaddle, a pot and pot hooks, a piggin or small wooden pail, a chest, a handsaw, a currycomb, a drawing knife and augur, a branding iron, and a saddle tree, objects that came together piecemeal over a lifetime. During his life McCaleb probably went to estate sales himself or bartered with neighbors for objects like the ones in his estate. As he contemplated purchases, he would have had a mental inventory of his present tools, so he would know what to add when things came up for sale. Every farmer's mind contained an inventory of the tools and furniture stashed away in house and barn.

At death, McCaleb's assemblage of objects was disassembled. At the sale, buyers added to their own collections of things, according to their own mental inventories of their current possessions. The diversity of estate inventories suggests that there was no model of a complete inventory to go by. No one collection represented an ideal set of possessions. Farmers put together what they thought they needed. Since no nearby store stocked everything, a farmer had to pick up items where and when he could, in estate sales like McCaleb's or by barter. Each person's assemblage assumed new shapes from month to month, as items came and went. If the deed and the promissory note project a flow of land and money about the county, the estate sale implies household objects and farm tools moving from hand to hand, each person's inventory constantly being refigured.

The Will and the Reproduction of Society

The stories and operations implicit in deeds, promissory notes, and estate sales culminated in the will. Death dropped like a cleaver across the worlds of deeds, notes, and estate sales, marking the end of a person acquiring objects. Family and friends were then invited to cannibalize the decedent's inventory. Although settlement could take years, death ended the ownership of land by one person and transferred it to someone else. Debts were ordinarily paid off and the movable estate dispersed. Both space and time changed. The landscape of plots and ownership took on a new shape as parcels were assigned to the heirs. The settlement of debts dissolved the deceased's portion of debtor-creditor dualities woven through the community. The world was reconstituted in a new way.

The task of organizing this reconstituted society fell to the dead person. The heirs and the probate court only carried out his intentions. The will was necessarily a complex family document that took into account the age, health, marital status, and character of the children, the viability of the farm if divided, the testator's sense of justice, past gifts to heirs, and innumerable idiosyncratic considerations. All these had to be weighed and the testator's intention reduced to who got what. In 1790 John Armstrong of Orange County gave his son William two hundred acres, his daughter Elisabeth a plantation of one hundred acres, his daughter Mary forty pounds, his daughter Margret a brown mare with saddle and bridle, and his daughter Rachel maintenance for life from the land left to William and Elisabeth. Armstrong's wife Margret was to receive all the income from his land until the older children came of age and thereafter one-third.

The justice of those divisions, with one daughter getting a plantation of one hundred acres and another girl one brown mare, can never be understood outside of particular circumstances in John Armstrong's family. For whatever reason, Armstrong assigned plantation properties to two of his children, making them possessors in a society of landowners, and gave one daughter a nominal gift and the other support but no tangible bequest. Possibly she was already married and recipient of a dowry. The two hundred acres William received was "the tract of Land wherein I now Live," making him John's successor as patriarch-farmer. Elisabeth would be a more attractive bride with one hundred acres of land in her possession, the potential wife of another substantial planter. So would Mary with forty pounds. John seemed most anxious to see that Rachel was cared for, though not left with goods to enhance her marriage prospects. John fastened his hopes for perpetuating a family of possessors into the next generation on William and Elizabeth.[8]

The intention of the court, the legal system, and all of society was to put the testator in control of the future. The court honored the will and enforced the testator's purposes even though he was gone. Nothing exemplified more fully the patriarchal position of the farmer-father-husband than the will. The text he produced mapped his portion of the future. Like every ruler, he had to consider the needs of each individual in his little kingdom; but he had the right to distribute his property among them and thus control their fates. Although often subverted by contingencies and by contests among the heirs, the men of property in each generation remade society—largely in their own images. No son, servant, or wife could successfully contest the father's authority. The father-husband's rule seemed natural, inevitable, and irresistible.

Court documents—deeds, promissory notes, estate sales, and wills—open windows into various segments of farm minds. In running a farm, the farmer called upon them all. He had to understand the directions and lengths of survey lines, foresee enough of the future to predict his ability to pay, hold in his head all the tools he owned as he purchased items at an estate auction, and constantly rebalance the justice of property distributions to family members to achieve equity at his death. Mistakes in any department could hamper the realization of his goals. The integration of each part was necessary to the success of the whole.

Tax Lists

Next to court records, tax lists are the most abundant sources of information about farmers. Colonial assemblies, which had the responsibility of levying taxes, determined the total financial need of the colony and distributed the tax burden among the towns (in New England) or counties (elsewhere), according to their populations and capacity to pay. This distribution inevitably led to controversy over how to determine each jurisdiction's fair share, and so to assure equity, legislatures over the years devised more and more detailed estimations of the wealth of each town or county. The 1771 Massachusetts "List of the Polls and of the Estates, Real and Personal of the several Proprietors and Inhabitants of the Town" was an elaborate attempt to measure the actual wealth of each town by appraising the wealth of each household. This knowledge gave the assembly an objective basis for dividing the tax burden. Each "rateable" (meaning taxable) male, sixteen years and older, was asked to report on his holdings in thirty-one categories, among them number of houses, shops, warehouses, wharves, mills and ironworks, slaves, tons of vessels, store inventories, money at interest, animals, acres of pasture, tillage, and meadow, and the fertility of the land determined by its yield.[9] The list offered a comprehensive assessment of the productive strength of each household, a basis for determining the tax burden of each town, and eventually the tax for each family. Every seven years or so, the information was assembled again to take into account the changing fortunes of each town.

So bounteous a source of information can be approached from many directions. The tax lists have been ably explicated by Bettye Pruitt in a classic essay on town economies. Pruitt calculated the kinds of property a farmer would need to produce all his family required and then demonstrated from the tax assessments that most farmers lacked some of the necessary components. Almost no one was self-sufficient. Farmers had to enter into exchanges to live.[10]

Surprisingly, the tax lists also yield to an analysis from the perspective of the postmodern French philosopher Michel Foucault whose seminal work on state power, *Discipline and Punish,* also illuminates the lists.[11] Traditionally, Foucault argues, power had been manifest through display. To elevate authorities in the eyes of the people, attention was focused on the king, the courts, and the military. Every effort was made to make the holders of power visible through processions, portraits, costume, and architecture. The modern national state, by contrast, undertakes to control society by putting the spotlight on each individual. The state recedes while each citizen comes to the fore. The state's method is to code social phenomena through a new form of power, statistics, the arithmetic of state affairs. Each person is named and measured according to prescribed attributes. The state puts the name of each person on a list, assigns qualities, and then sets a standard of normality. Through a seemingly objective examination, those who fall outside the norms, the dangerous or inadequate, may then be disciplined or disqualified. Foucault was thinking of schools, hospitals, and the military, but his insight applies to Concord.

The tax list was a form of examination. Every household in the town became visible through the qualities assigned to each person—his or her taxable estate. The assessors created knowledge about each household, making each visible to the gaze of the state. Payments were then collected according to this compiled knowledge. The tax list ingeniously and efficiently controlled everyone in the town without any overt coercion. The whole process seemed to be essentially objective. Assessors collected the information and transmitted it to the assembly, and with very little force, taxes flowed to the center in a wonderful manifestation of state power.

Foucault leads us to see the farmers as victims of the tax lists. Once they submitted their appraisals, they were in the state's hands. He does not observe that farmers were also beneficiaries. In another possible reading, the lists manifest the farmers' power as well as their subjection in that farmers had a place on the list; others did not. Only the heads of households were named. Women, children, and hired hands went unnamed. Servants were counted in the column for rateable polls, indicating they produced value and so should be taxed, but they were not named. They had the same standing as the oxen and swine in other columns. Married women and underage children were not even numbered except in the infrequent instances where a woman was the head of household. Although their labor was essential to farm production and in the work of the house and the kitchen garden, they were subsumed into the household head.

Thus being named on the list, as one scholar has put it, "made these named people something more and other unnamed people something less than individuals." The named individual represented more than a single person. He was linked to all his unnamed dependents on the assumption that the named individual was responsible for the unnamed. "The assessment lists recorded a corporate consciousness where heads of households stood in for their dependents."[12] To Foucault's observations about state power flowing from the list must be added, then, the implied power position of the household heads. The list of polls and estates, in the process of collecting taxes, implicitly validated the authority of household heads over sons and daughters, servants and wives. Lesser authorities were implicitly sustained along with the greater.

These two readings of the tax lists open them up but still do not exhaust their meaning. Another implication is related to one of the list's peculiar features: the farmers themselves reported the value of their property. Information about the number of bushels their tillage would produce, the number of cows their pasture would support, the barrels of cider they pressed each year, came from the household heads themselves. The assessors did not go to the farms to make the appraisal. The Act required each person to give "in writing . . . a true account of his rateable estate and improvements" to the assessors. The farmers reported voluntarily. If the assessors had doubts, they could administer an oath that the writing was a "full account," but few disputes turn up in the records.[13] Adjustments were made, but the issues were not hotly contested. The voluntary listing of property seemed to work.

It worked because something like the assessment list existed in every farmer's mind. If called upon, virtually every farmer could appraise the worth of his neighbors' property. This was a farmer's business. Farmers had expert eyes for the fertility of the soil, the number of animals distributed about a farm, the amount and quality of land in each parcel, the anticipated yield. Farm livelihoods depended on a precise knowledge of farm productivity. Tax assessment only codified what every farmer knew from long experience. One farmer could not cheat when his farm was open to observation by a townful of farm experts.[14]

Something like a list of polls and estates existed then in every farmer's mind, at least for his immediate neighbors. Social identity was bound up with the image of a person's property. In accounting for the boundaries of the Moor property in Worcester, human names blended with the land. To establish the boundary of Moor's seventy-five acres, it was said to abut the land owned by Gershom Rice and Daniel Bigelo. Name and land merged, giving an identity to each. When a neighbor looked at the land, he thought of its owner. It was Rice's land. When he thought of the person, he thought also of his land. The equivalent of today's crucial question, "What do you do?" was "Where is your place?" except that within the town everyone already knew the answer.[15] They knew minute details about the state of the fences, the quality of the plowing, the height of the corn, the fatness of the cattle, and a hundred other small matters that a farmer's eye immediately observed.[16]

A farm's worth was probably even more exquisitely calibrated in neighbors' minds than on the tax list. Each individual knew the worth of one plot of tillage compared with another, the quality of hay produced in one field contrasted with the grass in another, the weight and value of each head of cattle. Town residents knew where each person stood in the list of his neighbors. They probably had some idea, moreover, of a person's debts, of who owed money to whom. All this knowledge came into play when a person rose to speak in a town meeting, or when a young man courted a young woman, or when an election was held. The authority of the speaker, the suitability of the marriage, and the eligibility of a candidate would be judged in part by the value of the farm supporting each person's social identity.

It would be wrong to say that a farmer worked to raise his status in town society. The purpose of a farmer's daily labor was to make his farm produce; he worked to keep his family alive. But he also knew his position among the town's farmers and the consequences of losing it. Farmers had words for the loss of a farm: "ruin" and "destruction." Falling out of the list of valued farm properties, or dropping down it, was a form of social death. Social life depended on maintaining a position as an independent householder in the matrix of town farms. As a part of farm culture, the tax list represented an exercise of power, a social structure, a way of life, a reason for existence.

Archival records offer glimpses from one angle and then another of how farmers thought. Each document opens a segment of farmers' minds. The documents remind us that even the most traditional and routine work lives were built up from layer after layer of ideational constructions. Farmers' minds consisted of complex hives of procedures and methods. The outcome was not only a system of production but a social order and a structure of meaning. That farming was grounded in the soil, in tools, and in practices did not lessen its power to form the mind and order life.

PART TWO

North America, 1600–1800

3. The Nature of the South

The Creation of Sectional Systems

A close observer looking down on the Atlantic in the middle of the eighteenth century would see ships from the southern half of the North American continent moving along two lines of trade: on one track, they sailed between American plantations and British ports, laden with cargo after cargo of a dominant crop: tobacco, rice, or indigo. On the other track, they moved between Africa and America, bearing cargo after cargo of chained human bodies. At the shipping routes' western terminals, the enslaved Africans labored under white masters to produce the crops; at the eastern terminals, the products of their labor entered British and European commercial systems where they were distributed to markets all over the continent. On further inquiry, the observer would learn that the products were in high demand because they were not grown in Britain. Like the spice trade that motivated global commerce for so many centuries, the trade dealt in exotic products not produced in the homeland. This assemblage of routes, shipping, markets, labor, and farming constituted North American plantation agriculture.

As a distinctive form of agricultural production, plantation agriculture in the North American South was the northern wing of an agrocommercial system that stretched from the coastal areas of Brazil, up through Guinea on the northern coast of South America, to the Caribbean islands, and then to the southeastern quadrant of North America as far as Maryland's northern boundary. The fateful question for the United States was why it stopped abruptly in northern Maryland. The farms on the northern side of the line practiced agriculture on distinctly different principles from the plantations on the southern side.[1] Why the halt at the Pennsylvania border, laying the foundation for the sharply defined sections, North and South, that divided the United States from its founding?

The Emergence of Plantations

Plantations, like the labor force that worked them, were imported from the Eastern Hemisphere. Plantations were first organized on Cyprus and Crete in the fourteenth century to grow sugar. To augment local labor, the growers introduced Russian and Mongol slaves and Tatars from north of the Black Sea. In the fifteenth century, the Portuguese and then the Spanish established sugar plantations on their Atlantic islands, Madeira and the Canaries, and on the African island of São Tomé. In the early sixteenth century, plantations crossed the Atlantic to the Western Hemisphere. They first gained a foothold on the northern coast of Brazil in the 1540s, an area that over the next century became the dominant world sugar producer.[2]

The spread of the plantation system after that proceeded slowly. The Brazilian example took decades to catch on elsewhere. The Dutch brought the secrets of sugar from Brazil to the Antilles in the early seventeenth century, hoping to produce for the European market, but knowledge of sugar's secrets and the Brazilian example were not enough to convert all the potential sugar planting regions immediately. Not until the 1640s did the British and French go into full-scale production on an island or two. Plantation agriculture then moved gradually from island to island depending on local circumstances. It took Antigua twenty-five years to get sugar production in high gear after a crop was produced in 1655. Martinique and Guadalupe produced only a limited amount of sugar with a small slave population until the early eighteenth century. St. Christopher experimented with sugar production as early as 1643 but did not reach its potential until the eighteenth century, when its shipments exceeded those of Barbados. Jamaica and Saint-Domingue were delayed about the same length of time. Spain, preoccupied with silver production on the mainland, did not develop sugar plantations in Cuba until the mid-eighteenth century.[3]

The North American Chesapeake colonies trailed the most forward British sugar islands by about fifty years. The Virginians had discovered their equivalent of sugar, tobacco, by 1620 but relied at first on indentured servants for labor, stopping short of full plantation agriculture. After the Caribbean sugar planters attracted slave ships to their ports, African slaves began to trickle into the Chesapeake. But in the 1650s only the wealthiest planters, the largest growers of sweet-scented tobacco, could afford them. Growers of inferior oronoco tobacco and small planters of every kind lacked the means. Charles Calvert complained in 1664, "I have endeavoured to see if I could find as many responsible men that would engage to take a 100 or 200 neigros every yeare from the Royall Company, but I find wee are nott men of estates good enough to undertake such a buinesse, but could wish wee were for wee are naturally inclin'd to love neigros if our purses would endure it."[4] The planters wanted more "neigros," but could not pay the price.

To purchase slaves, North American planters depended on credit from their London correspondents. Large planters who shipped big cargoes of high-value tobacco first won the confidence of English merchants. Smaller men with small crops and underdeveloped properties followed only slowly. Not until they brought in more land and increased their harvests did their credit improve.[5] Through the century, the planters made progress. The Chesapeake shipped a million pounds of tobacco annually in the 1630s, and twenty million pounds in the 1670s. Production increased twentyfold while population grew only sixfold, suggesting significant productivity improvements. In Virginia and Maryland, productivity doubled from 714 pounds of tobacco per worker in the 1620s to 1,565 pounds in the 1690s.[6] Gradually merchants found reasons to grant second-rank planters credit for slave purchases.

Growth in the English market for tobacco motivated merchants. Between the 1660s and the 1690s, tobacco imports into England and Wales rose from 0.93 pounds per person to 2.2 pounds. To satisfy this voracious appetite, heightened by the fact that tobacco was addictive, merchants had to keep the tobacco plantations supplied with labor. After 1680, improving work prospects in England reduced the number of indentured servants going to the Chesapeake, jeopardizing the vital supply of tobacco. Over the next thirty years, with the merchants' help, the Chesapeake underwent a transformation from servants to slaves. In Maryland estate inventories in 1680, indentured servants outnumbered slaves almost four to one; by 1710, the ratio had reversed: slaves outnumbered servants five to one. By 1700, more than 90 percent of the workforce of the Virginia elite was enslaved. The slave population in the Chesapeake shot up from 4,611 in 1680 to 39,059 in 1720. The termination of the Royal African Company's monopoly on the slave trade in 1698 allowed a swarm of smaller merchants to meet the growing demand.[7]

The Carolinas followed a different path to plantation agriculture. Slaves were not introduced to an established colony as in Virginia; they came with the first migrants. Settled in the last third of the seventeenth century, the Carolinas were partly colonized by British Barbadian planters, who in the same years were looking at Jamaica as a site for settlement of their surplus population. After receiving a charter from Charles II, the Carolina proprietors granted Barbadians 150 acres of Carolinian land in return for each transported freeman, servant, or slave. At the same time, the Fundamental Constitution established the absolute rights of masters over their bondsmen, as if anticipating slavery.[8]

The enterprise was not an immediate success. The Barbadians came to Carolina with slaves in tow but not in large numbers. By 1680, there were only 200 slaves in the entire colony. The colonists' original plan to provision Barbados, where sugar preempted the production of foodstuffs and lumber, faltered in the face of competition from New England and the Middle Colonies. Deerskins, naval stores, and wood all helped, but not until the 1690s did rice cultivation prove to be the answer, followed by indigo in the 1750s. Rice exports grew from 10,000 pounds in 1698 to 6.5 million pounds by 1720 and 43 million pounds in 1740. The slave population meanwhile grew from 3,000 in 1700 to 39,000 in 1750. The Carolinian rice belt was the best example of intensive plantation agriculture in all of North America.[9]

By 1750, the zone of plantation agriculture had extended its sway as far north as the Chesapeake, and there it halted. Plantation agriculture did not cross Pennsylvania's southern border. Slaves were purchased for house servants or artisans in colonial cities, and a few slaves did turn up on Pennsylvania and New York farms. Slave agricultural workers in numbers were also spotted along the northern coast, but the classic plantation system did not form in Pennsylvania as it did in Maryland, Virginia, North and South Carolina, and Georgia. A clear boundary in agricultural organization was drawn at the Pennsylvania line. Below the line, plantation agriculture linked the lower colonies to plantations in the Caribbean and Brazil. North of the line, small family farms growing mixed crops predominated.[10] Eighteenth-century planters and farmers had created a South and a North well before names were assigned to the sections.

The divide was visible enough for late-seventeenth-century imperial theorists to take note. Economists saw that North America split at the middle according to its major export crops. Below the divide, the colonies produced crops that England and Europe needed; above the line, the American economy imitated England's. In 1690 Sir Josiah Child, a governor of the East India Company and a tory mercantilist economist, listed Britain's American plantations as "Virginia, Barbadoes, New-England, Iamaica, and the Leward Islands." On this list, Child set off New England from the rest. "All our American Plantations," Child wrote, "except that of New-England, produce Commodities of different Natures from those of this Kingdom, as Sugar, Tobacco, Cocoa, Wool, Ginger, sundry sorts of dying Woods, &c. Whereas New-England produces generally the same we have here." The products Child named were the ones enumerated in the Navigations Acts of 1651, 1653, and 1660 for exclusive shipment to Britain. The most valuable commodities had to move in a British ship to a British port where duties could be collected before moving on to European markets. In a sense, the Navigation Acts first defined North and South. Identified by their leading products, the plantation colonies fell into one category and "New-England" into another.[11]

By the mercantile calculus, gains to the Kingdom increased as you went south. Writing in the same decade, Charles Davenant, a slightly younger mercantilist contemporary of Child, also spoke of the "Northward" and "Southward" colonies, but was thinking more of product than of location. He referred to "the northern planters, viz. the people of New England, Maryland, Pensylvania, Carolina."[12] Davenant lumped Carolina with the northern colonies because at that time it produced no exotic crops. Its deerskins and naval stores were not enough to link the colony to the plantation regions, and its provisions trade to the islands made it seem more like New England. Carolina's rice production, an immensely valuable staple, would soon change the economists' view. In 1704 rice was added to the enumerated products in the Navigation Acts.[13]

Confusion about the exact definition of sections persisted into the Revolutionary period, but the division at the Pennsylvania-Maryland border was ultimately the one that most impressed James Madison.[14] In the midst of the debate about representation, he cut through the fears about large states dominating the small with his judgment that "it seemed now to be pretty well understood that the real difference of interests lay, not between the large & small but between the N. & South States. The institution of slavery & its consequences formed the line of discrimination. There were 5 States on the South, 8 on the North side of this line."[15] Madison's "line of discrimination" lay along the Maryland-Pennsylvania border, where the plantation zone terminated. Madison offered a brief explanation for the formation of these broad sectional interests. "The States were divided into different interests not by their difference of size, but by other circumstances; the most material of which resulted partly from climate, but principally from the effects of their having or not having slaves."[16]

Climate

Later historians agreed with Madison that the material reasons for the divide were partly climate and principally slavery.[17] In the much-quoted opening lines of *Life and Labor in the Old South,* U. B. Phillips blended the two: "Let us begin by discussing the weather, for that has been the chief agency in making the South distinctive. It fostered the cultivation of the staple crops, which promoted the plantation system, which brought the importation of negroes, which not only gave rise to chattel slavery but created a lasting race problem. These led to controversy and regional rivalry for power, which produced apprehensive reactions and culminated in a stroke for independence." In three sentences Phillips summed up two and a half centuries of southern history, beginning with climate and ending with the Civil War. Although he failed to elaborate his insight, Phillips's explanation remains to this day the simple, commonsense explanation for southern distinctiveness: the South was warmer than the North.[18]

Climate maps graphically corroborate Phillips. He spoke of two southern growing regions, one with six months between killing frosts, and the other, immediately below it, with nine months, corresponding roughly to the tobacco and cotton regions, and that divide clearly appears on the climate maps (fig. 3.1). The line of the 180-day growing season on the climate maps cuts across northern Maryland from the Atlantic Ocean to the Appalachian Mountains, and then drops south through the piedmont, curls around the bottom of the mountains, and heads north again to the Ohio River, whence it goes more or less directly west. Without comment or explanation, the map strikingly demonstrates Phillips's point. The 180-day growing season comes close to defining the slave region of the United States and the South that functioned in American politics up until the Civil War.[19]

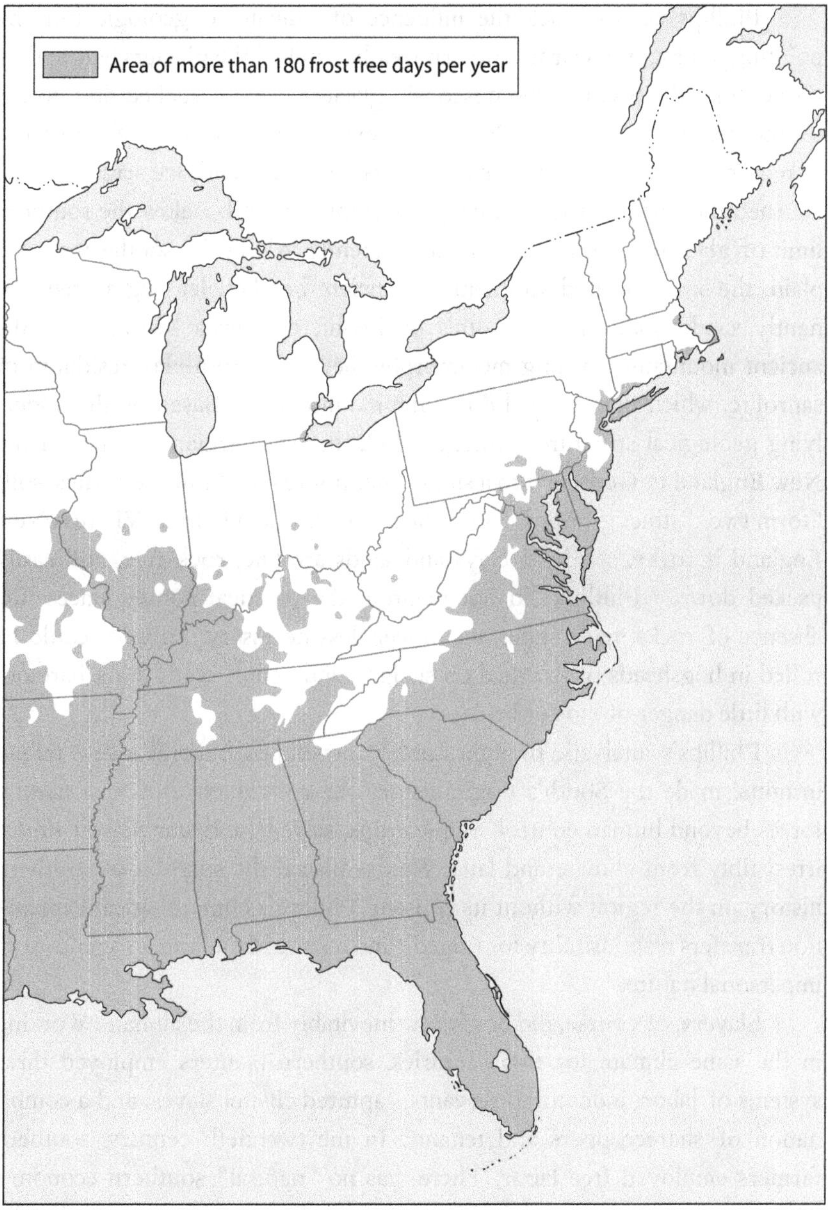

Figure 3.1 The northern limit of the 180-day freeze-free period. National Climate Data Center (U.S.), S. E. Love-Brotak, United States, and National Oceanic and Atmospheric Administration (2005). Selected maps from the climate atlas of the contiguous United States (Asheville, N.C.: National Climate Data Center), map 12, http://www1.ncdc.noaa.gov/pub/data/images/olstore/SelClimMapsPubOnlineReduced_3.pdf.

Phillips carried back the influence of climate to geologic time by pointing out that the warm southern weather melted the glaciers before they pushed into the South. The Wisconsin glaciers, which reached only to the southern boundaries of New York and New England, made a vast difference in regional topography. Where glaciers covered the land, ice scratched and churned the earth's surface, mixing rocks into the soil. Below the southern limit of glaciation, soil was formed differently. Along the southern coastal plain, the sea deposited sediments on ancient beaches, leaving a predominantly sandy soil. In the South's piedmont, chemicals "weathered" the ancient mountains, turning metamorphic bedrock into a clay residuum or saprolite, which then eroded down the mountainside. Based on the underlying geological structure, geologists link the Appalachian piedmont from New England to Georgia into a single "natural region," but the surface soils "form two distinct groups," above the glacial line and below. Whereas New England is rocky, southern clays and sands are fine, rock-free, and easily packed down.[20] Phillips did not mention the practical consequences: the absence of rocks made shoes and wheels less necessary. Tobacco could be rolled in hogsheads or dragged on sledges, and people could walk barefoot with little danger of cuts or bruises.

Phillips's analysis, though scarcely developed beyond a few telling insights, made the South's tragic history the consequence of vast natural forces beyond human control. Staple crops, slavery, and war flowed almost irresistibly from climate and land. Nature placed the sorrows of southern history on the region without its consent. Phillips's climatological explanation transfers responsibility for tragedy and horrors from human agents to an impersonal nature.[21]

Slavery, of course, did not follow inevitably from the climate. Working in the same climate for two centuries, southern planters employed three systems of labor: indentured servants, captured chattel slaves, and a combination of sharecroppers and tenants. In the twentieth century, southern farmers employed free labor. There was no "natural" southern economy. The South's greater warmth had little effect on Indian agriculture, which did not change substantially going from North to South. Beans, corn, squash, fish, and game, with seasonal berries and nuts were the foundation of the Indian diet up and down the coast.[22] Only European farmers, under the influence of the Atlantic market, saw the value of exotic exports and launched a plantation economy to satisfy European demands. The most valuable crops were not even the natural products of the land. Rice, indigo, and cotton seeds were initially imported, and even the tobacco plant was not the Nicotiana Rustica of the Indians but Nicotiana Tabacum, brought to North America from South America because it better satisfied European tastes and commanded a higher price in Atlantic commerce. The Virginia tobacco industry went nowhere until John Rolfe came by those famous seeds.[23] Prompted by markets, the colonists fundamentally reshaped the configuration of plants under cultivation. The conjuncture of two economies, the meteorological and the commercial, were required to crystallize the agricultural regimes of the two sections.

But nature did play its part. As farmers above all people know, the natural conditions for agriculture are not infinitely malleable. After ten years of farming in New York, Hector St. John de Crèvecoeur wrote plaintively, the "seasons brings along with them its Pains, Pleasures Toyls & unavoidable losses—often nature herself opposes us, what then can we do—? she is Irresistible."[24] Heedless of human will, climate limited the range of crops that could be brought to maturity from the time of the last killing frost in the spring to the first frost in the fall. The restrictions of the annual growing season set the limits; Maryland and Virginia plantations produced tobacco, the Carolinas rice and indigo, and the Caribbean islands sugar, only because the climate permitted. New Englanders could never grow those crops commercially. The South as an economic and social unit was partly nature's child.

Tobacco

Phillips's brief explanation of southern distinctiveness has other problems. The passage from climate to crop to slavery is not as smooth as he makes it appear. It is not immediately obvious, for example, why tobacco flourished in the South and not farther north. In the seventeenth and eighteenth centuries, only colonies well within the 180-day growing season grew tobacco, but climate did not exclude tobacco from regions with shorter seasons. Tobacco can be grown in 150 days or less. It was grown in England so readily that the monarch had to forbid its cultivation in order to encourage his American plantations. In the 1840s, Connecticut Valley farmers began to grow tobacco commercially. The tobacco plant can be grown as far north as Canada and in many parts of the northeastern United States. Indians grew it virtually everywhere.[25] Why then was its commercial cultivation limited to the South in the colonial period? If tobacco was commercially feasible in Virginia and Maryland, why not New England?

The key words are "commercially feasible." One plant can be set in the ground in early May and harvested in late September, well within the limits of the New England growing season. But the goal in the Chesapeake by the end of the century was for each worker to set ten thousand plants. Each plant had to be seeded in special beds and then the seedlings removed and set in a hill, which could be accomplished in a few days, except that the transplanting had to be done on rainy days, extending the planting time to several weeks. When it began to rain in May and June, workers dropped other tasks and rushed to the seedbeds to move the seedlings. Meanwhile in addition to raising tobacco, the tobacco workers had to produce enough food to support themselves. In the same weeks when they planted tobacco seedlings in the hills, the corn they were to consume had to go into the ground.[26]

The preparation of hills for both corn and tobacco was a demanding task. The worker pulled dirt up around his leg with a hoe, removed his leg, and flattened the top. During that time the ground could be neither frozen nor mired. Warmth had to come early enough to unfreeze the land and let the water drain away before the hilling could start. All of these complicated tasks required weeks of grueling labor after the last hard frost and before the last tobacco plant went into the ground. If the last plants had to be in place by late June to mature before the fall frosts, farmers needed to seed the tobacco beds in late February, start hilling in late March, and transplant the first seedlings in May. Another stretch of time at the end of the season for harvesting the leaves further extended the period required to grow a crop. It took eight to nine months to grow and harvest a crop large enough to be commercially feasible, much more than the actual growing time in the field.[27]

The region within the 180-day growing season had this broad window for seeding, hilling, planting, and harvesting. Above that line, tobacco growers did not have time in the spring to plant their corn and more than a few tobacco seedlings. To grow larger crops, the price had to be high enough to hire added labor to hurry the crucial processes. Connecticut grew only special tobaccos that commanded high prices. When the price dropped, farmers stopped planting. Without the leeway of a longer growing season, northern farmers could not grow ordinary tobacco commercially.[28] Tobacco cultivation flourished only in the longer warm season south of Pennsylvania, fixing the boundary that everyone recognized by the time of the Constitutional Convention.

Labor

Important as crops were in distinguishing southern from northern agriculture, slavery was still more important. The two were, of course, related. As Phillips understood, the production of valuable export crops in contrast to commonplace grain and cattle laid the groundwork for distinctive sectional labor systems. The key issue was exploitation in the technical sense of profiting from another's labor. Under what circumstances could a landowner profit from hiring labor to work the land? The primary requirement was an adequate return from his crops. Every full-time laborer on a farm (beyond family members) had to produce enough to feed himself and his family, plus enough more to pay the price of hiring or buying the laborer, plus a return for the owner. Family members cost only their subsistence. There was no cost in acquiring children and no wages beyond subsistence. Everything a son or daughter produced in addition to subsistence became part of family income. An indentured servant required subsistence like family members, but his or her labors also had to produce enough to pay for purchasing the indenture and yield a profit to the owner. Unless the worker's labor met all of these requirements, hired or purchased labor would be profitless or even cost more than it returned.[29]

Because New England lacked a profitable staple crop, returns on labor were low. The family farm, augmented by labor exchanges with neighbors and occasional hired labor, was the only feasible labor system. Tenancy appeared only here and there. In newly developing regions where speculators had taken up vast tracts and hoped to profit by reselling the land, owners granted developmental leases to tenants. Rents were minimal, yielding almost nothing to the owner. Instead, the speculator expected to profit from the increased value of land when the tenant had cleared and fenced it. More conventional tenancy, under which the owner profited from rents, also occurred in New England, but only on better land, near markets. Large landholders rented rich bottom lands to tenants in the Connecticut Valley in the seventeenth century, and tenancy appeared along the coast north of Boston, where the proximity of markets and the fertility of the soil enabled a tenant family to produce enough to live on with a portion remaining for the rent and a pittance for the tenant.[30] But tenancy flourished only in these special situations. Most farms yielded only enough to sustain the most economical form of labor—the family.

Going down the coast from New England, a rough labor gradient extended from the family farms in the North to the slave plantations of the South. The differences were accentuated by the breadth of the temperature range. As a geographer has observed, "eastern North America from Florida to Maine is distinctive for possessing one of the steepest temperature gradients for its length to be found in the world." The annual average temperature in North Carolina is fifteen degrees higher than in the region from Pennsylvania to Maine. In North America, "the products of tropical and polar lands are separated by less distance than anywhere in the world."[31] This sharp differentiation magnified the contrasts in labor organization coming down the seaboard.

Along the gradient, hired or purchased labor gradually increased as the returns on crops warranted the higher costs. Pennsylvania and New York did not fall into the region of exotic export production, but middle-colony grain found an eager market in both southern Europe and the West Indies, especially after 1740. As wheat prices went up, large landowners along the Hudson began to profit from rents where before they had chiefly issued developmental leases. In southeastern Pennsylvania, farmers purchased a few indentured servants, took on full-time live-in workers, and hired the labor of many cottagers who dwelled on the farmer's property and contracted to work for a specified number of days. The high returns on wheat enabled landowners to profit from the labor of a dense network of workers. After midcentury, about 30 percent of farmers in Lancaster and Chester counties in Pennsylvania were tenants who earned enough to pay rent and taxes and purchase necessary items from stores.[32]

Below the Pennsylvania border, large landowners also rented farms to tenants, but they benefited primarily from the full-time labor of slaves. The returns on exotic exports justified the expenditure on expensive labor. Tobacco, rice, and indigo farmers raised enough food to sustain slave families, grew market crops in sufficient quantity to pay the purchase price of slaves, and made enough in addition to realize a profit, making the entire operation worth the effort. Still farther south, in the Caribbean, sugar planters derived enough from their fabulously profitable crop to replenish their workforce when disease decimated its numbers, to hire supervisors, and occasionally to bear the cost of a genteel establishment in England. Going from North to South along the coastal gradient, then, the growing season, the market value of crops, labor costs, and returns to landowners increased together. Soil fertility and proximity to markets affected the detailed topography of this gradient—exactly what crops were grown in which localities. But in the broad outline, the selection of labor and crops in each region was a function of climate and the demands of the Atlantic market.[33]

The places where agricultural slavery existed north of Maryland, in apparent contradiction to the growing season pattern, only go to prove the rule. The line of the 180-day growing season actually does not end at the Maryland-Pennsylvania border. It moves northward along the coast well into New England, creating a narrow rim of warmer land as far north as Boston. In these areas, agricultural slavery flourished in the North. Chester County farmers along the Delaware River in Pennsylvania owned a total of 228 slaves in 1760, a substantial number but far fewer than in any Virginia county. Slavery appeared in Monmouth County, New Jersey, within the band of the 180-day growing season, and on Long Island. A large portion of rural slaves in Connecticut were found in a narrow coastal strip west of Milford in Fairfield County. Along Narragansett Sound, in another warm zone, slaves worked on the great dairying, sheep, cattle, and horse plantations. By 1760 there were more than 4,700 slaves in coastal Rhode Island.[34]

Slaves were present in the North, but agricultural slavery could not spread beyond this slender warm lip along the coast because the growing season quickly diminished going inland. In the northern colonies as a whole, the growing season was defined more by distance from the coast than by latitude. Slavery could not dominate any of these colonies, even though it had a toehold on the coast. South of Pennsylvania, on the other hand, the 180-day line left the coast and moved inland to encompass most of Maryland and Virginia. Large portions of both Chesapeake colonies produced staples, giving the whole region a common cast. Slavery could spread inland right up to the mountains. Where climate made tobacco production commercially feasible, the organization of labor followed, and the South began.

Winters

Within this framework, a warm climate, staple production, and slavery converged just as Phillips said. The capacity to use slave labor to cultivate exotic exports for the Atlantic market within the sheltering boundaries of the

180-day growing seasons seems to be the key to southern distinctiveness. Yet anomalies disrupt the pattern. In the middle of the eighteenth century, large portions of the Chesapeake tidewater, along with much of the eastern shore of Maryland, began a transition from tobacco to wheat. The increase of grain prices in Europe resulting from the explosion of population so improved the wheat and flour market for some farmers that grain was more profitable than tobacco. By the early decades of the nineteenth century, the zone of southern tobacco cultivation shrank, concentrating in southern Maryland, Virginia's Southside, and northern North Carolina. In the remainder of the former tobacco region, most tidewater and many inland Chesapeake counties turned to wheat. Virginia and Maryland were absorbed into the New York and Pennsylvania wheat belt.[35]

Strangely, the transition to wheat in the Chesapeake did not mark the end of slavery in those regions. Owners in Maryland's northern counties manumitted their slaves until the region's labor system came more and more to resemble Pennsylvania's. But wheat farmers in Virginia held on to their slaves. In Orange and Greene counties in Virginia's piedmont, where wheat had long displaced tobacco as the market crop by 1850, 70 percent of the farms were worked by slaves. So were wheat farms on Maryland's eastern shore.[36] Wheat and slavery were compatible in Maryland and not a few miles to the north in Pennsylvania.

The differences cannot be attributed to the high cost of slaves. The Pennsylvanians could afford the price. By the eve of the Revolution, the profitability of wheat exceeded that of tobacco in many instances, amply warranting the purchase of slaves.[37] Moreover, Pennsylvania farmers worked excellent land, far better than in the Tidewater, and were within reach of Philadelphia, the best wheat market in North America. Cost did not stop Pennsylvania farmers from buying slaves. Yet they held back. Despite the common crop across the North American wheat belt, slavery persisted in Virginia, declined in northern Maryland, and never took hold in Pennsylvania.

Quaker aversion to slavery in post-Revolutionary America must have influenced the Pennsylvanians' calculations, and racism probably reinforced the South's retention of slavery; but not all wheat farmers were Quakers, and northerners were racist too. One practical reason that the Pennsylvanians avoided slavery is that they had worked out a nonslave labor system that was much better adapted to their needs. Paul Clemens and Lucy Simler have shown how Chester County farmers precisely calibrated their labor system to meet their requirements. Chester County farmers purchased a few slaves or indentured servants for full-time labor but relied more on hired "inmates" and "cottagers." Inmates lived on the farmer's land and worked year round. Cottagers lived in small dwellings on the farmer's property and worked for wages during the specific periods when labor was in most demand. They were hired for precisely the months when the farmers needed help and no more. In the off seasons, when labor requirements lessened, they did not have to bear the costs of year-round workers.[38]

The system was so efficient, the question is why Virginia wheat farmers did not sell their slaves and adopt a similarly flexible arrangement, especially in the nineteenth century when demand for slaves was high in the newly opened cotton regions of the Southwest. Why employ laborers who had to be supported year round?

Once again, climate plays a role. As important as the growing season was to the farmer, the average winter temperature was of equal significance. Along with the 180-day growing season, another key line on the climate maps showed average day and night temperatures above 32 degrees all year round. North of the line, the average fell below 32 degrees for at least part of the year; south of it the average rose above the freezing point, night and day. This line of warm winters with average day and night temperatures above freezing outlines the South as accurately as the 180-day growing season. The South suffered cold snaps and snowstorms; ice froze on the ponds and was cut and stored. But below this line, thaws followed each freeze; the ground rarely froze hard. In Pennsylvania, the season of "frost and snow" lasted two months. Ships were frozen in the Philadelphia harbor for at least a month. But then at the Patapsco River below the fall line in Maryland, as a French traveler observed, "the dominion of snow" ended. "He who travels southward may notice the *sleigh* before every farmer's door, till he descends the steeps, at the foot of which rolls the Patapsco, after which he will see that vehicle no more."[39]

This difference in winter temperatures underlay the differences in labor systems, and the usual explanation for the linkage of tobacco and slavery suggests why. Tobacco and slavery have seemed like natural companions because tobacco requires yearlong attention; slaves could be kept busy every month. The seeds went into the beds in January or February (depending on how far south the plantation), and after harvest and curing, the tobacco often was not prized into hogsheads until December or later. Winter and summer, slaves had profitable work. Wheat required less attention, only twenty-five days of labor from planting through threshing, leaving long gaps in the annual schedule without employment for the slaves.[40] It has seemed obvious that slavery only worked if slaves could be kept busy year round.

The need for year-round labor is the key point, however, not the crop. The long stretches without work in the winter cold prevented slavery from spreading north of Maryland, not the wheat cycle. Work shut down in the northern winters because the land was frozen. Johann David Schoepf came across a poor German who said he would move from Pennsylvania to Kentucky except that "he had heard that in Kentucky there was no real winter; and where there is no winter, he argued, people must work year in, year out, and that was not his fancy." The German farmer's welcome recess from farmwork, however, was a problem for slave owners.[41] With the land hard and unworkable, their workers would lie idle for months at a time. The Pennsylvanians found it much more sensible to let their inmates go when cold weather shut down the farms.[42]

In the warmer South, slaves kept as busy on a wheat farm in the winter as on a tobacco plantation. Without hard freezes, slaves could plow in January or February as well as butcher hogs, repair fences, haul wood, and dig ditches. In Virginia's piedmont, Jefferson complained in a farm book entry for January and February 1795, "not a single ploughing day in either of these months. a degree of cold of extraordinary severity." The next year he plowed 136 acres in four fields by January 1. In 1760 Washington was plowing by late February.[43] *The Virginia and North Carolina Almanack for the year 1802* suggested among other gardening tasks for those months to "sow cresses, mustard, radish, lettuce, and other small herbs in warm, rich soil, plant out endive for seed in warm borders. . . . Dig up the ground that is to be sown with spring crops, that it may mellow; sow a few beans and peas."[44]

By March in the South, slaves could plant vegetables and grasses. In northern climes those tasks had to be postponed until April and May. Virginia's Landon Carter began preparing his fields in February and March and was putting corn in the ground by April. The corn was picked between November and February of the next year. The particular crop the slaves grew did not matter so much as did finding profitable work, and in the warmer South there was always plenty to do. Work expanded to fill the time when the weather permitted work to be done.[45] William Strickland, an English agricultural reformer who toured the United States in 1794 and 1795, observed that the Virginia and Maryland climate "admits of nearly equal labour throughout the year." In estimating labor costs, he calculated that New England labor was 42 percent less valuable in winter; in Virginia and Maryland, its worth was the same year round.[46]

Warmth affected the entire system of agriculture in the South. Conditions that made slavery feasible had many other advantages. The fact that Virginia farmers could plow the land on many days in January or February when the temperature rose above freezing meant that each worker could manage more land than in the North. Shorter winters gave southern farmers in effect 20 percent more work time each year than northern farmers, affording them more time to plow, more time to hoe, more time to plant, more time to harvest. Because the longer working year allowed more time for each stage of cultivation, each worker produced more.

The warm climate also simplified cattle raising. Animals could feed longer in southern pastures, because vegetation will grow a little so long as the temperature is above 35 degrees, and rapid plant growth begins at 43 degrees. In the South below Virginia, the temperature is permanently above 35 degrees on average. In most of Virginia, the mean daily temperature is below that level only for a month or a little more, from approximately January 1 to February 1. That meant that Virginia cattle and hogs browsed in the woods or on pastures for as many as eleven months of the year and in the Lower South for the whole year. Most animals did not have to be brought into barns for shelter during any part of the year and required supplementary feed only for a short period. "The climate of these colonies is so mild that the cattle run out all winter," *American Husbandry* observed, an "amazing advantage to the planter."[47]

In New England, the annual crisis in stock raising came in March, before grasses were growing naturally and when the supply of winter feed neared exhaustion. New England mean temperatures were below 35 degrees from December 1 to late March, three to four months.[48] Pennsylvania mean temperatures ranged between 29 and 33 from December through late February or March. Farmers could support sizable herds through the spring, summer, and fall, when the animals grazed in the woods or in pastures, but a limit on herd size was fixed by the amount of hay available to feed the animals when vegetation stopped growing in the winter. New England farmers valued salt marshes and natural meadows because they provided a natural source of hay. Otherwise, farmers had to devote large portions of their lands to hay production and spend much of their summers putting it up.[49] George Washington understood the problems of a northern climate: "In the New England States, and to Pennsylvania inclusively . . . the climate, especially to the Eastward of Hudson river, is cold, the winters long, consuming a great part of the Summers labour in support of their Stocks, during the Winter." The author of *American Husbandry* noted that "a large portion of every farm in New England consists of meadow and pasture land." In New York, farmers "make it a rule to mow every acre that is possible for hay," even if much of the cutting was "rubbish." The limitations restricted the number of cattle New England farmers could sustain. The value of livestock per person in New England was a third of the value per free person in the South.[50]

In the South hay production was minimal, partly because in the hotter climates grasses did not flourish, but equally because cattle needed so little winter feed. For the most part, animals foraged in the woods or in the fallow fields.[51] During the bridge weeks in late winter before grass took hold again, many let their animals starve. English observers were aghast to see cattle shivering in the fields with no protection from winter storms. In bad winters, many animals perished. Not until the mid-eighteenth century did larger farmers bring in pastures and begin growing clover. In the nineteenth century, Virginians used fodder more to facilitate manure collection than for winter feed. Cattle were enclosed on a rundown field and fed while the animals distributed manure. Although reformers pressed southerners to feed their animals better—and a few gentlemen who were "fond of improvements" responded—hay figured only marginally in the farm economy.[52] There were no hay barns harboring a store of winter feed, or vast hayfields, and still more important, no long and arduous haying season.[53] Workers produced food for humans and market crops that enriched the landowner.

What underlay the South's agricultural prosperity, then, more than any other factor was the long agricultural work year. Crops did not make the difference; Virginia's wheat did not make it a northern state. What distinguished the South were the laborers who could be put to work year round. Northern farmers devised ways to let workers go in the winter when cold weather shut down the farm. Southern farmers employed their workers through the winter because the land was workable nearly every month.[54] Climate did lead to slavery, as Phillips said, partly because of high-return staples, but equally because of the practicality of slave labor in the long work year.

The American South can be thought of as an "agrosystem."[55] Landforms, climate, an international market for southern products, a European habit of seeking gain, and the availability of forced labor from Africa converged to make the South what it was. Climate and markets together fixed a sectionalized economy on North America. By the time of the American Revolution, the South was clearly seen as a distinct society.[56] William Henry Drayton, chief justice of South Carolina, wrote in 1778 that "from the nature of the climate, soil and produce of the several southern states, a northern and southern interest naturally and unavoidably arise."[57]

Imperial theorists at the end of the seventeenth century had invented sections to aid them in comprehending the empire as a whole; a century later, nationalists employed the same terminology to understand the nation as a whole. Some regretted what they found. Joseph Ward wrote to John Adams in December 1775, "wish[ing] the distinctions of Southern and Northern were lost in the glorious name of American."[58] But the differences were real, and the labels enabled the Founders to account for the variations in interests, manners, and society.

Ward was not the only one to regret the division into sections. Charles Pinckney spoke of "the two great divisions of Northern & Southern Interests." "Nature," Pinckney wrote, "has drawn as strong marks of distinction in the habits and manners of the people as she has in her climate and productions. The southern citizen beholds, with a kind of surprise, the simple manners of the east . . . while they, in their turn, seem concerned at what they term the extravagance and dissipation of their southern friends, and reprobate, as unpardonable moral and political evil, the dominion they hold over part of the human race."[59] Nature, climate, crops, and slavery had yielded a southern disposition, Pinckney thought, giving reason, even then, to wonder whether union was possible between peoples so different.

4. Generation of Violence

A Population Explosion Ignites Conflict

After a long period of flat or slow growth, world population took an upward turn in the eighteenth century. England and Wales, the most prolific European nations, grew by around 75 percent. France increased by a third, Spain by about a fifth. British North America grew too, but by an entirely different order of magnitude. Fed by large families and a flood of immigrants, the population of Britain's American colonies from 1690 to 1790 increased by almost 1,800 percent.[1] Every part of British North America felt the pressure.

Writing at the end of the eighteenth century, when English growth had become evident, Thomas Malthus predicted that the nation's economy could not bear the strain. Population would always outstrip available resources. Favorable economic conditions, Malthus argued, encouraged marriage and childbearing, yielding an increase in population that drove up the cost of food and drove down wages. If the economy improved, people would only multiply more rapidly and then be as badly off as before. Only poverty and dim prospects would prevent people from marrying and bearing children. Poverty was inevitable and permanent.

Despite the fantastic population growth in North America, Benjamin Franklin had a sunnier outlook. In a brief treatise, *Observations concerning the Increase of Mankind, Peopling of Countries, &c*, Franklin predicted a doubling of the North American population every twenty-five years—growth about five times as fast as England's—but with no ill effects. "Land being thus plenty in America, and so cheap as that a labouring man, that understands Husbandry, can in a short time save money enough to purchase a Piece of new Land sufficient for a plantation, whereon he may subsist a family; such are not afraid to marry." There was sufficient land to serve the burgeoning population for generations. "So vast is the Territory of *North America*, that it will require many ages to settle it fully; and till it is fully settled, labour will never be cheap here."[2]

In his speculations about "the Increase of Mankind," Franklin thought mathematically and theoretically, not practically. He ignored the strains that population growth placed on American institutions. Between 1690 and 1790, the population of Britain's thirteen North American colonies increased from 210,372 to 3,929,214. Every year, thousands of people had to obtain land, some in nearby tracts, some at great distances. Land had to be located, surveyed, purchased, and developed. Indian titles had to be obtained and conflicts mediated. Families uprooted themselves and moved long distances into forbidding environments. Franklin said nothing about the hardships and obstacles to making new farms.

In actuality, the demand for land in the middle of the eighteenth century precipitated a crisis in family life. The shortage of land drove some families to take great risks. They moved onto properties with insecure titles or into regions exposed to Indian assault. Their ownership was challenged and their lives threatened. To protect themselves, farmers became reckless. Violence was more common among farmers in the decades after the French and Indian War than at any time since the Glorious Revolution. In some places, the social order broke down for months or years. Franklin's plentitude of land did not guarantee social peace.

In the midst of these pressures, institutions had to be invented to cope with the huge demand for farms. Land had to be distributed in an orderly fashion, and controversies over titles and boundaries resolved. In the hour of crisis, the imperial government proved to be of little use. Instead of recognizing the problem, it attempted to shut down expansion, an impossibility in view of the need. Solutions had to be conjured just when the Revolutionary movement was mounting. After Independence, the problem was dumped on the fragile new government, with the fates of thousands of families in the balance. Only because of the plentitude of land, the determination of the migrating families, and the ruthless expulsion of the native population was the crisis resolved.

Herman Husband

Herman Husband, the son of a slaveholding planter in Cecil County, Maryland, first visited North Carolina in 1751. Apparently satisfied with what he found, he returned in 1754 as a scout for ten Maryland investors looking for land. He came in advance of a wave of migration that would sweep into North Carolina in the next decade, as the much denser populations in Virginia and the colonies northward moved into the lightly populated Lower South.[3] Six colonies had a larger population than North Carolina in 1750; by 1780 only Virginia and Pennsylvania did. Within the colony, Orange County, where Husband looked for land, was one of the fastest-growing regions. The population tripled between 1750 and 1770. By 1767 Orange County, with 3,870 taxable residents, was the most populous county in the colony.[4]

When Husband visited in 1754, he was not happy with what he found. Orange was still largely unsettled; the first towns appeared in the late 1750s and 1760s. The land itself was "wholsome pleasant air, good water, fertile land," and enjoyed a moderate winter, but the method of land distribution struck him as unworkable.[5] Always voluble about his dissatisfactions, Husband wrote a letter to John Earl Granville Viscount Carteret in August 1756, listing the difficulties. Granville had held on to his eighth of the colony after the other Carolina proprietors sold out to the king in 1729. In 1754 Granville owned most of Orange County and was the logical man to write about flaws in the land office.

Husband harbored no romantic views of migrant farmers. He acknowledged that among the recent arrivals were the idle and poor from northern parts, including "the rogueish sort as had been forced to fly the law." On the whole, they were "poor and of low capaciaties," and were exhausted from their journey. But even "honest industreous people," Husband found, had trouble getting land. He reported to Granville that "Haveing travelled 4, 5, 6, and 7 hundred miles by land to come here," they are "so reduced and their horses so farr spent as renders them unable to take a new journey to the land office 200 and odd miles to Edenton," where they could enter their claims and obtain a title. Meanwhile, they had to stay alive. While readying themselves for the long trip, the farmers settled where they could. For "one, two or three years" they worked land they did not own "until they can procure stock and grain to sustain their famalies (as generally they have large famalies of children etc.)."[6]

That was the first of Husband's gripes: titles could not be purchased in Orange County. Meanwhile, in an effort to obtain titles, the settlers often became entangled with what Husband took to be sharp operators. Having paid fees to Granville's "Deputy Surveyor," a man named Jared Carter, to survey their land, the settlers expected a deed in return. Farmers on the best lands, however, ran up against an obstacle. Almost always one of Carter's "friends" had already claimed the tract and required payment of "10, 12, or 15 pistoles" to clear the title, money that Husband suspected they shared with Carter. Unfortunately, even the payment did not result in a title. Granville's Edenton land office took forever to process the surveys. To help break the logjam, Husband took the farmers' purchase receipts to Edenton himself. There he found many of the receipts not recorded and no deeds entered for any of fifteen purchases. Husband saw around 170 land receipts in the office and estimated that upwards of a thousand, representing the payments of hundreds of gullible farmers, had yielded no titles. Only Carter's favorites could get control of the lands.[7]

Always distrustful of the powerful, Husband suspected bad faith all along the line, but at the very least, Granville's land office had fallen down on its job. The squatter-settlers were left in limbo, without legal rights to their lands and no way, especially given their "low capaciaties," of obtaining title. Husband worried that the squatting settlers would lose hope and slacken their efforts. Lacking title to the land, they would "become heartless and quite careless to improve their lands or buildings, whereby idleness grows amain which is ever the case where they have not a shure foundation and title in those Americian parts." Even the most industrious "begrudge to bestow their labour" when all their hard work could be lost by a court decision. Instead, the settlers' minds wandered to other places. There "being so many places, always a new setling, our ears are daily full of news that such and such a place is the best and finest."[8]

Growth

Granville's cavalier treatment of new arrivals and their difficulty in obtaining titles were details in a much larger picture of confusion and conflict. In the years when Husband moved his family to the South, an ongoing upheaval of unprecedented dimensions was disrupting the colonies. Everywhere there was an ever-increasing demand for land, rising prices, migration, and controversy over jurisdictions. The mechanisms for distributing lands that had worked for a century or more no longer functioned. They had been undergoing a major transition for half a century and by the 1760s had reached a breaking point. Husband's encounter with Granville in 1754 was a comparatively mild version of struggles up and down the colonies that in the next decade would turn violent.

In the first generation of European settlement land was easily come by. Seventeenth-century colonial governments used land as a lure to attract settlers from Europe. They needed a population to develop their colonies and to defend the settlements against hostile natives; land was the magnet. From New York to Georgia, the colonies practiced one form or another of head rights, distributing free land to anyone who paid the passage to America. Those with rights selected a plot in an unoccupied tract, had it surveyed, and applied for a title to the colonial government. Most of these head rights (or "land rights" in Maryland) went to the ship captains, merchants, and large planters who transported indentured servants to the Chesapeake, but they were also available to ordinary migrants. Indentured servants had a harder time of it, but on completion of their terms, they could earn fairly high wages or rent farms for a time and save to purchase land. Some received land as part of their freedom dues.[9] The owners of head rights often disposed of them at reasonable prices.

East of New York in New England, the land went to proprietors in township-sized parcels for distribution to the inhabitants who settled the place in return for minimal fees. The migrants often came in groups from their English hometowns and applied for grants as a body. Once granted the land, the proprietors admitted new inhabitants to the town, granting each a house lot near the center and parcels of woods, meadows, and plow lots in the outskirts. Individual families could gain admittance by paying a small fee and moving to the town.[10]

The holdings of disappointed land magnates added to the supply. The crown had initially distributed land to aspiring gentlemen who were granted the land in the expectation they would develop it. They envisioned the creation of huge estates on the model of English manors, with imported tenants and laborers working the soil on the landlord's behalf. When migrants refused to accept land on these terms, the grantees resorted to sales to recover something from their investments, usually at low prices by English standards.

In one fashion or another, land was easily acquired. Through most of the seventeenth century, land flowed to farm families through one of these channels—head rights, town grants, inexpensive purchases, or tenantry. Farmers could pursue the customary life cycle of bearing and raising children, benefiting from their offspring's labor in their late teens and early twenties, and then assisting them to set up for themselves on new farms which were to be had inexpensively in relatively close proximity.

The pressures on these systems grew as population inexorably increased. Since at least three-quarters of the population lived off the land in the North American colonies, the imperative to reproduce families meant farms for as many sons as possible. The purely mathematical implications of family reproduction were explosive. As Gloria Main observed in her study of New England family culture, the production of children, even in a bounteous land, was "like a time bomb quietly ticking." Five-sixths of the meteoric population growth was due to births in the colonies. Each family had to support itself and find land for the rising generation. With families averaging five or six children, each family was like a molecule of water turning into steam.[11] Multiplied by tens of thousands and augmented by accelerating migration from Great Britain and Europe, farm families put unbearable pressure on the available land supply. In John Murrin's words: "To achieve the patriarch's goal in a society that doubled its population every twenty-five years, each successive generation had to take over as much new land as all of their ancestors combined had occupied since the beginning of European settlement." For the first century, that process barely got colonists past the tidewater, but in the eighteenth century, this geographic rate of growth began to engulf everything east of the mountains and was starting to invade the Ohio Valley.[12]

By the end of the seventeenth century, land was no longer immediately available in nearby areas. New lands in distant and only vaguely known places had to be investigated. Some migrants went to less desirable empty sections like sandy and swampy central New Jersey and hilly central Pennsylvania. The number of towns in mountainous western Massachusetts (Berkshire and Hampshire counties) increased from fourteen to sixty-two between 1740 and the Revolution. Other migrants pressed outward at the edges of European settlement. New Englanders moved north into Vermont, New Hampshire, Maine, and the Maritime Provinces of Canada and west into northern Pennsylvania. Pennsylvanians spread westward and filed south down the Appalachian valley into western North and South Carolina. Southern farmers spilled over the mountains into the Ohio Valley.[13]

Families moved even though departure disrupted their lives. For many farmers the movement into new territory along every edge of European settlement offered the only relief from the pressure to find farms for their children. Everyone knew someone who had chosen to leave. Farmers who did not move had to consider it. The inability to provide for children could become a crisis of fatherhood, perhaps manhood. Meditating on the consequences of the midcentury land shortage, Robert Gross wondered whether Concord parents on the eve of the Revolution were not questioning their own fitness: "They were failing as parents: failing to pass on their property and status to the next generation, failing to direct their children to their proper roles in life."[14] The West loomed in everyone's imagination as a tantalizing and frightening possibility. A migration mentality fixed itself on farm culture.

Increased costs heightened the migrants' difficulties. Under the pressure of population growth and the increasing scarcity of nearby land, prices inevitably rose. In every section from Virginia north, land values increased as much as four times in less than three decades. In coastal Ipswich, Massachusetts, land prices rose 40 percent between 1720 and 1749 and another 20 percent between 1750 and 1771. Land prices in Andover, Massachusetts, doubled between the 1740s and the 1770s. It was the same in the Upper South. "Between the 1750s and 1770s, a time of no inflation, land prices multiplied four times—from 10 to 40 shillings an acre—in Prince George's and Anne Arundel Counties," Maryland's Western Shore tobacco-growing areas. In southeastern Pennsylvania, land prices also went up from ten to forty shillings an acre between the 1730s and the 1760s.[15]

The value of the crops could not keep pace with the increasing cost of land, making it harder and harder for fathers to accumulate sufficient land to pass on farms to their sons, or for their sons to accumulate land on their own.[16] In every area, from Massachusetts to the Carolina Lowcountry, Allan Kulikoff reports, "the proportion of farm families owning land dropped and farm sizes diminished while poverty and tenancy grew." "New England swarmed with transients too poor to go to a frontier." In Prince George's County, Maryland, the proportion of landholders decreased from two-thirds in 1705 to just under a half in 1776. By 1787 only two-fifths of householders in Virginia's Northern Neck owned land. A parallel decrease in landholders occurred in Chester County, Pennsylvania, where the proportion dropped from three-quarters in 1760 to 63 percent by 1775. The landless could rent farms, but rents rose as the number of tenants increased. In Anne Arundel County, Maryland, rents went from 450 pounds of tobacco at the beginning of the century to 800 pounds by 1750.[17]

As prices rose, the governments began to see their unoccupied land as a source of revenue. The thousands of families seeking to reproduce themselves constituted an immense market. Instead of giving townships to migrating farmers, Connecticut began to sell township plots at auction, seeking ways to pay for the wars of the early eighteenth century. In Virginia, powerful magnates gained control of huge tracts in the West, where they made fortunes by selling land to needy farmers. Small farmers themselves became land speculators. In view of the steady inflation of farm prices, they bought up more acreage than they needed for their families in the expectation the surplus could be sold at a profit. In the eighteenth century, land became a big business. This commodification of land altered the whole system of land acquisition. The cost of purchase became an obstacle to the pursuit of farmers' normal life cycle. To acquire land that previously had been available at low cost, they or their children had to go into debt. Money, banks, loans, and all the perplexities of finance became as important to farmers as the weather.[18]

Herman Husband caught a glimpse of the opportunities for speculation on his 1754 visit to Orange County. He told Granville in his 1755 letter that the high cost of land in Pennsylvania, higher even than in Virginia and Maryland, caused farmers to "move out and settle those high and back lands of Virginia and Caralina; and as farr southwest as to Georgia." Herman's friends read the situation and bought a thousand acres each in Orange County, probably with no intention of ever moving in, knowing they could resell at a profit.[19] After Husband returned to settle in Orange County in 1762, he bought and sold land at a sprightly pace. In May of 1764, he registered a deed from Granville for 696 acres. By then he held more than 10,000 acres. In the same month, he sold 208 acres to Henry Linterman and four months later tracts totaling 2,664¼ acres to eight purchasers. To replenish his inventory, Husband in August 1765 bought from Granville another 2,116 acres, which he continued to sell off in smaller parcels over the next few years.[20] Husband's sympathies for the plight of the squatters did not stop him from profiting from sales to the very people he defended.

His dealings were dwarfed by the land-marketing organizations that came into being under the stimulus of midcentury expansion. Land companies had existed earlier, especially in New England, but with restricted purposes. They mainly bought and sold large tracts to one another, or attempted to settle tenants on their lands on the model of English manors. But these companies usually foundered. In New England, farmers could barely support their own families, much less pay rent to a landlord. The early companies succeeded along the coast or near cities, where urban markets provided adequate returns, and almost nowhere else.[21]

As prices shot up and the need for land increased, land companies and private speculators looked anew at small-farmer sales. In the eighteenth century, real estate entrepreneurs organized for the very purpose of selling retail to the hordes of migrants moving west, north, or south. In a great swirl of activity, the companies entertained fantastic schemes to engross huge western tracts, sweet-talk Indians into selling their lands, and wield political influence to confirm their purchases. In so doing, they became potential facilitators of migration and expansion. Permutations and combinations of companies blending and separating make an exact count difficult, but at least ten land companies were organized in the quarter century before the Revolution, and this number leaves out the countless individual speculators who devised schemes for settling tracts from Nova Scotia to Florida.[22]

The companies potentially served the very useful purpose of clearing titles with the natives and the governing jurisdictions. They purported to solve the problems like those of the Orange County squatters in obtaining titles from the land office in Edenton. In actuality, the land companies' titles frequently rested on shaky foundations. The company proprietors wielded their political influence to make large purchases from the Indians, then tried to get confirmation from the imperial and colonial governments, but slippage all along the line delayed the opening of land offices and in some cases thwarted the venture entirely. The North Carolinian Richard Henderson sent Daniel Boone into the area later designated as Kentucky to survey land in 1769. Henderson's group spent ten thousand pounds to purchase land from the Cherokees and soon after set up an independent government under the name of Transylvania. After Independence, Henderson petitioned to have Transylvania numbered among the "United Colonies." Then in 1779, the Virginia legislature declared the original Indian purchase void, and the whole venture collapsed. In compensation for his expenditures, Henderson received 200,000 acres in Kentucky, but his original plan failed.[23] As happened to many of his fellow speculators, Henderson's bubble burst, and those who trusted his promises went down with him.

Henderson's Transylvania was typical. In all but a few cases, the pre-Revolutionary land companies and speculators settled few farmers and were of little use in actually getting settlers onto the land. For the most part, the colonial governments carried the burden of dispensing land. Massachusetts and Connecticut were the most successful. They continued to grant townships to individuals just as they had been doing since the 1630s, but with a difference. In the eighteenth century, the governments themselves became quasi-companies, auctioning land to augment tax revenues, as in Connecticut and Massachusetts, or to line the pockets of colony officials, as in New Hampshire. Moreover, the recipients of the town grants functioned as companies, speculating in land and reselling property, often without settling themselves. In the South, early grants to the proprietary colonies had languished for decades until the price rise revived hopes for profit. Granville in North Carolina was among the rejuvenated proprietors who exploited grants first bestowed on an ancestor. The heirs of William Penn and the New Jersey proprietors profitably combined government of their colonies with land sales. By becoming de facto land companies, these governments facilitated migration more than the flimsy private organizations whose chief contribution was to pave the way for more enlightened private land companies after the Revolution.

In the 1780s and 1790s, land companies began to serve their intended purpose. William Cooper in the Otsego region of New York was the model proprietor. He surveyed tracts, opened stores and roads, extended credit, and rented land to the indigent. He failed to maintain the control of politics as he would have liked, but he was instrumental in opening a large tract in upstate New York.[24] Enlightened proprietors like Cooper recognized the importance of long-term development rather than short-term profits.[25] They offered rentals to migrants with insufficient funds or credit to purchase land.[26] The proprietors were more interested in developing the land than collecting immediate rents. Some tenants paid no rents for a decade as they cleared fields and put up houses and barns. Land companies eased the migrants' entry on to the land on the theory that the value of land around the pioneer settlers rose as a result of their work.

Contested Boundaries

Until the institutions for distributing land began to jell late in the century, the frontier was in turmoil. The period of greatest tension was the 1760s, following the French and Indian War. This was the generation of violence. In those years, pent-up demand, higher prices, and inadequate distribution mechanisms converged to create unbearable pressures. For a moment, neither governments nor private companies could manage the formidable growth in population. Title difficulties troubled settlers along virtually every North American frontier. At every edge of settlement where new tracts were being opened, the land was entangled in controversy. The largest obstacle was not corrupt or dilatory officials, as in North Carolina, but competing claims to jurisdiction or ownership. Huge swaths of unoccupied land fell under two jurisdictions—two colonies, or two land companies, or Native Americans and English, or one tribal faction versus another, each side claiming rights to the same tract. In many cases, not just one land office, as in Edenton, but two, each in a different colony, issued titles.

In the aftermath of the French and Indian War, as demand pressed against every frontier, conflict broke out all over the western landscape. A willingness to take up land in territory still claimed by Indians was one measure of the pressure farmers felt. From the late 1740s on, migrant farmers moved onto Indian lands in the Allegheny and Ohio valleys to build their cabins and open small fields. Cheap land titles or free squatting privileges attracted them, but they paid a price of another kind. In the decade after 1754, thousands lost their lives or were taken captive. Exaggerated or not, one horror story after another percolated back from the frontier. The *Pennsylvania Gazette* published accounts of children's heads bashed against cabin door posts and women tied to trees and forced to watch their husbands tortured.[27] Yet the stream of migrants kept flowing directly into the circuits of Indian war parties on contested lands. Both British and Pennsylvania officials tried to hold them back, promising the Indians no more intrusions. But the pressure was too great. The need for land drove the migrants into the danger zones. In 1768 the Pennsylvania Assembly imposed a death penalty on people convicted of trespassing on Indian lands, and still they came.[28]

Indian hostility was but one of the hazards to be overcome. Everywhere farmers became embroiled in title controversies. The problems originated in crown patents to the original proprietors. The first patents were notoriously confused. Boundaries specified in London did not hold up on the ground. Pennsylvania's northern, southern, and western boundaries were contested by Connecticut, New York, Virginia, and Maryland. New York and New Hampshire fought over Vermont for three decades. It took years to settle the line between North and South Carolina.[29]

The boundary problems lay in abeyance for the first century of settlement when ample land well within the colony's boundaries sufficed to meet the settlers' needs. As the century wore on, however, and population kept growing, settlement of the borderlands became a necessity. People purchased titles from their home government and moved onto the land, probably aware that their titles would be contested. Farmers took the chance in the belief the colonial governments would back them in the inevitable suits for trespass. The colonies, for their part, hoped to strengthen their claims by putting bodies on the ground. When neighboring farmers with title from an adjoining colony complained of someone harvesting their corn or pasturing animals in their fields, suits were entered. Since the cases turned on conflicting claims of colonial governments, rather than individual trespasses, governments ultimately prosecuted the cases, which were carried up the chain of courts and commissions and eventually settled in London. Eventually to halt the flow of cases, governments commissioned surveyors to mark the boundaries, the expedition of Charles Mason and Jeremiah Dixon along the Maryland-Pennsylvania-Delaware border being the most famous instance.[30] This sequence of events was enacted on one stage after another on nearly every colonial boundary.

The French and Indian War blocked westward movement for a decade, but at its conclusion the floodgates opened and settlers poured into the western and northern regions. Many squatted at least temporarily while they waited for the owners to catch up and offer title. Ultimately, however, as the land filled in, conflicts occurred, first farmer against farmer and then colony against colony. The results were predictable: hot spots at every friction point and commonly violence.

A typical outburst occurred along the Virginia-Pennsylvania border in what is now southwest Pennsylvania. Virginia interpreted the sea-to-sea clause in its 1609 charter to designate a northern boundary angling northwest from the coast across the southwest corner of Pennsylvania to a point above the forks of the Ohio. Squatters who moved into the area after the British drove out the French in 1758 confronted confusing and dangerous conditions: Indian tribes jealous of their presence, speculators offering titles under conflicting Indian deeds, and, overarching all, Virginia's claim to Pennsylvania territory. In the summer of 1771, Virginia settlers associated under an agreement to drive off Pennsylvania law officers and imposed a fine of fifty pounds on anyone who refused to follow their rules. In 1772 the settlers expelled Thomas Woods, a sheriff from Pennsylvania's Bedford County, and one of his deputies. The associates stripped the officials naked and threatened to kill them if they returned. Two hundred twenty squatters signed a petition charging the Pennsylvania government and its officials with oppression and injustice. The settlers demanded that no sheriff's process be served against trespassers until a definite boundary had been run to ascertain the jurisdiction of Pennsylvania. The dispute carried over into the Revolution and set the stage for conflicts between Tory and Patriot partisans.[31]

In a still more dramatic encounter, Connecticut's farmers moved to the Wyoming Valley within Pennsylvania's boundaries on the slim chance that the sea-to-sea clause in Connecticut's charter would hold up against Pennsylvania's. These Wyoming Valley settlers worked under a double jeopardy. Both the province of Pennsylvania and the Delaware Indians claimed the land. The first of the Connecticut settlers were massacred or driven out in Pontiac's Uprising of 1763, but others returned after the area was purchased from the Indians in connection with 1768 Treaty of Fort Stanwix to face opposition from Pennsylvania. The arrival of 240 Connecticut settlers to the Wyoming Valley in 1769 set off a two-year war between people from the two colonies.

Conflicts on the pattern of the Virginia-Pennsylvania struggle and the Wyoming Valley wars occurred in nearly every British colony.[32] In New Jersey, a mix-up at the time of settlement in the 1660s resulted in two groups claiming the same land. The duke of York's emissary, Richard Nicolls, granted the duke's land to settlers from New England and Long Island and confirmed the purchases that these settlers had made from the Indians. Meanwhile, unbeknownst to Nicolls, the duke conveyed most of eastern New Jersey to Sir George Carteret, who sent over his cousin Philip as governor. Philip Carteret acknowledged Nicolls's grants, but later Carteret's heirs insisted on quitrents before recognizing the titles. This demand, which many settlers resisted, threw all their titles into question. By the 1730s, hundreds of thousands of acres in northern New Jersey were in contention. To protect themselves, farmers formed committees to represent them in court and to take whatever action was necessary to prevent subversion of their titles. When some of their number were arrested, the farmers took action. In July 1747, two hundred of them descended on Perth Amboy armed with clubs and led by fiddlers and a pennant bearer. The sheriff read the riot act to no avail; no one dispersed. The crowd assailed the officers with staves and clubs and set the prisoners free. Five times in the following months, protesters freed popular leaders from jail by force. If resisted, they threatened that "there should not have been a Man left alive, or a House standing in . . . Perth Amboy." It is estimated that 90 percent of the populace stood with the rioters.[33]

Some of the most forthright protests occurred in New York, where migrants from New England had lived peacefully for decades, some as tenants, some as squatters, on the large patents stretching east from the Hudson River. Initially, the Dutch and English manor lords were happy to have their lands developed and permitted the New Englanders to settle on favorable terms. As the price of land went up in the 1750s and 1760s, however, the landlords recognized the rising value of their property and tried to collect rents from the longtime occupants. Outraged at this imposition, one of their number, William Prendergast, organized a couple of hundred club-bearing Dutchess County farmers to expel rent-paying farmers on the theory that those who acquiesced in the landlords' demands threatened everyone else. From the offending farmers, the protesters turned on the judges who took evidence against "mob men." They felt they could bring the landlords to an accommodation by preventing their compliant tenants from paying rent and stopping judges from prosecuting cases. If any of the "mob men" were sued for their rents or imprisoned, Prendergast's forces promised to free the prisoners, "or we will lose Our Lives." Prendergast kept protesting that he wanted to accommodate the landlords and was a good subject of the king, but "*they had made him a desperate man.*" At his trial a witness remembered him saying "it would not do to be overcome by Laws in their Circumstances. Their Estates—lay at risque—and they must either Quit their Estates or not be overcome."[34] After his capture, Prendergast was convicted of treason and sentenced to death, but at the governor's behest George III pardoned him.

The outbursts up and down the continent were farmer uprisings. In all of them farmers took the law into their own hands, even to the point of forming alternate governments. Prendergast marched his followers around a field like a militia band while he stood by with sword in hand. He laid down laws which he enforced in a mock court formed from four fence rails with punishment consisting of dragging offenders through a mudhole. In the midst of the guerrilla warfare against the landlords, he proclaimed that "he had the name of heading a Govt. of his own and that since he had the name of it he might was well exercise it."[35] The eccentricities, the violence, the suspension of the law, all grew out of farmers' defense of their livelihoods. The phrase "economic interests" does not do justice to their motives. Everything depended on the land they occupied. They were battling for their families' well-being, for continuation of the life pattern on which their existence was based, for the avoidance of ruin. When their control of land was jeopardized, these ordinarily placid people resorted to desperate measures.

Orange County Regulators

Of all these uprisings, the Regulation movement in Orange County led by Herman Husband was the most violent. After Husband moved to Orange County in 1762, he put his talent for protest to use against court officials. The word "corruption," a republican mainstay, came into play in a conflict between Orange County farmers and the courts. Husband and his compatriots believed that justices, sheriffs, and lawyers were cheating people. The controversy ended in a pitched battle in 1771, with nine dead and seven executed.[36] Husband, charged with treason, was forced to flee as a fugitive from justice.

The farmers' complaints began with the debt they incurred when buying new land and setting up farms. The number of debt cases rose astronomically in the years of Orange County's growth after 1763. On average, the courts heard 68 cases a year between 1753 and 1762; between 1763 and 1765, they heard 280 a year.[37] With currency hard to come by, nearly every economic exchange—purchasing a cow or buying an ax—involved a lingering debt. For farmland, the largest of a farmer's purchases, a loan secured by an interest-paying bond was unavoidable. Buyers promised to pay in a few years, and if they failed to meet their obligations, the holders of the bonds could take them to court. Nearly every newcomer carried around a load of debt and stood at risk of a suit should the lender choose to collect.

Although the farmers' distress began with debt, the Orange County protests were not directed at creditors. Farmers did not dispute the validity of their debts or impugn the people who lent them money. Rather than accuse money lenders of chicanery, Husband turned his wrath on court officials: lawyers who prosecuted the cases, clerks who recorded court action, and sheriffs and their deputies who distressed and sold property. The process of collecting debts, not the debts themselves, was the issue.

In 1766, not long after his arrival, Husband organized the Sandy Creek Association to oppose official corruption. It soon dissolved in the face of government intimidation, but Husband did not give up. He was particularly outraged at exorbitant fees imposed by the county recorder, Edmund Fanning, a New York–born politician who studied briefly at Harvard and Yale before migrating to Orange County, where he served as register of deeds, militia colonel, and two-term member of the colonial assembly. Husband titled a 1771 essay *A Fan for Fanning,* making him the archetypical corrupt official, bleeding the meager resources of the Orange County poor. In 1768 Husband was charged with organizing a hundred farmers to shoot their guns at Fanning's house. Husband never came to trial because 700 farmers sprang him from prison. Two years later, in September 1770, still angry at the venality of court officials, 150 "regulators" led by Husband, James Hunter, and others stormed the superior courthouse in Hillsborough, the Orange County seat, and beat up court officers and attorneys in the street. The next day, they invaded Fanning's pretentious new house, burned his papers, broke up his furniture, and finally demolished the whole structure. To express their contempt, the crowd "took from his chains a negro that had been executed some time, and placed him att the lawyer's bar, and filled the Judge's seat with human excrement."[38]

Unable to stand by with the county in a state of insurgency, Governor William Tryon called out 1,185 provincial militia and marched to Orange, where he met a motley army of 2,000 poorly armed Regulators at Alamance Creek on the western border of the county. Husband and a local minister tried to mediate between the two, but the farmers refused to disperse on the governor's command. "Fire and be damned!" was their response to the governor's ultimatum. His own troops hesitated to fire on the hapless farmers, but Tryon insisted: "Fire on them or on me!" For two hours the troops fired guns and artillery, and the Regulators, crouching behind rocks, fired back. Nine men were killed and many wounded. Tryon took fifteen prisoners and executed one on the spot to strike fear in the Regulators' hearts. A court martial in Hillsborough condemned six additional prisoners and saw them executed.[39] Then overnight the Regulator movement collapsed, and most of the farmers moved on to other frontiers.

Historians have read into the Regulator conflict a clash between elemental forces in colonial American society. So violent an outbreak, involving so many ordinary people—by some counts, three-quarters of the farmer population joined the Regulators—must have originated in some painful stress in agricultural society. On the whole, historians have seen in the struggle the fundamental cleavages that they happen to find in eighteenth-century America. The nineteenth-century historian George Bancroft detected rumblings of the coming Revolution. Historians under the influence of frontier historian Frederick Jackson Turner saw evidence of an east-west conflict, involving underrepresented, unpolished backcountry citizens versus indifferent coastal elites. After the decline of consensus history in the 1950s, conflict historians found class conflict between yeoman farmers and powerful, slaveholding planters. In a variant of class conflict, James Whittenburg depicts the Regulators as farmers displaced from power by merchants and lawyers and fighting to regain control. In the days of the republican synthesis, the instability of backcountry society coupled with a heavy dose of republican ideology accounted for Regulator action.[40]

Every explanation of underlying causes, however, must start with Husband's 1770 *Impartial Relation,* his wordy account of what happened and why. Husband was quite explicit about cause: the agencies of government, and particularly the county court, were in the hands of corrupt officials who were illegally charging excessive fees and collecting excessive taxes. Husband began his tract by quoting extensively from a 1759 pamphlet by George Sims from adjoining Granville County, who graphically portrayed the plight of farmers who were subject to court fees.[41] Sims evoked a hypothetical poor farmer who goes in debt four or five pounds for a few family necessities, hoping to escape "the lash of the law" until he can sell a few effects to pay the debt. He gives a "judgment" bond to a merchant, who takes him to court. The clerk of the court enters the case on the court docket and issues an execution "the work of one long minute." In return the poor man must pay the clerk—a Fanning-like officer named Colonel Benton—forty-one shillings and fivepence. Unable to raise the cash, the poor man accepts Benton's offer to weed Benton's corn at the rate of one shilling, sixpence a day, typical common labor wages. According to Sims's calculation, the poor man must work twenty-seven days to repay Benton for the work of a minute. The poor man asks what about his wife and parcel of small children at home. He loses a month's work and has yet to pay the merchant. Resigned to his lot, he turns to go but is stopped by the "damned Lawyers" who confessed the debt on the poor man's behalf and for so doing charged thirty shillings. Thus he must go to work nineteen days "for that pick-pocket" and then as many days for the sheriff for his trouble. Only then can you "go home and see your living wrecked and tore to pieces to satisfy your merchant."[42]

That inescapable dynamic of exorbitant fees drove Husband and the Regulators to distraction. Taken to court, farmers "must employ Clerks to register their Deeds, &c. and these men have demanded six times the legal Fee, and will not do the business for less. And what is the consequence? The Land becomes forfeit. The Clerks, and Lawyers, & c. watch their opportunity and seize the forefeiture and possess the Lands, and the people, when they have improved them must turn out, or pay for them the demand of these Men."[43] The strain that drove the farmers to violence came not out of an overriding social or ideological conflict but from the unjust and illegal fees exacted by court officials. The protesters fought official corruption not as members of social class or as frontier inhabitants but as farmers against court officials who jeopardized the farmers' livings.

In Orange County, suspicion focused on a particular man, Edmund Fanning, who was suspected of stopping at nothing to line his own pockets. Strangely, no specific instances of abuse of office were detailed in Husband's diatribe. No one sued Fanning for a particular misdemeanor. The basic problem was a lack of trust. The charges were based on a general suspicion, as if his fraudulent conduct were patently obvious. Perhaps no one could be trusted completely in Orange County in 1770. The residents had piled in too recently for a mutual confidence to develop. There was no Joshua Hempstead, the steady, experienced New London justice of the peace, whose wisdom, prudence, and fairness was proven over many years. Edmund Fanning was a New Englander and careerist politician, neither quality endearing him to Carolinians.[44]

With his law training and pedigree, Edmund Fanning stood out from the ordinary farmers in Orange County. On Long Island, where his family was well known, he would have ascended naturally to leadership. Even in Orange County, his abilities sufficed to win a popular election to the legislature. But he was not deeply enough entrenched in county society to bear up under the fear and anxiety of farmers unable to pay their debts and in danger of losing their land. This society had formed too quickly in the burst of immigration after 1760. Thrown together overnight, no one knew who was to be trusted. Those in power had not been tried and tested. Fanning was a victim of a society that had grown too rapidly to sort itself out. The county lacked a body of local men who had earned the trust of their neighbors. If Fanning had spent more time in his neighbors' fields, lent them money, and bought their wheat, he might have suffered less. Instead, he set himself apart by building a large house in Hillsborough, the Orange County seat, which the mob trashed. Known primarily as a friend of Lord Tryon, he reeked of patronage and ambition. It remains doubtful to this day whether Fanning committed the crimes he was accused of, but his unstable position in this freshly formed society made him a target when tempers flared.

The nature of the Orange County protests did not lead to any deep reforms in government. The complaints against Fanning were personal, not institutional. Orange County farmers participated in the revolt against imperial power along with everyone else and supported the installation of a republican government at home, but they did not take advantage of the Revolution to demand economic equality or a redefinition of property or reform of the courts. In the coming century, as the Orange County social order settled down, courts and court appointments proceeded smoothly. Magistrates were selected by custom from the county's various neighborhoods, assuring adjudication not only by one's peers but by one's neighbors. There were no more complaints about official malfeasance.[45]

Farmers and Slaves

Husband's involvement in the settlement of new land ultimately led him to a new perspective on slavery. Even though his own father was a Maryland slave owner, Husband objected to the importation of slaves into Orange. He did not find fault with the abusive treatment of Africans or condemn their enslavement as an affront to the human spirit. Neither Enlightenment rationalism nor his attenuated Quakerism moved him. He disliked slaves for the space they occupied. In a time when he and his friends needed more land, slaves occupied tracts that should have been given to poor whites. In Husband's mind, blacks and whites competed for places on the land. He had a farmer's sense of the land's carrying capacity. "As lands being capable of maintaining but such a number of inhabitants, for each of those Negroes the publike is deprived of a white person." Moreover, slaves did work that poor migrants could have performed to earn money for buying farms. If the English were stopped from keeping slaves, he told Granville, there would not only be "a white person employed and encouraged to settle for every black so bought, but that money which goes to purchase those blacks would be put into their hands for their labour, wherewith they soon would become able to procure a farm to themselves, and thereby become able to employ more poor."[46]

Husband's take on slavery was the view of a farmer in need of land. He was not concerned about large planters overshadowing small farmers, or about the dangers of racial mingling. He does not even allude to the inferior natures of the captive peoples. He was concerned about competition for space. As farmers listened for news that "such and such a place is the best and finest" land, they worried about aliens filling that space first. Husband's was an expansionist racism, directed not against slavery but against slaves—and most likely black people in any condition—whose presence on the land blocked white settlement.

Husband's anger evoked violent images of how to prevent slaves from engulfing the land: "Unless the white people take to beat out their brains as they do the piggs when over stocked, as Egyptians did the Hebrews, they must unavoidably (according to the naturall course of things) wholy over run . . . the whole provinces." If they were but animals, the surplus slaves could be disposed of, but "being of human shape and understanding [they] are not to be stoped from breeding or destroyed when overstocked with them." His nightmare was a North Carolina become another Jamaica where, he estimated, the ratio of black to white was twenty to one.[47]

His projections, while extravagant, were prescient. Husband believed some slaveholders were so "stupified" as to desire an occasion to destroy the remaining Indians and fill the land with slaves.[48] He pictured slave owners, in their eagerness to fill up the land with slaves, provoking needless wars to rid the land of Indians. He envisioned the future occupation of the South as a four-part racial competition, with white slaveholders and their black slaves on one side and Indians and white farmers on the other. The slaveholders aimed to expel Indians, and stock the land with slaves.[49] As it turned out, Husband was right. Over the next century, slave owners did drive out Indians and fill their places with slaves. Multitudes of northern white farmers fought slave occupation of western lands, not out of sympathy for slaves or outrage at the breach of republican liberty, but from jealousy of black people occupying space rightfully due to whites.

After the Revolution, outbursts continued: Shays's Rebellion in Massachusetts, the Liberty boys' revolt in Maine, the Whiskey Rebellion, and risings by Fries in Pennsylvania and the Green Mountain Boys in Vermont. Between ongoing struggles over land titles and controversies over currency, there was plenty to complain about. But none of these snowballed into a mass movement against the government. Farmers survived the eighteenth-century agricultural crisis. In Orange County, the populace eventually installed trustworthy officials in the courts. At the other sites of violence, the courts settled contested titles. In older settled areas, farm communities avoided the strife and class divisions that a land shortage might have provoked. Robert Gross's summary of the situation in pre-Revolutionary Concord applied to many towns: "Concord by mid-century had managed to work out a rough balance between numbers and resources and to escape the worst social consequences of overpopulation. Farms were not split up into smaller and smaller parcels. The proportion of the landless remained stable at about 30 per cent. The concentration of land holdings in the hands of the big farmers actually lessened. . . . In this case, the historian Frederick Jackson Turner was right: the west provided a safety valve for the pent-up pressures of an overcrowded civilization."[50]

All along all the frontiers, land companies facilitated movement into new territories. After Independence, the national government was even more instrumental in meeting the insatiable need. The weakness of the Confederation in the 1780s did not prevent the passage of land legislation. Every state understood the necessity of opening territory for the expanding population. Both North and South rallied behind the Land Ordinance of 1785 and the Northwest Ordinance of 1787. The 1785 ordinance provided for the appointment of a government "geographer" to supervise the surveying teams, facilitating the occupation of the land.[51]

Because of the colonies' long experience with expansion on a scale unmatched by any European nation, the new government devised far more workable solutions than any of the imperial government's. Recognizing the importance of children in farmers' minds, the second paragraph of the Northwest Ordinance of 1787 set the rules for dividing intestate estates, granting to all children, male and female, equal parts and saving a third for the widow's dower. The Land Ordinance of 1785 specified the exact methods for surveying townships so as to prevent the confusion about boundaries that had roiled settlements up and down the continent for more than a century. Each surveyor and chain bearer was required to take an oath to faithfully discharge his duties, and the ordinance specified that "the geographer and surveyors, shall pay the utmost attention to the variation of the magnetic needle; and shall run and note all lines by the true meridian." Too much misery had resulted from sloppy and dishonest surveys.

Within a decade of the new government's establishment in 1789, the machinery was in place for turning open land into farm properties. The government bought land from the Indians, surveyed it, and offered tracts in farm-size plots that grew ever less expensive. There were four government land offices in the Northwest Territory in 1800; by 1812 the land office system had been extended to the Mississippi Territory and the number of offices increased to eighteen. The system was hindered mainly by the temptation to make the government itself into a land company. Alexander Hamilton, as secretary of the treasury, expected public lands to become a major source of revenue for the debt-ridden nation. Situating responsibility for land sales in the treasury indicated that the government thought of public land as a source of income. The ideal appealed equally to a frugal Republican administration under Thomas Jefferson and his secretary of the treasury Albert Gallatin, who as a land speculator himself understood the potential for profits. When Gallatin admonished a Mississippi Territory surveyor to get a move on—"I will only repeat, what I had often urged to your Predecessor that the speedy completion of the surveys of the private claims & public lands in the Mississippi Territory is an object of great national importance"—he had in mind the need for revenues as well as the welfare of farmers starved for land.[52]

Over the next half century, the demands of farmers gradually won out over the needs of the treasury. William Findley of western Pennsylvania spoke candidly of the land office as "a retail store," meaning it was to cater to individual small farmers rather than large speculative purchasers who bought land in large chunks.[53] The farm population of course pressed always for reductions of cost, until eventually in the Homestead Act of 1862 the government gave away land to bona fide settlers. A little ungainly and always subject to private manipulation, the land laws did their job. Aided by the new institutions for distributing land, farmers found their way to open space where their children could make farms and take on the responsibility of provisioning their families.

When Husband left North Carolina in 1771, he put slaves and the problems of farmers behind him. After failing to mediate an agreement between farmers and the governor at the battle of the Alamance, he had ridden away from Orange County. Charged with treason, he was forced to flee without his family. Governor Tryon offered a reward of a hundred pounds and a thousand acres of land to anyone who would take Husband dead or alive, leading him to introduce himself to strangers as "Toscape Death." To conceal his identity, Husband purchased land in western Pennsylvania in the names of his children and brothers. He settled in Bedford County with his wife Amy and their children, and there envisioned a great inland empire bounded by the Allegheny and Rocky mountains, where a vast city, called the New Jerusalem, the largest and most glorious the world had known, would rise. He told inquirers that the natural geography of the continent conformed to specifications in the book of Ezekiel. Like a land developer working on a biblical scale, Husband envisioned his task as locating the route of a great highway through the mountains for "princes of the east" to enter this internal realm. While these visions were opening to him, he took a role in county affairs. Bedford County elected him to the state assembly in 1789. In 1795 he was mistakenly arrested as a leader in the whiskey uprising and taken to prison in Philadelphia. As part of his defense, he sent to North Carolina for certificates of his character. After he was cleared, ill health compelled him to stop at a tavern on the outskirts of the city. There Amy came to nurse him as he died. Husband was buried on June 19, 1795, and soon forgotten as a prophet of American expansion.[54]

PART THREE

Connecticut, 1640–1760

5. Uncas and Joshua

The Acquisition of Connecticut

Turning now from North America as whole to farming in New England, we begin the story with an event in the administration of President Andrew Jackson. In the summer of 1833, the old Indian fighter took a side trip to Norwich, Connecticut, during a presidential tour of New England. Accompanied by Vice President Martin Van Buren, members of his cabinet, and Henry Edwards, governor of Connecticut, President Jackson drove from Hartford in an open carriage with an escort of cavalry. A large crowd of townspeople, including bands of children with banners and mottoes, assembled to watch him lay the cornerstone of a monument to the Indian chief Uncas in the Norwich town cemetery. The orator of the day, local lawyer N. L. Shipman, rehearsed the history of Uncas's family and described the current state of Uncas's people, the Mohegans, who had once hunted on the site of Norwich and the larger part of New London County. The town historian, Frances Manwaring Caulkins, who probably was in attendance, observed that "a few scattered Indians from Mohegan, received the visitors with martial salutes and joyful acclamations."[1]

Caulkins understood the development of the town as a story of one people displacing another. She titled her book *History of Norwich, Connecticut: From Its Possession by the Indians to the Year 1866* and began with a chapter on the "Aboriginal History of the Nine-Mile Square," noting the Indian names that still marked major features: Quinebaug, Shetucket, Mashipaug,

Waweekus, Pautipag. She knew the Indian title to the land was once "paramount to all others."[2] Yet by 1833, the Indians who once hunted freely from the Connecticut River to the Rhode Island border were confined to less than two square miles of planting ground called Mohegan. White European settlers occupied the rest of the area.

The town did not complete Uncas's monument in the town cemetery until 1842, when it was finally funded by "female gifts." William Stone, the orator at the dedication on July 4, honored Uncas in the way conquerors often exalt vanquished native peoples when they are safely disposed of. Stone pointed to the spot where Uncas's remains were supposed to lie and told his hearers "we may there tread upon the dust of kings." The Mohegans' downfall did not arouse guilt in Stone or his hearers. The Indians were doomed from the start. "Such has been the design of an all-wise Providence—a design which the strong faith of the Puritans enabled them to foresee." The disappearance of the Mohegans did not appear as a crime to Stone, or even as a tragedy. It was destiny, an act of God.[3]

Stone acknowledged that Uncas had taken the side of the English in the 1637 war with the Pequots and for twenty years defended Connecticut against war parties from Rhode Island. The Mohegans never engaged in armed struggle on the side of the Indians. Uncas and his successors peacefully collaborated with the Connecticut government, all to no effect as far as his people were concerned. In 1842 the Connecticut wilderness was no longer theirs. The Mohegans had not been compelled to move away as most displaced Indians were. They remained peaceful coinhabitants of southeast Connecticut and still lost the battle. In less than half a century, without force or violence, the colony's English settlers had vanquished Uncas and nearly obliterated his descendants. Uncas and his tribe served only as Norwich's heroic history, its ruins, and its lost kings.

Contact

New London County, where Uncas's hunting grounds were once located, was the residence of Joshua Hempstead (1678–1758), the surveyor, gravestone carver, shipbuilder, and farmer who from 1711 until a few months before his death in 1758 kept the most extensive farm diary in eighteenth-century New England. Hempstead's grandfather, Robert, arrived in New London when Uncas was in his prime and obtained lands where the Pequots once roamed. Robert's fortunes were the reverse of Uncas's. While the Mohegans and Pequots were reduced to a vanishing point, the Hempsteads flourished in New London.

Robert Hempstead (d. 1653) came in 1645 with the first group of settlers under the leadership of John Winthrop, Jr. Even before receiving an official grant from Massachusetts Bay, a small band of eight or ten men cut hay in the New London meadows and salt marshes.[4] In May 1646, the General Court officially allowed them to open a plantation "in the Pequot country, which appertains to this jurisdiction, as part of our proportion of the conquered country." Massachusetts and Connecticut soldiers had both participated in the defeat of the Pequots in 1637 and now shared jurisdiction over the land by right of conquest. The court minutes noted that "some Indians who are now planted upon the place, where the said plantation is begun, are willing to remove from their planting ground for the more quiet and convenient settling of the English there"—as if they went willingly. But the elder John Winthrop's journal spoke more candidly of danger. From a strategic point of view, he wrote of New London, it was "of great concernment to have it planted, to be a curb to the Indians."[5]

On the ground, tensions with the Mohegans in the early years kept the New London settlers in a state of fright. Ordinarily cooperative and loyal, Uncas reacted ferociously to John Winthrop, Jr.'s, settlement at Nameag, the Indian name for New London. In the summer of 1646, the Nameag settlers asked two Pequot sachems, ostensibly under Uncas's regime, to hunt food for them on the east side of the Thames River. Not only did the hunters trespass on Mohegan hunting grounds, the two sachems appeared to be yielding to the authority of the English rather than to Uncas. He should have given permission, not the Connecticut authorities. Furious, he set upon the Pequots with three hundred men, chased them back into their village at Nameag, and then humiliated them in front of the English. Before a crowd of settlers, Uncas took away the Pequots' wampum, skins, and baskets and ordered his Mohegans to tear off the Pequot men's clothes, cut their hair, and beat them. Turning on the English, Uncas threatened them with guns, plundered their corn and wampum, and drove off their livestock. As Uncas strode up and down before them, the women and children cried and Winthrop and the men prayed. At last, Uncas said in English, a language he rarely used, "I am the victor."[6]

Uncas did not want to drive off the new settlers, only to show them that he was boss. Robert Hempstead and the other settlers stayed on to build their huts, fence their land, and cultivate the soil. Robert's wife, Joane Willey, bore the first English child in New London, a daughter, Mary, born in 1647. The town granted Robert a home lot in town and two hundred acres in the Mystic part of Stonington, which he passed on to his offspring. Robert's son Joshua (1649–83) lived while Uncas and his son Oweneco still commanded large tracts in New London County. Joshua bequeathed one hundred acres of "land promised by Oweneco" to his four daughters, "if that promise be performed." Joshua gave his son another two hundred acres promised by Uncas to five partners—"if that farm be enjoyed."[7] Land dealings with the Indians were conducted in a tentative mode. Neither of these properties came to the Hempsteads, but they had plenty to provide for their families. Joshua built a two-story frame house in New London in 1678 that still stands, the oldest structure in town, its diamond-paned windows and steeply sloped roofs giving it a medieval cast. Joshua's son, also named Joshua (1678–1758), lived in the house all his life, adding a wing in 1728. By then the Hempsteads were thoroughly entrenched in New London County and, for the most part, put the Mohegans out of their minds.

The younger Joshua, the diarist, recorded one encounter with Uncas's descendants. On November 15, 1722, he rode up to the Mohegan Indian village along the Thames River just north of New London, all that remained to the tribe of its once vast lands. There, with six or seven local men and the county sheriff, he witnessed the execution of a Pequot named Robert by the Mohegans. Young Ben Uncas, the Mohegan chief, shot the Pequot "Through ye Body" for having scalded old Ben's sister during a "drunken frollick."[8] Apparently the town had kept Robert in jail for seven or eight months for his own safety, then determined to let young Ben carry out Indian justice. Scalding old Ben's sister, even if by accident during a drunken frolic, called for punishment. Old Ben was the illegitimate youngest son of the venerated Uncas, the sachem who had established Mohegan power in southeastern Connecticut in the seventeenth century. An affront to old Ben's sister, daughter of Uncas, could not go unpunished.[9]

Uncas

The first Uncas deserved the respect that his descendants afforded him. He had not yielded Indian lands to the English settlers out of stupidity or venality. From the time of the first encounter, he adroitly managed the affairs of his people with an eye for his own honor and their well-being. His son Oweneco was less responsible and canny. After his father's death in 1684, Oweneco proved incapable of carrying on the sachem's office, despite having lived under Uncas's tutelage for three decades.

Oweneco was not solely responsible for Mohegan decline. The dissipation of Indian land and power began in the time of the estimable Uncas. Circumstances had compelled Uncas to master the intricacies of international diplomacy. When the English presence began to be felt after 1630, Uncas, who was probably born in the late sixteenth century, was a lesser chief among the bands of Indians under the hegemony of his brother-in-law Sassacus, the imperious Pequot sachem who controlled the southern New England coast between Pawcatuck (later the Rhode Island boundary) and the Connecticut River. Uncas's group was one of twenty-six principalities that paid tribute to Sassacus and followed his dictates concerning trade and hunting grounds. Although married to Sassacus's sister, Uncas resented Sassacus's domination of the Dutch and English trade and the tribute he exacted from his vassals. Restive and proud, Uncas had made five attempts to throw off Sassacus's domination before he recognized the potential of an English alliance against his enemy.[10]

In 1636 and 1637, a complicated series of events gave Uncas his opportunity. When Block Island Indians murdered a Massachusetts Bay merchant named John Oldham and five of his crew, the General Court sent John Endicott to demonstrate that Indians could not kill English with impunity. Unable to apprehend the real culprits, Endicott raided a Pequot village, firing wigwams and destroying corn. The Pequots appealed to their neighbors the Narragansetts to join them in a war on the English. The Narragansetts refused. They had formed an alliance with the English in Massachusetts Bay and had no love for the Pequots. Determined to wreak vengeance, the Pequots turned westward to the new, little Connecticut River town of Wethersfield. With a force of two hundred warriors they attacked the town, killed several men, and took two English girls captive.

The Connecticut General Assembly had to respond. Uncas told the Puritan divine Thomas Hooker that unless the English made war, "we had delivered our persons unto contempt of base feare and cowardise."[11] In 1637 Uncas went to Hartford with seventy warriors to egg the English on. By that time, the Connecticut General Assembly had already commissioned Captain John Mason, an experienced military man, to lead an expedition into Pequot country. In May 1637, Mason assembled a small army of soldiers from Connecticut and Rhode Island, to which he added Indian warriors, including Uncas's seventy men. To mislead the Pequots, Mason sailed by their fort at the mouth of the Mystic River and then returned overland to catch the Indians with their guard down. While the Pequots slept, Mason attacked the fort, broke through the gates, and fired the tepees within the walls. As Pequots fled, Uncas's men helped Mason cut them down. Between four hundred and seven hundred Indian men, women, and children perished. Sassacus, who occupied a nearby Pequot stronghold, realized he was at the mercy of the English and fled west across the Connecticut River. The English forces tracked most of the Indians down and captured or killed them, clearing the field for Uncas.[12]

It was an impressive if horrifying victory. Uncas could not understand the English willingness to kill women and children and go on slaughtering Indians after they were clearly defeated. On the other hand, his longtime foe had been obliterated in one stroke. After the Pequot defeat, he saw the wisdom of an alliance with the English. By 1638 he was ready to enter into permanent arrangements for mutual government of the area, and he never backed away from that decision. For its part, the infant Connecticut government wished to make sure that its interests in Pequot country were secured. Sassacus had been disposed of; the new powers were Uncas of the Mohegans and Miantonomi, head of the Narragansetts farther east. These two had to be brought under control.

When they were called to Hartford in September 1638, Miantonomi traveled with 150 men and Roger Williams. To hinder Miantonomi's passage and to show his own power, Uncas sent out warriors to harass the approaching Narragansetts. At Hartford, the sachems accused each other of harboring Pequots who had killed white colonists. The English insisted the two sachems shake hands, for Indians a meaningless gesture, to which they reluctantly agreed. Uncas, however, refused Williams's invitation to eat with Miantonomi, a ritual that did mean something.[13]

The "Covenant and agreement" signed at Hartford designated the English as arbiters of Indian disputes. "Injuries or wrongs" committed by one tribe against the other were not to be avenged. The settlers knew Indian justice required revenge, which would perpetuate the cycle of warfare. By this provision they sought to bring this practice under English rules of arbitration. The English also claimed the Pequot territory by right of conquest and forbade either Mohegans or Narragansetts to "possess any part of the Pequot's country without leave from the English."[14]

All in all, it was an astounding pair of concessions from Uncas and Miantonomi. Uncas no longer acted as a sovereign power with right to enforce his own edicts. The English were to mediate major intertribal conflicts. For the rest of his life, Uncas never took action against his enemies without consulting the Connecticut government. Modern critics of his strategy ask why the two sachems did not unite against the English, their real enemy, and New England Indians did toy with the idea of combining against the English until the maelstrom of King Philip's War made that possibility moot. At the time, the Indians' own rivalry was too bitter to permit cooperation. The sachems chose instead to deploy the English against each other, with Uncas manipulating English power better than anyone. For this policy he has been called a traitor, but he entered the English alliances to protect his people, not out of deference to white men.

Even though subsumed into an English system of adjudication, Uncas came out of the Hartford conference stronger than before. The slaughter of the Pequots at Mystic created a power vacuum, which he immediately filled, replacing Sassacus as the dominant Indian power in southeastern Connecticut. To cement strategic alliances, he married one of the widows of his father-in-law Tatobem, Sassacus's father, as well as half a dozen other high-born women. Whatever the agreement said about English control, Uncas ruled on the ground. Little villages throughout his territory now looked to him as sachem. Combined with his own possessions, Uncas's claims reached twenty-five miles into the interior north of Long Island Sound and westward to the Connecticut River.[15]

Uncas's struggle with the Narragansetts for control of Pequot territory did not end with the Hartford agreement of 1638. Miantonomi was determined to put Uncas out of the way. In 1643, Miantonomi invaded Mohegan lands with a massive force of perhaps a thousand men. To fend off nearly certain disaster, Uncas met Miantonomi face to face between the two bodies of warriors and proposed individual combat. Whichever of the sachems vanquished the other would rule both nations. When Miantonomi refused, Uncas fell to the ground and his warriors let fly with a volley of arrows. The surprised Narragansetts fled, and Miantonomi, weighed down with a chain mail corselet given him by a Rhode Islander, was captured.[16] Now the desperate one, Miantonomi proposed an alliance to drive out the English.[17]

As a token of his sincerity, Miantonomi offered to marry one of Uncas's daughters. To further strengthen their forces, Miantonomi's younger brother Pessicus would marry Massaoit's daughter to bring in the Pokanoket Indians to the north and east of the Narragansetts' domain.[18]

In keeping with his policy of cooperation with the English, Uncas refused Miantonomi's proposal and delivered him to the Connecticut authorities under the terms of the Hartford agreement. The United Colony commissioners, a body formed by four New England colonies in 1643 to deal with the threat of Indian warfare, determined that Uncas would never be safe so long as Miantonomi lived. They ordered the Connecticut authorities to return the Narragansett sachem to Uncas, who promptly dispatched him, probably delivering the death blow in person, as required by custom. Miantonomi lost out in the diplomatic maneuvering, and Uncas triumphed. For the next twenty years, Uncas relied on the English for arbitration and support.[19]

With hindsight it is obvious that Uncas's English allies posed the greater threat to his people. The menace arose not from English firepower but from the spread of the English population. Uncas began to feel overwhelmed by the complexities of managing his lands. Through the 1650s, the New London population spread like kudzu over Indian territory. In 1654 the General Court took the unusual step of warning the white inhabitants "not to mollest the Inyons in their planting ground or other rightfull possessions." The court sent out surveyors to draw the boundary between the New London and Mohegan lands and settle the conflicts breaking out along that line. At the same time, Uncas was granting and selling land in Mohegan country, among the largest the nine-mile-square township of Norwich in 1659.[20] Resisting English expansion and yet giving way, it was hard to devise the best strategy for developing while protecting his land.[21]

Recognizing his own inability to cope with the demand for Indian land, Uncas turned to Captain John Mason, who had led the 1637 attack at Mystic. In 1659 Uncas entered into an agreement with Mason to manage Mohegan land transactions. The English style of negotiating for land rights called for skills Uncas never understood. Exact surveys of land were not part of Indian practice. They relied on natural land features to define boundaries, which, though precise, were incomprehensible to the English. Williams said the Indians "were very exact and punctuall in the bounds of their lands, belonging to this or that Prince or People," but when Indians described their hunting grounds, the English understood none of it. By the same token, surveying instruments and the concept of precise lines on map were outside Uncas's ken. The Indians had no courts for registering deeds and adjudicating boundaries. A later lawyer in the Mohegan case summed up the problem when he noted that Uncas and his sons were "unskilled in letters." Uncas signed his deeds with a mark, a kind of torso with looped arms and a stroke between the arms.[22] Needing an adviser and a protector, Uncas put his trust in Captain John Mason.

Through the 1650s, Uncas entered into a series of agreements with Mason that in effect made Mason the Mohegans' guardian. In 1659 Uncas deeded all the Mohegans' lands in trust to Mason for the mutual benefit of the Indians and Mason. The deed was the real estate equivalent of Uncas's agreement to submit Indian disputes to the Connecticut government. Mason's supposed role was to stop the Indians from disposing of land against their own best interests out of confusion or in a state of intoxication. Uncas's son Oweneco in particular waxed generous when in his cups. Partly because of his son's weakness, Uncas saw the merits of reliance on the English for guidance and protection. Mason in effect became a substitute father for Uncas's sons when it came to land transactions. Other Indian tribes explicitly called white leaders "Father" as they sought protection.[23] When seeking the support of Governor John Winthrop and the Massachusetts Bay Colony, Uncas had used language that approached a father-son relationship. Laying his hand on his breast, Uncas told Winthrop, "This heart is not mine, but yours; I have no men; they are all yours; command me any difficult thing, I will do it; I will not believe any Indian's word against the English; and if any man shall kill an Englishman, I will put him to death, were he never so dear to me."[24] Perhaps Uncas only used the language of diplomacy—Winthrop later thought Uncas had outwitted him in this encounter—but the words showed a willingness to pledge everything like a son to a father. It was as if the commitment required a family dimension.

Oweneco was at his father's side during the meetings with John Mason. Uncas probably saw Oweneco's involvement as preparation for the role that would fall to him when the father died. He was trying to teach his sons the art of diplomacy with the wily English. After 1665, Mason received half of the returns on every sale to Connecticut residents, tempting him to dispense Indian lands for his own profit. Still, Uncas needed Mason's help. Connecticut farmers looked for every opportunity to encroach on Indian lands. In 1663,

Uncas sued New London for trespassing on Mohegan lands, demanding twenty pounds in compensation and receiving fifteen. In 1671 Uncas and another of his sons, Joshua, asked Mason to write the General Court about Lyme taking over Mohegan lands.[25]

In the confusion of surveys and overlapping claims, the English had ample opportunities to absorb one parcel of Indian land after another. The Mohegans were powerless to stop the tide. For one thing, by the 1670s they had few sources of income other than their lands. Fur-bearing animals had been largely eradicated, and in 1663 and 1664, the English colonies "demonetized" wampum, which the Mohegans had once manufactured, meaning it had no money value in the English trading system. Uncas, Oweneco, and the rest of the family had no recourse other than to dole out land piece by piece to eager white settlers. Recognizing their plight, Mason stepped in from time to time to restrain the Mohegans. In 1671 he stopped Uncas from selling part of the basic "planting grounds" at the core of the Indian's holding. To avoid further temptations to dispense these core properties, Mason entailed a tract of eight thousand by four thousand feet as what came to be known as the "sequester lands," which the sachems were forbidden ever to alienate.[26] The once vast Indian holdings in the end came down to that.

Uncas paid another price for his alliance with the English. Responding to strong pressures to fight with the colonists against King Philip in 1675, Uncas sent off two of his younger sons, John and Joshua, to war and lost them both.[27] By the time he died in 1683, Uncas was much reduced. King Philip's War was the last occasion for Mohegan warriors to serve in English military campaigns. Thereafter they counted for nothing as a military presence. Uncas had already turned over his lands to his guardians, relinquishing most of his bargaining power. The vast holdings he had once commanded were nearly gone. In 1682 he petitioned the town of Norwich adjacent to the remaining Mohegan planting grounds for relief. He felt that he had not been properly compensated for a small parcel of land within town bounds. With the magnanimity of victors, the town fathers "Considering of his Request and of him as an Old Friend, *see Cause to Gratify him* with the said Land as a Gift to him." They did not grant it as a right to the onetime proprietor of their township or as the chief of an adjoining independent nation. They saw nothing in the records that showed they owed him anything. "Yet notwithstanding the Town have Granted his desires as not willing to dissatisfie an Old Friend in such a small matter." Uncas also expressed "some fears

Respecting his Posterity, whether they may not be infringed of their Liberty of Fishing and making use of the Rivers." Fifty years earlier when Uncas was a boy, the Mohegans had fished every river and every pond for miles around at their pleasure. Now the town granted to him "full and free Liberty to make use of the Rivers and ponds, with other Royalties as abovesaid, not debaring Ourselves."[28]

After his father's death, Oweneco ruled alone as sachem. Oweneco is blamed for selling 1.7 million acres of land in the Quinebaug in 1680 and 1684 to James Fitch, Jr., the son of an earlier Mohegan protector, the Rev. James Fitch. The move appears less misguided when the frailty of the Indian's title is kept in mind. The huge tract along the Quinebaug River north of Stonington and Groton was not a hereditary property of the Mohegans. They had claimed it because of their suzerainty over the Wabaquasetts who occupied the area. Connecticut had confirmed the titles when they feared that Edmund Andros, governor of the Dominion of New England, would soon attack titles to all unassigned land, and the colony was distributing their unclaimed holdings to individuals as fast as possible. The Mohegans were the beneficiaries of these desperate measures. Their claims to Quinebaug, however, ran up against the counterclaims of the powerful Winthrop clan, who had long dominated that section of the colony. Oweneco did not give away much when he gave up Quinebaug. The sale to Fitch was a case of easy come, easy go and not a sign of Oweneco's ineptitude.[29]

Oweneco failed himself and his people more seriously in his inability to stop selling land to which the Mohegans did have clear title. To protect himself, Oweneco had petitioned the New London County court to invalidate deeds that lacked the signature of Samuel Mason, who had succeeded his father, John, as guardian. The county accepted the petition and ruled in 1679 and 1682 that purchases from the Mohegans required Samuel Mason's "assignment." In 1682 Oweneco made the same request to the Connecticut General Court, which officially appointed Samuel Mason as guardian. Yet despite the rulings, the alienation of Indian lands went on. It was the old story of Oweneco out of control through liquor granting deeds to importuning colonists. A lawyer, Nathaniel Foot, obtained title to the Mohegans' precious planting grounds from a "cheerful and magnanimous" Oweneco while under the influence. Oweneco recovered from that error when the court ruled against Foot but was less successful against Governor Fitz-John Winthrop, who insisted on his right to a farm in the Mohegan grounds. When

Samuel Mason stood up against the governor on behalf of the Indians, Mason lost his seat in the General Court at the next election, and the General Court proceeded to take over the Mohegan reservation. Mason carried the case to England, where in 1703 he initiated a suit that was to last for seventy years before it was finally settled in the colony's favor.[30]

In 1710 Oweneco, with his brother Ben Uncas and his son Caesar, conveyed virtually all that remained of Mohegan lands between Norwich and New London, several thousand acres in all, to four men. Many Mohegans objected to the sale. Old Ben Uncas, Oweneco's brother, and fifty-four other Mohegans signed a paper in May 1714 declaring that Oweneco had wrongfully sold a great part of their lands. By 1721 the Mohegans possessed only four or five thousand acres of "sequestered lands." In 1722 the Connecticut legislature noted that the acts forbidding private purchases from the Indians had "been broken repeatedly and with impunity." By then Oweneco, Uncas's proud son, wandered about the Connecticut settlements with a blanket, a pack, and a wife, asking for food.[31]

When Ben Uncas shot Robert the Pequot in 1722, the Mohegan sachems were without influence and land. Politically they figured mainly in their appearances before London commissions in suits that the Masons brought against the colony. In March 1737 Hempstead noted the death of Capt. John Mason, the grandson of the first John, and Mamohet, Uncas's great-grandson and current sachem, in London, where they had been pursuing their case against the colony. The name Ben Uncas appeared only twice more in Hempstead's record. He noted the death of the older Ben Uncas, son of the first Uncas, in March 1725 during a plague of deaths in New London. In 1742 the young Ben Uncas was "propounded for Baptism," and his "Confession of Excessive Drinking" was accepted. Sixty years earlier Uncas and Oweneco, after listening to the Rev. James Fitch, had decided against conversion to Christianity.[32] Uncas's grandson Ben, the descendant most inclined to assimilate, yielded.

Joshua and Uncas operated in a field of social action that was not purely economic, political, social, or military, but a combination of all. To this space, the English brought paper: wills, deeds, land surveys, diplomatic agreements, and contracts, which they used to dictate the rules of the game. The Indians began with none of these. They had no written resources to put up against the English documents. The Indians preferred oratory, gifts, and strategic friendships, and relied on customary claims embedded in memory. The Connecticut English recognized Indian claims and showed their respect through references in the deeds and agreements, but the moment the Indians put their marks on paper, they had given away the game. Once Indian customs were expressed as rights and reduced to writing, the English had the advantage. English expertise in the management of written records, backed by legal and military systems, overwhelmed the Indian's appeal to custom and fairness. The documents' strength lay in their power to mobilize the English courts, and behind the courts, law-enforcement officers, local militias, and, in the extremity, colonial armies. These papers ultimately stripped the Indians of authority. Ben Uncas had to have permission from the Connecticut authorities to execute his rival because he knew that he stood helpless against the array of forces backing up official words.[33]

In 1710, Norwich settled the Mohegans' sequestered tract on them forever "so long as there shall be any Mohegans found or known of alive in the world." According to the act, once the Indians disappeared, the lands would escheat to the town of Norwich. That day never came. The Mohegans did not disappear and have not to this day. They have been stubbornly resilient. They rose, fell, and held on.[34]

Joshua

Hempstead lived safely within the wall of paper shielding English settlers from Indian claims. He did not have to practice diplomacy to protect his land. Deeds registered in the county courthouse secured everything. Even though all he owned was once in the Indian's possession, he had no sense of wresting land from them. He fought no battles, entered into no treaties, engaged in no shady land transactions. Most of his land came through the division of town lands granted to the inhabitants bit by bit as their capacity for working more land grew. All that connected him to the bloody destruction of Indian titles was a phrase in the original Massachusetts Bay grant of New London calling it "a part of our proportion of the conquered country." That his titles went back ultimately to the destruction of the Pequots in 1637 meant nothing to him. He prospered under the protection of actions that took place before he was born. Had he lived to hear it, Hempstead might have found satisfaction in the 1842 orator's observation that the Indians' forests were now the site of "the bright cities and villages of new England."[35]

Yet ultimately Hempstead was complicit in English domination of the native people. In Connecticut, the European settlers did not outwit the

Indians or, after the Pequot slaughter, overcome them by force. The English obtained the land legally by their lights, then secured their gains by covering the colony with a dense web of farms. The settlers laid down a social and economic matting that foreclosed any hopes of the Mohegans' recovering their space. Hempstead wove his small part of this web by growing his own household economy. He did no more than farm families everywhere, but by providing as well as they could for themselves, farm families created an impermeable network of tightly woven legal and agricultural attachments to the land.

By comparison, the Indians were loosely organized, widely dispersed, few in numbers. They did not grip the land as the English settlers did. The native people are lauded for their light footprint, but they paid a price. They were too permeable, too vague about boundaries, too invisible, too mobile. The settlers' hold on the land was not easily loosened. With their sharp sense of boundaries, the settlers were quick to protest trespasses. The economy's capacity to support more people gave the English the advantage of numbers. Their work yielding more food, they did not have starving times. Their production of commodities allowed them to trade for guns and powder. All told, household economies like Hempstead's walled off the people of Uncas and Oweneco from their former land.

Although the Hempsteads flourished by comparison to the dwindling Mohegans, Joshua the diarist suffered his share of slings and arrows. His wife, Abigail Bailey Hempstead, bore her husband nine children between 1698 and 1716, first six boys and then three girls. Their last child, Mary, was born July 30, 1716.[36] One week after Mary's birth, Joshua recorded in his diary, "Sund 5 fair. my Dear Wife Died about half an hour before Sunrise." Abigail was thirty-nine and Joshua nearly thirty-eight. He never remarried, perhaps frozen by his losses. And his sorrows were not at an end. A week after Abigail left him, "my Dutyfull son Joshua Died about Noon like a Lamb being 17 years & 20 days old a patren of patience." The next day at about two in the afternoon, the father Joshua buried his eldest son beside his mother.[37]

For twelve years, Joshua filled the gap left by his wife's death with combinations of serving girls and relatives. Two weeks after Abigail's death, he wrote her sister and brother-in-law across Long Island Sound. A month later, "Brother Tallmage & sister is gone home & hath Carryed away my pritty babe," Mary. Thomas Tallmage's wife was Mary Bailey, Abigail's sister. The Tallmages also took Hempstead's daughter Elizabeth, age two, and

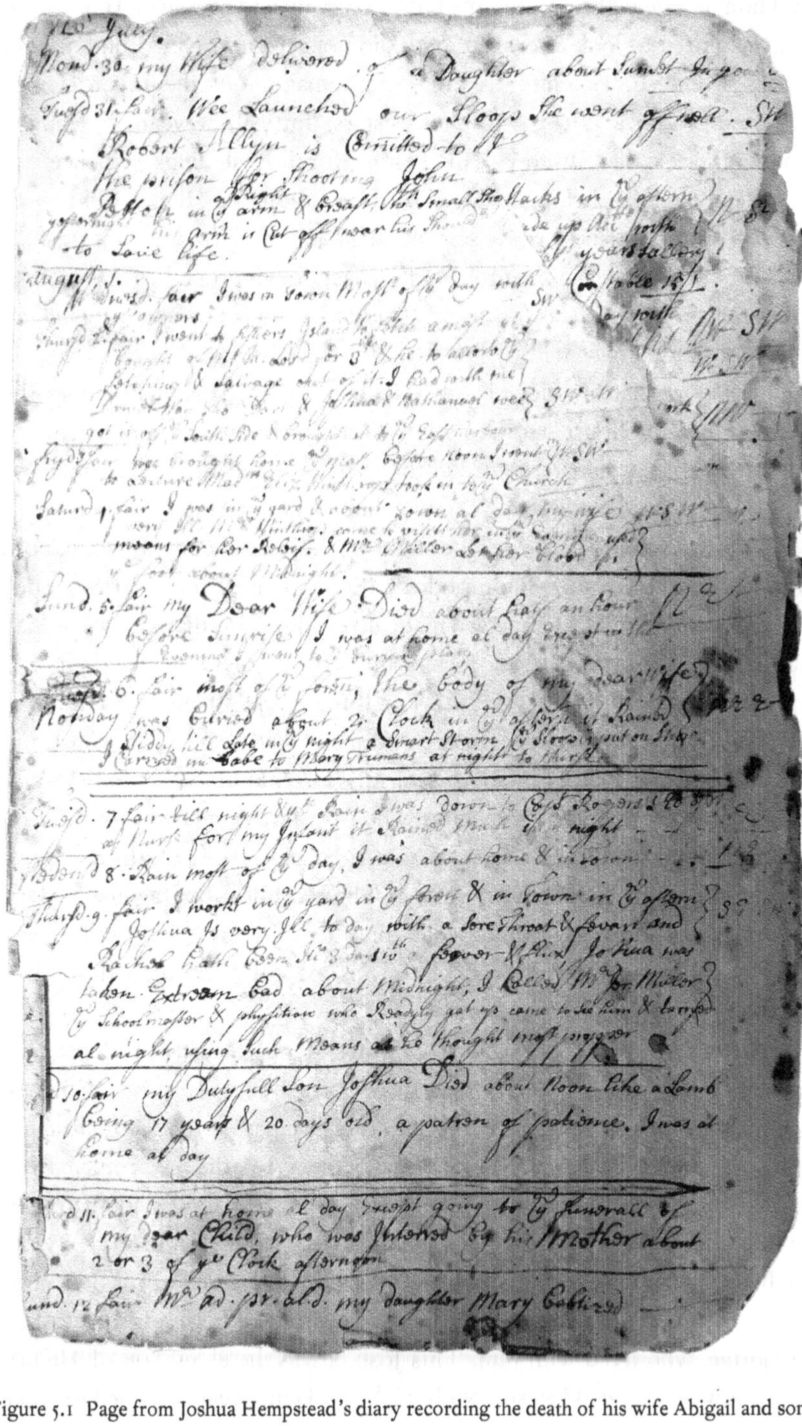

Figure 5.1 Page from Joshua Hempstead's diary recording the death of his wife Abigail and son Joshua in August 1716. Courtesy New London County Historical Society.

son Thomas, age eight, to keep the baby company and to relieve Hempstead of two children to look after. Elizabeth did not return to New London until she was seventeen. Two months after the Tallmages took the infant, Hempstead arranged for another of Abigail's sisters, thirty-three-year-old Hannah Salmon, to nurse the baby, now called Molly, for three shillings, sixpence.[38]

Meanwhile Rachel, a serving girl, stayed on in the Hempstead household to help.[39] Phoebe Lee, a serving woman, and Elizabeth Cornish, a kinsman, also stepped in to fill Abigail's place for the time being.[40] Hempstead's long-term plan was for his son Nathaniel and his wife, Mary Hallam, to move into the household, which they did after their marriage in 1723. As the eldest now that his older brother Joshua had died, Nathaniel was the logical heir to the house and home lot. The construction of a new wing in 1728 indicates that their residence in the house was meant to be permanent. Mary Hallam could manage the complex household in Abigail's absence.

But it was not to be. In another fatal week in the summer of 1729, both Nathaniel and his brother Thomas died. "Something of the fever & Ague" had stricken the family. Hempstead made no entries in his diary between May 11 and June 7. The two boys, Joshua himself, another son, Stephen, and Hempstead's daughter Mary fell ill. For three weeks, they were all ailing. Then on July 4, "Thomas my dear & dutyful Son died about 4 in the Morning being Aged Twenty one years (Apr. ye 14.) Two months & Twenty days." Five days later, "my Eldest Son Nathll who Lived wth me Died about Ten of ye Clock at night. a Dear & Dutyful Son Aged 28 years 6 Months & 3 days: Leaving a Sorrowful Widow 2 Sons & She near her time againe." Mary Hallam Hempstead gave birth to a daughter the next day.[41] At age fifty-one, Hempstead had lost his wife and three sons, two of them the eldest when they died.

After four years, Nathaniel's widow, Mary, departed Hempstead's household, leaving Hempstead with three sons, Robert (b. 1702), Stephen (1705), and John (1709), and two daughters, Abigail (1712) and Elizabeth (1714), to manage for their father. Elizabeth (1716) did not return from Southold until 1733. The three girls married between 1731 and 1736, and Stephen, the last of the three sons to marry, wed Sarah Holt in 1737. By the time he was fifty-nine, Hempstead's household was cleared of his own children. In their absence, Hempstead had taken custody of his grandsons Joshua and Nattee, who lived with him. This Joshua was the eldest son of Hempstead's now deceased eldest son Nathaniel, and Hempstead intended to make the boy his primary heir. He personally taught him the arts of farming, and at death granted him the largest farm in his possession. As a sign that this Joshua had succeeded to the place of the lost two eldest sons, Hempstead gave title to the New London house to him, making Joshua heir to the symbol of the family's position in the town.[42]

Hempstead's Economy

Although shorthanded for most of his life, Hempstead pieced together a thriving domestic economy. Like those of Matthew Patten of Bedford, New Hampshire, Hempstead's diaries show him engaged in a number of occupations. Beside surveying and shipbuilding, he cut gravestones and constructed coffins. From the diary pages, it would appear that Hempstead was at most a part-time farmer. In 1716, the year Abigail died, he worked a total of seventy-seven full days and twenty-one part days in his shipyard and spent another twenty-one days hauling in timber and assembling other materials. In May, June, and July, critical months for farmers, he was in the shipyard or collecting materials sixty-four days of a possible seventy-seven (excluding Sundays). Hard at work on a sloop, for twenty-five days in July 1716 he repeatedly made the same entry: "I workt in ye yard al day." Occasionally he noted the progress of the work: "wee finished planking Starboard Side." There was no letup to work the farm, save for one day when he fetched a calf from Joseph Cheapells.[43]

Work on the sloop commanded his attention even when illness invaded the household. On Monday, July 30, 1716, he wrote, "I was all day Getting Waylogs & Launching Timber. my wife delivered of a Daughter about Sunset In good. . . . Tuesd 31 fair. Wee Launched our Sloop. She went off well." The next day he was in town most of the day "with ye owners" and the next day off to Fishers Island to fetch a mast. He made no mention of wife or their new daughter. By Friday noon the mast was in New London. Hempstead spent all Saturday in the shipyard and about town but noted: "my wife very Ill. Mr. Winthrop come to visit her in ye Evening used means for her Relief & Mr Miller Let her blood in." That was the only notice of Abigail's precarious condition. Clearly the burial three days later occupied his mind, but he could not help noting on the same day: "It Rained Stiddy till Late in ye night a Smart Storm. ye sloop is put on Shore."[44] His wife meant everything to him, but the sloop meant something too.

The sloop later named *Plainfield* made one voyage, probably to the West Indies, and then Hempstead loaded it with 16,260 feet of plank in July 1717 and sailed it to New York, where he sold the cargo and the sloop. A few months later, he collected a £400 payment in Boston. To share the risk, Hempstead owned only part of the sloop and the cargo. A sixth of the payment went to a Mr. Whitney and £177, 16s to "Ms Coit." Hempstead received a larger share than the other partners, probably because he built the sloop, and he had to pay the workers out of his share.[45] The next winter he settled with the men he hired for the construction. The sloop made him many things: an artisan, an employer, a merchant, a capitalist. He was also a laborer. When a sloop in which he owned a share came into New London, he helped unload it before dividing the cargo among the owners.[46]

The sloop occupied so much of Hempstead's time in the summer of 1716, one wonders who was managing the farm. He had inherited a home lot from his father, along with parcels of 8, 6½, and 26 acres in various parts of town and, largest of all, 145 acres in the "general neck."[47] Most of this land was being worked. In the early summer, while Hempstead spent nearly every day at his shipyard, the meadows had to be mowed to put up hay for the livestock's winter feed. Hempstead's oldest son, Joshua, was seventeen that summer; the next oldest, Nathaniel, was fifteen. They could do the work; could they also manage the operation?

The sequence of events after 1716 offers a clue to family roles on the farm. The death of Abigail that summer, along with young Joshua's, marked a divide. After 1716 Hempstead never built another sloop. He put the finishing touches on the *Plainfield* but never again put down ways and laid a keel. He never again worked in the shipyard all day, day after day, as he had in July 1716. The sequence suggests that work on the sloop depended on Abigail and young Joshua managing the farm. Together they could see to the hay and crossplow the corn, supervising the younger boys and the occasional hired hands. Without them, Hempstead could not absent himself to the shipyard.[48] The enterprises of husband and wife were sufficiently interwoven that one could step in for the other. In 1716 she managed the farm while he built the *Plainfield*. After her death, he stepped in as best he could to rear the children and do the housework.

Sloop building was a mainstay for Hempstead in his first years, but he deployed an amazing collection of other skills.[49] He was an adviser and estate manager for the Winthrops, descendants of John Winthrop, the

Massachusetts Bay founder, and the largest landowners in the area. He surveyed lands for the colony and for private individuals. When someone died, he was ready with a coffin. To round out his services for the deceased, he wrote wills, lettered gravestones, and inventoried estates. He repaired the church belfry and framed window casements. He owned a whaleboat that he rented to whalers.[50] When you add in his civic duties as selectman, justice of the peace, and later deputy to the General Court, Hempstead can be considered an early urban man, like Matthew Patten, deeply involved economically and politically in the town.

Yet this man of many skills still owned land and worked a farm. Much of his time was spent on his land, plowing, hoeing, mowing, harvesting, slaughtering. The farm economy is only partly visible in Hempstead's diary. It pops up in entries when he has slaughtered a lamb or helped with haying, but the nature of the diary kept the bulk of the farmwork out of sight. As with Matthew Patten's diary, virtually none of the women's work is mentioned. Nothing about child rearing (unless there was an illness), cooking, dairying, kitchen gardens, spinning. The work the boys did at home, tending animals, cutting firewood, plowing, sowing, hoeing, haying, and harvesting rarely comes to light. The self-provisioning family economy, though essential, remained in the background.

Still, enough shows up in the diary to suggest how he distributed his resources—which productions took the most time, which occupied the most space. The entries for 1713, when he was in his early middle age and his eldest son Joshua was just fourteen, bring to light the central importance of livestock. More entries appear in the diary for mowing, raking, stacking, and pressing hay than for any other agricultural activity.[51] Between woods for summer grazing, meadows for cutting hay, and pasture for grazing, cattle claimed more land than any other of Hempstead's products, and they took more time. Haying occupied Hempstead for twenty-nine days in the summer.[52]

Grain came next in its demands. The 1713 diary entries mention oats and corn, which evoke the existence of tilled fields.[53] Hempstead does not mention how much land he tilled. Ten to twenty-five acres would be typical. He did not do his own plowing in 1713. He hired Amos Tinker for that work. Like other New England farmers, Hempstead may not have owned a plow and maybe no ox at this point, preferring to hire someone to do the job and avoid the cost of feeding an ox for a whole year. But he did work in the cornfields, weeding in June and harvesting and husking corn in September.[54] He also purchased grain, a little rye and corn and considerable wheat. With all his other sources of income, Hempstead had the flexibility to fill in the gaps in his own production with purchases from neighbors or exchanges of work and products with neighbors.

Orchards were still smaller than the tilled fields. Hempstead did not grow apples commercially, but he did set out apple trees in 1713, and thereafter harvested apples and made cider. Apples were the fruit he saw most commonly during the year, though he mentioned setting out pear and peach trees and enjoying "watermilions" with his wife in late summer at a kind of fête.[55] Cider afforded them a chance for a small respite. In a startling exception to the unrelenting record of labor, Hempstead's diary reported that on June 16 he and Abigail went off with two other couples in a boat "to drink Cydar & Recreate our Selves."[56]

The diary for 1713 says little about wood, though Hempstead was always bringing in timber for sloop construction. New England farms usually included large unimproved spaces where timber could be harvested. Hempstead recorded hauling in a cord of wood which would partially meet the requirements of the fireplace during the cold winter. Beyond that one cord, the boys and Ebe, a boy Joshua cared for as guardian, must have been cutting wood all through the fall and winter. Hempstead purchased shingles and clapboard, a form of timber that required special skill and equipment to produce.[57] If he did not have enough forest on his own land to supply his needs, there was plenty within easy reach. The water lanes along the coast and up and down the two rivers intersecting New London, the Thames and the Niantic, made it easy to reach forest areas and float timber to town.

Beyond food and fuel, the household manufactured most of the family's basic needs and solicited help from the town for the rest. Ebe made a pair of his own shoes, though this year Hempstead only repaired his. A few years later, Hempstead made five-year-old Abigail a pair of shoes. He constructed a tanning vat for his neighbors the Trumans, giving him ready access to leather.[58] Items the family could not manufacture themselves, they hired done in the household. In the midst of shearing time, "Eliz Mayhew & Joanna workt at our house making my wife a Suit." The next year "Mr. russell Come to work at our house to make me a Coat & Jacket."[59] Local people came in to tailor clothes probably made from fabric that the Hempsteads had others weave for them. Joshua took wool or flax and even cotton to spinners in the neighborhood, though only after Abigail died.[60] The production of clothing mixed work done in the home with the labor of imported workers or the help of neighbors. Clothing for the children was probably improvised at home. In 1716 after his wife died, Hempstead made a pair of breeches for eight-year-old Thomas, a job Abigail would probably have handled before. In October of that year, he spent a whole day in town "to ye weavers & Shoemakers &c."[61] The goal was to produce enough to minimize expensive purchase and barter for the rest with weavers, tailors, shoemakers, and the other actors in the town economy.[62] Like Patten, Joshua mobilized the town to complete the family's self-provisioning.

From all these details, the overall structure of Hempstead's domestic economy begins to emerge. Joshua himself was a constant source of income over the years, agilely shifting from task to task depending on the season and the opportunities of the moment. His reputation as a boatbuilder, stone-cutter, surveyor, and overall dependable laborer brought him work, perhaps a little more each year as his skill grew. He shared in the cargoes of the sloops he built, perhaps loading in casks of salted meat from his own farm or the oars that he shaped in the off seasons. Living in one of the busiest outports along the New England coast, Hempstead was anything but an isolated subsistence farmer. He produced for the West Indies and New York markets as well as for exchanges with neighbors. Besides his work in the exchange economy, an immense amount of labor, much of it by his wife and children, went into the farm, the base of the self-provisioning domestic economy. The household economy was the foundation of Hempstead's many other enterprises. It was interwoven in a seamless web with shipbuilding, gravestone carving, surveying, and many other works outside of the household. Almost nothing is said about purchases for family consumption. For years in the diary, no mention is made of storekeepers or merchants.[63] Nearly all of the family's consumption came from their own labors on the farm, augmented by work by their neighbors.

Hempstead never calculated the profit from the sloop's voyages—or anything else he did. There is no sign that he counted up his net worth or tried to estimate whether he had come out behind or ahead in a given year. The point of his many works was to help his family flourish, perhaps adding small luxuries like cuff links or a new dress from time to time, but never calculating profit. Hempstead accumulated exchange power so that he could function fluidly in the town's exchange economy. His aim was to produce things, not money. It required his constant attention to bring together the food, the clothing, the firewood, the animals, the farm equipment, and a host of other items like salt and barrels, to keep his family alive and the farm producing. Town service, work for the neighbors, shipbuilding, and surveying all pointed toward one end, the prospering of the family.

Hempstead thought locally—of his family, his kin, his fellow townsmen, and the colony. He could not see that his farm project was one stroke in the centuries-long, continent-wide displacement of the native population. He never considered that his work made Indian removal permanent. But his farm filled the land so thoroughly that it could never be retaken. On inspection that would not have been evident. Colonial farms did not look heavily occupied. Tillage, pasture, and meadow accounted for less than half of most farms. Most of the colonial landscape, even in settled areas, was heavily wooded or only partially developed. Farms looked rough and unfinished. But the land was not as empty as it appeared. Where there were no marks of the farmer's labor—tilled fields, fences, open pasture, felled trees—the land was occupied mentally. Deeds and titles recorded the surveyor's lines on the land. Within those lines, farmers had plans for every square yard. In their minds, empty areas were future pastures, cornfields, or vital wood lots.

In the seventeenth century, Indians ceded or sold vast tracts to the colonists; the exchange never went the other way. After settlers moved into New London, land once empty became full. Even heroic efforts to expel the English, such as King Philip's War, failed to remove them. In *Two Treatises of Government,* John Locke said that mixing labor and land turned unowned space into private property.[64] That transformation took place in New London in the century after settlement, as farmers like Hempstead took irreversible possession of Uncas's once spacious domain.

6. Sons and Daughters

Provision for the Young

Like every farm father of his time, Joshua Hempstead had to plan for his children's independence. As they grew older, children became both a resource and a problem. After twelve or fourteen, children substantially added to the family workforce; the older boys could do the work of a man and the girls of a woman. But by their mid-twenties, children would marry and strike out on their own. How were they to start their own families? What resources could a father provide, and how would the children assemble the rest for themselves? The family bonds that required the children to donate their labor during their teen years obligated the fathers to set them up as young adults, especially the sons, on farms or in shops of their own. Daniel Vickers found that in Essex County, Massachusetts "every rural householder in the county felt some obligation to assemble a patrimony large enough to endow his offspring with sufficient property to launch them on the road to comfortable independence. In a society where large families were the rule, moreover, this pressure could be serious enough to provide the organizing principle for a life's work. Farmers managed this by acquiring land and other forms of productive property through several decades of married life and then passing it along to their children in later years."[1] Sons could not sue their fathers—no laws required fathers to bestow a patrimony on their sons—but the obligation bore on everyone. In the prime years of family labor, most fathers did accumulate additional property; taxable property peaked in the 50–59 age group and then declined as land was passed along to offspring.[2] Farmers did their best to give their children a start.

Preparing the rising generation called for more than supplying sufficient land. Children had to be instructed in the ways of farming, its assumptions, its physical skills, its wariness, its great stores of knowledge. Farm parents had to transmit a culture across the generations. Schools provided a specialized set of skills for dealing with the outside world, but children learned how to attain a livelihood and govern a household, how to dwell in the community, how to shape a life, from their parents at home.

Uncas and Joshua were alike in bearing responsibility for rearing the next generation. Native people had to convey the intricacies of life in their beleaguered society just as Joshua taught his children to farm. The Indians' efforts to bring up their children were of little concern to Hempstead and his fellow townsmen. By Joshua's time the natives occupied the margins of white consciousness just as they lived at the margins of white settlement. Joshua had few occasions to witness the difficulties of transmitting a culture in crisis. Indian fathers and mothers had to prepare their children for life in a society that had been displaced and decimated by the European settlers. Perpetuation in any form was an achievement. That the natives survived at all is a tribute to the ingenuity and resilience of Indian parents.

Management of the Young

To assemble land for the next generation, farmers had to make the most of their children's labor while it was available. Hempstead had extra hands for the ten years or so before his children's marriages; how was he to put them to best use? One of his strategies was to turn the farm over to his boys while he built a sloop. For two years after 1714 he let them work the farm while he labored in the shipyard.[3] Hempstead also kept his eyes open for places where his sons could be profitably put to work. In July of 1714 he hired for twenty-five shillings from one "Woyat" "ye 6 acre Lot," which he and the boys mowed and fenced. Within a week, he had both a hay crop and pasture for ten animals. To support projects like that, Hempstead began to make small land purchases, leasing some of it to others while awaiting the boys' maturity.[4] His whole operation swelled as his sons entered their teens.

From around 1715 to 1731, when the boys were in their teens and twenties and still not married, the family possessed its maximum labor force before

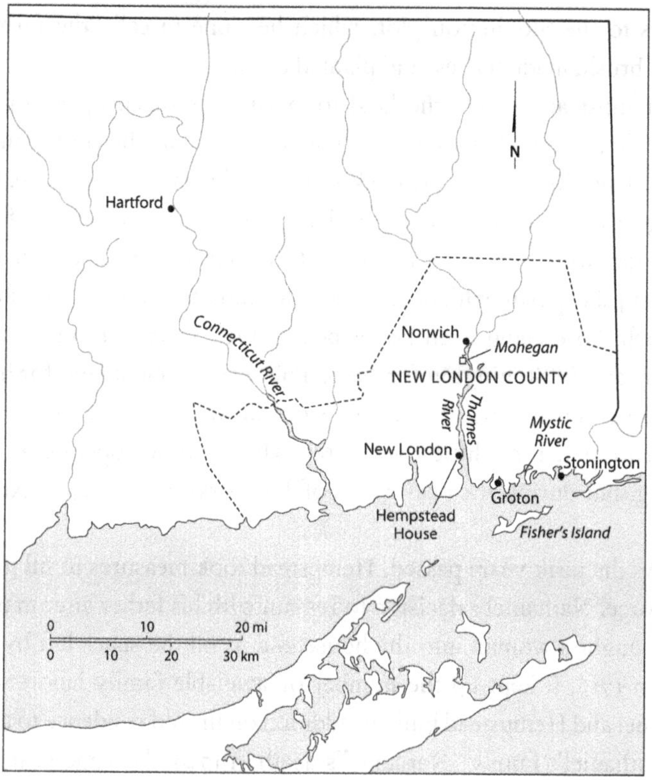

Figure 6.1 New London in the mid-eighteenth century.

thinning out. Joshua died in 1716 and Thomas and Nathaniel in 1729. The boys one by one married and took on responsibility for their own families: Nathaniel in 1723, Robert in 1725, and John in 1731. Stephen was not to marry until 1737, at the unusually old age of thirty-two, but he left the family workforce in 1730 to go to sea.[5] After 1731 Joshua had no sons at his behest except Stephen when he was in port.

To make the most of these growing boys, Hempstead did not need to look for land in distant places. He inherited two hundred acres in Stonington from his father and enlarged the plot to five hundred acres. After the death of the elder Hempstead, Joshua's mother had sold the property, apparently illegally under terms of the will, and Hempstead had to sue. He recovered his right to the land in 1709, but controversy lingered until March 31, 1719, when the court fully cleared the title.[6] That spring, he brought his corps of family workers to the Stonington plot, which he came to call "the farm." They burned brush, made fences, and planted corn.

Hempstead wanted the land to expand his sheep operation. He had been folding some of his sheep with a neighbor; now he could put them on his own land. To enlarge his flock to match the pasture available, he began renting sheep, 80 of them from William Walworth for a pound of wool per animal for two years, with a right to buy after a year. The next spring he rented 114 sheep (still with fleece) and 108 lambs, this time for one shilling per year each. Foreseeing even larger possibilities, in 1720 Hempstead bought another farm in Stonington for £180. This was sufficient land for his sons to work. In August 1721, he sold his wool in Wethersfield, the Connecticut River entrepôt, for a little over £260.[7] He could not operate at that level for long, but during the peak years of his workforce, sheep maximized his return.

As the peak years passed, Hempstead took measures to fill gaps in the labor force. Nathaniel's decision to remain with his father after marriage not only brought a woman into the household to fill the space left by Abigail's death in 1716, it kept up the number of available family laborers. In 1728 Nathaniel and Hempstead built an addition on the old residence to accommodate Nathaniel's family.[8] Nathaniel's death in 1729, the same year as that of Hempstead's son Thomas, suddenly decreased the number of available hands, and once again the family adapted. Nathaniel's widow Mary Hallam remarried and made their grandfather the guardian of her two sons, Joshua and Nathaniel. He raised them like his own boys, teaching them to hoe, and eventually giving Joshua the farm in Stonington.

The prospect of a shrinking labor force moved Hempstead to purchase a slave, Adam Jackson, in early fall 1727.[9] Nathaniel and Robert had married; the next son, John, was looking ahead to marriage and devoting himself to blacksmithing, the trade he took up when he went on his own. The purchase of a slave did not require complicated negotiations. There were black families and slaves in town. Coastal Connecticut was one of the northern regions amenable to slave labor. New London was situated in the thin rim along the Connecticut and Rhode Island coasts where the 180-day frost-free growing season approximated the growing season in Piedmont Virginia and Maryland. These congenial conditions permitted Connecticut farmers to raise tobacco and use slaves for agricultural labor. Hempstead mentioned "negroes" from time to time in his diary, evidence of their presence in New

London. Adam Jackson was available when Hempstead needed to build his labor force.[10] Adam appeared in the work record as often as Hempstead's own sons, filling a role in the family labor force just like one of the boys. Hempstead seemed to have trusted Adam completely. "Adm gone to Stonington," he wrote in 1737, referring to Hempstead's other property across the Thames River in a nearby township. He showed no fear that Adam might continue on to Providence and freedom. Adam stuck with Hempstead to the end. An entry a month before his death noted that "Adam carted home 2 load of Pumkin."[11] The inventory to Hempstead's estate listed "An old negro man named Adam, value £2."[12]

Save for Robert, who moved to Long Island, all of Hempstead's sons remained in New London after they married and were available for cooperative ventures. But they were no longer at Hempstead's beck and call. He could assign his younger sons to virtually any task he chose while they remained in his household, as if they were indentured servants or slaves. After their marriages, the sons' own families had priority. Any work they performed for their father had to be balanced by work or services he performed for them. John helped Hempstead load wood, and Hempstead helped him repair his house. In 1736, when Stephen was thirty-one and still unmarried, Hempstead's notation "Stephen mowed for me" indicated that he was keeping track.[13] After John's marriage in 1731, he raked hay for a half day for his father, but three weeks later Hempstead built a three-rail fence for John.

At his death in 1758, age eighty, Hempstead passed on everything to his children. He owned a little more than 1,055 acres of land in four towns. Thirteen of the seventeen parcels were in New London, the rest in Stonington, Groton, and Colchester, all in New London County. Still under the influence of the primogeniture ethos, Hempstead bequeathed more than half of his real estate to grandson Joshua. All of the other children found stable positions in life.[14] Abigail married Clement Miner, a third-generation resident of neighboring Stonington, where Hempstead had a 500-acre farm. Abigail bore eleven children, two of whom ended up in Vermont, but others remained in New London. Elizabeth married Daniel Starr, the scion of a family that had been in New London since 1673. Only two of her eight children lived beyond young adulthood. They lived in New London and Middleton, where the Starr family had first settled. The youngest daughter, Mary, did not fare as well. She married Thomas Pierpoint of Roxborough, Massachusetts, who first appeared in Hempstead's diary when he delivered a watch that Hempstead had sent out for repair. The couple lived with her father for a few years, then moved to Stonington, and finally to Middletown. Hempstead borrowed one hundred pounds to lend to Thomas in 1750, presumably because his son-in-law's credit fell short. Hempstead repaid the loan in 1754, but there is no record of Thomas repaying his father-in-law.[15]

Hempstead's sons lived respectable lives in the area. At age fifteen, Robert Hempstead was sent to Southold on Long Island, where the Hempsteads probably resided before moving to New London in the seventeenth century. In Southold, he was apprenticed to a blacksmith and inherited his mother's Long Island property. He married the daughter of Judge Benjamin Youngs, inherited his father-in-law's law practice, built a grand house, and later became known as Squire Robert Hempstead. John followed the example of his older brother Robert and married a cousin on his mother's side, Hannah Salmon, from a Southold family where the Hempsteads had so many connections. His wife's father, William Salmon, bequeathed his daughter a slave girl at his death in 1759. Stephen was more of a problem. He married in 1737 at age thirty-two, late for the Hempstead sons. He had previously gone to sea and had to be pressured to return to New London.[16] Stephen seems to have lived in his father's house for twenty years, until Joshua died. In his will Joshua granted Stephen use of a chamber and garret in the older part of Joshua's "Mansion House" until he "shall in Convenient time build himself a house on his own land."[17] Stephen was fifty-two at the time. Stephen and John both received New London lands from their father and raised their children in the town. Between the two of them, they had nineteen children, ten of whom died young.

The fortunes of Hempstead's six surviving children took their twists and turns, but within a fairly small circumference. Not until the generation of grandchildren and great-grandchildren did the family begin to disperse. Through most of the eighteenth century, Hempstead's offspring found space for their families in New London or the immediate vicinity. In January 1737/38, the colony auctioned off fifty rights to land in a western township. Hempstead attended the auction and noted the prices ranging from £132 to £137, but purchased nothing for himself.[18] One hundred twenty acres in Colchester just north of New London was as far as he ventured. The lands obtained from the Mohegans and Pequots served the Hempsteads for four generations.

Hempstead and His Sons

In deploying his little labor force about his properties, Hempstead also became the teacher of his children. They learned more on the farm than in the formal classroom, for which Hempstead helped to hire a teacher. Bringing up children was nearly synonymous with teaching them how to farm. They implicitly learned about manhood and womanhood in acquiring agricultural and household skills. Hempstead was a little more explicit about teaching his grandsons than his own boys, perhaps because in 1736, as they were coming of age, an epidemic of throat distemper struck down twenty-five children, their names all dutifully recorded in Hempstead's diary. Nattee, Joshua's little brother, fell ill, seriously enough to call in a nurse, but then recovered.[19] After losing three of his own sons, Hempstead had every reason to fear he might lose a grandson.

Fathering farm children called for more than nursing the sick, putting food on the table, and providing a warm room against the cold. Fathering meant transmission of skills and knowledge. Hempstead's laconic summaries of work often named his sons. In a November 1711 entry, Joshua at twelve was driving a dray loaded with the goods of a deceased villager. A few days later, ten-year-old Nathaniel drove the wagon, hauling timber for oars out of the woods.[20] When not named, they must have been often watching—and learning. On a frosty December day, Hempstead killed a red steer without mentioning the boys, but they would have been standing by to see the spurt of blood and watch their father's deft strokes as he sliced off the animal's hide and cut up the body. They had to learn how to plow parallel furrows behind an ox and cut hay with the long smooth motion called for by a scythe, stacking the hay to make it shed water. It took practice to sow oats properly, flinging the seeds evenly across the open earth, or to plant corn kernels at the proper depth in the hills. Later in the season, the diary found father and sons "mowing among the corn" to keep down the weeds, and then topping the stalks. The boys had to split rails, dig fence posts, drive sheep, search for lost animals on the village's open range, and on and on.[21] For even the simplest task, there was a smooth, easy, efficient way and an awkward, lumbering, sloppy way. The boys had to learn by watching and doing, gradually training their muscles to remember all the little tricks and maneuvers that worked best. When he grew older and was weighed down by other duties, Hempstead sometimes went into the fields with his grandsons simply to teach. "I hoed Corn with Josh & Natte part of the day to Larn them to hoe." Joshua was eleven and Nathaniel eight.[22]

The technologies of farming, the part learned by watching, imitating, and occasionally being corrected, could be talked about. The lesson of sheer endurance went unsaid. The will to labor hard had to be learned. A model of persistence himself, Hempstead rarely wavered from his work agenda. Six days a week his sons would have seen him leave the house headed for some task. Adverse conditions could not stand in the way. Hempstead recorded the weather but rarely let it daunt him. On January 17, 1712: "I was in town & att the mill all day. I got no meal. a Cold freezing day." The next day "very Cold in ye morn, ye Latr pt moderate. I was att work in maple Swamp Cutting wood." When it snowed and rained, he might stay home, at least until noon. Then back to the maple swamp to cut wood, "ye Boys draying."[23] They had to learn to harden their bodies against the cold and put the pain out of their minds.

Hempstead's mixture of husbandry and shipbuilding complicated his daily work schedule. The routine chores of milking, feeding animals, and chopping wood that set up a regular underrhythm to the day never merited an entry in Hempstead's diary. His diary noted only the variegated, seemingly unpredictable, and improvisational work that he chose for himself each day. In January and February 1712, the off season, Hempstead worked in the mill, went to his shipyard, made a coffin, cut wood, went to town to buy a saddle, went to a funeral, killed two hogs, worked on a window, finished "Capt Andrews oars," daubed his apple trees to prevent the calves from barking them, took an inventory of John Fox's estate, paid the schoolmaster, cut and salted pork, made a chest, restacked hay, cut poles and rails in the cedar swamp, made a door for the lean-to, broke up ground, dug stones.[24] Each day his mind had to run through all the segments of his work world and decide where to put his attention. Hempstead would have started thinking about the day's schedule in the haze of first awakening. He could plan only generally in advance because the weather of the day affected everything. As the family arose, he issued directives. By observing their father's choices, the boys learned to form a work agenda, their minds following the channels of his mind just as their muscles learned from his muscles how to cut and stack hay.

In a society that relied almost entirely on exchanges, the boys also had to learn prices. Hempstead frequently joined with two other appraisers to evaluate the estate of a deceased villager. In December 1711, they spent three days at Holloway's going through the furniture, the implements, the bedding and clothing, the crockery and tableware, the tools in the farm buildings, the livestock and fowl, the crops in the field, the records of debts and credits—every single item on the farm.[25] To each of these, the three appraisers assigned a monetary value based on the item's condition. They would examine an object, one would propose a number, the others would counter; eventually and quite efficiently they would concur and the value would go on the list opposite a brief description. They reached agreement out of long experience in auctions of estates, in bartering, and in observing prices for new items at the store. The appraisers' ability to arrive rapidly at a figure represented a huge body of economic lore stored away in each of their memories.

The diary follows an offbeat rhythm. The regularity of chores for the boys and the women, repeating a distinctive pattern daily or weekly, did not hold for Hempstead. The variability of his days, the diversity of his activities, the complexity of the many little stories running through the entries gives a strange jumbled quality to his reports. Through this blizzard of diversified work, one eventually can see the vague outlines of the institutions that structured his life. He attended church faithfully every Sunday, reporting without fail on who preached even if it was Mr. Adams most of the time. Hempstead never mentioned what Reverend Adams preached about, as if the fact of the preaching meant more than the substance. Government institutions took his attention many days a month as he sat in court or took on a surveying assignment. The neighbors' farms surrounding his own became scenes of work as he put up a tanning vat or a fence or sent a son to plow. His own family required attention when someone was ill or getting married or falling out of line in some way, as when Stephen went to sea or Abigail died. And there was nature itself, with which he was always engaged to bring forth crops and rear animals. The record of tasks can be largely categorized as responses to one of these framing institutions. He was not their victim; he was their collaborator. His life consisted of helping each one of them to work—the church, the government, the neighbors' farms, nature in his own land.

Ultimately his sons needed to assume responsibility for the world their father inhabited. Whatever happened in New London, Hempstead knew what to do. Puzzled or uncertain as he may have been as new circumstances impinged—like Abigail's death—by the time he made his diary entry he knew how to act. A line or two summarized his reaction to the most difficult events. With certain, skillful strokes, he met whatever came. Could that clarity be inherited or taught?

Daughters

We have no comparable diary for Abigail Hempstead before her premature death in 1716. Few farm women anywhere kept diaries. One who did was Mary Cooper, who lived in Oyster Bay, across Long Island Sound from New London, about twenty-five miles east of New York City. From 1768, when she was fifty-four, until 1773, Cooper made nearly daily entries in her diary.[26] The entries were usually only two or three lines, but they offer a glimpse of how mothers taught daughters to perform their duties as "huswifes."

Mary Wright married Joseph Cooper in 1729 a few days after her fourteenth birthday. It was not a happy marriage. On July 13, 1769, she noted her fortieth wedding anniversary. "This day is forty years sinc I left my father's house and come here, and here have I seene littel els but harde labour and sorrow, crosses of every kind. I think in every respect the state of my affairs is more then forty times worse then when I came here first, except that I am nearer the desierered haven." Family losses marred Cooper's life as they did Hempstead's. Of her six children, two died in infancy, two more in early childhood, and both of the girls who grew up to marry died before their mother, who lived until 1778, when she was sixty-three. She never forgot these lost children. Eighteen years after the death of a son, Mary noted "this day is 18 years since my dear son Caleb was born. O alas, how is my expectation cut off."[27]

Ester, the daughter who figures most prominently in the diary, had married her cousin Simon, but they soon separated, and Ester came home to live with her mother.[28] One wonders how Mary felt about her daughter leaving her husband. Did Mary disapprove or did she admire her daughter's courage in making the break? And on Ester's side, did she resolve not to suffer a bad marriage after observing her mother's misery? Mary witnessed Simon flying into a rage with Ester and striking her.[29] Mary did not have the heart to force her daughter back under his control. Her relationship with her other daughter, Bet Ann, was even more troubled. Mary opposed Bet Ann's wedding to a physician. When Bet Ann eloped, Mary refused to talk to her and forgave her only after she died. Only then did Mary allow Bet Ann's coffin to reenter the house—through the window through which she had eloped.[30]

One of the lessons for daughters was how to carry on through distress. Personal misery was no reason to stop working. The unrelenting demands of the farm compelled everyone to keep at their labors. No matter whether she was repelled by a husband or sorrowing from a lost child, the work had to be done. Mary recorded her feelings along with her work—her illness, her emotional distress, or fatigue. "I am much hured and feele very unhappy" was as likely to appear in the diary as a note that the green herbs had escaped the frost. "Much hard work and but little happyness this week" was often her feeling.[31] Her entries were a record of her endurance.

Mary was not laboring alone. The Coopers owned four slaves, and Mary had the help of her daughters. But the burden of the work fell on her. Growing up, Ester and Bet Ann would have watched their mother doing one task after another, each requiring practice to be performed properly. The Coopers probably marketed wheat and flour in the city, but they produced a great variety of other farm goods, which fell to Mary to process. In the spring, she helped with lambing, and Ester planted a garden. Ester raised ducks, which they sold in New York. In fruit season, they dried cherries and sold some. For four days in November, they cut apples for drying. They harvested peaches, dried pears, kept bees, and made pickles.[32] After the hogs were slaughtered in the fall, sausage had to be made. No fuss about mucking about in a pig's guts.

Sometimes the work was too much for Mary. "Oh, I am distressed with harde worke makeing sassages and boile souse, bakeing and cooking."[33] Yet she did not quit. In the same season, they made tallow for candles, boiled soap, and made mince pies. The fabric cycle went forward throughout the year. Retting and hatcheling the flax, cleaning wool, spinning flax, wool, and cotton. Ester sometimes went off to help others spin. Once turned into clothing, the fabric had to be cared for. "I am drying and ironing my cloths til almost brake of day."[34] By the time she was an adult, Ester's fingers and mind were stocked with multiple household skills.

Mary kept track of visitors who came and went almost as if the Coopers ran a tavern. Some were welcome friends; others were just a burden. "I am sore distreste with visseters from day to day." For all of them she had to prepare meals. She could not bear the repugnant Ben Hildreth and two friends who drank rum and kept a yapping dog in their room. "The first I herde this morning was Ben's dogs barking and yoling in the bed room. They did nothing but drink them selves drunk all the day long and sent for more rum."[35] Yet she had to prepare meals for them like everyone else. She complained sometimes that meals had to be put on the table when there was no food in the house. The task drove her to the end of her rope. "Much hurre and distrest with company" was a frequent refrain. Fatigue overcame her, but she had to get meals on the table however unwell herself. When the guests left, the house had to be cleaned. In a day before brooms were common, the nature of house cleaning is a little unclear, but Mary frequently mentioned her efforts to restore order. It did not help that Ester "fretted most greveously all day long about cleaning the house."[36]

Mary frequently said she felt distressed. Was that a reflection of unhappy relations with her husband or was she ill? Much of the time it was simply fatigue. "Very unwell and tired almost to death." "My feet ach as if the bones was laid bare. Not one day's rest have I had this weeke." Illness did overcome her from time to time, and she was terrified when she heard rumors of smallpox in the neighborhood. She walked to church across the fields to avoid meeting afflicted people.[37] When her granddaughter Salle and a friend went to Doctor Potter "to take the small pox," she prayed for their souls and bodies. "Bring them home to their mour[n]ing mother in helth and safty." Illness struck down everyone from time to time, and the burden of caring for the sick fell primarily on her. She was the one to prepare meals for the sick and nurse them. If she was debilitated herself, the household fell apart. When called, she and Ester went to help with the birth of a child.[38]

Daughters had to learn to carry this heavy load—the yearly round of tasks and the stress of doing the work, rearing the children, and caring for the ill—even when suffering from loss or family stress. There are not many happy entries in Mary Cooper's diary. She may not have had a happy nature.[39] Her chief surcease from sorrow came from her worship at a New Light Baptist church. "Some heavenly tranceports filled my soul this evening." After walking to meeting one June Sunday, Mary said, "I felt very happy parte of this day." Ester went with her and, when they had meetings at home, sometimes exulted.[40] From time to time, there were lighthearted moments. Mary noted frolics for spinning, quilting, sewing, and barn-raisings, though when they had a chopping frolic themselves, Mary had to cook for the workmen. She bought a new dress for Ester when a wedding was coming up. For two days in the fall in 1768, they went off to the horse races. Ester, despite her miseries, was capable of having fun; Simon had argued with her about her dancing. She had six girlfriends over to stay a couple of days, though

Mary "much freted" with the preparations.[41] Mary may have made entries when she was most under stress, leaving more peaceful moments out of the diary. At the very least, she taught Ester and Bet Ann to keep working however they felt.

Uncas and His Sons

Uncas had four sons: Oweneco, the eldest, destined to succeed his father as sachem, Joshua (also called Attawanhood), John, and Ben, who became sachem in 1723. Uncas had different lessons to teach his sons and grandsons than Hempstead. In the Hempstead household, every man had to know how to grub weeds. Although they ate corn, Uncas's sons did not hoe. The brothers Oweneco and Ben needed to know about farming. They directed the movement of the village to hunting grounds and fishing sites at the right season; they saw their father distribute the fields among the Mohegan villagers. But they would not have planted or cleared the ground of choking weeds. That was left to women, while men fished and hunted. Roger Williams said men planted tobacco, the only crop they worked on. Indian men also burned the woods to open spaces for small game; men and women together broke up the ground for new fields.[42] Otherwise only old men or occasionally an exceptional man out of regard for his wife would help in the fields. Women planted and kept the weeds down using what Williams called "naturall Howes," meaning shells and perhaps stones bound to sticks. Indian children, probably including boys, drove away birds from newly planted cornfields.[43]

In response to population pressures, the Mohegans had taken up agriculture well before English settlement.[44] Corn, squash, beans, pumpkins, artichokes, cucumbers, watermelons, and sunflowers entered their diet, augmented by fish and game. In Uncas's boyhood, the Mohegan men fished in the spring when the shad, alewives, eels, and salmon were running. Women planted at the same time and then through the summer cultivated corn and vegetables. At the end of the summer, the women harvested the crops. In the late fall and winter, when the animals were fattest, the men hunted deer and bear. The combination of hunting, gathering, and cropping minimized traveling and hunting space requirements, and provided a solid year-round diet.[45]

In Indian families, women's work produced two-thirds to three-fourths of the family food supply. When shelters were constructed, women mounted bark slabs or mats on pole frames built by men. Women ground the corn in mortars to produce meal and gathered shellfish. Williams speculated that Indian men took additional wives partly to add to their wealth. Victors in Indian wars valued women captives as much as men.[46] An additional adult woman in the household could double the harvest. Extra women meant as much to the Indians as Hempstead's boys meant to him. Edward Winslow, an early-seventeenth-century English observer, noted that among the Indians "where are most women, there is greatest plenty."[47] Williams attributed Indian women's hardened constitutions to their "extraordinary great labour."[48]

Roger Williams, Uncas's contemporary who became adept in the Indian language, is as good a contemporaneous reporter on the Mohegans as can be found. The Rhode Island Narragansetts whom Williams knew well lived within fifty miles of the Mohegans and spoke a closely related variation of the Mohegans' Algonquin tongue.[49] In the absence of closer observations of the Mohegans, we can extrapolate from Williams, at least for the period from 1635, when Williams began dealing with the Narragansetts, to 1643, when he wrote *A Key into the Languages of America* aboard ship on his way to England to obtain a charter for his colony.[50]

Much of the learning Indian boys had to acquire came no doubt by emulation and imitation. Williams thought that Indian fathers out of affection refused to discipline their children. Boys would have acquired skills, like the ability to find one's way in a pathless wilderness, by following and observing older men. Williams marveled that Indians knew "all the body and bowels of the Countrey (by reason of their huntings)," and navigated accurately without a trail. "I have often been guided twentie, thirtie, yea sometimes fortie miles through the woods," he wrote, "a streight course, out of any path." That would have required exquisite attention to landmarks, slopes, variations in flora, and a hundred other details by which to steer a course. At night the Indians probably depended on stars and planets to guide them. Williams said the Indians "much observe the Starres, and their very children can give Names to many of them, and observe their Motions."[51] The body of lore and technique to be absorbed was immense.

Williams reported on the construction of a canoe by burning out a chestnut log: "I have seene a Native goe into the woods with his hatchet carrying onely a Basket of Corn with him, & stones to strike fire[.] when he had feld his tree (being a *chesnut*) he made him a little House or shed of the bark of it, he puts fire and followes the burning of it with fire, in the midst in many places: his corne he boyles and hath the Brook by him, and sometimes angles for a little fish: but so hee continues burning and hewing untill he hath within ten or twelve dayes (lying there at his work alone) finished, and (getting hands,) lanched his Boate; with which afterward hee ventures out to fish in the Ocean."[52]

Along with boatbuilding, the boys learned the complexities of hunting and trapping. Uncas's sons, like every boy, would have progressed from small bows to ever larger and stiffer bows while practicing incessantly. Williams said Indians were "naturally excellent marks-men," overlooking the years of practice it took to shoot well. Skill with the bow went with the ability to stalk. He found the Indians "hardened to endure the weather, and wading, lying, and creeping on the ground." All the grisly techniques of warfare had to be learned as well. Williams marveled at Indians' skill in dispatching enemies. They fell quickly upon a foe wounded by an arrow, "and tearing his head a little aside by his Locke, they in the twinckling of an eye fetch off his head though but with a sorry knife."[53]

Critical as these technical skills were, for the sons of the sachem, diplomacy was far more important. Though the sachem was granted wide authority by Indian villagers, his power was far from absolute. Mohegan sachems ruled by a kind of consensus. As Williams explained, "the *Sachims,* although they have an absolute Monarchie over the people; yet they will not conclude of ought that concernes all, either Lawes, or Subsides, or warres, unto which the people are averse, and by gentle perswasion cannot be brought." Sachems needed wisdom and oratory to win assent.[54] The Indians Williams knew sustained a profoundly oral culture. "I have seene neere a thousand in a round, where *English* could not well neere halfe so many have sitten: Every Man hath his pipe of their *Tobacco,* and a deepe silence they make, and attention give to him that speaketh; and many of them will deliver themselves, either in a relation of news, or in a consultation with very emphaticall speech and great action, commonly an houre, and sometimes two houres together." Williams said the Indians insisted on attention when they spoke and considered it one of the greatest compliments to say "You speake true." These "are words of great flattery," Williams reported, "which they use to each other, but constantly to their Princes at their speeches, for which, if they be eloquent, they esteeme them Gods."[55] Uncas's sons could sit and listen and perhaps in time try out their oratory in the round meetings.

Uncas had to initiate his boys into the culture of tribal violence. A sachem had to avenge the deaths of his people. A sachem without the strength to protect villagers from humiliating defeats would soon lose support.[56] In 1656 Uncas became entangled in a tug of war over a warrior named Weaseapano who had killed a rival sagamore (a lesser form of a sachem) at Mattabesset. The murdered man was not one of Uncas's own people, but a subordinate of a sachem whom Uncas hoped to bring into his orbit. Once the subordinate sachem had appealed to Uncas for aid in avenging the murder, even though the victim was twice removed from Uncas, he had to insist on the murderer's delivery to maintain the respect of his tributaries. Protecting Weaseapano was a Podunk sachem with whom the warrior took refuge. The Podunk leader refused to give up the killer because of his many kin in the sachem's village. To achieve his ends, Uncas threatened to call in the dreaded Mohawks, who lived to the north and west of Mohegan territory. The Podunks thought Uncas was bluffing and stood firm. To prove his claim, Uncas attacked and burned a Podunk wigwam, leaving behind Mohawk weapons as if dropped by accident. The terrified Podunks immediately sued for peace and surrendered Weaseapano. That kind of cunning was hard to teach. Uncas's sons could learn only by watching.[57]

Imperial Families

All this was swept away by the wave of white settlers pressing into Connecticut in the seventeenth and eighteenth centuries. The treaties and purchases that bit by bit ripped away hunting and planting grounds from the native people disrupted a family life that was as intricate and regulated as Hempstead's. Without intending cruelty or dominance, English settlers such as Hempstead possessed a sense that their family project must prevail. The cost to the natives was scarcely contemplated by Hempstead, any more than southern farmers measured the toll when their governments refused to recognize slave marriages.

Hempstead would never recognize himself in the name "imperial family." As he taught Joshua and Nattee to hoe corn, he was only seeking to reproduce himself in the next generation. He had no intimation that one people was superseding another. His will, probated at his death in 1758, expressed only his desire to perpetuate the life that he had lived for eighty years. His diary showed little sign of a broad outlook on imperial affairs. It was confined to the local: his fields and animals, his children's illness and marriages, the admission to the church, the coming and going of sloops, business among the selectmen. It was a record of his ongoing engagement with a local world, not just his own family and farm but the affairs of his town and his neighbors. It was a rich, full world, but one strictly circumscribed. He expressed no ambitions for the British Empire or for American society. He wanted only to maintain and perpetuate the world his diary recorded.

The reason why his life finally could not be localized, why it inevitably went beyond itself to the nation, was the need for land for the next generation. In farm families, everything depended on the control of space. Hempstead could conceive the future of his family only spatially. Farms are rightly described as spreads; they filled up blocs of space. Hempstead thought of his own farm as a series of spaces, many of them with the names of previous owners: Holmes's lot, Crossman's lot. Hempstead created agricultural spaces nearly every year of his adult life by drawing survey lines around tracts of land and assigning them to owners. His children and grandchildren required space. This rudiment of Hempstead's existence is what made conflict between Joshua and Uncas inevitable and made all farm families in the last analysis the enemies of the native people.

The national project can be described as Hempstead's writ large. The creation of America involved the extension of survey lines deeper and deeper into the western wilderness, turning Indian lands into territories, then into tracts, into plots, and finally into farms where families such as Hempstead's could re-create their lives. The expansive impulse was driven less by raw economic necessity than by a judgment about the good life. It envisioned little societies like Hempstead's New London as the better way, perhaps the only way, to a fulfilled existence. Hempstead said nothing about wealth or fame or dominance. What he cared about was what he recorded in his diary, a record of making and growing, provisioning a family, managing the town, and working, working, working. It was this inauspicious life that ultimately defeated Uncas and his sons.

7. Farmers' Markets

How the Exchange Economy Formed Society

In 1720, Joshua Hempstead spent the end of the summer haying as usual in his New London fields. Through the final week of July, all of August, and much of September, he worked with Nathaniel and Stephen cutting hay for winter feed. It was arduous work. The grass had to be cut, dried, raked, hauled, and stacked before it was secure against the rot that would make it useless for feed. All the hay went through these stages, but some of it went through two additional steps: weighing and pressing. Weighing was required to ready it for sale. In August he sold seventeen hundred pounds to Widow Prentis for two shillings, sixpence per hundred. Pressing compressed the stack to take up as little room as possible in vessels headed for the West Indies. In March, Capt. Richard Christophers stowed Hempstead's hay in his sloop for sale in Barbados. In July, Hempstead agreed to supply Captain Christophers with another two loads for three shillings, fourpence per hundredweight, and in August, he carted twenty-seven hundred and forty-one hundred pounds of pressed and weighed hay to the dock.[1]

The double use of his hay—for himself and for sale—typifies the mingling of Hempstead's domestic economy with the town's exchange economy. Hempstead spun wool to make cloth for his children, but also sold wool worth eleven pounds, nine shillings in Hartford. Another shipment of wool delivered to the Widow Biddwell brought thirty-seven pounds, nine shillings in cash plus forty-eight yards of linen cloth.[2] Even self-provisioning, the production of food, clothing, and warmth for his family, required exchanges in the town. Over the years, he brought in people to make clothing and shoes from fibers and hides from his own farm. He took yarn of the family's making to Oliver Manwaring to make shirting. In the 1740s, Lydia Fox made breeches for his slave Adam and for Hempstead himself.[3]

In a port town like New London, local and international commerce also overlapped. Hempstead kept close track of the sloops leaving New London for the West Indies. He recorded five voyages in March, April, and May 1720 to Barbados and "Antegua," and two others left in August and December. He made no mention of putting cattle or barrels of beef on these ships, but he did make four sixteen-foot oars, which he shipped with Captain Manwaring on March 18 and for which he later received twenty-eight pounds of cotton.[4] A few weeks later, he gave five pounds in Barbados silver money to Captain Christophers to buy rum. When it arrived, Hempstead divided it into smaller portions to sell through the year.[5] Hempstead was not a merchant, but like many others, he was a trader who dealt goods and services with a ship captain as readily as with a widow needing help with her hay.

This interlayering of making and trading kept the family stocked with basics and enabled Hempstead to acquire a little more besides: luxuries like fine cloth, a comb, a mirror, or a walnut table. Hempstead owned a pair of gold cuff links, one of which he accidentally swallowed but later recovered by keeping his eyes open at the right moment.[6] Little luxuries were the farmers' reward for making all they could for themselves while still producing for exchange. Hempstead moved seamlessly from one economy to the other—from the domestic to the exchange, from raising food for himself to buying and selling when the opportunity arose.[7]

Exchange was essential to making a living on a farm. It also made rural society. The relationships formed in the exchange of goods and services went beyond trade. Exchanges were the way people came to know one another. Farmers learned how trustworthy, how competent, how easy to deal with their trading partners were. Experience in exchanges played into friendships, courtships, and politics. The exchange economy formed the bones and sinews of local society.

Exchange

Labor away from his farms was one measure of Hempstead's involvement in the town's exchange economy. He had the habit of noting when he was "at home al day" and when he was working for someone, or went to town or to

Hartford on business. In 1720 he was away more days than he kept to his own place. He was a somewhat exceptional case because of his various offices in New London and because his children carried on the household economy while he was away. Still, in 1720 he worked on his own property less than 40 percent of the time.[8] He was much in the employ of John Winthrop, the son of Wait Winthrop and owner of Fisher's Island off the Connecticut coast. Hempstead settled accounts, dealt with tenants, handled court proceedings, and ran errands for Winthrop.[9] Hempstead devoted seventeen days in 1720 to his chief patron.

Beyond his work for the Winthrops in 1720, Hempstead performed a wide variety of services for his neighbors in a New London variant of bricolage.

March 29	"I helpt Thos Harris al day about his boat"
April 2	"aftern at Sister Marys Seting up a well crotch"
April 5	"I was helping Divide Charles Hills Estate"
April 14	"Woiat helpt me finish Soll coits Window Shutts"
May 6	"I was at home al d. making a Tanfat [tanning vat] for Jos Truman"
May 7	"At Jos Trumans about his Tanfatt"
May 9	"aftern about J. Trumans Tanfat"
May 10	"I finished Jos Trumans Tanfat"
June 2	"Willm Holts Cow came" [to be impregnated]
June 3	"I hlpt Jno Pendal in apprizing Richds Land"
July 23	"I was at home al day mending Mr Hills fence"
August 17	"I was al day haying at Hills Lot"
August 23	"aftern writing Brother Plumbs will"
August 27	"I was al day Stacking hay & at Hills Lot"
September 3	"I wrote a Deed for Ja Harris to Capt. Ellery"
September 7	"I was at home al d. Making a Map of Capt Ellery farm"
September 8	"I was at home al d. writing a deed & Making a Map &c."
December 6	"I was mending Mr Hills fence most of ye day"
December 13	"aftern writing a deed of Mortgage for Samll Rogers. he pd me 3s"[10]

Hempstead carefully noted each service rendered, each item bought and sold, each place where he lodged on his trips, each day of labor by himself and boys down to the half day.

Wherever he went he left a trail of obligations: what he owed and what was owed to him. Repairing a fence for the widow Hill meant she was obligated to Hempstead. Staying with Ebe Williams in Stonington during haying season meant Hempstead owed Williams. The exchange economy created hundreds of these obligations every year. Every farmer was laden with a record of services rendered and services received. The town was bound together by invisible ties of person-to-person exchanges. They were entered in account books or recorded in memory or inscribed in promissory notes. In time they had to be balanced. "I went in to Town & Ballanced Accots with mr Shaw," Hempstead wrote of one of the periodic settlements.[11]

All the exchanges rested on judgments about how people would act, ultimately judgments of character. When Hempstead hayed for Widow Hill or made a tanning vat for Joseph Truman, he assumed they could be trusted to pay him. It took time for this trust to build up. By the time Hempstead made the vat for Truman in 1720, they had been interacting for at least a decade. An entry for September 10, 1711, one of the first in Hempstead's surviving diary, noted, "I went to work about casements & for Jos Truman att his house for him to make a pr Shoes for Joney." Here was an immediate quid pro quo, window casements for shoes. Soon after Hempstead made a "currying beam" and finished a bench for Thomas Truman, Joseph's brother. Over the next year, Joseph made three barrels of cider for Hempstead, and he lent Joseph three shillings, sixpence in bills. In 1714 Hempstead spent an afternoon "at Tho. Trumans Triming his Tanfatt."[12] The brothers Thomas and Joseph Truman had inherited a tannery from their father and began to employ the Hempstead to help out, beginning with a day trimming the vat. The next May, the month when the tanning vats were usually put in operation, Hempstead worked two days on the Trumans' tan vat. By the time Hempstead built Joseph Truman's tan vat in 1720, he had worked with the brothers for at least nine years, and in addition proved himself by building vats for William Rogers and Christopher Darrows. By then, the brothers had developed confidence in Hempstead, and he was sure of repayment from the Trumans. In 1722 he built two more vats for Joseph Truman.[13]

Memories like these were entwined around the webs of obligations covering the town. Everyone acquired an economic reputation constructed from scores of small exchanges. When Hempstead traded with someone, he knew the history of their dealings, certainly with himself and probably with others. He could steer clear of those who were known to be slow to repay or inclined to forget. This meant the whole town helped enforce payment. Those who fell down put their reputations at risk with everyone. Truman's ability to go on exchanging depended on how well he dealt with Hempstead.

If Hempstead suffered economically from misplaced trust, the defaulter suffered even more.[14]

Nearly everyone in town was a small-bore banker. Decisions about credit that now are passed on to experts like bankers were made by virtually everyone in the exchange economy. In New London, credit was everyone's business. Everyone had to have some impression of who among their neighbors could be trusted and who not. They had to keep an eye on their diligence, the state of their crops, the health of their children, the number of animals in their fields, the casks of meat they brought to the docks for shipment to Antigua. Trust was based on a constant evaluation of productive capacity as well as faithfulness in exchange.[15]

This trust functioned like capital. As Craig Muldrew explains in his study of economic obligation in early modern England, "most wealth, as it was earned and spent, existed in the form of household credit."[16] The farmer's credit reputation was as tangible an asset as cash in hand, land, houses, barns, animals, or tools. The neighbors' trust permitted a farmer to acquire the working capital he needed from year to year and eventually funds to acquire property for his children. Lacking that trust, he lost access to capital and could not launch ventures like Hempstead's Stonington sheep ranch. Hempstead flourished in the trust economy. Coupling work on his own farms with ventures in the exchange economy, he proved his worth over and over. With neighborly trust as his working capital, he bought land and sheep, purchased cider and pork, and hired hands to work in his hayfields.

Over the next century and a half, the local trust economy receded. The capital created by trust in Hempstead's character was transferred from neighbors to banks. Bankers took over the responsibility of lending money. As cash began to circulate, the question of trust passed to the bills. Were they to be trusted? Would the money, rather than the person, hold its value? Personal relationships were flattened out and simplified, and the integrity and wisdom of the issuers of the money came under scrutiny instead.[17]

In the eighteenth century, trust flowed into politics. Hempstead was appointed a justice of the peace in 1727, when he was forty-seven, and remained in office until his death in 1758. Because his mettle had been tested, he became a constant in town office.[18] In 1727 Hempstead was well established as a farmer and craftsman, and tried and tested as a town leader. He had already been chosen as selectman ten times beginning in 1709 and was elected to the General Assembly eight times between 1714 and 1730. He was not admitted to the Congregational Church in New London until 1726, and it may not be coincidental that he was first appointed justice of the peace the next year. Although an invariable attendee at the Rev. Mr. Eliphalet Adams's sermons twice each Sunday, Hempstead did not officially join the church until the requirement to relate a conversion experience was dropped.[19] With that one missing element added, he won the town's complete confidence.

Hempstead's name was never preceded by "Honorable" or "Worshipful," though as a justice of the peace, he merited the title of "Esqr." in his obituary.[20] But he had an unchallenged position among the body of solid citizens who were repeatedly chosen for town offices. The town trusted him with difficult negotiations over the boundaries of the Mohegan lands and with the disposal of a lump of money that fell into its hands through a court case. He paid the schoolmaster and the minister. People trusted him to appraise their estates and write their wills. In 1736 he was captain of the town's second company of militia.[21] He was one of the body of known men who inspired confidence, benefiting from a reputation that Edmund Fanning, the maligned county official in Orange County, North Carolina, lacked and, in consequence, suffered.

Two Economies

In one sense, the exchange economy and the core domestic economy in New London blended almost imperceptibly; they were part of a seamless, interwoven fabric. But in the farmers' minds, the two were not the same. Although functionally merged, the two economies served different purposes and remained conceptually separate. The account books themselves mark the divide. Hempstead's diary was a record of external obligations, not a comprehensive record of work. He noted only what he owed persons outside of his household. Work in the domestic economy made only spotty appearances. On three days in July 1714, Hempstead mowed and stacked hay at his home without mentioning his sons except on the day that "Josh cut his knee with a Sythe." It took an injury to bring him into the record. On neighbors' land, it was just the opposite. On a Tuesday in July 1714, he hilled corn at home, as usual saying nothing of the boys. But on Wednesday he did the same work for a neighbor, and then his sons appeared in the record. "I was hilling Corn al day at Jo Lesters & all ye boys."[22]

As in Matthew Patten's diary, the work done by women and children in the household economy is nearly invisible in Hempstead's record. This was the work that kept the family alive, produced most of what was eaten and worn, cared for the ailing, put a roof over most heads, and kept the family warm in cold weather. Yet it was not recorded. Women's work was excluded not because it did not matter in the life of the family but because it did not count in the exchange economy. In his diary, Hempstead kept track of his relationship with the world beyond the household. For purposes of his record, the two economies were separate.

The same distinction governed tax valuation lists. As far as possible, tax valuations avoided references to the domestic economy. No taxes were laid on kitchen gardens or the labor of women and children. Spinning wheels and dairying equipment were not listed. The assessors noted only goods that contributed to the farmer's capacity for exchange. In 1699 Pennsylvania taxed "all Lands & other rents as also the personal estates" a penny for "every pound of clear value," but specifically exempted "the household goods and implements they use." To be sure, a clear distinction could not always be made. Hay and animals served a double purpose, both for household consumption and for exchange; so did spinning wheels. But every item and every person that served the household alone was left out. In the mind of legislators, they existed in another category.[23]

Today governments tax "income." Eighteenth-century farmers had no category comparable to "income."[24] Hempstead never calculated how much "profit" he had accumulated over a year. Governments taxed wealth, by which they meant resources that produced goods for exchange—capital goods we would call them—land, animals, money at interest, warehouses, shops, and workers. Goods and people who produced for the household economy were excluded.

Perhaps the most compelling evidence of a distinct exchange economy is the use of money values in Hempstead's diary and other records of exchange. Nothing in the domestic economy had a price; everything in the exchange economy did. No one calculated how much Hempstead's son Thomas earned by plowing the family's fields or Abigail Hempstead by churning butter at home. Within the domestic economy, no one paid for anything—not for food, work, clothing, tools, or sleeping space. In the exchange economy, prices were attached to everything, to wool and rum, to pasturage and haying, to ferryage, to board, to transport, to surveying—and those prices were known and agreed upon. Hempstead sold Edmond Fanning a barrel of pork for ninety shillings, part to be paid in cash and part with a yearling worth thirty shillings. The exchange worked because both parties knew the value of a yearling and a barrel of pork. When Hempstead took an inventory of a deceased person's estate, the men surveying the property knew the value of everything. They could look at pile of chipped dishes and quickly estimate its worth. An old horse plow was clearly worth two shillings, an old desk forty shillings, a portmanteau with lock and keys one shilling, sixpence, saddle bags three shillings.[25] A brief inspection by the assessors, a proposed number, a comment or two, and the value was entered on the inventory.

That quick agreement on virtually everything implied a market. Somewhere each object had acquired an agreed-upon worth—everything in house, barn, and fields had a money value. Farm materials were monetized, even though currency was scarce and only occasionally came into play. The inventory takers must have remembered exchanges when objects like these had been bought and sold before. Money values had to be assigned to effect any kind of barter whether or not money was involved. There was no way to exchange a barrel of pork for a yearling unless a monetary value could be assigned. Monetization was required to determine equivalencies. Nothing like that happened in the core domestic economy. Family consumption existed in another sphere, and farm families knew the difference.

Stores

Had Hempstead lived in Virginia in the mid-eighteenth century, his economic life would have been more like the cash economy of nineteenth-century New England. In Virginia, a man of his eminence would likely not have expanded his inventory of skills to gain credit with his neighbors: no gravestones, no sloops, no tanning vats, no casements, no compressed hay. In Virginia, money grew on tobacco plants. Virtually everything could be purchased with tobacco. All the exchange power he needed lay in those leaves, as later it was to lie in cash. All that he accomplished by going to court for the Winthrops and writing deeds and wills for his neighbors, by surveying town lands and shaping oars, he could do in Virginia by raising tobacco.

Tobacco was a form of currency. Payments were delayed until the season's end, requiring a certain amount of trust, but once the tobacco was in hand, a storekeeper or a neighbor had only to appraise the quality of the leaf, not the character of the man. After 1730, the legislatively mandated inspection warehouses relieved storekeepers of even that care. Planters whose tobacco measured up to export standards received an inspection receipt when they deposited their crop in a colony warehouse, and these receipts functioned as currency.

"The merchants generally purchase the tobacco in the country, by sending persons to open *stores* for them; that is, warehouses in which they lay in a great assortment of British commodities and manufactures; to these, as to shops, the planters resort, and supply themselves with what they want, paying, in inspection receipts."[26] The receipts made storekeeping feasible. Stores flourished when some kind of currency circulated in the local economy. It avoided the problem of deciding how to exchange a batch of hay or work in the fields for goods in the store. The southern storekeeper did not have to work through these complicated transactions or wait until his customers had some form of payment that was "merchantable." Everything was paid for with tobacco.[27]

New London storekeepers made almost no appearances on Hempstead's map. Richard Shaw came closest. In 1721 Hempstead bought eleven bushels of corn and one of wheat from Shaw for forty shillings. In late October 1758, two months before his death, Hempstead bought four barrels of cider from "Capt Shaw." In the intervening thirty-seven years, Hempstead purchased a silk handkerchief from Shaw in May 1748, but otherwise mentioned him only a dozen times. His diary went for years without noting a purchase in a store. Apparently everything Hempstead needed, he obtained through exchanges. He brought in people to weave his cloth, tailor his suits, make his shoes. He bought rum directly from the ship captains who imported it from the West Indies. It is hard to identify the name of one proper storekeeper in his diary.[28]

The absence of store exchanges in Hempstead's diary cannot have been typical. Matthew Patten, the slightly younger version of Hempstead who kept a diary in Bedford, New Hampshire, from 1754 to 1788, made purchases on average three or four times a month. His most frequent purchases were rum, snuff, and sugar, followed by coffee and tea. Patten purchased nails for his active carpentry business and fabric and buttons to supply the tailor Mr. Hopper, who came to Patten's house for sixteen days in January at the same time as James McClure was there making six pairs of shoes. The store augmented Patten's household economy by supplying components he could not make for himself. It was also a place for buying little luxuries—nutmeg, pepper, and allspice, an ivory comb, and a jackknife. In late spring, when his own provisions were running low, Patten bought corn, peas, and shad.[29]

Still, stores did not loom large in New England before Independence. Patten did not sell his cabinets or his meat through the store. Stores augmented his economy rather than playing a central role, as they did in Virginia. The scholarship of the North and the South reflects this economic reality. Historians have reconstructed southern society by examining the brimming pages of storekeeper account books.[30] The same kind of study has never been made in New England. When Winifred Rothenberg wished to record commodity prices in eighteenth-century New England, she did not turn to storekeeper accounts, where prices might have been found. Such accounts from country towns are rare before the Revolution. Instead, she turned to farmer account books, with their multiplicity of references to exchange partners. Farmers rather than storekeepers were the nodes of the New England exchange economy.[31] They kept the records that facilitated the flow of local commerce.

Stores do have a place on the 1771 Massachusetts tax valuation list. The appraisers filled in a category for store inventories labeled "An Account of each Person's whole Stock in, in Trade, Goods, Wares and Merchandise, paid for or not paid for." The larger towns, especially the port towns, had a number of individuals taxed for trade goods, but in the country towns the sums were not great. Stores became the centers of trade in the nineteenth century as more currency made them practical. Earlier, most Massachusetts store inventories were valued at less than £100. If one considers that Hempstead paid £2.5 for one silk handkerchief in 1748, the inventory of a store with less than £100 worth of goods could not have been very substantial. Broadcloth in 1747 went for £3 10s a yard. Hempstead bought three and a half yards and paid £12 5s. What could a store stock with inventory worth £50 to £100? Perhaps tow cloth, which cost 3s 6d per yard, or Indian corn at 1s a bushel in 1734, or nails, pins, salt, sugar, or rum. In Talbot County, Maryland, in 1719, Edward Lloyd's stock of cloth alone was valued at £400. In his largest store, he carried 450 pairs of shoes, 130 hats, 200 pairs of gloves.[32] In Springfield, Massachusetts, by contrast, the entire inventory of the biggest store came to only £450, and in Lancaster £500. These were among the five largest towns in the colony after Boston and Salem.

Had Hempstead been born in Virginia, he would have concentrated on tobacco, all that was needed to establish credit and create capital. For substantial planters, Hempstead's Virginia equivalents, a good tobacco harvest solved all problems. He would not have been away from his farm more than half the time working for others as he was in New London. He would have tended his fields and tobacco barns and overseen ten or twenty slaves. Exchanges with his neighbors would have occurred less frequently, and his credit with the store or, if he was a great planter, with British mercantile houses, would have meant more to him than the trust of the county. Since Virginia was not part of the obligation and trust economy, he would have been more independent, less connected, more focused on his skill as a planter than as an entrepreneur who served his neighbors and the town in a score of ways. His reputation would have rested less on his dependability in meeting obligations and more on his crop.[33]

Debt

In 1720 Hempstead expanded his holdings in Stonington, the town immediately adjacent to New London, where the family had been settled for three generations. He was looking ahead to the time when his sons would need farms of their own, and nearby Stonington was a logical site. He had cleared up a dispute about ownership of an inherited Stonington tract and wanted to add to his holdings. On March 8, 1720, he bought a farm from Mr. Ashby for £180. "I gave him two bonds one for to pay £80 ye Midle of July and ye other to pay one hundred ye Last day of November."[34] Like all enterprising farmers, Hempstead went into debt whenever he began a new venture. Debt was not a mark of poverty or desperation. In Hempstead's case, it was a sign of favorable prospects.

Hempstead may have hoped to acquire the payment by selling something before the debt was due—rum or wool or hay—but the payment was not made as scheduled. The contract called for paying the debt which was incurred in March 1720 by the following July, and he did pay £40 not long after, but not until March 1724, four years after contracting the debt, did he make a second payment. "I went to ye farm & Stephen. I pd Mr Ashbey £57 8s od & £40 before & took up my £80 Bond. £100 Still due & £18 for ye Interest 3 year past to ye first of Nov Last." The payment of £57 8s plus the previously paid £40 covered the principal and interest on the first bond for

£80. The £100 bond with three years of interest at 6 percent remained outstanding. Ashby did not press for collection at the due date of the bond; so long as he was drawing interest on the loan, he was satisfied. Hempstead's bond was an investment. Fixing the repayment date soon after contracting the loan gave Ashby a legal right to call it in if circumstances required, but so long as he was not under pressure, he was happy to carry Hempstead for a few more years while the interest accumulated.[35] In a pinch, bonds assured the lender recourse to the courts if payment was not forthcoming.[36]

Over the next ten years Hempstead gave bonds in transactions with seven other parties to purchase land, a slave, and more sheep. Bonds served to finance capital improvements that a farmer could not manage within the normal bounds of the exchange economy. Hempstead made out a bond to the widow Elizabeth Crossman for £80 for the New London property he purchased from her. The slave Adam also cost Hempstead £80. The price of 114 sheep purchased from James Babcock came to £45. In Hempstead's case, bonds helped him add to his productive capacity: more land, more animals, more labor.[37]

At the same time as he was borrowing money to expand his Stonington holding, Hempstead accepted bonds in payment for land he was selling. He was both lender and borrower. Parties to large purchases necessarily became bankers for each other. In March 1723, he sold sixty-five acres in Stonington to David Cleaves and took two bonds for £18 and £48 toward a total price of £91. In March of 1728/29 he took two bonds from Nathaniel Warner for £100 and £95 in addition to £25 in cash for land at Aquebogue (or Occubank) on Long Island, where Hempstead owned property. In the same decade that he incurred debts, he accumulated almost as many debtors.[38]

In this tangled network of exchanges, it is difficult to identify a creditor class. Anyone selling land was likely to be a creditor for at least a few years. The 1771 Massachusetts tax valuation listed quite a number of people with money at interest "more than he or she pays interest for." These were net lenders. Only the smallest towns lacked lenders: Egremont, a town with 104 rateable (taxable) men in the far southwest corner of the state immediately adjacent to the New York border had none; Lincoln, nearer to Boston, with 68 rateables, had only one. Nearby Sudbury, by contrast, had forty-one lenders in a population of 461 rateable men, and Marshfield in southeastern Massachusetts with 250 rateables had forty-two. On the average, one person in sixteen in small and large towns in Massachusetts in 1771 listed money at interest. Since it was only the differences between amounts owed and amounts lent that were listed, the sums cannot be used to gauge the total amount of debt in a town. Hempstead owed hundreds of pounds while at the same time he was owed hundreds of pounds. The numbers in the evaluation were far smaller than the amount actually in play in the credit market.[39]

The lenders as a group do not seem to have come from conspicuously wealthy townsmen. The entry on the valuations list that named "The Annual Worth of the whole Real Estate without any Deduction" best reflected each person's worth. At the top of the Springfield list, three people had real estate whose annual worth was thirty pounds or more; none was a big lender. The median worth of the lenders was twelve pounds, and apart from the richest man in town, worth forty-eight pounds, the top real estate value among the lenders was twenty-six pounds.[40] The lenders seem to have been drawn from a middling range of householders who, like Hempstead's creditors, had property to sell and took bonds in payment.

Storekeepers and merchants turned up somewhat more frequently among the net lenders. Farmers could get into debt by overspending at the store. When the tab in the storekeeper's book went too high and the customer was slow to pay, "book debt," which drew no interest, could be converted into a note, which did. But book debts were not a major reason for indebtedness. The amounts of money at interest on the tax valuation list did not point toward the conversion of storekeeper book debts to a note or a bond as a frequent occurrence. The sums listed were usually rounded to numbers ending in zero or five, with no shilling and pence, not the odd-sized numbers that would result from a variety of small purchases in a store.[41] Moreover, according to the 1771 valuations, fewer than half the storekeepers and merchants had more money out at interest than they owed. In the inland towns, the percentages of merchants and storekeepers who were net lenders ranged from 25 percent to 50 percent. In the port towns, Salem, Charleston, and Newburyport, only between 10 percent and 19 percent of the merchants had money at interest. Most of the moneylenders were not merchants at all. In Springfield, the bustling entrepôt on the Connecticut River above the falls, only 10 percent of those who had more money at interest than they owed were storekeepers or merchants. In the port towns merchants and storekeepers made up a larger proportion of the net lenders: 23 percent to 53 percent. But in a 10 percent sample of inland towns, fewer than 15 percent of net lenders were merchants. Lending and trading did not necessarily go together.

Women were occasionally active lenders. The legend for the money at interest category was the only one to explicitly acknowledge women's part in the town economy. It referred to the "Money that any person has at Interest, more than he or *she* pays Interest for." In Springfield, the biggest lender by far was Elizabeth Dwight, a widow who had £4,400 at interest with very little other estate. Widow Elizabeth Bliss had 120 pounds, and two other Bliss women, Elizabeth Bliss, Jr., and Eunice Bliss, 180 and 50 pounds, respectively.[42] All were connected to important Springfield families. Elizabeth Dwight had been married to Colonel Josiah Dwight, a Springfield merchant who purchased a large house on Springfield's Main Street and added a large broken scroll front-door pediment that was the mark of Connecticut River Gods' dwellings. The addition of women to the category heading suggests that women such as these were not unusual. Hempstead owed money to Widow Crossman and Stephen Harris's wife. In lieu of other resources, cash bequests put out at interest supported widows and unwed daughters after husbands and fathers were gone.[43]

In a few cases, people with large resources on the scale of Elizabeth Dwight in Springfield made a living by lending capital. Most commonly, the amounts on loan suggest notes and bonds were granted in the course of buying and selling land or other costly items. On the whole, the distribution of money at interest on the valuation lists points to the issuance of bonds for purchases along the lines of Hempstead's purchase of land, a slave, and a flock of sheep. Bonds appear to have been given as normal part of the town exchange economy, rather than as instruments of creditors seeking to exploit the needs of the disadvantaged. The balance of interest owed versus interest owing was not large. The median amount of money at interest in a sample of fifteen towns from the 1771 valuation list was £33. The median for the four largest towns after Salem and Boston was £37. The "lenders" were probably both debtors and creditors, with the balance falling slightly on the creditor side in a given year.[44]

The value of Hempstead's bonds suggest the amounts required to make significant capital improvements on a New London farm in the first half of the eighteenth century. A whole farm could be purchased for two hundred pounds. You could buy a hundred sheep for less than fifty pounds. With credit worthiness in that range, a farmer could expand his operations, provide for children, go into a new venture like raising sheep. Twenty-three loans by the Queens County, New York, loan office for a slightly later period,

1756–60, ranged between twenty-five and one hundred pounds.[45] These were the amounts farmers needed to transact ordinary land purchases and make other capital improvements.

To prosper, farmers needed credit at least at these modest levels. In the wider commercial economy, where merchants often dealt with strangers, creditworthiness depended on reputation in the largest sense. Merchants dealing with backcountry storekeepers wanted to know about the character of prospective debtors, their probity, industry, and self-discipline as well as their wealth.[46] Within a town, even one as large and booming as New London, no inquiries were required. A farmer's character was on display every day in the state of his fields, his alacrity in returning work for work, and the quality of his crops and animals. Most of his capital resources were visible on his farmstead; habits of industry showed up in barnyard and field. Creditors had all the information they needed to estimate the degree of risk when they accepted a neighbor's bond.

For those who could not pass the test, the consequences were dire. The poor, the ill, the unfortunate, the improvident could not purchase land or other capital goods to provide for their children's futures. If they could not be trusted to repay eighty pounds in a reasonable period, they could not write a bond, as Hempstead did for his Stonington farm. Until his neighbors saw signs of such competence, a farmer's bonds were worthless and his prospects cramped. He might subsist, but he could not expand to meet his family's needs.

For those with sound credit, though, rather than marking defeat, debt was a sign of character and improving prospects. The growth in debt prosecutions in the eighteenth century measured increasing creditworthiness, not declining fortunes. By that measure the economy was making great headway in the first half of the century. In New London County, both the number of debt cases per capita and their value per capita rose more than tenfold between 1700 and 1730. If we assume that increase in debt prosecutions per capita indicated an increase in overall debt, the rising number implies that an ever larger proportion of farmers were becoming creditworthy. The debt cases indicated a deeper and heavier involvement in the exchange economy by an increasing number of farmers.[47]

New England was not unique in its rise in debt cases. The level of financial competence and the concomitant increase in debt cases rose everywhere along the seaboard. New York began issuing currency in 1709, the same year as Connecticut, lubricating the wheels of trade. Fast on the heels of increased currency circulation, debt increased. In New York, only 10 percent of estate inventories in the period from 1680 to 1699 included debts owed to the decedent. In the years 1760–75, 60 percent of the inventories listed debt.[48] Although estate inventories were skewed to the high side of the economic scale, the sample indicates how widely debt had become a part of ordinary economic life.

These were the decades when, for good or ill, debt became a fixed part of farm life. The increase of debt cases meant the farm population's level of financial competence was rising. But the news was not all good. The exposure to risk was growing too, resulting in prosecution in court, the burden of court costs, and the potential loss of property. Debt was always a risk, a potential disaster. The Long Island housewife Mary Cooper complained bitterly of her family's debts. "My hearte is burnt with anger and discontent, want of every necessary thing in life and in constant feare of gapeing creditors consums my strenth and wasts my days. The horrer of these things with the continuel cross of my family, like to so many horse leeches, prays upon my vitals." Eventually she put off her creditors, but at the high cost of mortgaging her farm.[49] Debt put the source of her livelihood in jeopardy. If growing debt marked increased production for the exchange economy, it also signaled the arrival of the sorrows that debt frequently brought.

Hempstead felt none of Mary Cooper's pain from his debts. Rather than bearing him down, debt and obligations worked in his favor. The constant rhythm of obligations incurred and obligations met built trust among his trading partners. His credit history paved the way for appointment as justice of the peace and election to the General Assembly. Having trusted him for years in the exchanges of everyday farm business, people trusted him with civic responsibility. Unlike Edmund Fanning, the much-berated Orange County, North Carolina, official who suffered the wrath of Herman Husband, Hempstead had proven himself above suspicion.

PART FOUR

Pennsylvania, 1760–76

8. Crèvecoeur's Pennsylvania

Farming in the Middle Colonies

Michel-Guillaume Jean de Crèvecoeur, the scion of a genteel French family, migrated to Canada in 1755, when he was twenty, to work as a surveyor and cartographer for the French military. After being wounded in Montcalm's defeat at Montreal in 1759, he was discharged and moved to New York. Long an anglophile, he became a British citizen in 1765 under the name of Hector St. John. For a decade, Crèvecoeur's work as a trader and surveyor took him all over North America, from the Atlantic to the Mississippi. In 1769 after his return to New York, he married Mehetable Tippet, the daughter of a prosperous Westchester family, and purchased land in Orange County, New York, west of the Hudson River. For ten years, he farmed the land he named Pine Hill, raised three children, and wrote.

While working his Orange County farm, Crèvecoeur scribbled incessantly, a habit his Jesuit schooling may have instilled in him.[1] When he left the country in September 1780, he carried a stack of essays in his baggage. On his way to France, Crèvecoeur stopped in England, where he sold some of his writings to a London publisher. The essays were published in 1782 as *Letters from an American Farmer.* The book immediately won Crèvecoeur a following in France. In Paris he was fêted by the intellectual aristocracy and invited by the minister of the navy to write a report on the North American colonies. So impressive was Crèvecoeur's work that he was appointed French consul to New York, New Jersey, and Connecticut. Returning to America in 1783, he learned that Indians had burned Pine Hill and killed his wife. By good fortune, he recovered his children, who had been taken to Boston by a stranger. In 1790, Crèvecoeur returned to France, where he died in 1813.[2]

His essays, especially an additional trove discovered in 1922, give us firsthand access to farming in the Middle Colonies. Crèvecoeur's farm lay near Chester village in Goshen Township, Orange County, New York, but he wrote about Pennsylvania.[3] His fictive Andrew, the archetypical migrant of one of Crèvecoeur's sketches, got his start in Philadelphia and moved to the Pennsylvania interior. In the dedication to the Abbé Raynal, Crèvecoeur located himself in Carlisle, Pennsylvania. He probably changed the purported site of his labors to heighten the contrast between the European and the American church. Crèvecoeur thought the absence of religious establishments in America one of the country's best features, and the prevailing tolerance in Quaker-dominated Pennsylvania served his purposes better than New York with its mixture of church establishments from county to county. The economies of the two colonies were close enough that he could safely draw on his New York experience to describe Pennsylvania. Goshen was twenty miles west of the Hudson and sixty miles north of New York City; Carlisle was twenty-five miles west of the Susquehanna and a hundred miles or so from Baltimore. The circumstances of the two were close enough that Crèvecoeur could extrapolate his New York experience to Pennsylvania and offer a report on farming in the Middle Colonies on the eve of the Revolution.

Crèvecoeur's essays were personal, impulsive, occasional. The published letters are famed for their rhapsodic idealization of Pennsylvania farm life. In Crèvecoeur's telling, America transformed the lives of the poor. The "crowd of low, indigent people who flock here every year from all parts of Europe . . . no sooner arrive than they immediately feel the good effects of that plenty of provisions we possess." There is food, work, and comfort. The European "begins to feel the effects of a sort of resurrection; hitherto he had not lived, but simply vegetated; he now feels himself a man." Before long he discovers he has credit to purchase land. "He is now possessed of the deed, conveying to him and his posterity the fee simple and absolute property of two hundred acres of land, situated on such a river. What an epocha in this man's life! He is become a freeholder. . . . He is now an American, a Pennsylvanian, an English subject. He is naturalized; his name is enrolled with those of the other citizens of the province. Instead of being a vagrant, he has a place of residence; he is called the inhabitant of such a country, or of such a district, and for the first time in his life counts for something, for hitherto he

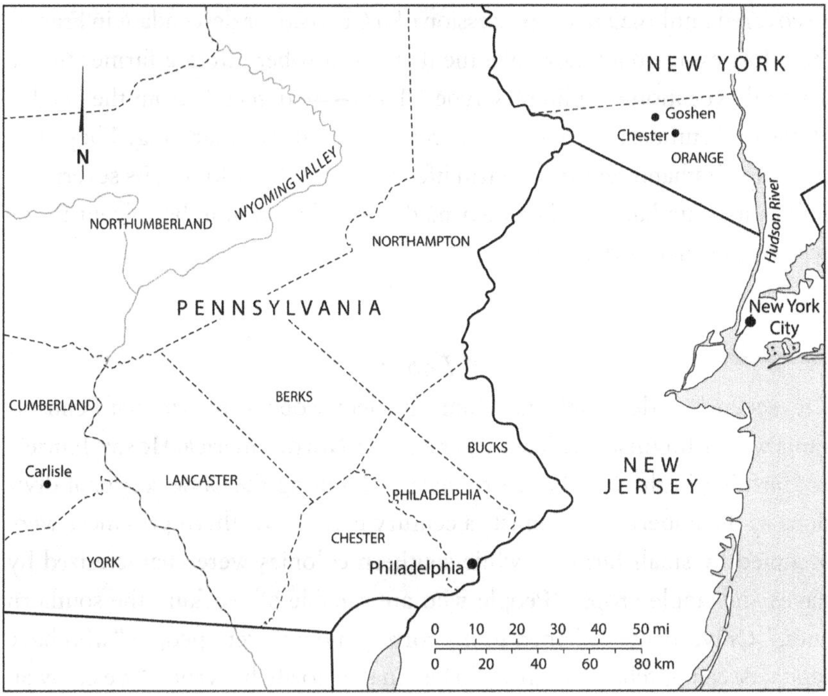

Figure 8.1 Crèvecoeur's New York and Pennsylvania.

had been a cypher." A few years in America worked wonders; the onetime vagrant has a place, a name, and a country. "From nothing to start into being; from a servant to the rank of master; from being the slave of some despotic prince, to become a free man, invested with lands to which every municipal blessing annexed! What a change indeed! It is in consequence of that change that he becomes an American." Lofted by his own enthusiasm, Crèvecoeur said simply, "we are the most perfect society now existing in the world."[4]

Crèvecoeur's depiction was not without basis in the realities of American agriculture. Pennsylvania earned its reputation as the "best poor man's country." As the literary critic Leo Marx said of Crèvecoeur, in America "under the singularly beneficent circumstances of native experience, the barrier between art and reality is likely to break down."[5] The colony's booming wheat trade and rich land enabled a broad segment of the population to prosper. At the same time, as one who had actually farmed in America, Crèvecoeur was not blind to the realities of farm life. Twenty two of his essays were written in a different vein than the published letters. Not discovered until 1922 in the possession of a Crèvecoeur descendant in France, these lost essays read more like the diary of a sober, literate farmer than a fictional evocation of a literary type.[6] The prose descends from the heights of pastoral enthusiasm to realistic accounts of American farming. They offer close-up, firsthand reports on farm life in the Middle Colonies, its severity as well as its abundance. Crèvecoeur made clear that even in beneficent Pennsylvania, farmers struggled.

Labor

Crèvecoeur's wide travels gave him sufficient scope to realize that Pennsylvania was distinguishable from other parts of North America. He saw himself as "farming in the Northern Provinces," adopting the same sectional divisions as the imperial economists a century earlier. Northern provinces were occupied by small farmers, while southern colonies were characterized by slaves and staple crops. "People who are capable of working the southern ones," Crèvecoeur explained to his correspondent, were people "who have capital & can purchase Negroes." Here in the North, he wrote, "we enjoy an happy poverty & a strong health."[7]

Although speaking of himself as a northerner, Crèvecoeur was equally aware that Pennsylvania actually lay between two climate regions. To the north, he said, settlers suffered a "Canadian or a Mohawk" winter, while to the south there was "a perpetual summer."[8] Pennsylvania, as he saw it, was nestled in the midrange of the temperature gradient running down the coast of North America. Pennsylvania did not produce southern exotics like tobacco or sugar, and did not invite investment in "Negroes" as the southern climes did, but Crèvecoeur was fully aware that the colony had a dominant market crop in wheat, as New England did not, and that in Pennsylvania slaves as well as tenants and hired labor augmented the family labor system familiar to New Englanders. Pennsylvania, Crèvecoeur realized, combined the agricultural systems of North and South into a distinct variant of its own.

Enough of Virginia had filtered into Pennsylvania, Crèvecoeur's essays make clear, to bring a substantial number of slaves to the region. He spoke casually of "Negro" slaves in Pennsylvania as if they were a part of every well-established household. When describing how to set up a farm, he assumed, one "must have a Team a Negro" at a cost of at least "3 or 400 pounds." He considered it a disadvantage that "their original cost is very high, their Cloathing & their victuals amount to a great sum, besides the risk of Loosing them." Yet he pictured them as commonly present. In a passage on the seasons, he drew a picture of slaves enjoying winter leisure. "They have their own meetings & are often Indulged with their Masters slays & Horses—you may See them at particular Places as happy & Merry as if they were freemen & Freeholders." Crèvecoeur devoted a full essay to praising a family friend who ended his life owning a "family of Blacks composed of 11 all born & reared in his house."[9]

Slavery had enough of a foothold in Pennsylvania to require a column in a 1779 Lancaster County tax list. The report reveals that slave numbers were fewer than Crèvecoeur's comments imply. Among the county's 7,125 taxable households, just 224—3 percent of the total—were assessed for slaves. The total number of "Negroes" in the county came to 421. Sixty-three percent of the slaves lived in six of the forty-two towns in the county; twenty-eight of the towns had 3 or fewer taxable negroes.[10] Except for a few centers, the small black population was thinly scattered over the county and constituted only a small fraction of the workforce.[11]

The bulk of the auxiliary labor force, beyond family members, appeared on the tax list as "inmates" and "freemen." Freemen were single men, including sons, who lived with the farm family. Inmates were live-in workers who were available during the year but hired only as needed. Often they were married people or widowers who rented a house and a small plot of land on the farmer's property, agreeing to work during harvests and at other demanding periods. In Lancaster County in 1779, inmates and freemen together numbered 1,575, nearly four times as many free workers as the 421 slaves. The great advantage of inmates was their flexibility; the farmer hired them when they were needed without incurring any fixed cost.[12]

Although commanding more labor than New England family farmers increased Pennsylvania's productivity, the colony never reached the wealth levels of the South. Here and there in Lancaster County, landholdings exceeded a thousand acres, but in most towns they topped off at around 500 acres, and the median was closer to 125, nothing like Jefferson's 5,000 acres. In a sample of five towns with a total of 783 landholders, only two households were taxed for more than 1,000 acres, and only eleven for more than 500. Even on the fabulous Lancaster Plain, some of the most fertile land in the world, no huge estates arose like the 1,000- and 2,000-acre plantations in Virginia and Maryland. No one accumulated hundreds of slaves. In all of

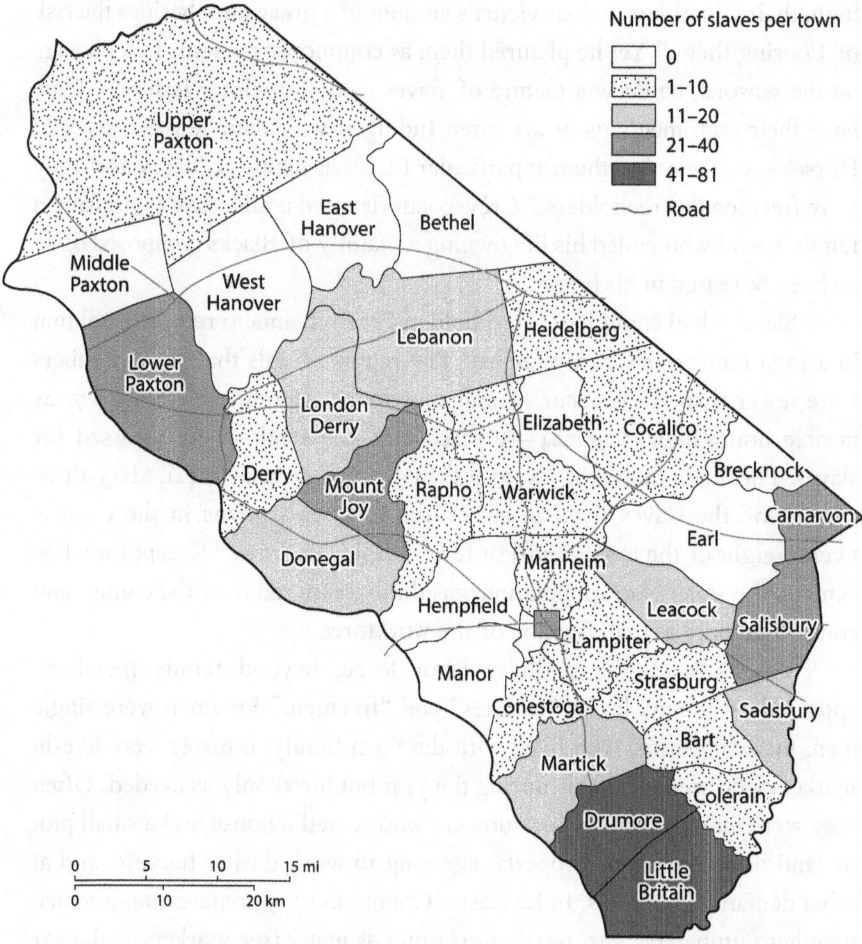

Figure 8.2 Number of slaves in Lancaster County Towns, 1779. "Return of the Effective Supply Tax of Lancaster County for 1779," *Provincial Papers: Proprietary and State Tax Lists of the County of Lancaster for the Years 1771, 1772, 1773, 1777, and 1779* ed. William Henry Egle (n.p.: William Stanley Ray, 1898), 491–684.

Lancaster County in 1779, the persons with the most slaves owned fifteen and eleven, respectively; the more usual highs in towns with slaves were two or three.[13]

Without slaves, incomes never reached the heights found in the South. Solid brick and stone houses graced the Pennsylvania countryside, not Westovers or Rosewells. Rural Pennsylvania stood firmly in the middle of

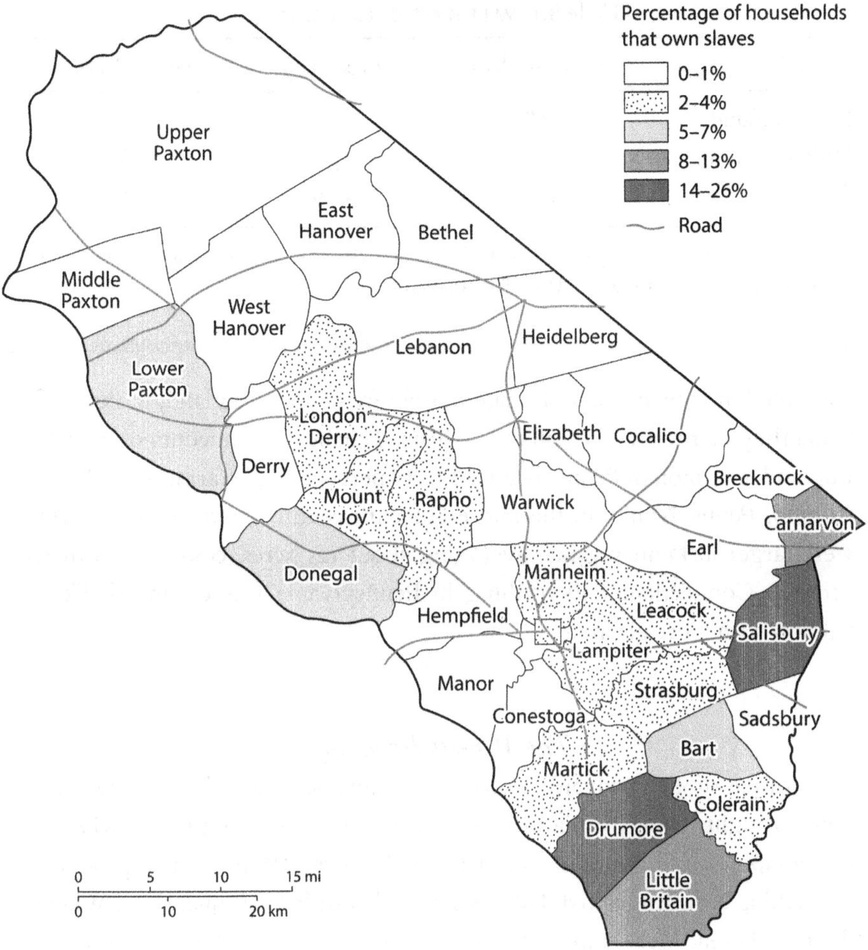

Figure 8.3 Percentage of slave owners in Lancaster County Towns, 1779. "Return of the Effective Supply Tax of Lancaster County for 1779," *Provincial Papers: Proprietary and State Tax Lists of the County of Lancaster for the Years 1771, 1772, 1773, 1777, and 1779*, ed. William Henry Egle (n.p.: William Stanley Ray, 1898), 491–684.

the North American wealth spectrum, just as it was in the middle of the temperature gradient along the coast.[14]

In size of holdings and reliance on family labor, Pennsylvania resembled New England more than Virginia or Maryland. The rudiments of the New England family farm system prevailed. The difference between Pennsylvania and New England was less in type than in degree: everything was

Table 8.1 VALUE OF ESTATES, 1774

	£400 or More	£100–399	£99 or Less
New England	16%	52%	32%
Middle Colonies	8%	83%	9%
South	43%	31%	26%

Source: Alice Hanson Jones, *Wealth of a Nation to Be: The American Colonies on the Eve of Revolution* (New York: Columbia University Press, 1980), 221–23.

magnified in Pennsylvania. Inmates were rare in New England; in Pennsylvania they merited a place on the tax lists. Tenancy was uncommon in New England, common in Pennsylvania. Thirty percent of the farmers in Chester County, Pennsylvania, in the mid-eighteenth century were tenants. Farms were larger in Pennsylvania, averaging about 125 acres, compared with 80 acres in Connecticut.[15] Everything in Pennsylvania was expanded, like a balloon with more air in it.

The Wheat Economy

The source of Pennsylvania's economic buoyancy was wheat. Wheat and flour brought Pennsylvania farmers into the international grain markets in Philadelphia, Wilmington, and later Baltimore. Pennsylvania produced everything New England did plus wheat and flour in large quantities. Wheat, flour, and bread were shipped to southern Europe to feed the growing European population, to the West Indies to provision sugar plantations, and even to New England where local production could not meet the demand. In 1770 (a good year), the value of Philadelphia exports of corn totaled £12,000, meat £25,000, and flaxseed £30,000. The value of wheat, flour, and bread exported from Philadelphia came to £554,044 in Pennsylvania money, eight times as much as the other three products combined. James Lemon estimates that probably half of a farmer's income came from wheat sales.[16]

On the eve of Revolution, Pennsylvania agriculture was rising on the crest of a boom. A series of crop failures from the West Indies to southern Europe and England, coupled with expansive population growth, converged to create a food shortage. By the 1770s, most of Europe could not feed itself.[17] The Middle Colonies, New York, New Jersey, and Pennsylvania, and increasingly Maryland and Virginia, became the breadbasket of the Atlantic world. Every small farmer benefited as the demand for wheat in the Philadelphia market burgeoned. As Philadelphia's shipping increased fourfold between 1740 and 1770, its wheat and flour exports grew sevenfold; and the increase in production did not bring down the price. A bushel of wheat, which cost less than a shilling in the first half of the century, rose to seven shillings in the 1770s and stayed there. The southern European market absorbed seemingly limitless amounts of Pennsylvania breadstuffs.[18]

In the same years, Philadelphia's increase in population from thirteen thousand in 1740 to twenty-nine thousand in 1770 heightened the demand not just for wheat but for all kinds of provisions. The biggest farmers catered to the Philadelphia market by producing vegetables, rye, corn, buckwheat, and flax, plus butter and cheese, women's entries in the exchange economy. Towns within ten or fifteen miles grew fruits and vegetables. Small farmers concentrated on wheat as their chief market crop and with good cause: wheat was twice as valuable as corn. It has been estimated that a typical 125-acre farm with 26 acres in wheat would yield 345 bushels annually. The farm family consumed about 290 bushels itself, leaving 55 bushels for sale. The grain could be taken to a local custom miller, who would grind the wheat into flour in return for a payment of cash or a portion of the grain. If the crop was carted to one of the great merchant millers, he would buy the wheat outright and market the flour in Philadelphia or Wilmington. By 1790, eight three- and four-story mills clustered along the lower Brandywine River in New Castle County, Delaware, attracting wheat from all over the region. Many Lancaster County farmers shipped wheat down the Susquehanna to Peach Bottom at the southeastern corner of the county, where it was transshipped across the peninsula to Christiana Bridge, Delaware, and thence by shallops to the Brandywine mills or Philadelphia.[19]

Wheat production led to substantially greater wealth in the Middle Colonies compared with New England. Alice Hanson Jones's analysis of 1774 estate inventories showed the total physical wealth of New England on average at £36.6 sterling per capita compared with £41.9 in the Middle Colonies. That was only a 14 percent difference for the two populations as a whole, but the number was much higher for farmers. The average per capita holding of livestock in New England was worth £2.8 and in the Middle Colonies £4.8, a 71 percent premium. The value of crops in the New England inventories was £0.2 and in the Middle Colonies £2.1, ten times as much.[20] Greater wealth buoyed up everything. Pennsylvania farmers could afford more hired labor. With more hands, they could work more land. The returns on wheat made it possible to charge higher rents and profit from land let to tenants. The increase of cash supported more craftsmen and stores. Women could dream of gauzy fabrics and men of fine suiting. Storekeepers flourished.

Pennsylvania had a wheat economy and from that came a wheat culture. Wheat was a demanding crop. Besides threshing, it had to be freighted from farms to ports, often via a mill, where it was ground into flour. It also required thousands of casks to carry the product and hundreds of coopers to make the casks. Lancaster borough alone in 1773 had fourteen coopers, and doubtless others were scattered throughout the county, especially near gristmills. The merchant miller firm Tatnall and Lea worked with over fifty local coopers, and smaller custom mills were known to work with a half dozen.[21]

Casks were strong. When well fitted, the staves formed a compound arch that could bear huge pressure when dropped or stacked. Coopering required expert skill: to round the staves to make them concave on the back and convex on the front, to bevel the edges so the staves fit snugly against one another, to heat the staves to the right temperature (200 degrees Fahrenheit) to bend them into a barrel shape, and to make the inside volume exact to specifications were complex tasks. Barrel, along with firkin, kierkin, and hogshead, was a measure of volume. A barrel held 31.5 gallons of wine and 200 pounds of meat. Pork and beef were measured by the barrel, wheat by the bushel even though transported in casks.

Coopers had to construct casks to fit these measures, not something every farmer could do. Farmers could produce staves, however. They could fell the timber, split or saw the log into quarters, saw the quartered log into the correct lengths, and then saw or split flat boards from the log to serve as the basis for coopered staves. From 1759 to 1762, one Lancaster carpenter/farmer, William Smedley, produced fifty-eight thousand staves. Philadelphia newspapers published stave prices along with the prices of other regularly traded items, such as bushels of wheat, barrels of pork and beef, hundredweights of flour and tobacco, pounds of sugar, and gallons of rum. Staves were sold by the thousands. In April 1761, the going rate per thousand was £13 for pipe staves, £6 for hogshead staves, and £3 for barrel staves. Smedley chose to sell his barrel staves to a local flour dealer; had he carried them to the city, they would have fetched £174 on the Philadelphia market, enough to cover almost half the cost of the 148 acres he purchased in 1759 for £374.[22]

The barrels in turn implied wagons and horses to haul the barrels of flour. Crèvecoeur admired Pennsylvania's "Two Horse Waggons . . . Executed with great deal of skill," and answering "all the purposes of a farm." Sixteen feet long including the tongue, they could carry "5 barrels of Flour . . . a Ton of Hay & often more." They could be lengthened to "bring home the body of a Tree 20 or 30 feet Long," for sawing into lumber or staves. "We commonly carry with them 30 Bushels of wheat & at 60# to the Bushel, this makes a weight of 1800# with which we can go 40 Miles a day." Lancaster County was the birthplace of the famed Conestoga wagon. On his way west from Philadelphia, Crèvecoeur's Andrew was flabbergasted at the sight of "several large Lancaster six-horse waggons, just arrived from the country." "At this stupendous sight, he stopped short and with great diffidence asked us what was the use of these great moving houses." "These huge animals," he exclaimed, "would eat all the grass of our island!"[23]

There was little evidence of all-purpose wagons in New England, where farm work fell to oxen and carts rather than horses and wagons. The New England household rarely had more than one horse but usually two and often three or four oxen. Of the 292 households on the 1771 Concord, Massachusetts, tax assessment list, 183 owned a horse, but only 20 households more than one. By contrast, of Concord's 153 households with oxen, all but one had two or more. The Pennsylvania tax lists did not mention oxen, and instead measured wealth by the number of horses along with acres, cattle, and servants. Of Lebanon's 351 households, 254 owned horses and 225 of those owned two or more. There were at least twice as many horses in Pennsylvania as in eastern Massachusetts. Seventy-three percent of Lancaster County taxpayers owned horses in 1771.[24]

Pennsylvania sported a horse-and-wagon culture.[25] Crèvecoeur said that on Sunday the wagon became the family coach, traveling as much as seven miles an hour. "I do not Know where an Am: farmer can possibly enjoy more dignity as a Father [or] as a citizen, than when thus all clad in good Neat homespun Cloathes Manufactured within his own house, he carries with him his wife & family & Trots along with a Neat Pair of fat horses of his own Raising."[26]

Underlying this dedication to horse culture was the economic necessity of moving produce and goods and the sustaining businesses that followed from the horse-and-wagon population. In 1773, out of 386 tradesmen in Lancaster borough, 30 were horse-and-wagon based: two saddle-tree makers, thirteen saddlers, four skinners, five wagoners, and six wheelwrights. If the twenty-eight tavern keepers are added to these numbers, Lancaster appears to be a town devoted to movement. The Lancaster-Philadelphia turnpike when it was completed in 1795 was the first paved highway in America.[27] The heavy flow of wheat, flour, and provisions to Philadelphia and shop goods to Lancaster made the route one of the most heavily traveled on the continent. Gates were constructed every five or ten miles and tolls collected by the gatekeeper according to the size of the rig. In the 1790s a single horseman paid 5½ pence per ten miles; a wagon with four horses drawing it was charged 2 shillings, 9¾ pence. Users complained the costs were too high, driving wagoners to the toll-free side roads, but the investors claimed that they derived an income of only 1.86 percent a year on an investment of $446,142.31.[28]

Southeastern Pennsylvania's wheat-horse economy sustained towns unlike any found in New England. Lancaster borough was designated as county seat in 1730 just as Lancaster County was being spun off from Chester County. Andrew Hamilton, the town's founder, envisioned Lancaster as a small city from the start. Land was divided into city lots, 64½ feet wide and 245 feet deep to accommodate outbuildings, gardens, and fruit trees. Because he knew settlers would want more land to support their domestic economies, Hamilton also offered 45-acre "outlots" outside the central town plat for more extensive farming.[29]

Hamilton's expectations proved accurate. By 1773, Lancaster had become strikingly different from other towns in the county. Traffic generated by the courts that were situated there attracted shopkeepers who, besides retailing their wares, distributed Philadelphia goods to country storekeepers.[30] The tax assessors in 1773 treated Lancaster as a species of its own within the county. The tax list provided the usual four categories of wealth—land, horses, cattle, and servants—but in Lancaster only one person among the 435 households on the list was taxed for his land, a brick maker who was assessed for six acres. Unlike in other towns, most names on the Lancaster borough list had a trade or profession attached. Three hundred thirty-one of 435 households, 74 percent of the total, were associated with trades. Lancaster had become a hive of small craftsmen and professionals, supporting themselves with their skill rather than by working the land.

Nothing like Lancaster developed in backcountry Massachusetts. The intricately detailed 1771 Massachusetts tax assessment lists had a category for

"Dwelling-Houses and Shops under the same Roof, or adjoining to them," and another for "Tan-Houses, Slaughter-Houses, shops separate from Dwelling-Houses, Pot and Pearl Ash-Works," but nothing to highlight specific crafts as in Lancaster borough. Only rarely did Massachusetts assessors pen in the trade of the taxpayer. Even in bustling inland towns like Springfield, which was half again as populous as Lancaster in the early 1770s, the tradesmen were taxed for land as no tradesman (save that brick maker) in Lancaster was. Hartford, the busy entrepôt on the Connecticut River, had seventy-one buildings on its main street but only twenty-three tradesmen.[31] Inland New England towns could not muster the dense, rich assemblage of tradesmen living from their trades that Lancaster borough supported. The wealth introduced into the Pennsylvania economy by its commerce in wheat sustained a corps of artisans unlike anything found in New England.

Rural Realities

Because of its good land and high productivity, Pennsylvania merited its reputation as "the best poor man's country." It was deserving of Crèvecoeur's plaudits. In the eighteenth century, Pennsylvania was the destination for more immigrants than any other colony. The wheat economy blessed both town and country. But no one knew better than Crèvecoeur that prosperity was not achieved without struggle. He knew that even in plentiful Pennsylvania, it required careful management to prepare for old age and the departure of children.[32] "It is our duty to provide for our eldest children while we live in order that our homesteads may be left to the youngest, who are the most helpless." Often this responsibility drove families to the frontier. The farmer's aim in "removing to [a] New District" was to "purchase as much Land as will afford substantial Farms to every one of his Children." This is what "Causes so many even wealthy People to sell their Patrimonial Estates; to enlarge their sphere of action & Leave a sufficient Inheritance to their Progeny."[33]

Even on the frontier, Crèvecoeur saw, land came at a price. "Lands are not purchased for nothing, a Man must have a beginning a certain capital without which he may Languish and Vegetate." To make his point to his supposed European correspondent, Crèvecoeur compared farmers venturing onto new land to colonial merchants purchasing European goods. They both needed credit. Just as "the Credit of England, enables our Merchants to

Trade & to get Rich," so "the credit & wealth of the father enable our Children to form new settlements." One of the farmer's most valuable assets was his credit rating. "The foundation of a good name" was "the most useful acquisition he can make." When Andrew wanted to buy land, "his good name procures him credit." On top of the purchase price, development was costly. Swamps had to be drained, and "they are in general so Expensive & difficult to Clear that it cannot be done in the ordinary course of Husbandry; it is generally done by the acre & in order to pay those extraordinary Expenses the proprietors of them [are obliged to borrow Money]."[34] To keep moving ahead, a farmer had to continually invest in his own enterprise.[35]

The result of all these demands was a mountain of debt. "The Number of debts which one part of y' country owes to y' other," Crèvecoeur wrote, "wou'd greatly astonish you." This was the downside of American farming. "Flourishing as we may appear to a superficial observer, yet there are many dark spots which on due consideration greatly Lessen that shew of Happiness which the Europeans think we posess." Debt was the darkest spot of all. As new settlements on fresh land "are allways made by people who do not posess much, they are obliged to borrow, & if any accidents Intervenes they are not enabled to repay that amount in many years." And that is the beginning of sorrows. "The Interest is a canker worm which consumes their yearly Industry, many never can surmount these difficulties the Land is sold, their Labours are Lost & they are obliged to begin the world a new." A visitor who judges the American landscape by the appearance of houses and fields "without descending to deeper particulars," he wrote, should "feel the Pulse of every farmer." The farmers' debt payments were "the great & the Enormous Taxes" they were obliged to pay one another.[36]

More than the hard-headed Hempstead or the enterprising Patten, Crèvecoeur saw the dramas of debt and family perpetuation being played out on the stage provided by the natural environment. Perhaps because he was a romantic, Crèvecoeur took note of nature, but he saw it as harsh and demanding, not generous and welcoming. Adverse weather always threatened. "The Horrid Mountaneous waste which overspreads or North" brings cold blasts each winter with devastating effects. Summers grow "Exceedingly dry." "The grain Turns Yellow & soon dies—a Severe Mortification for the American farmer [thus] to see crops which have Escaped all the Severities of y' Winter, Entirely Perish in the spring." Creeks begin to fail as a result of clearing the swamps so that mills lack water. "Our antient woods

Kept the earth Moyst & damp, & the sun cou'd èvaporate None of the waters, contained under their shades."[37] With the woods gone, the creeks dry up.

Crèvecoeur detailed a long list of natural enemies of the farmer: mosquitoes, birds, squirrels, insects, poison ivy. Corn crops have to pass through a gantlet of evils before producing a single ear. In dry seasons ants form societies in the cornfields "& Establish themselves in the very Hills in the Midst of which the corn is Germinating—there they Live on the young succulent sprout." Those sprouts that make it through germination are likely to become victims of worms. "No sooner is it above the Ground than it becomes Exposed to the Rapacity of a black worm, which cuts its Tender Stem, a Little below y' surface of the Earth." And then when "it has no sooner reached 2 or 3 Inches above the Ground . . . its greatest Ennemies, the Crows & black birdes come in order to Eradicate it, by means of their strong bills." Once standing, the corn is subject to more marauders. If the fences are not kept up, they will not stop "the Intrusion of hogs & Pigs." "Their Inclination to Mischief, & their singular Ingenuity in finding out those vacancies is such" that they will always find their way into crops.[38]

"From this imperfect sketch," Crèvecoeur concluded, now miles away from his earlier optimism, "you'll Easily conceive that if we enjoy Some happiness, we are made to pay for it." In the end he was philosophic. After complaining about the mice which came out of their burrows to attack stacks of grain, he reflected that "if Nature has formed Mice she has created also the Fox and the owl they both prey on them." "Thus one species of Evil is ballanced by another," and "in the Midst of this great this astonishing Èquipoyse Man struggles and lives."[39]

In his brighter moods, Crèvecoeur captured the optimism of the farm idea. With land, a family could provide for itself and achieve a modicum of dignity. But he recognized that farm lives were fraught with pitfalls and hardships. More than the stolid Hempstead, Crèvecoeur acknowledged the risks, temptations, and hardships of farm life. He knew the allure of luxury and the agonies of debt. He knew that there was no persuading, no resisting, no overpowering nature. Nature was warm and giving at one moment and relentless and unfeeling the next. Farmers could only pray for nature's grace and yield helplessly when it heedlessly disregarded their pitiful efforts. The sky, the soil, the trees and plants, the varmints and insects, the blights and diseases all had to be waited upon for what they dispensed to the creature struggling to live in "this astonishing Èquipoyse."

Paxton

In his optimistic moods, Crèvecoeur believed that American plentitude would create good citizens as well as prospering farmers. Once vested with land and the title of Pennsylvanian, the newcomer would willingly pledge allegiance to the government. A man could scarcely love a country where "existence was a burthen to him," as in Europe. Here he happily conforms to the law. "With a heart-felt gratitude he looks toward the east, toward that insular government from whose wisdom all his new felicity is derived and under whose wings and protection he now lives. These reflections constitute him the good man and the good subject."[40] America gave him an existence, and in return the new migrant yields happily to its government.

Pennsylvanians had every reason to be as content as Crèvecoeur in his happier moods imagined them. The tax lists bear out a picture of comfortable farmers, working middling farms, earning disposable income from the wheat and flour market, sometimes practicing a trade besides. A substantial majority of property holders on virtually every town tax list owned more than a hundred acres, were taxed for at least two horses, and grazed four or five cattle. Of the 246 property-owning households in Lancaster County's Cocolico Township in 1771, 144 owned one hundred acres or more, and only eight owned no land.[41]

There were differences, of course. Wealth in Lancaster County was strung out between rich and poor. In Cocolico Township, 106 cottagers rented land from the property holders and made their livings by hiring out their labor. All but 13 of the 106 inmates paid only two shillings in taxes, the lowest amount levied on anyone, and close to the poverty line. Most property holders in Cocolico paid five times as much in taxes as the inmates, and 33 paid ten times as much or even more.[42] If assessed taxes were a measure of wealth, as they were meant to be, there were discrepancies in prosperity in these idyllic little Pennsylvania villages.[43] Some farms were less well developed, with fewer cattle in the field, less land in tillage and meadow, smaller and shabbier houses. In Upper Paxton, pushed up against the mountains in the northern section of Lancaster County, the land was less workable and the tax assessments showed it. The median was three shillings, sixpence per person, a third of Cocolico's.[44]

The divisions between rich and poor in this prosperous country, however, did not lead to conflict. The poor did not square off against the rich. Crèvecoeur's contented immigrant seems to have prevailed in most towns. The great gulf in Lancaster County fell between established farmers in older towns and settlers living along the edges of Indian territory. Social conflict erupted at this boundary, not at the junctures of rich and poor. Crèvecoeur saw frontiersmen as almost a different species. "It is with men as it is with the plants and animals that grow and live in the forests; they are entirely different from those that live in the plains." "Back settlers" in the Carolinas and Virginia, Crèvecoeur reported, "have been long a set of lawless people; it has been even dangerous to travel among them." In Pennsylvania, the few magistrates among the backcountry population were "in general little better than the rest; they're often in a perfect state of war." "There men appear to be no better than carnivorous animals of a superior rank, living on the flesh of wild animals." "There, remote from the power of example and check of shame, many families exhibit the most hideous parts of our society."[45]

The gulf between the settled regions and the frontier was measured in December 1763, when fifty-seven frontiersmen descended on a tiny band of Indians, consisting of seven men, five women, and eight children living on a five hundred–acre tract of land at Conestoga Manor in Lancaster County. The Conestoga Indians subsisted by crafting baskets and brooms for sale in nearby towns. When the frontiersmen invaded the village, most of the residents were away peddling their wares.[46] The men killed the six Indians who happened to be at home, scalped them, and burned their houses.

Two weeks later, learning that the remainder of the Conestogas had been sequestered in the Lancaster borough workhouse for their own safety, fifty frontiersmen broke into the building at noon on a bitter cold day and in fifteen minutes slaughtered the remaining fourteen Indians, including the eight children. In February, the Paxton Boys, as they almost immediately were named, marched at least two hundred strong on Philadelphia to wreak the same havoc on a peaceful band of Moravian Indians in custody in the city barracks. The city ordered ferry ropes cut and the Paxtons' boats sunk to impede their progress. Cannons were placed in the streets near the barracks. The armed men were stopped at Germantown outside of the city, where a promise that the assembly would hear their grievances persuaded them to return to their homes.[47]

It was a peculiar as well as a ghastly series of events. The very ferocity of it was stunning even then. The Paxton men ruthlessly destroyed eight children and five women along with the adult men who had lived peaceably among the white population for decades. Not content to kill the Indians, they mutilated their bodies by scalping. The response in print was astonishment and horror. Even Benjamin Franklin lost his customary cool as he described the scene in the Lancaster workhouse when the Indians "fell on their Knees, protested their Innocence, declared their Love to the *English*, and that in their whole Lives, they had never done them Injury; and in this Posture they all received the Hatchet!——Men, Women, and little Children—were every one inhumanly murdered!—in cold Blood!" The butchers "to the eternal Disgrace of their Country and Colour, then mounted their Horses, huzza'd in Triumph, as if they had gained a Victory, and rode-off."[48]

Pamphlet after pamphlet spoke in the same voice. The Paxtons were universally condemned in print as if the country could not find words strong enough to repudiate the villainous act.[49] Yet the Paxton men themselves showed no shame. Rather than fleeing the wrath that seemed certain to fall on them after Lancaster, hundreds of them brazenly marched on Philadelphia. They exposed themselves to the forces of law and order as if guiltless and unafraid of punishment. Defenders of the culprits appealed to the court of public opinion in published pamphlets. On January 2, 1764, immediately after he received news of the massacre, Governor John Penn issued a proclamation charging all civil officers and all "liege subjects" to apprehend the perpetrators and offering a reward of two hundred pounds for the arrest and conviction of each of the three ringleaders.[50] Yet no one was caught or tried; the names and residences of the great bulk of the Paxton men still are not known. They returned to their farms and resumed their ordinary lives with the blood of the slain Indians still on their hands.

The Paxtons' defense of their actions rested on a single point. They believed that the slaughtered people had been in communication with the hostile Indians who had long harassed the Pennsylvania frontier. Without any actual evidence other than inference, the Paxton apologists accused the Conestogas of conspiring with Indian enemies all along the border. "Experience has taught us that they are all Perfidious, and their Claim to Freedom and Independency puts it in their Power to act as Spies, to entertain and give Intelligence to our Enemies, and to furnish them with Provisions and warlike Stores." It seemed absurd to the Paxton men that "altho' the *Wyalusing* Tribe is at War with us, yet that part of it which is under the Protection of the Government may be friendly to the *English*, and Innocent. . . . Who ever proclaimed War with a part of a Nation, and not with the Whole?" Even the pacific Moravian Indians were suspected of carrying on "a Correspondence with ou[r] Enemies on the Great Island." "These things put it beyond doubt with us, that the *Indians* now at *Philadelphia*, are His Majesty's perfidious Enemies." Benjamin Franklin reduced the Paxton defense to a simple-minded racism. "The only Crime of these poor Wretches seems to have been, that they had a reddish brown Skin, and black Hair; and some People of that Sort, it seems, had murdered some of our Relations." Franklin was not far from the truth. A Paxton apologist admitted that "the White People most in General, hates any Thing that Savours of the Name of an Indian."[51]

The settlers were obdurate against all appeals to justice and humanity. But if so hardened, why? Their bitterness cannot be attributed to social distress. The two towns named as their home base, Paxton and Donegal, were not noted for economic hardship. The residents owned land in the same quantities as other Lancaster County towns and paid taxes at about the same rate. The pamphlets written in the Paxtons' defense said nothing about poverty, debt, or mistreatment. They spoke of the period before Indian warfare as a time when "the Province of Pinsylvania was flourishing in Prosperity & Plenty." Even frontiersmen were prospering. Before the Indian onslaught, the defenders said, the frontier consisted of "near *one Hundred Miles* of as thriving a Settlement as any in Pennsylvania."[52]

The apologists offered their own explanation of the outrage. They said the Indian onslaught had changed people. Franklin went to the heart of the matter in noting that there were "some (I am ashamed to hear it) who would extenuate the enormous Wickedness of these Actions, by saying, 'The Inhabitants of the Frontiers are exasperated with the Murder of their Relations, by the Enemy *Indians*, in the present War.'" "Exasperated" did not begin to capture the fury and despair left from "the Murder of their Relations." Crèvecoeur, who had suffered from British-inspired Indian attacks, put it well. After years of danger it began to appear that "we must perish, perish like wild beasts, included within a ring of fire!"[53]

The accounts suggest that a distinctive mentality was forged in the fires of war. An undercurrent of rage ran through the frontier mind, fed by the frequent retelling of atrocity stories. The tellers of these stories, the curators of memory, relived the terror that had permeated the frontier throughout the war. One pamphlet, *The Conduct of The Paxton-Men. Impartially represented*, said "the Miseries of the back Inhabitants are really beyond the Power of Description." The writers laid out the bloodiest, most revolting scenes they could imagine. "Here lies the provident Father welt'ring in his own Blood, his Scalp tore off, his Body ript up, his Bowels dragg'd out, and his private Parts stuffed into his Mouth!—*There* the virtuous tender Mother lies stretched on her Bed, dreadfully mangled, with her new-born Infant scalp'd and placed under her Head for a Pillow, and a Stake drove into her—Modesty forbids me to name it!"[54]

The typicality of such events—or even their accuracy—was not weighed by the storytellers. Critics complained that "numberless Stories have been raised and spread abroad" against the Indian victims, "all which Stories are well known, by those who know the *Indians* best, to be pure Inventions contrived by bad People."[55] Indian attacks triggered a cultural mechanism which turned suffering into a mentality. Horror stories were collected, prized, and distributed. People in the danger zone formed into a band of outraged victims. Few of the hearers had witnessed such atrocities, but for the frontiersmen, such moments of horror stood for the dangers that all were exposed to. They justified any form of retaliation. Stocked with such stories, the group memory invested the frontiersmen with the authority of pain. They were justified in taking any dire action because the frontier had suffered so dreadfully at Indian hands.

The codification of experiences like these made ordinary farmers capable of extremes that appalled everyone else. Memories of Indian terror set frontiersmen apart in ways that others could not understand. "None but those who have been Spectators or Eye Witness of these shocking Scenes can possibly have any adequate Ideas of our Sufferings," one apologist wrote. Philadelphians "lived at their ease and in plenty, and had no idea of the distress and trouble of the poor frontiers." "A True Countryman" called the experiences a "Heart scald." They could only hope that in time, as the pamphleteer put it, the scald would "weare away."[56]

All this bitterness was turned against the colony's rulers as much as against the native people. Remote as they were at the edges of settlement, the settlers had not forgotten the distant government in Philadelphia. The Paxtons' march from the Lancaster frontier to the city traced a connection that existed in every frontiersman's mind. By their own accounts, the onslaughts at Conestoga and Lancaster were political acts, directed against the current regime. The destruction of the Indians was a statement that the government had failed in its most elemental duty—to protect the people. The attack on Conestoga Manor resembled all mob actions: the government having failed in its responsibilities, the people as a *posse comitatus* had to take the law into their own hands.

What infuriated the frontiersmen most was "the publick Money lavishly prostituted to hire, at an exorbitant Rate, a mercenary Guard, to protect his Majesty's worst of Enemies, those falsly pretended *Indian* Friends," while "hundreds of poor distressed Families of his Majesty's Subjects, obliged to abandon their Possessions . . . were left to starve neglected." The government coddled the Moravians in Philadelphia while the exposed frontier was bleeding. "To protect and maintain them at the public Expence, while our suffering Brethren on the Frontiers are almost destitute of the Necessaries of Life and are neglected by the Public, is sufficient to make us mad with Rage, and tempt us to do what nothing but the most violent Necessity can vindicate."[57]

The crisis of confidence had begun in 1755, when Indians swept through Pennsylvania frontier settlements before the French and Indian War. The chief target of frontier wrath, then, was the Quaker-dominated assembly, which had refused to appropriate funds for military action. The Paxton Declaration and Remonstrance spoke of "that Faction, which for so long a Time have found means to enslave the Province to *Indians.*" Despite the hundreds of deaths and captures along the frontier, the petitions from Lancaster for protection went unheeded. John Elder, the Presbyterian pastor in Paxton and Derry, complained in November 1755 that "we seem to be given up into the hands of a merciless Enemy." To drive home the point, the frontiersmen paraded the bodies of a murdered family through the streets of Philadelphia to remind the assemblyman of the price of inaction. Had the assembly not declared war on the Indians in April 1756, the backcountry was prepared to march on the city in a rehearsal of the march in 1764.[58]

In the summer of 1763, as tension rose again, Edward Shippen, the scion of the great Philadelphia merchant family who had moved to Lancaster in 1752 to conduct trade, wrote his son that the Indians "have laid a deep plan for the extermination of us all." A month later depredations began again and Shippen reported that "every body . . . that are at Paxton, must be in great Terror, night and day." He foresaw the debacle that was to come. When disagreement over how to raise funds for defense paralyzed the Pennsylvania assembly, the frontier went mad with rage.[59] Wartime encounters with the native people, shaped into stories by the curators of memory, transformed family farmers into Paxton men, furious with the supine government and capable of unspeakable atrocities against native people.[60]

Susquehanna

After the Conestoga adventure, some of the Paxton people moved to the Wyoming Valley in northern Pennsylvania, where the divide between government officials and frontier settlers opened again. In Wyoming, they became involved in another kind of violence, one between white and white. In the Pennamite wars, the white minions of opposing colonial governments faced off against each other. Pennsylvania and Connecticut claimed the same wide swath of land between the 41st and 42nd parallels in northern Pennsylvania by virtue of conflicting grants in their original charters. The controversy began in 1753 when Connecticut-based land companies took title to vast tracts in Pennsylvania on the basis of grants from the Connecticut government, backed up with questionable titles purchased from the Iroquois. On the eve of the Revolution, the disputes broke out into armed conflict between the Connecticut and Pennsylvania settlers. The competing claims to jurisdiction and ownership turned into settler wars of unbridled violence.[61]

In the 1760s and early 1770s, a few Paxton men in search of land migrated up the Susquehanna River to the Wyoming Valley formed by the river's east branch. They purchased land under Connecticut's claims, pitting them against the authorities of their own colony, whom they had come to detest. Among the migrants was Lazarus Stewart, the leader of the raid on the Indians in the Lancaster workhouse in 1763 and one of the few Paxtons whose name is known. In 1769 Stewart signed a petition with sixty-two other "poor people," protesting Pennsylvania's advance sale of Wyoming Valley land in big lots to speculators. The petitioners said they were "straitly bounded, enjoying but small Tracts of land & mostly Barrening Ground," and needed the land themselves. When Pennsylvania sent in Colonel Turbutt Francis with twenty men and a four-pound cannon to drive them off their newly acquired lands, the settlers fought back.

To defend the Connecticut claimants, Stewart offered to bring in his Paxton Boys. Forty of his old friends marched to the Wyoming Valley under Matthew Smith of Paxton town to plunder and destroy the houses of Pennsylvania settlers. A year later on September 15, 1770, Stewart was arrested while visiting Lebanon, back in Lancaster County, but escaped by beating the constable with an axe handle. Backed by twenty armed men who had ridden into town to support him, Stewart warned a tavern keeper not to stand in his way or he would tear him "to Pieces, and make a Breakfast of his Heart." A month later, he was detained again in York County until parties of Paxton Boys armed with rifles and pistols came to his rescue. Riding with twenty-three residents of Hanover, Lancaster County, Stewart moved north to capture Fort Durkee, one of the strongholds of the Pennsylvania forces in the Wyoming Valley. When opposed by a posse of Pennsylvanians, the armed men opened fire, and Stewart killed one of the opponents. Governor John Penn offered a reward of three hundred pounds for his arrest, but he was never apprehended.

At the end, Stewart's life took a surprising turn. He became a respected leader of the Connecticut forces and helped establish the first permanent New England settlements in the Wyoming Valley. One of them was named Hanover in his honor. He took up residence in Westmoreland and was elected a selectman, choosing instead to accept the position of "Sealer of Weights and Measures." During the Revolution, he fought on the Patriot side and died on the battlefield fighting the forces of the British colonel John Butler, still in opposition to unfeeling government.[62]

Glimpses of Stewart petitioning for land and serving as sealer of weights and measures are startling alongside of his tales of axe handles and pistols. Was he best described as a farmer or a warrior? Paul Moyer, the historian of the Wyoming Valley's "Wild Men" who for half a century resorted to kidnappings and destruction of their enemy's property, concludes that these insurgents were motivated by a simple desire to obtain land. Most of the participants in the attacks on Pennsylvania officials had share rights in the Susquehanna Company. They wanted one thing: the "ability to acquire enough land to achieve for themselves and their heirs agrarian independence."[63] The Wyoming Valley insurgents resembled the Paxtons, who had always insisted that they had done "Nothing inconsistent with our Duty to the best of Kings, with our Privileges as British Subjects, the Dignity of Government, or the Character of good Subjects."[64] They did not relish their roles as warriors. Yet when their lands and their families were in jeopardy, they placed no limits on the violence they would wreak.

Ambiguity hangs over the stories of the Paxton Boys and the Wyoming settlers. Were they thugs or frustrated husbandmen? They appear to have been ordinary farmers who went rogue, provoked by circumstances.

Crèvecoeur felt the same ambivalence toward the Pennsylvania farmers he wrote about. Carlisle, Pennsylvania, his fictive home in *Letters from an American Farmer,* lay in the heart of Paxton country. He made no mention of the Conestoga Indian slaughter or the march on Philadelphia; cruelty and rebelliousness did not fit his image of contented American farmers happy in their prosperity. But he was less reticent in talking about the conflict between Connecticut and Pennsylvania in the Wyoming Valley of northern Pennsylvania, where he attempted to reconcile his idealistic vision of American farming with the realities of frontier life.

One of the routes from New England to the Connecticut claims passed through Orange County, New York, where Crèvecoeur's farm lay. On one of his exploratory tours, he apparently followed this road over the mountains into the Susquehanna River basin. In "Susquehannah," an essay not discovered until 1922, Crèvecoeur described the region as he knew it in the 1770s during the years when Stewart was on the loose. The region was the epitome of American promise. The immensely fertile farmscape adjoining the Susquehanna typified the potential of American soil. Here quite ordinary people could thrive on their little farms and live peaceably together free from European oppression. Even isolated farmers in little glens were "Seemingly happy & unconcerned at their Hermit situation. . . . That round of Labour & perpetual Industry which fills the Measure of their Time Supplies the Place of every deficiency. They Seem'd to have no wants, their victuals were as Good & Wholesome as those I had Seen in More opulent Neighborood."

An entire population of Andrews was rising to dignity and prosperity on the beneficent American soil. "Immense were the difficulties which these people had to Encounter." Roads and bridges to build, families to transport, houses to erect, grain to plant. They faced "Herculean Labours & difficulties." But the "vivid hopes of greater Prosperity" and the "strong desire of providing for our Posterity" animated their efforts. Underlying it all was the fabulous fertility of the soil, a veritable valley of the Nile where no dung was required. Here the settlers enjoyed "the most fertille Lands in y' World." "Undebased by servile Tenures, horrid dependence a Multiiplicity of unrelieved wants as it is in Europa," mankind may "rea quire its former & antient dignity; now Lost all over the world Except with us."[65]

Crèvecoeur heard of still more valleys beyond Wyoming. One day, he was convinced, they would be the "Garden of this part of the World." And this was only the beginning. "What is all this Region of Susquehannah when compared to the heads of the Oyio, the Monongahela & the Innumerable Rivers which falls into it during its astonishing course to ye Missipi." He envisioned countless other valleys extending indefinitely into the American West, "a Spectacle reserved for Posterity."[66] A new and enlightened empire was coming into existence on the western landscape.

But after this moment of exultation, the light on this beneficent scene suddenly dimmed, as if he had stretched his optimism beyond its limits. In the next paragraph, Crèvecoeur launched a long meditation of all that went wrong in the valley. Poor people suddenly prosperous "found themselves Inspired [to] a degree of Pride & consequence to which they had hitherto been strangers." The underlying contradictions in their land titles began to surface. "Chicannery, contention the Love of Party & Tumults had follow'd them from Connecticut," and these passions "flourished very Rapidly." The farmers fell into disputes among themselves. His happy husbandmen rapidly deteriorated before his eyes. The good land attracted "a Strange Variety of sects & Nations, all Equally filled with that pride which Sudden Ease & consequence Necessarily Inspires."[67]

Hovering over their little local fights was the ongoing struggle between Pennsylvania and Connecticut over ultimate command of the territory. New Englanders now "think of disposessing by arms the Pensilvanians who were settled on the W. Branch." Pennsylvania retaliated and "open'd war was declared on both sides," accompanied by "shocking retaliations." These battles were only prelude to still more vicious encounters when the contest with the mother country spread "among the Lower Class Like an Epidemy of the Mind." Solitary farmers launched into the "Intricate mases of this grand Quarell" which "disseminated among them the most horrid Poyson which has Torn them with Intestine divisions." The war led to Indian attacks with their customary tales of atrocity, of husbands killed before the eyes of the wives and children, of fallen victims scalped, and bodies floating in the river.[68]

At the end, Crèvecoeur described the mournful retreat of the settlers eastward along the path that they had so hopefully followed into the West not many years before. "Here you might see a poor Starved horse as weak & Ematiated as themselves given them perhaps by the Ennemy as a last boon, the poor beast was Loaded with a scanty feather bed serving as a sadle, which was fastened on him with withes & barks, on it sat a wretched Mother, with a child at her breast, another on her Lap, and 2 more placed behind her, all broyling in the sun, accompanied in this pilgrimage of Tribulation by the rest of the Family creeping slowly along." The scene moved Crèvecoeur to ask "don't we blaspheme then when we dare pronounce man to be the Image of God—such a reptile, so restless so vain, so cruel so vindictive?" He offered no answer to his own question.[69]

The Susquehanna story completed Crèvecoeur's vision of Pennsylvania and America. The country was a potential paradise. The absence of feudal oppressions offered boundless hope to downtrodden Europeans. Its rich soils allowed hardworking farmers to flourish. But at some point, contention invaded paradise and the countryside fell from grace. Nature itself proved cruel and unfeeling, and even more often, human nature darkened the scene. Evil crept in to disturb the peace of the happy farmers.

The unhappy endings seem to have been arrived at contrary to Crèvecoeur's will. He did not set up his readers for disillusionment. As he began to write, he seemed genuinely confident and hopeful. But in the end, America could not sustain his high hopes. He did not single out particular villains to close his stories; evil took many forms. The happy paradise deteriorated, as if Adam was not destined to live in the Garden of Eden forever. Crèvecoeur did not explain why; he could only assert that "the Facts it contains are related with my usual Veracity & scrupulous attention."[70]

9. Revolution

Why Farmers Fought

The publication of Crèvecoeur's *Letters from an American Farmer* in 1782, as the American Revolution was winding down, came at exactly the right moment. The collection's seminal essay "What Is an American?" offered an account of American society just as the new United States was taking its place among the nations of the world. Crèvecoeur answered the question: What is life to be like in the new country? He described an America free of European feudalism and lavish in opportunities for personal independence in the nation's bounteous hinterland. He pictured a poor farmer's paradise, a free and open society that was a perfect match for the nation's free and equal government.

But Crèvecoeur himself felt no need to replace the monarchy with a republic. The Revolution had brought only sorrow to him and his fellow Loyalists. "I am conscious that I was happy before this unfortunate revolution. I feel that I am no longer so; therefore I regret the change." Feeling respect for "the ancient connexions," he would have preferred that America avoid war.[1] Like so many others, he had flourished under British rule. Why endure the turmoil and miseries of war? His aversion to Independence implicitly poses a question: What was at stake for farmers in the Revolution? Not only Crèvecoeur, but thousands of farmers were thriving as colonists. If an American farmer's aspirations could be realized within the Empire, why revolt? Why did so many farmers fight?

Farmers were notoriously slow to join the agitation against parliamentary measures. On the whole, they held back until the Boston Port Bill of

1774, when almost overnight they entered the fray. Not that farmers favored the stamp duties; no one in America did, including future Loyalists. Assemblymen from rural areas voted for delegates to attend the Stamp Act Congress and were happy to open courts without stamped paper, contrary to law. But farmers did not actively campaign against the act. They were far more likely to practice passive disobedience. After a year of urban resistance to the stamp tax, Boston's Sons of Liberty worried that "our friends in the country towns are cold and negligent."[2] Rural people did not form associations or humiliate stamp distributors. Only in eastern Connecticut, eastern Massachusetts, and Westmoreland County, Virginia, were there major actions in the countryside.[3] The Sons of Liberty, the organizations behind the colonial protests, were made up of professionals and artisans rather than farmers. After making an exhaustive study of Sons of Liberty up and down the coast, Pauline Maier observed that "it is noteworthy that the occupations of the Sons of Liberty were generally urban in character. No simple farmers are listed—and, indeed except for Virginia, hardly any whose livelihood came from the land."[4]

Rural Sons of Liberty

The farmers' restraint is all the more striking in light of their vigor in fighting for their land titles. During the decade of popular resistance to Parliament, farmers were closing courts, beating up officials, and springing fellow protesters from prison to protect their holdings against rival claimants. In place after place, they showed themselves capable of forcible resistance when their livelihoods were threatened. None of this anger was turned against the British. The Paxton Boys, noted for slaughtering Indians, never directed their zeal against stamp men.[5] Hudson River farmers drove off the surveyors who threatened their titles but did not prepare a single petition against British taxes.

It was as if two chronologies of resistance proceeded independently of each other in the decade after 1764. One consisted of the colonial protests against British measures that defined the path to Revolution, beginning with the Sugar Act in 1764 and the Stamp Act in 1765 and culminating in the Intolerable Acts of 1774. The other chronology lists the rural outbursts that broke out in nearly every colony from South Carolina to Vermont in the same period: the Regulators in the Carolinas, the Virginia Pennsylvania border controversy, the New Jersey land claims disputes, the Paxton Boys and the

Pennamite wars in Pennsylvania, and the battles over titles and rents in New York and Vermont. Each chronology proceeded by a logic of its own quite independent of the other. One was instigated by parliamentary legislation and precipitated debate over colonial rights. The other brought farmers to defend their lands against various forms of encroachment. One was rooted in disagreements over the British Constitution, the other in the social distress of small farmers struggling to protect their livelihoods. One only mildly engaged farmers; the other drove them to violent action. The two did not merge until 1774.

Until then, the two chronologies intersected only here and there. The Connecticut claimants to Pennsylvania lands in the Susquehanna Valley were among the few farmer-protesters to resist the Stamp Act. Needing government backing for their claims to Pennsylvania lands, the party won control of the Connecticut Lower House but met resistance from the governor and Upper House. They were seeking to break the grip of the conservative faction on the legislature when the Stamp Act agitation in 1765 gave them their opportunity. In September, hundreds of men from the eastern towns where the Susquehanna supporters were concentrated confronted the stamp distributor Jared Ingersoll on his way to the assembly and forced his resignation. A month later, the conservative governor Thomas Fitch, who had opposed the Susquehanna claims, took an oath to enforce the Stamp Act against the wishes of the people. In the next spring's election, Fitch and all the councilors who had sided with him were defeated. One of the Susquehanna party's own, Jonathan Trumbull, was elected lieutenant governor. The Susquehanna faction's particular interests and opposition to the Stamp Act happening to coincide, farmers became Sons of Liberty.[6]

That blend of interests turned out to be rare. Hudson Valley farmers made a stab at joining forces with New York City's Sons of Liberty, but without success. The farmers had two complaints. Some battled for clear title to land in New York based on Massachusetts's claims to the area; others resisted rent increases by their landlords. Resistance reached a peak in 1766 at the very moment when New York City Sons of Liberty were taking their stand against the Stamp Act. Riots in both places were going on simultaneously. In an attempt at an alliance, the agrarian radicals called themselves "sons of liberty" and marched on the city in hopes of winning support from their urban brethren. To the dismay of the farmers, the city Sons of Liberty turned the upstate radicals away. In a study of the Revolution in New York,

Edward Countryman concluded that "at least two distinct patterns of upheaval were working themselves out. One was urban, turning on political, social, and imperial discontent. The other was rural, springing primarily from problems of land ownership and the local dominion that went with it."[7] Although the two launched protests simultaneously, they never joined forces.

From 1764 to 1773, farmers were actively involved in the Revolutionary cause only in a few places. In eastern Connecticut, as we have seen, farmers drove Jared Ingersoll from office.[8] A few counties in eastern Massachusetts also voiced opposition. John Adams persuaded the Braintree town meeting to accept his draft of instructions to the town's representative to the Lower House condemning the Stamp Act. Much later, he claimed that forty towns adopted the resolves, although no corroborating evidence of such action has been found.[9] In what may have been a purge, Massachusetts voters in 1766 failed to return seventeen of the thirty-two representatives to the General Court who were known as friends of the Stamp Act, eight to ten more than can be accounted for by ordinary turnover.[10]

In Westmoreland County, Virginia, the revolutionary leader-to-be Richard Henry Lee led his fellow planters in signing the "Leedstown Resolves." One hundred twenty-two men put their names to a statement declaring that "we will exert every faculty, to prevent the execution of the said Stamp Act in any instance whatsoever within this Colony."[11] A Westmoreland merchant at Hobb's Hole who attempted to use stamped paper suffered the same humiliations as his compatriots in New York and Boston. He was compelled to walk a gantlet between 400 angry planters before yielding his post. The Virginia House of Burgesses representing planter interests also took a stand. With the help of the Westmoreland group, Patrick Henry was able to ram resolves opposing the Stamp Act through the Virginia House of Burgesses. Before proposing the resolves, Henry waited until most of the delegates had gone home. Only 39 of 116 remained, and of these, just 22 voted for the resolves in what Jefferson called a "bloody" debate. Many of the favorable votes came from Lee's Westmoreland.[12]

That is a spotty record for American farmers in the opening years of the Revolutionary movement. Until 1774, antiparliamentary protests found little footing in the countryside outside of eastern Massachusetts, eastern Connecticut, and one county in Virginia.[13] The mild response cannot be attributed to farmer passivity; they rose in wrath when their vital interests were endangered. But parliamentary taxation kindled little active resentment.

Taxes

One reason for the passivity was that the Stamp Act favored farmers. The framers of the Stamp Act purposely chose a tax that operated at one remove from rural taxpayers. The stamp duties were an excise tax that bore most heavily on city dwellers, unlike property and poll taxes, which affected farmers directly. The act required that "every skin or piece of vellum or parchment, or sheet or piece of paper, on which shall be ingrossed, written, or printed," for any official court document be subject to a duty. This included deeds, mortgages, and contracts, licenses, ship clearances, leases, bonds, and diplomas.[14] It also applied to playing cards, almanacs, pamphlets, and newspapers. All were to be printed or written on paper that had been embossed with a stamp for which a duty had been paid. The paper was marked in England and shipped to America, where the so-called "stamp men" or distributors sold it to users.[15] Some of these documents, like deeds and titles, did intrude into farmers' everyday lives, but only to raise slightly the costs of entering a deed or going to court. British tax men never came to the door. The distribution and collection machinery would have ground away in the port cities, not in country towns.

In the battles over which kind of tax to levy—property taxes, poll taxes, excise taxes, or duties on exports and imports—country people had a history of favoring excises. In 1754 the Massachusetts assembly sought to tighten up collection of the excise on distilled spirits over the objection of merchants. Sales of liquor in quantities less than thirty gallons had long been taxed in licensed taverns and inns, but many barrels of smuggled liquor and Massachusetts-made rum flowed outside these channels. The reform bill sought to collect the tax on this stream by requiring each household to declare annually how much it had consumed from sources other than the licensed outlets. Invasive as it was, the bill passed in the assembly by a strictly sectional vote—seventeen representatives from the coastal cities against and fifty-four from inland towns in favor. The port towns were sure the excise was a plot of the country towns to reduce property taxes by enlarging excise income.[16] The farmers did not seem to care about intrusive excise men.

In 1772 the Pennsylvania assembly took the same course. To enforce the liquor excise, a new law called for a tax to be paid on sales of less than seventy gallons as a discouragement to "immoderate use" by "persons in low circumstances." By custom, the excise men had overlooked these small sales, allowing merchants and tavern keepers to avoid the tax. The effort to crack down met furious resistance in Philadelphia. Pamphleteers moaned that enforcement was "the Hydra of corruption and slavery," comparable to Parliament's unconstitutional tax on wines imported into America. No voices were raised in the countryside. As in Massachusetts, excises and duties were city problems. Sympathetic though they may have been to the Stamp Act protests, farmers were not moved to action.[17]

1774

A change in attitude came in 1774 after the Boston Tea Party in December 1773 set off a chain of events that finally registered with colonial farmers. Parliament retaliated against the destruction of 342 chests of taxed tea in Boston harbor with a series of acts to exact repayment and quash the rebellious Bostonians. The Massachusetts Government Act put the selection of the provincial upper house wholly in the hands of the governor and reduced the power of town meetings to the regulation of trivialities. It gave the governor the right to appoint justices to county courts without any input from elected officials and authorized appointed sheriffs to choose juries. The Quebec Act establishing a royal government with a powerful governor and a puny popular assembly seemed to foretell the future of all the British colonies.

These measures had an impact, but the act that impressed farmers most was the first in the series, the Boston Port Bill which passed in both houses of Parliament "by a very great majority in both," as Franklin reported, and received the royal assent on March 31, 1774. The bill closed Boston to both exports and imports until the city compensated merchants for their lost tea. The bill provided, as a Boston broadside on May 12, 1774, put it, for "blocking up the Harbour of Boston, with a Fleet of Ships of War, and preventing the Entrance in, or Exportation of, all Sorts of Merchandise."[18] Though not redcoats beating their drums, the armed forces of Great Britain were stationed at the mouth of Boston harbor to stop the passage of ships. Parliament deprived Massachusetts of its chief outlet for the products flowing from farms, fisheries, and forests into the Atlantic trade. That was the imperial action named most frequently and with greatest alarm in the statements coming out of rural gatherings in the Pennsylvania hinterland beginning in June 1774.

Copies of the Port Bill reached Boston on May 10, 1774. On May 12, the Boston Committee of Correspondence called for support of other colonies and dispatched Paul Revere to carry their plea to New York and Philadelphia. On June 4 the inhabitants of Hanover, Lancaster County, Pennsylvania, met to declare that the "recent action of the Parliament of Great Britain" is "iniquitous and oppressive." Another group of Lancaster County inhabitants met on June 8 and resolved that "it is an indispensable duty we owe to ourselves and posterity to oppose with decency and firmness every measure tending to deprive us of our just rights and privileges." On June 15 the tradesmen and merchants in the borough of Lancaster conferred about stopping imports of British goods as a form of retaliation. Lebanon and adjoining townships met on June 25, and by July 9 a county meeting was held.[19] In the next six months Lancaster County's inhabitants chose delegates to provincial congresses, agreed to an association to stop imports, set up committees of observation to detect departures from the nonimportation agreement, and were soon to form military associations to defend themselves against British troops. The lassitude of the previous decade was gone; the countryside was abuzz with activity. After 1774, "central Pennsylvania provided the core of the state's support for the cause."[20]

The same thing was happening elsewhere in Pennsylvania, in nearby Maryland, and in Virginia. Chester County, Pennsylvania, formed its first Revolutionary committee on June 1, despite the conservative influence of its Quaker population. York County gathered food and blankets for Boston. Several hundred people gathered in at the Northampton County courthouse to form a committee of correspondence. In Maryland, antiparliamentary meetings were held in Talbot County, as well as Kent, Anne Arundel, Frederick, and Charles. At least half the counties in Virginia held mass meetings and passed resolves printed in the *Virginia Gazette*.[21] The reliable Westmoreland County planters under Richard Henry Lee's leadership resolved that "every Man of us," will "keep our Produce, whether Tobacco, Corn, Wheat, or any Thing else, unsold, on our own respective Plantations; and not carry, or suffer them to be carried, to any publick Warehouse or Landing Place." Jefferson later remembered that on the day of fasting and humiliation set for June 1, "the people met generally, with anxiety & alarm in their countenances, and the effect of the day thro' the whole colony was like a shock of electricity."[22]

The same response occurred in New York, where county after county reported its resistance: East Hampton, Southampton, Tryon, Suffolk, Dutchess, Shelter Island. According to Robert Taylor, Western Massachusetts "did not come solidly to the support of the Whigs until after the passage of the Intolerable Acts in the spring of 1774." In 1768 only one delegate from Connecticut Valley and Berkshire County towns attended the convention to oppose the coming of British troops. After 1774, the Massachusetts west surged to the forefront of revolutionary action. "Town after town assembled and chose committees of correspondence." Conventions were held in Berkshire, Hampshire, and Middlesex counties. Crowds of people shut down courts presided over by the hated governor-appointed justices, then proceeded to set up courts of their own.[23]

Why after a decade of urban resistance to Parliament did the countryside rise up in 1774? The militant response from the countryside amazed John Dickinson. In late June 1774, he wrote to Josiah Quincy, Jr., that "what never happened before, has happened now. The country people have so exact a knowledge of facts, and of the consequences attending the surrender of the points in question, that they are, if possible, more zealous than the citizens who lie in a direct line of information." After failing to react to previous appeals such as Dickinson's own *Letters from a Farmer in Pennsylvania,* the countryside was as aroused as the city. As the Philadelphia committee wrote the counties in mid-June, "all the colonies, from South Carolina to New Hampshire, seem animated with one spirit in the common cause."[24] Something had ignited rural suspicion and anger.

The explanations given for the antiparliamentary surge in 1774 had a familiar ring. The Lancaster County meeting on July 9, 1774, recapitulated the tax controversies of the preceding nine years. "We do further declare that no power is constitutionally lodged in the hands of any body of men to give and grant our money, save only our representatives in assembly . . . that the acts of the British Parliament for divesting us of such right, and assuming such power to themselves, are unconstitutional, unjust, and oppressive." A month earlier, Middletown foreshadowed Lancaster in asserting that "the acts of the Parliament of Great Britain in divesting us of the right to give and grant our money, and assuming such power to themselves, are unconstitutional, unjust and oppressive."[25] The Pennsylvania countryside may not have risen up against the Stamp Act and Townshend Duties, but it had been listening. Town and county statements in 1774 drew on a decade of antiparliamentary writing to explain their opposition.

But all this was by way of background. The topic most on the minds of country people in 1774 was not taxes but the Boston Port Bill. Pennsylvania and Maryland counties began meeting in June almost immediately after

Philadelphia heard of the bill and well before news of the other acts, signed into law on May 20, reached the colonies. On June 4, Hanover's inhabitants could only have meant the port bill when they complained of "the recent action of the Parliament." The Lebanon resolves spoke explicitly of "the late act of the British Parliament, by which the port of Boston is shut up." The Lancaster County meeting expressed its sympathy for "our brethren of Boston, who are suffering in the American cause by an unconstitutional and oppressive act of the British Parliament, called the Boston Port Bill." Lancaster borough declared that "the act of Parliament for blocking up the port and harbor of Boston is an invasion of the rights of the inhabitants of said town" and proposed nonimportation as the most effectual means "to obtain a repeal of the said act." In nearby Berks County, a convention resolved that "the Boston Port Bill is unjust and tyrannical in the extreme."[26] The Port Bill, more than any other of the Coercive Acts, precipitated rural action.

The reasons for the rapid response are not entirely clear. Farmers, it could be conjectured, understood the vital role of ports in conveying the wheat that left their farmsteads for flour markets in New York, Philadelphia, or Baltimore, and thence to ultimate sale and consumption in the West Indies and southern Europe. They saw that the Boston closing might spread to their own ports, arousing both sympathy and fear. But if port closure was fatal, why their willingness to close ports voluntarily by nonimportation and nonexportation agreements under the Association soon to be recommended by the Continental Congress? The pain of port closings could not have been excruciating if farmers willingly inflicted it on themselves. Moreover, closing Boston alone would have little impact in Pennsylvania and might even increase Philadelphia's commerce. None of the county resolves mentioned the effects of the Port Bill on farmers outside New England. All the danger was potential. There must have been a more subtle and powerful logic in play than economic suffering alone.

The common theme running through the county and town resolves in the Middle Colonies and Virginia was indignation with the injustice and cruelty of the Port Bill. The protesters referred to the bill as a "cruel edict." Samuel Adams wrote Arthur Lee in May that "for flagrant injustice and barbarity, one might search in vain among the archives of *Constantinople* to find a match for it." The resolves of Maryland's Prince George's County echoed the same refrain: "The late cruel, unjust, and sanguinary Acts of Parliament, to be executed by military Force and Ships of War upon our

Sister Colony of the *Massachusetts Bay,* and Town of *Boston,* is a strong Evidence of the corrupt Influence obtained by the *British* Ministry in Parliament." All the laments for the suffering of the people of Boston implicitly condemned the British ministry for their harsh treatment.[27] Colonists up and down the seaboard took up collections to aid their brethren in New England, and every shilling raised for Boston's succor registered a protest against Parliament for causing the hurt.

The Port Bill had a different tenor than the other Intolerable Acts. The others affected the process of government—selection of judges and juries and the Upper House. The Port Bill put ships in the harbor to stop outgoing vessels. Its enforcement depended on arms. Troops were camped on the Boston Common. The armed forces of Great Britain stood ready, and who knew how far they would go? In Virginia, Landon Carter summed up his feelings in a diary entry for June 3, 1774. "Great alarms in the Country. The Parliament of England have declared war against the town of Boston and rather worse; for they have attacked and blocked up their harbor with 3 line of Battle Ships and 6 others, and landed 8 regiments there to subdue them to submit to their taxation; as this is but a Prelude to destroy the Liberties of America, the other Colonies cannot look on the affair but as a dangerous alarm."[28] It did not help that with the Port Bill, Governor Thomas Hutchinson had been replaced as governor by Gen. Thomas Gage, the commander of the British Army in America. One observer called it "a studied insult." Simultaneously it was reported that eight British regiments were in readiness to embark for Boston.[29]

Implicitly the Port Bill turned the people of Massachusetts into enemies of the Empire. It punished the entire colony for the work of a few in dumping the tea. Instead of arresting and prosecuting the guilty parties in the tea incident, as is normal in civil society, the government punished the entire population. That is the way nations treat enemy populations in times of war. And if Massachusetts could be dealt with in that fashion, was any colony safe? A Philadelphia writer speculated that "when the spirits of our brethren in *Boston* are subdued, our rivers and shores will probably be crowded with men-of-war."[30] Within six months virtually every Pennsylvania county was organizing military associations as if they anticipated that British troops would soon enforce the iniquitous laws on them.

The reaction seemed to stem less from ideas about constitutional rights or republican ideologies of corruption than from a basic sense of government's obligations to its people. Government was to protect people, not to attack them. Parliament's crime was to send fleets and armies to war on Boston. It did not require political instruction to understand that wrong. The government's cruel action severed the bonds of loyalty between king and people.[31]

Dickinson marveled at how well the country people understood the consequences of resistance. They knew it could end in combat. "Our country people appear to me to be very firm. They look to the last extremity with spirit." Already in June, reports circulated in colonial newspapers of two Massachusetts men from Worcester County who said "by the Acts of the British Parliament lately passed, and the Bills now depending therein, our Charter is utterly vacated, and the Compact between this Province and the Crown of Great Britain being dissolved, they are at full Liberty to combine together, in what Manner and Form they think best for mutual Security."[32] Although not yet advocating independence, newspapers now dared print revolutionary sentiments.

The Port Bill cannot be said to have endangered the vital interests of farmers in Pennsylvania. A different cultural mindset underlay the reaction to the bill than spurred the land riots of the 1760s and 1770s. The earlier protests had grown out of stresses in the family economy. When farmers battled for Susquehanna rights or fought New York for titles in Vermont, they were driven by their need for land. Again in the 1780s, farmers were to protest high taxes and a shrinking money supply in order to preserve their farms. Those protests were based on material family needs. Seventeen seventy-four was different. The farm economy figured only slightly in the resistance. Farmers were not fighting to hold on to their land. They reacted against the imperial government for political, not economic, reasons. The government had turned on its own people. In 1774 farmers resisted Parliament not as distressed husbandmen but as outraged subjects.

Rural Democracy at War

The writings coming out of town and county meetings in 1774 and 1775 reveal a countryside prepared for resistance. Though slow to respond in the previous decade, when they were at last aroused, farm communities articulated their objections in one clear statement after another. Frequently the statements ended with a set of resolves that set the community into action, leading to Independence two years later. Somehow the men who drafted the resolves had learned the language of politics, perhaps in the Pennsylvania assembly, or during business visits to the capital, or through heeding the political correspondence coming from Philadelphia. They knew what to say and how to say it in such a way that the local populace would come along with them.

Behind the statements to which the freeholders and inhabitants "unanimously resolved" to subscribe was a social process. It began with a sense of who should take the lead when the community chose to act. The county meetings knew how to select a committee to "act for us and in our behalf as emergencies may require."[33] In the minutes of the meetings, the names of six or eight men followed, often with titles like "colonel," "esquire," or "mister" attached. These few wrote to the committee in Philadelphia and represented the people in congresses and on committees. In all things political, these leaders acted for the whole.

The committeemen's names often had a military equivalent in the names of officers and privates in the militias. Each company had a captain, a first lieutenant, a second lieutenant, an ensign, three or four sergeants, in some cases a clerk, and the rest privates—up to a hundred of them. Battalions of at least two companies were led by colonels. The people chosen for military office were often the same as those chosen as committee members in the county meetings. Anthony Wayne was the leading figure in Chester County's revolutionary movement, the person the people turned to for the most demanding offices. Wayne did not earn the people's trust through long service, as did Joshua Hempstead in New London. His father, Isaac Wayne, owned sixteen hundred acres and the largest tannery in Pennsylvania. Anthony learned surveying at an academy in Philadelphia and then attended the College of Philadelphia. Though only twenty-nine when the Port Bill was passed, he was chosen colonel of the Chester County Battalion and chairman of the committee of correspondence.[34]

Although there must have been plain men among the town leaders, the plodding kind who earned their standings through long service in local government and proven integrity in business, figures like Wayne turned up in every county. By dint of wealth, experience, family standing, or education, they took their places as heads of local society. Knowing the language of politics, these eminent figures could speak for their fellow inhabitants. At its July 9, 1774, meeting, the Lancaster County freemen and inhabitants moved to thank George Ross, "the worthy chairman for very proper and spirited address made by him to this assembly." The motion "was agreed to by a general holding up of hands, and the thanks of the assembly were then presented to Mr. Ross for his patriotic conduct." Ross, the son of an Anglican clergyman, was born in 1730 in New Castle, Delaware, studied law, and was admitted to the Pennsylvania bar in 1750. Soon after, he established a practice in Lancaster County just as it was beginning to grow. He served as crown prosecutor for twelve years and was elected to the Pennsylvania assembly in 1768. Initially a Loyalist, he was converted to the colonial cause. As a member of the Continental Congress, he signed the Declaration of Independence. In 1775 George Ross, Esq., headed the list of colonels in the Lancaster County battalion, and on July 4, 1776, he presided over a meeting of all officers and privates from Pennsylvania to elect a brigadier general. He came in fifth in the balloting but was nonetheless thanked for "the cheerfulness, celerity, and Impartiality with which he conducted the Business of the Day."[35] Ross was Lancaster County's Anthony Wayne.

In a sense the revolutionary movement made visible the unseen structure of farm communities from the top through the middling ranks. There were colonels, captains, and lieutenants, and there were sergeants and privates. At the top stood eminences like Ross and Wayne. Below, less luminous figures with more stolid backgrounds served as lieutenants and sergeants.[36] The officers spoke, and the privates mostly listened. In Philadelphia, the privates claimed a committee of their own to speak their minds, and once during the Revolution a battalion of county privates made an appeal for greater equality. Representing the twelve companies in the Cumberland County militia, they asked for annual elections of officers, "for annual election is so essentially necessary to the liberty of freemen." The incident was unusual. Except for infrequent outbursts, ordinary farmers for the most part went along.[37]

Considering the influence of local leaders, the county protests of 1774 are not to be thought of as raw expressions of the popular will. The resolves were a filtering of widespread political sentiments through the minds of trusted local leaders. The Philadelphia committee of correspondence referred to these eminences as "proper persons." The minutes of a Philadelphia meeting spoke of the forty-four people chosen for the committee of correspondence as men "to whose approved integrity, abilities, and sincere affection for the interest of this immense Empire, their constituents look up for the most propitious events."[38] These leading figures were looked to for a suitable response to events in the wider world. Although they could not stray far from the sentiments of ordinary people, they could win over the undecided and provide words for common feelings. These local hierarchies were critical to the functioning of grassroots democracy. They were the ones to shape popular opinion in open meetings. Once written down, the agreed upon words came to represent the will of the people and could be used to enroll popular support and punish dissenters. The Revolution worked because functional democracy had become political habit long before Pennsylvania and the nation became republics in name.

Over the next two years, from July 1774 through July 1776, county and provincial committees assumed ever broader authority. From May through December 1774, the committees mainly stated their opinions, formed committees, and elected delegates to provincial bodies. In July and August, both the county delegates and the provincial assembly agreed to elect delegates to the Continental Congress that met in Philadelphia on September 1, 1774.[39] Out of the Congress's deliberations came an agreement—the Association—to halt imports from Great Britain immediately and exports after a year. The Association was adopted on October 20 and sent to the colonies to implement. On December 10 the Pennsylvania assembly urged the counties to comply. The terms came down from the Congress via the provincial legislature, and elected committees in the counties put them into effect.[40]

Northampton named its group the Committee of Observation and Inspection in order to clarify its responsibilities. The only effective form of enforcement of the ban on exports and imports was to expose transgressors to public shame. That called for a committee to spot the offenders and bring them to public notice as "foes to the rights of British-America" and "enemies of American liberty," as the Congress put it, and henceforth to "break off all dealings with him or her."[41] Offenders could not be punished by law. The resolves of the Continental Congress had no legal authority. In the absence of law and courts, the people themselves were the only enforcers.

As the months went by, the local committees stopped merchants from taking "advantage of the scarcity of Goods that may be occasioned by this Association." They were to sell goods "at the rates we have been respectively accustomed to do for twelve months late past," and if any storekeeper raised his prices "no person ought, nor will any of us deal with any such person." When Robert Ferguson took "an unusual and exorbitant price" for some of his goods, the committee forced him to "solemnly promise in future to be governed by said Association in all my mercantile dealings." In keeping with a provision in the Association, a few counties also stopped the slaughter of sheep in order to protect wool production, doubtless with blankets for the troops in mind.[42]

The skirmish between British troops and Massachusetts militia men at Concord on April 19, 1775, dismayed the Pennsylvania countryside as much as the Boston Port Bill a year earlier. At Chester County on May 15, the committee with Anthony Wayne in the chair lamented that the British Parliament "have proceeded to fresh acts of tyranny and oppression, which added to an Address of both Lords and Commons to his majesty, declaring the inhabitants of the Province of Massachusetts Bay to be in a state of open rebellion . . . have induced the soldiery under the command of General Gage, at Boston, to commence a civil war, by wantonly firing upon and murdering a number of the inhabitants of that Province." The Chester committee believed the address of the Lords and Commons declaring Massachusetts in a state of rebellion "militates equally against all the inhabitants of the other Colonies," and "if suffered to take effect, must inevitably reduce these Colonies to a state of abject slavery, from which in all probability, no human efforts would ever be able to rescue them."[43]

The Provincial Congress recommended that counties organize military associations, and the counties immediately associated into militias to defend themselves against the next stroke of British power. In Northampton County, the committee "unanimously *Resolved,* That the several Townships in this County should Associate & form themselves into Companies, choose their proper Officers, & provide for each Man one good fire lock, one pound powder, four pounds of Lead, a sufficient quantity of Flints & a Cartridge Box." Besides enlisting men and electing officers, arrangements had to be made for gunpowder, flintlocks, and uniforms.[44]

Battalions were raised at the Congress's behest to join the continental army. Recruiters had no trouble raising men for a year of service. "The spirit of the people on this occasion gave the committee much encouragement," York County reported. About 75 percent of the male population between fifteen and seventy-five in the county—some 3,349 men—was enlisted for service. In Cumberland County about 3,000 men enlisted.[45] Over the next year, counties learned "the military art," collected arms and gunpowder, and equipped the soldiers for war.

As warfare between the Continental Army under George Washington and British troops heated up through 1775 and 1776, the countryside with little debate or evident distress accepted the idea of a new government. By the late spring of 1776, the towns expected a government to be organized under the "authority of the people." Local records give no evidence of debate or soul-searching, save for the non-Associators who had dragged their feet from the start. County meetings followed the lead of the Continental Congress, which in mid-May 1776 recommended that government under the authority of the crown should be "totally suppressed, and all the powers of government exerted, under the authority of the people of these colonies."[46]

By the end of May rural people knew that a conference of county delegates was meeting in Philadelphia on June 18 to select delegates for a provincial constitutional convention and that "a Government will shortly be founded on the authority of the people in the room of the present."[47] The committees showed no anxiety about the change in government, only about how to keep order in the meantime. On July 4, upon receiving news of Congress's resolve to declare independence, Yorktown patriots called people together for celebration by ringing a large bell owned by the Church of England.[48]

Although the conceptual leap from monarchy to a republic was huge, little farm communities had lived democracy too long to be anxious about taking the fateful step. They knew how to gather the inhabitants, identify leaders, formulate opinion, and organize committees. They had associated for protest, for nonimportation and nonconsumption, and finally for war. They had enforced the ban on commerce with Britain, learned to make gunpowder, formed militia companies, stopped the butchering of sheep, and kept order for two years while imperial government crumbled around them. They knew each other's minds and who was competent to lead. Government under the authority of the people held no terrors for them.

10. Family Mobility

The Lincolns of Massachusetts, New Jersey, Pennsylvania, Virginia, Kentucky, Indiana, and Illinois

Not everyone who went to war in Pennsylvania in 1776 fought for a familiar homeland. Many had resided in one place for a few years and moved on. Over the course of six generations, the ancestors of President Abraham Lincoln lived in seven colonies and states as they made their way from Massachusetts to Illinois. Most of the Lincolns were farmers whose chief incentive for moving was to obtain land for their children. The first Samuel Lincoln who migrated to Massachusetts in 1637 began as a weaver but then turned to farming. From then on, all of the Lincolns in President Abraham's direct line owned land, and to keep on farming, they had to move. The Lincolns were typical of many farm families. Studies of eighteenth-century New England communities find from 30 to 50 percent of the population moving after a decade. The same held true in Virginia and South Carolina.[1] Although they stuck with farming, the Lincolns were part of this shifting population. They were examples of the most elusive American farm type, the migrant family.

Movers are hard to follow as they migrate from place to place. Families that stay put generate a small pile of information over a lifetime that enables historians to reconstruct their lives: birth and death dates, land purchases, jury duty, service in public office, signatures as witness to a will, wills and estate inventories. People on the move are much more slippery. Their destinations are not always known, and when a name appears on a tax list in a new place, historians can never be sure that this is the person they are looking for. Genealogists do the hard work of tracking down these migrant families. They scour the sources for data and painstakingly collate the information to be sure they have the right people. More than any other source, genealogies help historians to recover the lives of migrating farmers and explain why and how they moved.[2]

The Lincolns were both movers and stayers. The first Samuel Lincoln made the big leap from Hingham, Norfolk County, England, to Massachusetts Bay in 1637, migrating with his master. Then after completing his weaving apprenticeship, he joined two of his brothers in Hingham, Massachusetts, where a number of his countrymen from Norfolk had settled. The three of them, with the help of two other Lincoln migrants from the English Hingham, initiated the numerous Lincoln clan in America.[3]

After Samuel's great leap, the Lincolns settled down. All of Samuel's eleven children born in Hingham between 1652 and 1673 remained there or in nearby Scituate, save for one son who trained as a tailor in Boston. Outmigration began in the next generation. In the first decade of the eighteenth century, two grandsons, Mordecai and Abraham Lincoln, born in 1686 and 1688, moved to New Jersey and then Pennsylvania. They were exceptional in that generation. Their two brothers and two sisters who grew to adulthood, plus twenty-three first cousins, married and died in Hingham, content to find mates and bear children among familiar faces in the Hingham parishes. Their deep roots helped them to claim substantial places in town government, serving as constables, selectmen, and town moderators.[4]

The two migrants left kin and familiar neighbors for places where they were scarcely known. The genealogists have turned up no clues as to why the brothers chose Monmouth County, New Jersey, as their destination, but the New Jersey ties could not have been strong; within a few years both had moved on to Pennsylvania. Mordecai and Abraham seemed to be responding to opportunity rather than familiarity. They did not even remain near each other. Mordecai ended up in Amity, Philadelphia County, and Abraham in Chester County.[5]

Some measure of economic calculation may have entered into the brothers' decision to go. Their father, also named Mordecai, was a miller and iron forger on a "puny" stream in Hingham named Bound Brook, which he

Table 10.1 MALE AMERICAN ANCESTORS OF PRESIDENT ABRAHAM LINCOLN

(Italicized names are direct ancestors)

First Generation—England to Massachusetts

Samuel b. 1622, Norfolk County, England; d. 1675, Hingham, Massachusetts
Siblings: Thomas Daniel

Second Generation—Hingham, Massachusetts

Mordecai b. 1657, Hingham, Massachusetts; d. 1728, Hingham, Massachusetts
Siblings: Samuel b. 1650 Daniel b. 1652/53 Mordecai b./d. 1655 Thomas b. 1659/d. 1661 Mary b. 1662 Thomas b. 1664 Martha b. 1666/67 Sarah b./d. 1669 Sarah b. 1671 Rebecca b. 1673/74

Third Generation—Hingham to New Jersey and Pennsylvania

Mordecai b. 1686, Hingham, Massachusetts; d. 1736, Amity, Pennsylvania
Siblings: Abraham b. 1688-9 Isaac b. 1691 Sarah b. 1694 Elizabeth b. 1703 Jacob b. 1708

Fourth Generation—Pennsylvania to Virginia

John b. 1716, Freehold, New Jersey; d. 1788, Linville's Creek, Virginia
Siblings: Deborah b. 1717/18 Hannah Mary Anne b. 1725 Sarah b. 1727 Mordecai b. 1730 Thomas b. 1732 Abraham b. 1736

Fifth Generation—Virginia to Kentucky and Tennessee

Abraham b. 1744, Berks County, Pennsylvania; d. 1785, Jefferson County, Kentucky
Siblings: Hannah b. 1748 Lydia b. 1748 Isaac b. 1750 Jacob b. 1751 John b. 1755 Thomas b. 1761 Rebecca b. 1767

Sixth Generation—Kentucky to Indiana and Illinois

Thomas b. 1778, Augusta County, Virginia; d. 1851, Goose Nest Prairie, Illinois
Siblings: Mordecai b. 1771 Josiah b. 1773 Mary Nancy b. 1780

Seventh Generation—Illinois and Washington

Abraham b. 1809, Hodgenville, Kentucky; d. 1865, Washington, D.C.
Siblings: Nancy (or Sarah) b. 1807 Thomas b./d. 1813

Eighth Generation—Illinois and Washington

Robert Todd b. 1843 Edward Baker b. 1846/d. 1850 William Wallace b. 1850/d. 1862 Thomas b. 1853

Source: Waldo Lincoln, *History of the Lincoln Family: An Account of the Descendants of Samuel Lincoln of Hingham Massachusetts, 1637–1920* (Worcester, Mass.: Commonwealth, 1923).

exploited to the utmost by constructing a gristmill, a sawmill, and an ironworks. The stream powered a trip-hammer that the elder Mordecai used to forge iron smelted from the bog ore obtained from the neighboring town of Pembroke. As Mordecai and Abraham entered their teenage years in 1700, their father was forty-three, with presumably another twenty years of working life ahead of him. As they entered their twenties, they made a calculation that was not uncommon among elder sons. With little prospect that the mills would come to them during their father's work years, Mordecai and Abraham looked elsewhere for opportunities.[6]

In the next century the Middle Colonies were to become the center of iron forging in North America, and by 1700 the signs were beginning to appear. The two young men may have sensed opportunity. The migrating Mordecai purchased land in Monmouth County, New Jersey, on Machaponix Creek, which flowed into the Manalapan River. Later in the century, the Spotswood forge was constructed on the Manalapan near the mouth of the Machaponix. By midcentury enough ore had been discovered to warrant investment in the forge.[7] Mordecai also purchased three hundred acres on Cranberry Brook, which today rises near Iron Ore Road in Middlesex County, New Jersey, and drains into the Millstone River. He seemed to have been scouting out lands with milling and forging possibilities. In 1723 Mordecai entered into a partnership to mine and forge iron in Chester County, Pennsylvania, which two years later he sold for five hundred pounds. Although both Mordecai and Abraham owned farms, they were known as "blacksmiths."[8]

In the course of their lives in New Jersey and Pennsylvania, Mordecai and Abraham established Middle Colony outposts of the original Lincoln clan.[9] The Pennsylvania Lincolns adopted different strategies for setting up their sons. Abraham took advantage of Philadelphia to give his older boys a start. Apparently unwilling to deed them a part of his own farmland while he was still working, he bought lots for them in Philadelphia and saw his son Abraham trained as a cordwainer, another son, Isaac, as a carpenter, and a third son as a scythe maker. Two younger sons received the traditional gift of land from their father and went on to become solid citizens in their rural communities.[10]

Mordecai's eldest son, John Lincoln, adopted another strategy. He headed for Augusta (later Rockingham) County in Virginia's Shenandoah Valley. Unlike Mordecai and Abraham, who moved from Hingham in their twenties, John left Pennsylvania in 1768, when he was fifty-two years old. He was not seeking a start in life like his father and uncle; he was thinking of the five sons who had come along in quick order, four of them between 1750 and 1761.[11] By 1768 the oldest were on the verge of setting up on their own and needed farms.

The family's needs came to a head at a critical time. The population was booming and land prices were skyrocketing. In the 1760s, thousands of people were on the move as the French and Indian War came to an end. Herman Husband moved into Orange County, North Carolina. Virginians claimed land in southeastern Pennsylvania under Virginia titles. Connecticut people swarmed onto Vermont lands claimed jointly by New Hampshire and New York. These were the years when settled areas were bulging, and people took risks with shaky titles and threats of Indians along the frontier. John joined the swelling mass of migrants in search of land for their children.

John had a workable strategy. By 1765 he had sold all his Pennsylvania lands, and three years later he paid £250 for 600 acres in Augusta County. Five years later, in 1773, he was able to sell 210 acres to his son Abraham (then twenty-nine) and 215 acres to Isaac (twenty-three) for £20 each. That was not exactly a father's gift, but it was less than a quarter of the market price, which would have been about £90 for each parcel in 1773. That arrangement provided for two of the five boys. After John died, a third son, Thomas, received the farm and house where his father had lived. John's will makes no mention of the remaining two sons, another John and a Jacob, but father John must have provided them land while he was still alive. Later documents show Jacob living on property adjoining Abraham, and John farming in Turleytown, twelve miles away.[12]

Father John was more successful than most in fulfilling his obligation to his sons. Their holdings would have put them squarely in the middle ranks of Augusta County society in the 1780s, when 35 percent of landholders owned more than 300 acres of land and 40 percent owned less than 200. The daughters received small cash bequests and some of the household furnishings. Yet it was scarcely a triumphant life. When father John died, his estate inventory recorded a modest household. He owned a wagon and threshing fan in partnership with someone else, probably Jacob, who lived next door. For serving food he had "Five dishes and 8 pewter plates." The house had five chairs, two of them "old ones," and no table. No bedding or beds are named, though children may have carted them away before the inventory.[13] John had not risen in the world; he had survived and done his duty by his sons.

John Lincoln's effort to provide for his wife and children can be considered only partially successful. Youngest son Thomas and his mother were burned out of the family dwelling. In the 1780s, two other sons, Abraham and Isaac, moved to Kentucky and Tennessee, where Abraham was killed by Indians and Isaac tragically lost his only son by drowning. One of John's daughters sued the executors of the estate, who were her own mother and two brothers, for depriving her of her just due. Two of John's sons did better. They seemed to have prospered in Rockingham County. Jacob, who worked his father's farm as well as his own after Thomas left, rose to prominence in the county. He served as a lieutenant in the continental army during the Revolution and later as a captain in the militia, and by the end of his life had moved from his log cabin into a brick house, which he furnished with mahogany furniture imported from Pennsylvania. His wife received three slaves as a bequest from her father, and Jacob owned slaves of his own. His brother John reverted to the family business of milling. He owned a gristmill, a bark mill, and a tanyard, and was appointed deputy surveyor of the county.[14]

The brothers who migrated before building up their assets in Virginia fared less well. They dealt in large tracts of land without accumulating much wealth. Abraham, the president's grandfather, was given a farm by his father, John, in Rockingham County, Virginia, and was respected enough to be elected a captain in the county militia while he remained there. He was on a par with his brother John in the 1770s, but even before the Revolution, he seemed determined to move west. In 1776 he made an entry for one thousand acres in Kentucky, and in 1780 he paid the Commonwealth of Virginia (which still claimed Kentucky) for twelve hundred acres. Subsequently, he patented another five hundred acres, probably thinking not only of his sons but of the flood of eager settlers who were anxiously waiting for Kentucky to open. Around 1784 he moved his family to Lincoln County, Kentucky, near Louisville. The written record says nothing about how he died, but family tradition held that he was attacked by Indians while working a field with his three sons. The eldest son, Mordecai, seventeen, ran to the house for a gun; Josiah, fifteen, dashed off for help from the militia; and Thomas, age ten, stayed with his father. Mordecai returned in time to shoot an Indian who was about to seize Thomas, but too late to save their father, who was killed.[15]

Abraham's plans for a massive array of Kentucky properties never came to realization. He paid the price for venturing into the line of fire along the Indian frontier. When he died, his personal estate was valued at only sixty-eight pounds. The inventory of his belongings was meager: one axe, two beds, a flax wheel, a dozen pewter plates, and two pewter dishes; a Dutch oven and a small iron kettle; a smoothbore gun and a rifle; a plow but no ox; one horse; and no tables or chairs. His widow, Bathsheba, left for Washington County, Kentucky, where her family lived, taking Thomas, the president's father, and the other children with her. Because Abraham died intestate, his land under the laws of primogeniture all went to Mordecai, the eldest son, who had saved Thomas's life.[16]

That stroke of fate pretty much determined the lot of the next generation. Mordecai, who received all the land, flourished; the two younger brothers, Josiah and Thomas, floundered. By his early thirties Mordecai (born 1771) was dealing in large parcels of land from his father's estate. His wife's inheritance in Washington and Madison counties added to the property received from his father. As a badge of his prominence, Mordecai was elected sheriff. With none of his brother's advantages, Josiah lived at a much lower level. He is not known to have owned any property until 1809, when he was thirty-five and purchased 60 acres near his brother.[17] The third brother, Thomas, the president's father, did no better. In 1803, when he was twenty-five, he purchased 238 acres with barns, stables, and houses for £118. In 1814 he sold this land for £100. Thomas Lincoln inscribed a signature on the papers, a mark of literacy, though his wife, Nancy Hanks, made only her mark. He learned the trade of carpenter in the shop of Joseph Hanks in Hardin County and practiced carpentry until his removal to Indiana in 1816. Thomas got by but never found an upward path. In 1830 he moved from Indiana to Macon County, Illinois, and a year later to a forty-acre farm on Goose Nest Prairie, where he died in 1851.[18]

All the sons of grandfather Abraham moved, one measure of how times had changed. Migration was exceptional in their great-grandfather's generation. In the sixth generation of Lincolns in America, the movers outnumbered the stayers. Thomas's son President Abraham was among the movers, but not to new lands like his father and uncle. This Abraham followed the urban path to his life work. Despite being "raised to farm work," as he said of himself, he had no interest in farming.[19] The supposed security of family farming had not worked for Thomas Lincoln. He barely supplied a living for his children and had no prospects of setting up young Abraham on his own land. Like the children of the earlier Lincoln who gave three of his sons trades in Philadelphia, Lincoln chose to take his chances in Illinois in

New Salem as a storekeeper, postmaster, lawyer, and politician. He was part of the 1850s generation of presidents, the first who never farmed as adults—Millard Fillmore, Franklin Pierce, and James Buchanan. Migration to the frontier no longer promised to satisfy their ambitions. Like many young men of ability in Lincoln's generation, they turned their backs on fresh land in the West and made their careers in the towns and cities now spotting the land.

The story of the prolific Lincoln clan offers a microhistory of the explosive social and biological forces propelling American expansion in the early years. Parents like the Lincolns ultimately accounted for the uncontrollable expansion of American boundaries and for the sorrows that went with it. Some of those sorrows were national—the displacement of the Indian populations. Others were personal—loneliness and separation. With all the leave-taking and resettlement over seven generations, Abraham Lincoln of New Salem seems to have lost sight of his ancestry. His active memories went back no farther than his grandfather Abraham. His law partner William Herndon opened his biography of Lincoln by noting that Lincoln "had but little to say of himself, the lives of his parents, or the history of the family before their removal to Indiana." William Dean Howells's 1860 campaign biography said there was only "incertitude, and absolute darkness" about Lincoln's ancestors.[20]

A casual comment to Herndon indicated that Lincoln sometimes wondered about his origins. When a law case of theirs touched upon a question of "hereditary traits," he opened up about his own origins. "During the ride he spoke, for the first time in my hearing, of his mother, dwelling on her characteristics, and mentioning and enumerating what qualities he inherited from her. He said, among other things that she was the illegitimate daughter of Lucy Hanks and a well-bred Virginia farmer or planter; and he argued from this last source came his power of analysis, his logic, his mental activity, his ambition, and all the qualities that distinguished him from the other members and descendants of the Hanks family. . . . His better nature and finer qualities came from this broad-minded, unknown Virginian."[21]

Seeming to have come out of nowhere, Lincoln could account for himself only by fastening on a well-bred Virginia planter engendering an illegitimate child by Lucy Hanks, his mother's mother. It was a sad plight for a striving young man to imagine that his intelligence and character were illegitimate. But constant moving and innumerable broken ties left him with little else to work with. The Lincoln line was invisible to him. After he spoke of his mother's illegitimacy, Herndon said, Lincoln lapsed into silence.[22]

PART FIVE

Virginia, 1776–1800

11. Founding Farmers

The Contradictions of the Planter Class

By a quirk of historical fate, the genealogical lines of two presidents, Abraham Lincoln and Thomas Jefferson, converged briefly in Virginia in the late eighteenth century. Abraham Lincoln's great-grandfather John Lincoln purchased land in Augusta County, Virginia, in 1768, one of thousands moving to the Shenandoah Valley after the French and Indian War. Three decades earlier, just to the east of Augusta over the mountains, a similar flood of newcomers moved into Virginia's Piedmont. Among the first was Peter Jefferson, who in 1735 received a patent for land in Goochland, later Albemarle, County, less than sixty miles east of John Lincoln's later holdings.[1] During the Revolution, Peter's son Thomas Jefferson lived within a two-day ride of John Lincoln along the road passing through the intervening Blue Ridge Mountains.

John Lincoln and Peter Jefferson were carried along by the tide of farmers moving to the frontier in the mid-eighteenth century. The population was booming and land prices were skyrocketing. As the French and Indian War came to an end in the 1760s, multitudes were on the move in search of fresh, cheap land. Virginians were claiming land in southeastern Pennsylvania under Virginia titles. Connecticut people were swarming on to Vermont lands claimed jointly by New Hampshire and New York. These were the explosive years when settled areas were bulging, and people took risks with shaky titles and threats of Indians along the frontier. John Lincoln and Peter Jefferson were part of the swelling mass of migrants in search of land.

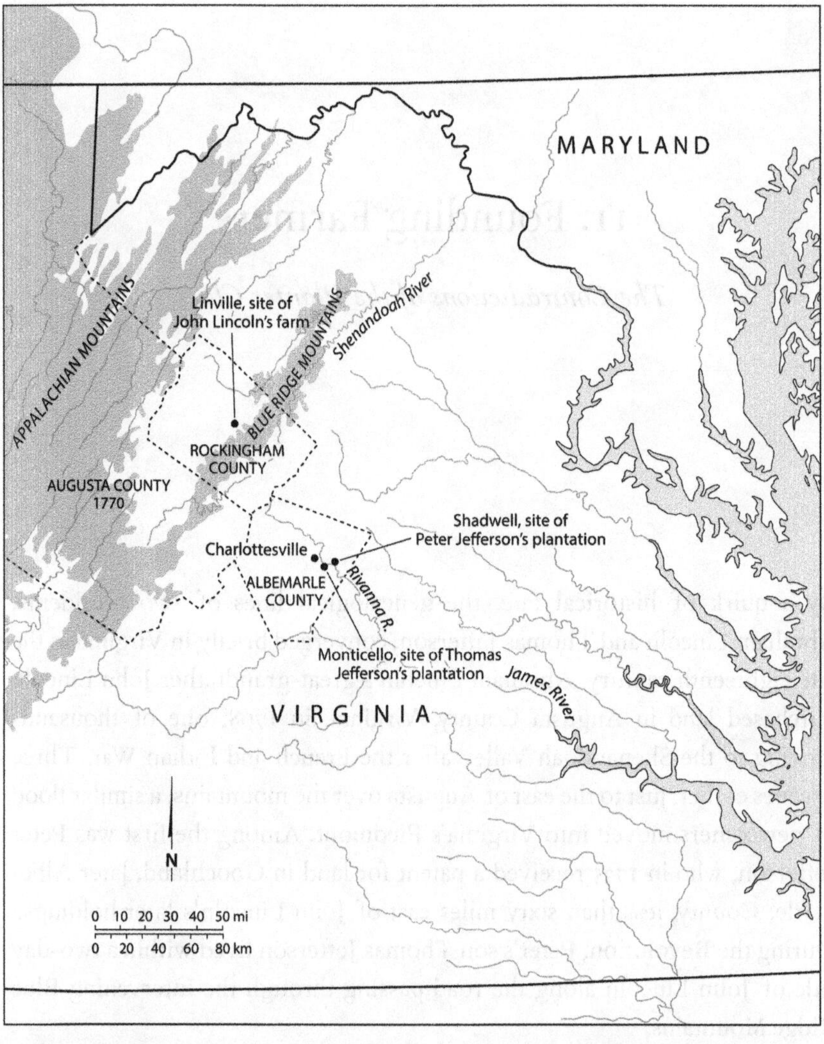

Figure 11.1 Farm of John Lincoln and plantations of Peter Jefferson and Thomas Jefferson.

While both saw expanded opportunities at the edges of settlement, they followed widely divergent paths. One family, always scrambling to provide for the next generation, was generally prosperous but never wealthy. The other family rose steadily to ever greater heights of wealth and power. Both families were ambitious and capable but came to occupy different stations in life. The Lincolns, as we have seen, expended their energies moving horizontally in space and achieved at best middle-class respectability. The Jeffersons moved upward in every way—socially, economically, politically, culturally. Peter Jefferson provided large plantations for his two sons and an education for Thomas that made him one of the most accomplished men of his generation.

How was it that the Jeffersons so far exceeded the Lincolns? Do tobacco and slaves alone account for their rise? Were the Jeffersons more astute or more lucky? Did they adopt a more propitious farm culture? In the nineteenth century, the fortunes of the Lincolns and the Jeffersons took strange twists. Thomas Lincoln descended into rural poverty, but his son Abraham became president. Peter Jefferson's son Thomas became president but died bankrupt. How could it be that one so favored as Thomas Jefferson ultimately failed as a farmer and at his death lost his estate?

The Lincolns and the Jeffersons

The Lincolns and the Jeffersons began their American sojourns at about the same level. The first Jefferson in America, another Thomas, was at first no more eminent than Samuel Lincoln of Hingham, Massachusetts. This first Thomas Jefferson's English ancestry has never been reconstructed, one sign that his lineage was not particularly distinguished. He squatted on the land he worked until he purchased it from William Byrd I in 1679; his wife could not sign her own name. He seems to have moved ahead modestly from there, serving on a jury and as surveyor of highways, like other middling planters. By the time of his death in 1698, he owned several slaves.[2]

The gradual rise of the Jeffersons continued in the second generation. The first Thomas boosted the second Thomas just far enough for him to marry well. His wife was the granddaughter of the speaker of the House of Burgesses. Thomas II was appointed justice of the peace, a sign of public trust. By then the Tidewater and much of the Piedmont had been cleared of natives, opening new land for settlement. After two massive Indian attacks in 1622 and 1644, the English had waged wars of extermination. The natives who remained after these campaigns dwelled on small reservations, much like the sequestered Mohegan land near Norwich, Connecticut. As in the North, Virginia claimed onetime Indian lands by right of conquest. These acquisitions supplied the government with ample land to distribute to settlers.[3] In 1718, Thomas II received fifteen hundred acres on Fine Creek south of the James River in the expectation that he would help develop the frontier area.

Then Thomas II suffered a reversal of fortunes. After suffering from a fire late in life, he seems to have been forced to liquidate some of his holdings; he appealed to the assembly for succor as if he were desperate. When he was unable to satisfy a debt of 6,480 pounds of tobacco, his property was attached. Neither of his surviving sons, Peter and Field, lived on his father's home plantation. A third brother, Thomas, died at sea at age twenty-three.[4]

Thomas left Peter Jefferson two slaves, the Fine Creek land, and something more valuable still: gentry standing. Exactly how he acquired the trust and respect of the rising cadre of Virginia gentlemen remains unclear, but Peter enjoyed the privileges commonly afforded the Virginia elite. In 1734, when he was twenty-six, he was appointed justice of the peace, and three years later he was named sheriff. Peter married the daughter of Isham Randolph, a ship captain and member of the most distinguished clan in the colony. His wife's dowry consisted of two hundred pounds sterling. She brought him no land, but Peter had access to land by dint of his position in society.[5]

He acquired part of the land by importing persons into the colony under the long-standing head right system of fifty acres per imported person. In addition to head rights, Peter Jefferson, along with hundreds of others, received outright grants. These apparent gifts had the appearance of pure favoritism; influential men received rights to tens of thousands of acres on the basis of their standing in society. Actually, they were beneficiaries of a long tradition that grew out of Elizabethan practices. In hierarchical society, rulers believed that the best way to accomplish a project was to entrust it to leading men. Great men received royal charters and large patents in the belief that they could turn them into fruitful colonies. The English followed this system in settling Ireland, as they did early New Hampshire, Maine, Pennsylvania, Maryland, and the Carolinas. Before the first Virginia Company was dissolved in 1624, it granted "particular plantations," probably averaging about five thousand acres each, to individuals or companies that brought over a hundred settlers. Although not all were taken up, the colony issued seventy patents. Virginia's eighteenth-century land system carried on in this tradition.[6]

No one questioned the basic assumption that reliance on leading men was the best way to open settlements. The crown was quite willing to dispense land "according to the merits and qualifications of the person." William Gooch, who governed with unusual success from 1727 to 1749, pointed to the good results in areas where "the greatest tracts have been granted and possessed, and thereby given encouragement to the meaner sort of people to seat themselves as it were under the shade and protection of the greater."[7] To rank among "the greater," an ambitious planter needed only to acquire a reputation for competence and character that would bring him into the ranks of the colonial gentry. Honorable parents and education helped, but practical abilities as a surveyor or military leader served as well. Peter Jefferson's stock went up when he completed the torturous survey of the western boundary of the Fairfax's Northern Neck and produced an accurate map of the Virginia backcountry. He could confidently apply for thousands of acres in the knowledge that he was numbered among the colony's elite.

The Governor's Council began granting tracts in western Goochland County in the area that was to become Albemarle in 1727. The Treaty of Albany in 1722 had prohibited members of the Five Nations from passing south of the Potomac to visit tributary tribes in Virginia, reducing the fear of Indian harassment that had previously inhibited settlement. This final touch unleashed a flood of applications for patents in the western regions. The first grant in western Goochland was for 3,100 acres, followed by a massive grant of 13,762 acres. From then until 1744, when Albemarle was separated from Goochland, the Council issued 191 patents, 46 of them for more than 1,000 acres, many more of around 400 acres.[8] Peter Jefferson, now identified as a person with the qualifications, located 1,000 acres on the Rivanna River in 1734, five years before his marriage. The next year he received a patent for this tract and added to it by purchasing another 400 acres from his boyhood friend William Randolph, his wife's cousin. Eventually he acquired more than 2,500 acres. Peter was one of the first settlers on the Rivanna and quite naturally was appointed a justice of the peace and judge of the court of chancery when Albemarle County was separated from Goochland. A year later he was a lieutenant colonel, second in command of military forces in the county.[9]

Still not sated, Peter petitioned the council for additional grants to the point of exasperation. On May 5, 1741, the Council granted him and others 37,000 acres in Brunswick County. When he went back for more, the Council ruled that "The Pet[itio]n of Peter Jefferson & others for 40,000 Acres in Goochland on Black water Creek is rejected as being judged too great a grant to what is already granted the Pet[ition]ers."[10] Meanwhile, he turned the Rivanna properties at Shadwell into productive plantations. At the behest of his friend William Randolph, Peter moved his family to a Randolph plantation, Tuckahoe, to help raise William's children after he died, but after a half dozen years, Peter returned to Albemarle to make Shadwell home for the rest of his life.

Peter's land had a potential beyond anything available to the Lincolns in either Hingham or Pennsylvania. In Massachusetts, owners of large tracts had few choices other than to sell the land. They lacked the labor force to clear land and put it to work. In the South, besides profiting from land sales, great proprietors could work the land themselves—thanks to the availability of bound labor. The author of *American Husbandry* calculated that Virginia and Maryland planters were in a position to earn 13–15 percent on their investment by growing tobacco with slave labor.[11] Planters like Washington and Jefferson set up "quarters" wherever they came into possession of land and worked their property with slaves. In the early seventeenth century, when planters relied on small contingents of indentured servants for labor, grants to private individuals were small—hundreds of acres rather than thousands. Between 1626 and 1632 the largest grant was 1,000 acres, and the average ranged from 100 to 300. Once slavery was established at the beginning of the eighteenth century, 10,000-acre grants were not uncommon. Planters could multiply their wealth by acquiring land and multiplying their workforce.[12] This advantage propelled the Jeffersons ahead of the Lincolns. Easy access to land via gentry status, coupled with the feasibility of slavery, enabled Virginia planters to rise to the heights of a Jefferson or Washington, far above anything the Lincolns could aspire to.

Peter Jefferson did not have sons to provide for when he built the first house on his property in Goochland in 1737. He was thirty and not yet married but looking ahead. He was to take his wife, Jane Randolph, and their two daughters to Shadwell in 1741 in time for the birth of their first son, Thomas, in 1743. Peter's holding on the Rivanna River, the north branch of the James, was large enough to eventually support four plantations, a good start for his male heirs. Over the next dozen years, Jane was to bear three more sons and four more daughters. Of the boys, only Thomas and Randolph survived infancy, and by the time of Peter's death in 1757 there was more than enough for these two. Peter acquired another estate on the Fluvanna River, the south fork of the James, fully as large as his plantations on the Rivanna. Peter's will allowed Thomas to choose between the two, and he selected the 2,650 acres bordering the Rivanna.[13]

Peter Jefferson's sons aspired to a life beyond the ken of John Lincoln's boys and a step above their father's. Early in Peter's life, the title "Gent." appeared beside his name, but though he was a skilled surveyor, an expert mapmaker, an entrepreneur, and a civic and military leader, he was not polished. He was securely located among middling gentlemen, well below the likes of William Byrd II at Westover, in his mansion stocked with books and walnut furniture. Peter's story-and-a-half frame house at Shadwell had four rooms downstairs with a hall down the middle. His library contained nearly a hundred books, but nothing like the collection his bibliophile son would accumulate.[14] Thomas Jefferson was the one to seize the cultural acquisitions that his father Peter was just beginning to achieve. Thomas could think of himself as a provincial version of the English gentry, in a class with the sugar planters of the Caribbean or the rice growers of the Carolinas. He played the violin, learned to dance from a dancing master, attended college, studied the classics, and when he finished his law studies and returned to take over the Rivanna plantations in 1768, immediately began construction of a mansion. He chose a site on a hilltop, impractical for a farmhouse because the wells ran dry in the summer and water had to be hauled up the hill, but valued for its view.[15] He was among the most cosmopolitan Americans of his generation, the logical outcome of his father's ambitions. When John Lincoln's son Abraham, the president's grandfather, was shot by Indians in Kentucky in 1785, Thomas Jefferson was living in Paris as the United States minister to France.

The Washingtons

From age nine until nineteen, Thomas Jefferson spent a good part of the year away from Shadwell, first studying the classics with the Rev. William Douglass and the Rev. James Maury, then attending William and Mary College for two years from 1760 to 1762. After he began to read law with George Wythe, he returned home for much of the year, but labored under a study regimen that kept him at his books most of the time. Not until 1767 did he end his studies and begin his life as a lawyer and planter. Shadwell became his full-time residence until 1770, when a fire forced Jefferson into a premature move to Monticello, then rising on a hill just south of the Rivanna River. From this commanding site, he directed work on his various plantations on both sides of the river.

Until he was fifty or so, Jefferson's interest in day-to-day farm management was spotty in contrast to that of George Washington, who wrote his farm manager virtually every week, even while commanding the army or presiding over the nation.[16] Jefferson rarely sent instructions or asked questions.[17] His unacknowledged slave son, Madison Hemings, remembered that "unlike Washington he had but little taste or care for agricultural pursuits. He left matters pertaining to his plantations mostly with his stewards and overseers." Jefferson showed an interest mainly in the general state of things: "I will thank you if in all your letters you will be so good as to give me a particular account of the seasonableness of the weather and the state and prospect of crops of wheat, corn and tobacco as these things are very interesting."[18] George Washington and Landon Carter kept detailed daily diaries of their farm practices: the weather, the work of the day, the seeds used, plowing, seeding, hoeing, the manuring of fields. Their logs were active attempts to figure out what worked and to keep on top of the crop cycle. Jefferson kept such a diary for only two years, 1795 and 1796. Even then his entries were thin. The amount Jefferson recorded for the entire year of 1796 was less than Washington regularly recorded for a month.[19]

Washington switched from surveying and the army to farming in 1752, when his half-brother Lawrence died of tuberculosis without a leaving a son or daughter, and Washington by terms of his father's will came into the property. The Washingtons had followed pretty much the same path in Virginia as the Jeffersons, but started earlier and rose higher. The first Washington arrived in Virginia in 1657 as mate and partner in a ketch, the *Sea Horse of London*. When the ship ran aground and sank during a storm with a full cargo aboard, John Washington helped salvage the tobacco. Attracted to a young woman, he bargained with the vessel's master to remain in Virginia when the ketch sailed for England. John Washington must have been an appealing figure because in a society where women were at a premium, Anne's father Nathaniel Pope gave Washington seven hundred acres and lent him eighty pounds to begin life in the colony. On his own, John began accumulating property, some by head rights, some by purchase, and a great deal by grants from the governor, acquiring in all more than five thousand acres. He also began acquiring the offices that came inevitably to men of his class. He was the son of an Oxford-educated English clergyman and had been schooled himself. In Virginia, he began as coroner and county justice and ended as colonel of the militia and member of the House of Burgesses.[20]

For the next three generations, the Washingtons were stayers, like the Hingham Lincolns who remained in Massachusetts when Abraham Lincoln's direct ancestor left for New Jersey and Pennsylvania. Succeeding generations of Washingtons came to maturity in a dense matrix of cousins, uncles, and aunts, reaping the benefits of familiarity and connection just as the Massachusetts Lincolns did. The Washingtons acquired land and office, built mansions, and assumed the prerogatives of a classic elite. John Washington's eldest son Lawrence (b. 1659) went to England for schooling and on his return was appointed a justice of the peace at age twenty-one and elected to the House of Burgesses when he was twenty-five. At age twenty-seven he married the daughter of the speaker of the House of Burgesses, who was also a member of the governor's council. Lawrence was less ambitious than his father about land acquisitions. He apparently added only 400 acres or so to his inheritance. But he educated his two sons, John and Augustine, in England, as he had been educated, and left them each more than 1,000 acres. Augustine (b. 1695), George Washington's father, had 1,740 acres to work with by the time he married Jane Butler in 1715 or 1716.[21]

Augustine was more ambitious than his father. He came of age during the period of extravagant land acquisitions following the 1722 Treaty of Albany with the Five Nations, the opening of the Shenandoah Valley, and the confirmation of the Fairfaxes' control of the Northern Neck's backlands. Augustine did not look west, as Peter Jefferson did. Instead, he added to the lands along the Potomac acquired by the first John while purchasing tracts elsewhere in the Tidewater. By the time of his death in 1743, Augustine owned more than 10,000 acres and an ironworks. Each of his six living sons received substantial properties, though the bulk went to the eldest son Lawrence. George's share was the 260-acre Ferry Farm opposite Fredericksburg on the Rappahannock, where Augustine had moved his family in 1738 to be near his ironworks. The will contained complicated provisions about the devolution of his bequests in case his heirs died before bearing children, not an unlikely event in death-ridden Virginia. If the eldest son Lawrence died young, for example, Lawrence's half-brother George by Augustine's second wife, Mary Ball, was to receive Lawrence's land at Little Hunting Creek on the Potomac—unless George's full brother Augustine preferred Little Hunting Creek to Mattox Creek, another of Lawrence's inherited properties. With many twists and turns, the will strove to take into account unpredictable contingencies while respecting the privileges of birth order.[22]

At age twenty-two, Lawrence was selected by the colony as one of the four Virginia commanders sent to assist Adm. Edward Vernon in the assault on the Colombian stronghold at Cartagena in 1740/41. He survived the fruitless battle but not the tuberculosis that afflicted him soon after. After years of trying for a cure, he died in 1752. Given a choice by their father's will, George's brother Augustine selected Lawrence's land at Mattox Creek, and George received the property at Little Hunting Creek, which Lawrence had named Mount Vernon in honor of his commander at Cartagena.[23]

For eight years, George leased the land from Lawrence's widow, Anne Fairfax, until at her death in 1759 Mount Vernon came to him. From then on, Washington applied himself to planting, buying more land, and learning husbandry. Like Jefferson, he also worked on his house. He enlarged Mount Vernon from a story and a half to two and a half stories in 1758–59 and later built additional wings, improving it by stages until the very end of his life. To bring himself up to date on the latest methods, he ordered books on agriculture, including Jethro Tull's *The Horse-Hoeing Husbandry* (1751), whose recommendations Washington copied into his diary and put into practice in the fields at Mount Vernon. War and politics took him away for eight years during the Revolution, and the presidency for another eight from 1789 to 1797, but his mind was on his farm even from a distance. When he was at Mount Vernon he rode the twenty-mile circuit to each of his six plantations every day and came home to record what he had said and done. When away, he received nearly weekly reports from his farm managers and sent them detailed instructions in reply.[24]

Farm Thought

Washington was doubtless more conscientious about tending his farm than most. He was impatient with overseers who stayed at home rather than going to the fields with the hands each day.[25] He seems to have been an experimentalist by nature. In 1760 he tested various composts to see which yielded the strongest wheat, oats, and barley shoots, and he kept up such trials to the end of his life. He was forever experimenting with seeds sent from friends abroad.[26] One year he planted seeds from China, carefully noting their Chinese names and exactly where he planted them so as to compare their growth.[27] Using the same method, he sowed clover, lucerne, and rye grass "to try their Goodness."[28] His prolific correspondence and farm diaries reveal an energetic agricultural mind at work.

Though Washington was doubtless more active and entrepreneurial than most, his instructions to Anthony Whiting, his farm manager at Mount Vernon, offer clues to how Virginia farmers thought. The workings of his mind come through in the simplest comment, such as Washington's response to Whiting's report of an offer to rent the Potomac landing where Washington netted fish to feed his workers. "Your letter of the 9th came to my hands last night, and though I am much hurried, will briefly observe, that I had rather repair my Seins, and fish myself, than hire the landing with the Negros. If a good price could be obtained for the Landing without the Negros, and an express prohibition of Waggons coming thither, I should like, & would prefer that. But at any rate repair, & keep the Seins dry and out of the way of Mice."[29]

Apparently, Washington's seines had fallen into disrepair, and to take advantage of the landing would require work. Someone wanted to rent the landing, repair the seines, and hire Washington's slaves to collect the fish. Washington had to decide whether he could spare the workers and risk them to someone else's supervision. He decided not to let the slaves and to repair the seines himself. Then he adds a precaution to "keep the Seins dry and out of the way of mice." Stored in his mind was a memory of mice having caused the breakage by gnawing at the netting. A little matter like gnawing mice had undermined his whole fishing operation and denied him a valuable food source for his slaves. Information of that order, multiplied thousands of times, constituted the farmer's most important asset, his encyclopedic knowledge.

It was dynamic knowledge, never fixed or final. Every bit of it was subject to modification by experience. Every year brought a series of small experiments. Hauling in herring from his landing one day in April, Washington noted: "Hauld the Sein but without Success. Some said it was owing to the wind setting of the Shore, which seems in some Measure confirmd by the quantity we catchd Yesterday when the Wind blew on upon it." Washington wondered whether the wind in effect blew the fish toward his seines along the shore. Keeping that observation in mind, he kept an eye out the next day. "My Negroes askd the lent of the Sein to day but caught little or no Fish. Note the Wind blew upon the shore to day." The hypothesis about wind driving fish to the shore was stored away one day and the next met a contrary observation. Even then the wind hypothesis could not be totally discarded until tested by multiple observations down through the years.

None of this knowledge ever attained mathematical certainty. Farmers' minds were stocked with thousands of contingent items about places and things and processes, all of it subject to reexamination and reevaluation. Though always tenuous, this great store of experiential knowledge eventually gave them judgment. Washington accumulated thousands of pieces of tested information on which he based his decisions each day.[30]

Much of that information was organized into a four-dimensional map in his head. In the same month he wrote to Whiting about the landing, Washington sent directions for clearing land that had once been devoted to corn and putting it in grass and trees.

> I shall again express my wish, and, as the raising of corn at the Mansion-House is given up, will also add [*sic*] my anxiety, to have all the ground (except single trees and clumps here and there) cleared, and well cleared, as mentioned in a former letter, between the old clover lot and the sunken ground quite from the wharf to Richard's house and the gate; but, previously, do what has been desired from the cross fence by the spring, to the wharf. In clearing the whole of this ground, let all the ivy and flowering trees and shrubs remain on it, over and above the clumps, and other single trees where they may be thought requisite, for ornament. The present growing pines within that enclosure might be thinned, and brought more into form. When this is done, and all the low land from the river up to the gate laid down in grass, it will add much to the appearance of the place, and be a real benefit and convenience, as it will yield an abundance of grass.[31]

Although far distant from Mount Vernon at the time, Washington had engraved in his mind detailed information about the slope of the land, the markers, the structures, and the vegetation on this one plot. His mental map was much more complicated than any survey he might draw. There were fixed markers on this plat, like "the wharf to Richard's house and the gate" and the spring, information that could be plotted on a map. But these bounded places not only had dimensions, they were populated with grass, corn, flowering trees, ivy (probably mountain laurel), shrubs, pines, clover. Washington came close to having a plant-by-plant image of the land.

In addition to vegetation, the map had a time dimension. Calling a piece of land "the old clover lot" gave it a history. Washington had in mind what the property had once been—a lot seeded in clover—along with what it was now. Moreover, he saw it, as all gardeners and farmers must, for what it would be. His comment that planting the low land from the river up to the gate in grass "will add much to the appearance of the place" envisions the plot's future. As he rode about his property, Washington saw each plot as it once was and perhaps even more vividly as he was willing it to become. Anywhere he stopped, he stood between the past and a future that he was wresting from nature.

His mind had to encompass not only one future but many. In every field every year, multiple possibilities lay latent. Should this field be plowed or left fallow? Should grass be laid down or can it bear another planting of wheat? As an experimentalist and investigator, Washington saw more possibilities than most. In Philadelphia, he met a Mr. Lambert who believed in keeping fallow land plowed rather than letting it run to rubbish.[32] Washington listened to Lambert because he seemed an experienced "sensible man." Washington was not persuaded sufficiently to practice naked fallow, but neither was the idea so trivial that it could be discarded. He stored the notion along with many others in a tentative file that held alternate prospects for his land. He mapped not just one future but many. His land was a chessboard on which he was forever plotting his next move.

Rational Agriculture

After his resignation as commander in chief in December 1783, when he once again threw himself into farming, Washington ordered copies of Arthur Young's volumes on farming. Like other planters of his class, he was in touch with the progressive farm reforms then gaining momentum in England. He was in the mood to heed the reformers because of his own discontent with Virginia's methods. In their first exchange in 1786, Washington had told Young: "The system of Agriculture (if the epithet of system can be applied to it) which is in use in this part of the United States, is as unproductive to the practitioners as it is ruinous to the landholders."[33] By system, he meant the practice of opening new land, wearing it down with crops for five or six years, and then leaving it alone for twenty years while a new plot was cleared and worked. He was sure the planters were destroying the soil by overworking it and allowing erosion to gully the surfaces, and he knew enough about agricultural reform to realize that guidance was to be found in England.[34]

While Washington was looking to England, Young was curious about the United States. He was contemplating a move to America and was hungry for information about the profits to be made. He sent a set of inquiries to Washington about land prices, labor costs, and the value of American products in the market. His aim was to work up a series of calculations concerning the return on investment. Washington relayed Young's inquiries to a half dozen American correspondents, including Jefferson, who could write with authority about Virginia's Piedmont.[35]

Young's inquiry puzzled Jefferson. Young wanted to know about the return on capital investment, and Jefferson was of little help. "I had never before thought of calculating what were the profits of a capital invested in Virginia agriculture," Jefferson wrote Washington, "yet that appeared to be what mister Young most desired."[36] The two Virginians were certainly calculating agriculturalists. They conducted experiments, invented farm equipment, maximized labor, but calculating a return on investment never occurred to them. Young in turn was amazed that so obvious an inquiry had never been made. "Is it possible that the inhabitants of a great continent[,] not new settlers who of course live only to hunt, to eat and to drink[,] can carry on farming and planting as a business and yet never calculate the profit they make by *percentage* on their capital?"[37] It seemed to him that American planters, like any other businessman, would naturally calculate return on investment.

The exchange gives an idea of how far American and British farming had diverged. The agricultural revolution had infused English farmers with a capitalist mentality that judged success in much the same way a button manufacturer would: by return on investment. The family mentality still prevailed in America, even among the wealthiest planters. The planters' aim was to sustain their establishments for themselves and their descendants. They wanted to pay their debts, speculate in land, purchase more slaves, erect worthy houses, live well, and provide for their offspring, but not to maximize their returns compared with alternate investments.[38] To be a planter was the highest form of life in Virginia society, the best they could imagine for themselves and their children. To sell out and abandon a plantation for a more profitable pursuit would defeat the very purpose of economic endeavor. Planters were interested in flourishing on their farms, not in maximizing profit.

Young was equally perplexed by the neglect of manure. He could not credit Jefferson's account of Piedmont agriculture. The reported yields and the returns were far better than Young believed possible. He had been informed by Washington and others of American farmers' heedless exhaustion of the soil, and Jefferson's rosy picture clashed with what Young had heard. Young doubted Jefferson's figures on wheat yields in the Piedmont because of the small number of animals on the plantation. "How can Mr Jefferson produce anually 5000 bush. of wheat worth £750 by means of a cattle product of only £125? I do not want to come to America to know that this is simply impossible."[39] Young believed that cattle were essential to the production of dung and to the cycling of land from tillage to grass. Nor could he believe the yields could be kept up without more sheep to renew the soil.

In the face of Young's skepticism, Jefferson did not back down.[40] English lands had been worked for centuries and had to be continually renewed with manures and clovers. The fresh land still available in Virginia altered agricultural reasoning. "Mr. Young must not pronounce too hastily on the impossibility of an annual production of £750. worth of wheat coupled with a cattle product of £125," Jefferson insisted. "Mr. Young has never had an opportunity of seeing how slowly the fertility of the *original soil* is exhausted, with moderate management of it. I can affirm that the James river low grounds with the cultivation of small grain will never be exhausted: because we know that under that cultivation we must now and then take them down with Indian corn, or they become, as they were originally, too rich to bring wheat."[41]

Jefferson admitted that he based his estimates on plantation agriculture at its best. "My object was to state the produce of a *good* farm, under *good* husbandry as practised in my part of the country." But by putting forward the colony's best, Jefferson rather brashly promoted Virginia methods against the wisdom of England's leading agricultural reformer. "*Good* husbandry with us consists in abandoning Indian corn, and tobacco, tending small grain, some red clover, fallowing, and endeavoring to have, while the lands are at rest, a spontaneous cover of white clover."[42] In Jefferson's mind, tobacco was the villain and clover the hero. Switching to wheat was one way to stop soil exhaustion, and interspersing clover between wheat crops doubled the effect. By claiming that good yields could be achieved without manure, Jefferson politely challenged the central dogma of the English reformers.

Washington held himself above the fray during this exchange and simply passed along the reports and the queries to the parties involved, but by the 1790s he had largely come around to the reformers' view. Something had to be done to refresh the fields. To crop them too hard, he told his farm manager, "is like pushing a horse that has a long race to perform to his full speed at first; the result of which must be, that he will grow slower and slower every round he takes, until he is unable to move."[43]

Washington kept searching for sources of manure. He dug up mud from the bottom of the Potomac to spread on his fields and noted discoveries of calcium-rich marl. As early as 1760, he was experimenting with various fertilizers. He dug marl, cow dung, and mud from the marshes, shoreline, and river, put them into pots, and planted oats to test the efficacy of each soil. He constructed a "stercorary" for storing dung.[44] Along with all the progressive farmers in the Chesapeake at midcentury, Washington harvested hay to feed his cattle through the winter rather than letting them half starve in the woods or in pasture, the traditional Virginia way. That enabled him to collect dung through the coldest months. After all his experiments, however, Washington, like Jefferson, in the end felt that his best hope was rotation.[45]

Although he had sparred with Arthur Young via Washington, Jefferson was ready for rational agriculture as he took up farming in earnest in 1793.[46] For the next three years before his election as vice president necessitated a return to Philadelphia, he threw himself into farmwork. The basic thrust of agricultural reform appealed to his deepest nature. He loved the application of reason to practices long governed by tradition. Reform agriculture had the added advantage of being an occasion for writing notable figures on both sides of the Atlantic, Jefferson's forte. He relished opportunities to address a distant figure on some aspect of the public good. He wrote George Logan in Philadelphia, Lafayette, Charles Willson Peale, James Madison, E. I. Du Pont, Robert Fulton, and a variety of other less notable names. Although he limited his practical involvement, he was pleased to be named an associate of the London Board of Agriculture in 1798 and a member of the Agricultural Society of Paris in 1808.[47]

Rational agriculture in this period was an extension of the traditional farmer's reliance on scattered bits of knowledge collected over a lifetime. Jefferson's excursion into reform involved collecting and systematizing information. One large segment of Jefferson's farm book consisted of pages and pages of individual topics related to farm production—threshing machines, granaries, houses for laborers, roads, fences, timber, horses, mules, oxen, cattle, sheep, goats, hogs, and on and on. Under each category he recorded tidbits of knowledge: Under "Hogs," for example, he entered: "keep a breeding sow to every 2. Laborers," and "a hog of a year old takes 1. Barrel of corn to fatten him. he will weigh 100. lb. he eats a bushel of corn a week while fattening." Under "Fallow": "Young's experiments shew that ploughing in fall gives from one to three bushels per acre produce more than ploughing in the spring."

Farming required a huge stock of specific knowledge, and Jefferson did his best to acquire it wherever he could, often noting the source: "Ronconi. Voce 'Medica,'" or simply "A. Cary." Occasional entries were credited to "Logan," most likely George Logan, a Philadelphian farming expert. Much of the information probably came from Jefferson's own experience on his Rivanna plantations.[48] For Jefferson, the rationalization of agriculture involved the collection of facts followed by categorization, much like botanists who collected specimens and then divided them into varieties and species. Practical farmers collected this kind of information instinctively; Jefferson verbalized it and wrote it down. His study of agriculture was book learning twice over. He gathered information from books, and then wrote what he learned in a book to stabilize the knowledge and make it his own. The farm book was the mediator between Jefferson's experience, his reading, and his practice. The end result of Jefferson's studies was an embryonic encyclopedia of agriculture.

Jefferson's design of a plow moldboard called for another and more satisfying form of ratiocination. He had conceived the idea while touring northeast France in 1788 and roughed out plans, including a sketch, among his notes on the region. Most plows at the time had no moldboards because they added resistance and required more pull.[49] Jefferson aimed to design a board that would lift the sod upward after it had been cut by the share (the horizontal knife cutting below the surface) and turn the soil over without causing too much drag. He wanted, as he said, "a mouldboard of least resistance." The next year Jefferson revealed what mattered most about his invention in a letter to John Taylor: "I have imagined and executed a mould-board which may be mathematically demonstrated to be perfect, as far as perfection depends on mathematical principles." Doubtless at Jefferson's request, the eminent Philadelphia mathematician David Rittenhouse declared that it was mathematically demonstrable that the moldboard offered the least possible resistance.[50]

Washington's attempts at plow improvement were carried on with much less fanfare. On March 26, 1760, he noted in his diary, "spent the greatest part of the day in making a new plow of my own Invention." The next day he reported "Sat my Plow to work and found She Answerd very well in the Field in the lower Pasture."[51] Jefferson's plow also proved to have practical value. When he tried the moldboard at Monticello in 1795, it met his expectations. By 1810 he was using five of the plows in his own fields. But Jefferson was conducting a scientific experiment as well as improving a farm implement. To prove his point, he looked for "one of those instruments used in England for measuring the force exerted in the drafts of different plows." He wanted measured confirmation of his plow's low resistance. In 1810 Robert Fulton lent him a force gauge, and he put his plow to the test.[52]

The experimenting, measuring, rationalizing impulse carried over into everything on the plantation. To figure out how much plowing cost him, Jefferson estimated every expense: the plowman's annual hire (ten pounds), his clothes (two pounds), food (three pounds, eight shillings), tools (one pound), supervision (two pounds). Then he divided the total (eighteen pounds, eight shillings) by three hundred days to arrive at the cost of plowing: one shilling, threepence a day. From there he went on to the annual cost of the horse—its corn, fodder, and pasture—multiplied by six, the work life of a horse, plus the initial cost (fifteen pounds) and three years' interest on this expenditure (two pounds, five shillings). Finally, he arrived at the figure he wanted, the cost of a horse for one day's work plowing: one shilling, eight-pence. When he looked over his fields, Jefferson saw pounds and shilling. He was by nature a cost accountant. He wanted to attach a price to every movement of the plow, every step of the harvest, every aspect of turning corn into meal. Precise information about costs gave Jefferson the sense he was farming rationally.[53]

Debt

Jefferson was concerned about costs for the same reason he was interested in yields. He was heavily in debt, and the best way to make payments was to maximize production and minimize costs. The only alternative was to sell land or slaves, which he was extremely reluctant to do. The creditors' constant demands kept him focused on the bottom line.[54]

He accumulated debts to English merchant houses in the way common to all the planters: every purchase of furniture or fabric from England incurred an obligation to be paid in future years with tobacco or wheat shipments. When the crop was "short," the planter fell behind, and debt began to pile up. In addition, Jefferson had inherited the debts of his father-in-law, John Wayles, whose huge estate valued at thirty thousand pounds was encumbered with obligations, primarily eleven thousand pounds owed to the Bristol partnership of Farrell and Jones, which over the years Wayles had incurred in the usual fashion and never repaid. When Wayles died in 1773, Jefferson and the other two heirs, husbands of his wife's sisters, had to devote virtually all the returns from Wayles's properties to satisfying his creditors, especially Farrell and Jones.[55]

Jefferson's anguished negotiations with his creditors over the next fifty years and his ultimate failure to avoid bankruptcy exemplified the treacherous ground on which planters walked. Despite a generous income from his government posts, Jefferson could not elude his creditors. The state of planter credit became evident in Jefferson's first attempt at repayment. Much as he disliked selling property, he did dispose of a portion of the Wayles estate in 1774 for forty-two hundred pounds, with the intention of using the proceeds to satisfy Farrell and Jones. To his dismay, the firm's representative, knowing the perilous financial condition of Virginia's planters, refused the bonds given to Jefferson by the purchaser as payment.[56] The firm did not trust the purchaser's credit. Although planters produced hundreds of hogsheads of tobacco each year, they were so entangled in obligations to one another and to their English creditors that their ability to make payments on any given bond was always in doubt.

Washington ran into the same problem in collecting debts owed his wife's estate. English firms rejected a note for £100 from the largest debtor, Bernard Moore, as they did another for £194 on the estate of William Armistead. Washington complained to his English agents, the firm of Robert Cary, that his failure to pay was the result of "Mischances rather than Misconduct." How could he know that "the Debts which I thought I had collected, and actually did remit to you shoud be paid in Bills void of credit." English firms advanced credit to planters for the goods they ordered as a necessary condition of conducting business with farmers whose crops were harvested annually. But when it came to collecting a debt owed to a planter, as the purchasers owed Jefferson, the firms' trust ran out.[57]

Jefferson further suffered from a chance misfortune that affected many planters. The sale of land to satisfy the Wayles debt occurred on the eve of the Revolution. As the war got under way, state governments issued currency, as they always had done in wartime to finance soldiers' salaries and the purchase of supplies. Knowing that they risked rapid depreciation of the money's value, the legislatures required all parties within the state to accept the currency in payment of debts. This was a golden opportunity for debtors like Jefferson's purchasers to repay obligations that might otherwise have taken years to satisfy. Jefferson received a bushel of depreciated paper money in payment for the land he had sold in hopes of satisfying Farrell and Jones. But currency accepted within the state was useless for retiring his English debt. Farrell and Jones insisted on sterling or worthy bills of exchange. Jefferson's attempt to satisfy the Wayles creditors ended in disaster. He had lost the property and made no headway with the debt, defeated in large part by paper money.

Jefferson was deeply concerned to be thought of as an honorable debtor. Inability to pay debts, or worse, a reputation for defaulting on one's debt, was a condition he could not bear. The shame of not paying a debt was reflected in the word "embarrassment" as a common term for the inability to pay. "We are now therefore clear of embarassment to pursue our principal object," he wrote to William Jones.[58] He wished to avoid embarrassment at all costs. As Herbert Sloan has explained in his study of Jefferson's debt, "Jefferson was especially anxious to obtain his creditors' recognition that he was complying with the most stringent standards of virtue and morality." The agreements usually involved the creation of bonds for substantial amounts of the debt with interest on the principal. The agreements did not speed repayment but implied recognition by the creditor that Jefferson intended to repay. "Once the creditors accepted his position, it was then as though his debts were as good as paid, and he could rest easy."[59] His standing as a man of honor had been preserved.

Jefferson was insulted when he was dunned by an aggressive creditor who implied that Jefferson was not to be trusted. His letter, Jefferson told the creditor, was "mortifying to me. It was in a tone of complaint to which no action of my life has ever justly exposed me. I think I may say with truth that no man on earth has been readier to do every thing possible to discharge that debt, of a portion of which you are become the representative."[60] Creditors had to press their Virginia debtors with sensitivity and tact for fear of insulting them. Through the intricate negotiations, the debtor could never be made to feel he was acting dishonorably. It was not only the planters' economic viability that was at stake in debt management, but the honor that they valued as life itself. Jefferson's letters stressed his good intentions. "I am desirous of arranging with you, such just and practicable conditions as will ascertain to you the terms at which you will receive my part of your debt, and give me the satisfaction of knowing that you are contented. What the laws of Virginia are, or may be, will in no wise influence my conduct. Substantial justice is my object." He could not have borne being hauled into court and put on display as financially incompetent or remiss in keeping promises. An inability to reach an agreement with a particularly aggressive creditor caused him "torment of mind." "I am miserable till I shall owe not a shilling."[61]

Jefferson, and before him John Wayles, incurred the debt in the first place to sustain their places as gentlemen in Atlantic society. Jefferson went into debt to build Monticello, to furnish it, to entertain suitably, to clothe himself as a gentleman, to ride in a carriage. The necessities of genteel life, the fine horses, the china and silver, the books and prints, the mahogany furniture involved more and more debt. Jefferson understood this and advocated greater simplicity; he may even have consciously simplified his own clothing as a gesture toward frugality. He told his daughter Mary that "nothing can save us and our children from beggary but a determination to get a year beforehand, and restrain ourselves vigorously this year to the clear profits of the last."[62] But the demands of his position required him to continue his purchases. He had to maintain his personal appearance to support his standing as a gentleman.[63] Jefferson could not bring himself to stint on his house or his person. His style of living defined him as a gentleman, the core of his social identity. Gentleman status was his blessed privilege and a cursed burden. Clinging doggedly to the material embellishments of his social class drove him at last into bankruptcy.[64]

Like Jefferson, Washington started work on his house as soon as he took up farming at Mount Vernon. His order to Robert Cary and Co. for 1760 reveals how he expected to live. Among scores of items he asked for were:

1 Tester Bedstead 7½ feet pitch, with fashionable blew or blew and white Curtains.
1 Fashionable Sett of Desert Glasses, and Stands for Sweet Meats Jellys & ca[ke]
6 Carving knives and Forks—handles of Staind Ivory and bound with Silver
2 pair of fashionable mixd, or Marble Col[ore]d Silk Hose 6 pair of finest Cotton Ditto

Half a dozn pair of Men's neatest Shoes and Pumps
One neat Pocket Book, capable of receiving Memorandoms & small Cash
Accts to be made of Ivory[65]

The fortune that came with Martha Custis from her first marriage to Daniel Parke Custis entitled him to live at that level, but much to his dismay, after two years he discovered that his obligations on Cary's book were mounting at an alarming rate. He owed £1,871 on his own account and another £2,038 for his wife's estate. Knowing he must cut back, he tailored his order accordingly. He asked for no glass or fine fabric, although through another London merchant, he ordered a livery. In a telling comment about the balance he sought to maintain, Washington had told Robert Cary that he would pay off his debts "so fast as I coud make remittances without distressing myself too much."[66] When he spoke of distress, Washington was not talking about insufficient food or clothing; there was always plenty to eat. He meant dignity in keeping with his rank, which meant suits and uniforms, tables and chairs, chandeliers and tableware, carriages and horses. These were not vain indulgences; they were requirements second only to food on the table.[67]

For both men, everything was at stake in preserving their positions in Virginia society. Their privileges, including their access to land, depended on their standing. The second Thomas Jefferson and the first Lawrence Washington had elevated their families into the ranks of the privileged. Once they were considered gentlemen, land was virtually theirs for the asking. Both families were trusted with thousands of acres to be developed for the benefit of the crown and for their own gain. Their great estates, their access to public office, and the general respect afforded them all hinged on achieving and defending their status. At all costs, gentlemen had to live as gentlemen, exhibiting largesse, appearing liberal and free, stylish and polite.

Viewed from a distance, Virginia gentleman appear to have been ensnarled in an inescapable dilemma. To enjoy the privileges that came with their status, they had to live like gentlemen, but the costs of high living threatened to bring them down. Even those who adopted the best agricultural methods, as Washington and Jefferson did, and held off the ravages of erosion and soil exhaustion could not keep their creditors at bay. They were caught in a contradiction of their class. A Virginia matron advised one of Jefferson's grandsons to "live on bread and water" to avoid debt.[68] That was something planters could not do. They went on spending until debilitating debt left them hollow at the core. In the end, some like Jefferson succumbed to bankruptcy.[69]

Inheritance

Jefferson's embarrassment made it impossible to fulfill the obligations he had to his children. He died with debts of more than $100,000. A few months before his death in 1826, he had proposed a lottery for his benefit with his Albemarle County land as the prize. The Virginia assembly approved it, and his grandson Jeff Randolph went to New York, Boston, and Philadelphia to drum up interest. He hoped people would purchase tickets out of regard for their former president. But the scheme fell flat after Jefferson died. Over the next five or six years, Jeff Randolph gradually liquidated his grandfather's holdings without satisfying his creditors. Monticello, the most prized of his possessions and the hardest to relinquish, went for only $7,000.[70]

Washington had far more to offer his heirs than Thomas Jefferson. If at the end Jefferson faltered as a planter, Washington was the exemplar of success. In the last will and testament that Washington drew up in July 1799, he dismissed his debts in one line: "All my (deb)ts, of which there are but few, and none of magnitude, are to be punctu(al)ly and speedily paid." He is a reminder that not every Virginia plantation was sinking under the weight of debt. Washington did provide liberally for his heirs, though none received slaves. He set all his slaves on a path to freedom after the death of Martha. He gave generous bequests to five nephews and to Martha's two grandchildren, who were already richly endowed from the estate of her first husband. All the rest of his property was to be liquidated, the proceeds divided into twenty-three equal parts, and distributed around a larger family circle.[71]

Beneficent as the will was, it delivered a death blow to his plantation.[72] By dividing the land and releasing the slaves, he made it impossible for anyone to live on the estate as he had lived there. Washington apparently did not believe the plantation as he had managed it was viable.[73] As early as 1794, he was thinking of how to break it up. In 1796, he distributed advertisements to friends in the United States and England, offering to lease his Mount Vernon lands except for the central plantation. He hoped he could attract migrating Englishmen whose farming skills he trusted more than those of "the slovenly farmers of this country."[74] When that plan failed, he considered laying down grass on all his fields in order to "turn my farms to Grazing principally."[75] This would require him to sell most of his slaves, driving them from the land as England's enclosure movement drove out the peasants. Well before he died, Washington realized that something was wrong; Mount Vernon as he had known it must go. In his will, he voluntarily dismantled the monument he had spent a lifetime building.[76]

Years later Abraham Lincoln was to follow the course of his two predecessors. Like his ancestors, he might have gone west in search of new land, but impatient with the marginal existence of his father, he left farming altogether. He moved to town and turned to politics and the law. Even when he prospered, he made no effort to purchase land. Like the other two presidential families, Lincoln gave up farming. Their withdrawal did not signal a general breakdown in the farm economy—anything but. Family farming would govern the life plans of a majority of the nation until the end of the nineteenth century. But the fate of farming in these unusual instances suggests that there were weak points. Even with the nation's vast land reserves, even where great resources were available, even with the adoption of rational methods, farmers failed. Under the best of circumstances, the farm idea, for all its promise, did not always yield the security farmers dreamed of.

12. Jefferson's Neighbors

Economy, Society, and Politics in Post-Revolutionary Virginia

Compared with life in the other North American colonies, southern society was a land of extremes. At the top of the scale, the South was much wealthier than the North. The physical wealth of southern property holders in 1774, minus slaves, averaged 63 percent more than the wealth of property holders in New England and 46 percent more than in the Middle Colonies. If the value of slaves is added in, southern per capita wealth was more than twice that of the two northern regions.[1] The richest man to die in New England in 1774 was a Boston esquire with an estate of £15,303.2; the richest to die in the South in 1774 was a South Carolina esquire and planter worth £32,737.8. The others on the southern list were likewise men of great wealth. Only that single richest New England decedent, had he died in the South, would have been listed among the ten richest there. None of the Middle Colonies' ten richest would have made the southern list.[2] At the peak of society, southern agriculture sustained a style of life unknown in the North, even among the wealthiest urban merchants and gentleman.

At the other end of the social scale, the lowest orders of southern society appear to have been less prosperous than their northern counterparts. Although exact comparisons are hard to make, southern poor farmers lived less well, despite the beneficence of their climate. Gouverneur Morris contrasted the "rich & noble cultivation" in the middle states with "the misery & poverty which overspread the barren wastes of V[irgini]a Mary[lan]d &

the other States having slaves." Prejudiced as he was, Morris's impressions are borne out by the analysis of 1774 estate inventories in the South and Middle Colonies. The average net worth of the estates in the bottom two deciles in the population was 29 percent and 40 percent lower in the South than in the Middle Colonies.[3]

The extremes show up in the tax lists of Jefferson's Albemarle County. In November 1781, near the end of the American Revolution, the Virginia General Assembly levied a new tax in hopes of "establishing a permanent revenue."[4] Abbreviated and stylized as it was, the personal property tax list gives us a black-and-white snapshot of Virginia society at the end of the Revolutionary War. Thomas Jefferson's name stands out. He was taxed for 2 free males, 129 able-bodied slaves, 23 horses and mules, 106 head of cattle, and for the six wheels on his carriages. His total tax bill for goods and chattel was the second highest in the county. The highest tax was paid by Edward Carter, grandson of Robert "King" Carter, who inherited 9,350 acres from his father, John Carter, the colony secretary. John had patented Albemarle land in 1730 just when Peter Jefferson was accumulating property for his children. Edward Carter named his estate Blenheim after the duke of Marlborough's grand mansion and built a house sixty feet long. He owned 237 slaves, and his taxes were 80 percent higher than Jefferson's. The estate of another Carter grandson, Robert Carter Nicholas, who died in 1780, occupied the same heights with 120 slaves.[5] The three of them headed a dozen or so Albemarle County families who owned slaves in the scores, with horses and cattle to match, and claimed the county's leading offices in the militia and the government.

The tax numbers tailed off quickly from there. In Jefferson's tax district (one of eight in Albemarle County), 83 families owned slaves, but only 6 households out of 132 owned 20 or more. The median number was 5, which meant half of the slaveholders owned 1 to 5 slaves. They occupied the great middle range of white society in Albemarle. Since 63.5 percent of the county's property holders owned between 100 and 400 acres, the middle third of slave owners probably held land in that range. Above them were slave owners with numbers ascending from 6 to Edward Carter's 237. Below the middling farmers was the third of white households with no slaves. Albemarle white society in 1782 divided into thirds: one-third with 6 or more slaves, one-third with 1 to 5, and one-third with no slaves.[6] This lower third must have been the group that drew Gouverneur Morris's scorn for its misery and poverty.

This was the society that bore the burdens and strains of Revolution and the hard years that followed in the 1780s. It was a time of conflict over taxes, the draft, and currency, controversies that brought out hidden resentments and assignments of blame for social suffering. Could the elite leadership retain the loyalty and subservience of the lesser orders? All the ligaments that held together this society of extremes were tested and tried, yet the society did not fall apart. There was no outburst in Virginia comparable to the protest led by Daniel Shays in Massachusetts. No army had to march to put down an uprising. Bitter and frustrated as farmers were when faced with the draft or a shortage of currency, their protests were contained. The Virginia social order survived the Revolutionary ordeal nearly intact.

The Poor

The third of the taxed households who owned no slaves stood at the bottom of Albemarle white society, many of them probably landless tenants. They seem to occupy a tenuous position, not servants, not bound, but not masters either. Were they alienated from the society rising above them? It is tempting to think of them as the dregs of white society, barely holding on to their places at the bottom of the heap, the segment a visitor characterized as "abject."[7] Yet this stratum was not entirely cut off from the slave owners above them in the wealth scale. Virtually all the slaveless farmed a little.[8] Of the 132 households in Jefferson's district, 123 owned cattle and 126 at least one horse. Even the poorest must have owned a little land or rented a plot to pasture their animals. At the outbreak of the Revolution, a lieutenant in the Albemarle County militia spoke of an imagined poor man as an "industrious labourer, who counts a cabin his dwelling, a single cow and a small parcel of land his whole estate."[9]

Slaveless households were, of course, poorer than the great body of middling farmers who owned from one to five slaves. The median wealth of the slaveless at death, judging from probate inventories, was around £40 worth of goods and chattel, much less than the £191 of farmers with one to five slaves, but the slaveless did not live in another world. Much of the wealth of small slaveholders was invested in slaves. When the value of their slaves is subtracted from the total, the median value of small slaveholders' goods and chattels was £100, still substantially more than the £40 of the slaveless, but not enough to set them apart entirely.[10]

Table 12.1 VALUE OF GOODS AND CHATTEL IN A SAMPLE OF 1774–75 VIRGINIA PROBATE INVENTORIES OF SLAVELESS FARMERS AND SMALL SLAVE OWNERS

Value of Goods and Chattel Not Including Slaves	Inventories of Slaveless Farmers	Inventories of Farmers with 1–5 Slaves
£1–25	3	0
£26–50	5	4
£51–100	6	5
£101–150	2	6
£151–200	0	4
Total	16	19

Source: Virginia estate inventories, 1774–75, in Alice Hanson Jones, *American Colonial Wealth: Documents and Methods*, 3 vols., 2nd ed. (New York: Arno, 1977), 2: 1300–1400.

Moreover, not all slaveholding families were superior in their wealth to all nonslaveholding households. The wealth of the slaveless and the small slave owners overlapped. Owning a few slaves was not enough to elevate a farmer into a new way of life.

The lines blurred between people with no slaves and those with a few. Did the "1 old negro fello" owned by Daniel Farguson when he died in 1779 really make that much difference in his life? Or did the "One Negro Woman" valued at £35 in Alexander Fitzpatrick's inventory make him think like a master? Fitzpatrick's only animal was one black mare; he had no hogs, no cows. His inventory listed no hoes or tools of any kind, no gun, nothing but two beds, an iron pot, and a few table utensils. He was no better off than the no-slave household of David Edwards, with its horse and cow and no tools of any kind save a sley used in weaving and an old hatchel. Edwards had nothing to farm with, only eating and cooking utensils, a chest and bed, a looking glass and a "pair of taro candles."[11] One slave or two did not bring much change in the level of living in these households. They were brought together by their common poverty.

Some slaveless households, on the other hand, were as well furnished as the houses of people with a half dozen bound workers. The inventory of slaveless John Woodson registered in 1780 included:

2 working stears and a cart
12 head of cattle
7 head of sheep
1 hatchel
5 pecks of flaxseed
1 loom
17 yards of cloth
7 hoes
3 axes
2 scythes
30 barrels of corn
A quantity of tobacco worth £500.

And much else besides, but no slaves.[12] The list reads so much like the inventories of slave owners that we are inclined to believe Woodson once owned slaves and distributed them to his heirs or sold them before he died. The seven hoes in the inventory suggest many hands at work hilling or weeding. The hoes put him in the category of owners of six to nine slaves, who frequently had seven to nine hoes. (The biggest slave owner in the sample had forty-two hoes.) Woodson's slaveless condition when the inventory was taken does not separate him from the middling farmers who surrounded him.

Estate inventories seem to show that farm households of Albemarle County were interwoven with one another without sharp demarcations anywhere along the line—save at the top. Among Albemarle County estate inventories from 1779 to 1788, the greatest of the decedents was Charles Lewis of Frederick parish. With fifty-four slaves, ninety-four cattle, and the forty-two hoes, not to mention eighteen china plates, a volume of "Flaveals Works," and four tablecloths inside the house, Lewis was set off from the rest.[13] He was miles above the next wealthiest decedent, with twenty-one slaves and twenty-two cattle. But except for a few towering peaks at the top where Jefferson and the Carters dwelled, Albemarle society ascended gradually in a gentle slope.

Work and Society

Like social relations in all agricultural societies, work defined the relationships among Jefferson's neighbors in Albemarle County. Social ties took concrete form in day-by-day exchange of works, borrowing and lending, bartering and selling. Few account books remain as records of such transactions, but remnants of farmers' day-to-day living can be recovered from probate inventories, which contain compilations of a farm family's possessions at death. Many of the objects provide clues about how people worked. They serve as points of reference from which, by triangulation, the decedent's household economy can be reconstructed. The objects enable us then to imagine the work relationships of family to family and person to person in Albemarle.

Nicholas Gentry's ownership of six slaves when he died in 1779 put him near the middle of Albemarle society. To settle his affairs, four men swore in court to "value and appraise" his estate. During their rounds of Gentry's barnyard and house, the appraisers named everything they saw and assigned a monetary value. At the top of the list as they moved through his barnyard were "One cow and calf £25," followed by another cow and calf at twenty pounds, and a third cow with a yearling at twenty-five. Later the appraisers listed ten pounds of wool and five sheep, sheep shears and reap hooks, and a parcel of old sieves.[14] The two cows with calves suggest that Gentry's cows produced milk, and perhaps that his wife was making butter that went into the butter pot in the inventory. The reaping hooks were to cut grain, and the sieves sifted the chaff from the kernels. Gentry was probably raising barley, rye, or wheat.

But strangely, no hoes, plows, or axes appeared in Gentry's inventory. Can that be right? How committed to farming was a man without the basic implements to clear land and cultivate the soil? What work did his six slaves perform? In its lacks, Gentry's inventory was not unusual. John Woodson's estate, with its seven hoes, appeared to lack slaves. Many inventories were missing expected implements, animals, or people. In one sample of Virginia inventories, a third of owners with eleven to twenty slaves and a quarter of owners with twenty-two or more slaves lacked hoes.[15] How did they grow tobacco or corn without the basic instrument of Virginia husbandry? The estate inventories, we are forced to conclude, while useful, are not necessarily a straightforward guide to a household's work routines. We must take precautions in reconstructing the household economy from this flawed source.

There probably was seepage from an estate during the extremities of death. A 1691 Surry County inventory named five slaves and a horse that the appraisers said were "given by will therefore not appraised." Parts of an estate may have been distributed before death. Friends or family may have walked off with desirable items in the belief they had a right. Decedents may have given away valued items to a needy child or friend. There are many reasons why the collection of possessions at the moment of death may have been smaller than the inventory of belongings at the peak of life.[16] We should allow for perhaps 10 percent or 20 percent more possessions than the appraisers recorded in the inventories.

On the other hand, we do not want to furnish a family with items we believe it must have had because we think life would have been untenable without them. We must at least consider the possibility of farm families surviving without a full complement of kitchen or farm tools. They may have been more ingenious or long suffering than we imagine. We have to ask how a family managed if the inventoried possessions were in reality all they had.

Table 12.2 PERCENTAGE OF ALBEMARLE COUNTY ESTATE INVENTORIES WITH CERTAIN ITEMS, 1779–88 BY NUMBER OF SLAVES OWNED

(Number of Cases in Parentheses)

	Number of Slaves			
Item	0 (13)	1–5 (9)	6–9 (11)	10–54 (7)
Hoes	46%	89%	67%	100%
Hogs/pigs/sows	54%	56%	67%	100%
Cattle/cows	69%	67%	73%	100%
Spinning wheels	77%	64%	55%	100%
Sleys	62%	56%	36%	57%
Cards	38%	56%	45%	71%
Looms	46%	33%	27%	57%
Carpenter, smith, shoemaker, cooper tools	54%	36%	45%	100%
Bells	31%	56%	45%	14%
Guns	54%	33%	27%	71%
Churns	31%	11%	18%	14%
Carts	31%	33%	27%	71%
Casks/hogsheads	23%	22%	9%	71%
Horses	85%	67%	100%	100%

Source: Virginia County Court Records, *Will Book: Albemarle County, Virginia, 1752–1756, 1775–1783* (n.p.: Antient, 2002), 46–103; Virginia County Court Records, *Will Book: Albemarle County, Virginia, 1785–1798* (n.p.: Antient, 2002), 2–46.

The inventories of forty decedents in Albemarle County in the ten years from 1779 through 1788 define the problem. Fifty-four percent of slaveless inventories listed no hoes; 46 percent had no hogs or pigs. How could households have survived without key items? We can imagine them carrying on without a loom or carpentry tools, but could they survive without hoes and hogs? The puzzling gaps in the inventories suggest that poor to middling people were following alternate strategies within Albemarle's farm economy. One of the notable numbers in the tabulation of inventory items is the number of households owning spinning wheels but no slaves: 77 percent. Half again as many poor men owned wheels as owned hoes. That figure does not match the 100 percent spinning wheel ownership in households with ten or more slaves, but it exceeds the number in households with six to nine slaves: 55 percent. The high percentage of wheels is matched in poorer households with the other accoutrements of spinning, sleys, cards, and looms. Households with no slaves were more likely to have a sley, the slotted frame through which yarn was threaded as the loom was prepared, than were the biggest households. The discrepancy suggests that poorer families were carrying their sleys with them to weave on the looms of larger planters. The sley attached to a harness determined the pattern of the cloth, so weavers installed a particular sley to produce the kind of cloth they wanted. Instead of owning many sleys to meet particular needs, loom owners could hire the person with the desired sley to come weave.[17]

Nicholas Gentry, the six-slave decedent without hoes, owned two wheels, three sleys, and a card, showing he was in the spinning business. Hence the five sheep, the wool, and the shears in his inventory. In the absence of farm tools, his four female slaves were probably as profitable to him as his two male farmhands. He was not working the land in a big way; he was spinning and dairying, tasks for which women performed the labor. It must have been true for many poorer households that women came to the forefront in bringing in income. An Albemarle man advertising for work as a steward noted that "his wife is also well acquainted with the management of a dairy, &c."[18] A larger percentage of the slaveless households owned churns (31 percent) than the households with ten or more slaves (14 percent). Churns allowed the women in the household to go into the butter business. In Albemarle in the 1780s, with war interrupting the commerce in English cloth, they also produced yarn and may have knitted.

Artisan tools tell the same story. People with no slaves owned more carpentry tools than households with up to nine slaves. These part-time artisans would probably find little need for their services on the big plantations, where the right tools abounded, but they could get work with middling planters who concentrated on agriculture using slave labor. The poorest third of society was in a sense the service sector, spinning yarn for people with looms, making barrel staves and coffins, and occasionally cobbling shoes. They were as likely to be on the road, working at other farms, as hoeing their own fields. No wonder that they mostly kept up with the rest of the county in owning horses. Eighty-five percent of the slaveless households owned a horse, more than owned hogs or cows. Though not slaughtered for its meat, the horse was a vital possession, needed to get to work.

Thus out of the pervasive farm culture of Albemarle County emerged specialties suitable for those who lacked the labor, the land, or the tools to focus on corn and tobacco. Fewer of these people owned hogs or cattle; without hoes they may not have grown much. What they had to offer was their labor, either in the fields or at the spinning wheel or loom or wielding carpentry tools. With their labor they built up credit, which enabled them to borrow tools or procure bacon or corn. Lund Washington hired a carpenter to work at Mount Vernon during the war in return for thirty barrels of corn. "Lanphier was here some little time past, after some conversation with him I found he had very little thoughts of working here much more—he said money woud not purchase the necessarys of Life and that he must endeavour to make them—findg I coud do nothing better with him, I told him if he wou'd stick to his worck and endeavour to finish it—I wou'd make him a present at shearg time of 40 Wt of Wool and next Fall 30 Barrels of Corn—he has promised that he will be here very shortly and stick close to the worck."[19]

The poor were the great improvisers of the community. They had to be on the lookout for work opportunities where a tool that had fallen into their hands, like a reap hook, a scythe, or an axe, would make them valuable. They were not entirely dependent on exchanges and services for their livelihoods. In the classic Crusoe fashion, they exploited all the resources at hand to provide for themselves. For good reason, the poorer two-thirds of the farm population—those with no slaves or up to five—owned bells. Thirty-one percent of slaveless households and 56 percent of one-to-five-slave households possessed a bell, compared with just 14 percent of the wealthiest. Bells were useful for locating animals in the woods, where cattle roamed for most of the year. Animals could stay alive even in winter in the free range of the Virginia woods, but they had to be located when the time came for calving or slaughter. Bells and the brands licensed by the county court helped with the roundup or identification when animals were lost. "Taken up in Orange, a red cow with a middle sized bell on, and marked in the ear with a crop and slit," read an ad in the *Virginia Gazette*.[20]

The woodlands were an unnamed resource of the poor, useful not just for foraging but for game. Besides domesticated cattle and hogs foraging in the woods, forested land supported wild animals, which for purposes of meat and skins were as valuable as the farmer's own stock. In 1782 the legislature added deerskins to the list of commodities acceptable in payment of taxes. The gun was the tool for harvesting this natural bounty, and slaveless households owned as many guns (54 percent) as did modest slaveholders (33 percent). For many, the gun was perhaps the most efficient instrument for producing food. It served also for driving off wolves, the settlers' rivals for the bounty of the woods. In winter, wolves would sneak into the pens at Monticello and kill five or six sheep in a night.[21] Farmers had to protect their own animals as well as slay forest creatures for food. Bounties on wolves gave the poor an added reason to keep a gun. Occasionally guns served military purposes, but more commonly they were another agricultural tool, adding to the small farmer's reliance on meat in his diet.[22]

Plantations were centers of wealth, and the poor took advantage. The big establishments served as markets for such services as weaving and carpentry. In late June 1782, Jefferson received three young turkeys from Mrs. Gray and paid her with six pounds of sugar. A few months later, he bought another seven turkeys from her, and in the same months he was buying ducks and turkeys from "Mic. Defoe." Bob Chatsworth sold him eight toothbrushes for eight shillings, and James Pleasant cards for his loom for thirty-six shillings.[23]

Some of these people, like Mrs. Gray with her turkeys, appear once or twice in Jefferson's accounts and then disappear. Other names appear more frequently. William Beck, a handyman and errand runner, appears in scores of entries. In 1768 he sold Jefferson oysters for four shillings. Three decades later, he spent two days "setting lime kiln," for which he received two dollars. In between, he performed all manner of services, subsisting on the little jobs Jefferson sent his way. In 1782 Jefferson sent Beck to fetch the household slaves that the British had carried off during their occupation of Richmond. Beck was a poor man who was useful to the rich. In the 1782 tax lists, Beck's assessment showed no slaves, six cattle, and two horses. His taxes came to fifteen shillings when Jefferson's were more than eighty-two pounds.[24]

The lives of the poor intermingled with the great plantations through multitudes of small exchanges. For some, the plantation provided a living. In 1782 Bartholomew Kindred contracted to weave for another year for Jefferson in return for five hundred pounds of meat, five barrels of corn, a half bushel of salt, and fodder, plus half the earnings of the shop beyond what Jefferson himself required. Kindred was one of the slaveless in Albemarle County in 1782, with no cattle to tend but three horses, which enabled him and his son to reach the weaving shop each day. Later Jefferson contracted with Richard Durrett for a year of carpentry. "Jefferson agrees to pay the said Durrett forty pounds, and to find him four hundred and fifty pounds of pork, and a peck of corn meal a week." In case Durrett has three in his family, Jefferson will provide "three pecks a week, and to find him a cow to give milk from 17 April to 15th November." Durrett took his offer, even though he owned thirteen slaves and nine horses in 1792.[25]

Ordinary neighbors like these are almost never mentioned in Jefferson's correspondence. In letters to his wide range of acquaintances, he dealt with people who led the militia, ran for the legislature, and had a voice in national policy. In his memorandum book, however, ordinary people appear by the dozens. The local exchange economy was the place where Jefferson got to know his neighbors. Over the course of a year from November 1, 1781, to October 31, 1782, he dealt with fifty-nine persons, purchasing whiskey, hogs, pork, wheat, sawing, weaving, ferriage, dinners, horses, wax, clover seed, gun stock repairs, sugar, beer, ducks, a mare, paper, smithing, a side of leather, beef, shoes, turkeys, cloth, distilling, and a basket called "a leap."[26] All this in a season that began with the defeat of the British at Yorktown, was soured by an investigation of Jefferson's conduct as governor, and concluded with the death of his wife, Martha, in September 1782, age thirty-three. Through it all, life went on at Monticello.

The poorer half of Albemarle County lacked the resources to provide entirely for themselves. They had to fill the gaps in their domestic economies with the products of a spinning wheel, their skill with an adze, or butter from a churn in exchange for corn, pork, and borrowed tools from larger farms. Merely to survive, the poor located niches where their work would be valued.

The services which they performed wove the community together much as the exchange of works did in New England farm villages.[27] Although Jefferson lived high on a hill, Monticello was not out of reach or beyond sight. Many were familiar with its precincts and knew its master. One cannot tell whether these exchanges bred respect or resentment, but isolation did not mark Jefferson's position in Albemarle society. The poor brought him into the neighborhood's exchange society.

Albemarle at War

Out of the farm economy grew a society that was both populist and aristocratic. Great families stood at the summit but not entirely detached from the rest. Ties of exchange for mutual benefit wove the whole together. Differences at the top were clearly marked and respected, but even the poorest woman could sell Mr. Jefferson a pair of turkeys. Every family had its place on the landscape of exchange. After 1776, exigencies of war brought these customary relationships into the open. High and low were measured and named, and the resilience of the social bonds was tested.

George Gilmer, a voluble physician who took a leading role in the county's military during the Revolution, resorted to a familiar class vocabulary to describe how Albemarle worked. Gilmer was one of the neighbors who knew Thomas Jefferson personally. Trained in medicine at Edinburgh, he was physician to the Jefferson family from 1771 to 1775, and stood in for Jefferson in the fifth Virginia convention in 1776.[28] In 1775, after his election as lieutenant in one of the Albemarle volunteer companies, Gilmer became an exhorter in the Revolutionary cause. He recruited for the militia, rebuked the disorderly, warned of British perfidy. In explaining events, he fell back on the language of class.

News of Governor Dunmore's removal of the colony's powder from the public magazine in Williamsburg reached Albemarle in April 1775. This confiscation of public arms was Virginia's equivalent of General Gage's attack on Concord that same month. Both were efforts to neutralize the military strength of the colonial protesters by gathering in their arms and ammunition. In response, Gilmer was quick to propose "a Plan" for organizing an "Independent Company" of militia. Gilmer judged the situation of affairs was "sufficiently alarming to rouze the indignation of every man that is capable of feeling for the publick welfare." His proposal for a militia conformed to the standard format for the companies forming in all the colonies that spring: a captain, a lieutenant, an ensign, two sergeants, a drummer, and twenty-five to thirty men.[29] It was a structure designed to mirror the outlines of hierarchical society, with its aristocrats and commoners.

The Albemarle elite flowed easily into the upper layers of this structure. Charles Lewis, the man with fifty-four slaves and ninety-two cattle when he died in 1779, was a logical candidate for captain. Gilmer, notable for his Edinburgh education and his estate at Pen Park, was well suited for the lieutenancy. Members of the elite occupied all the military and committee positions that opened up later that year. In this group of officials, the median number of slaves owned was between sixteen and twenty. The largest planter among the officials owned forty-eight slaves. They were the substantial people in the top third of Albemarle society.[30]

But some confusion ensued in filling the ranks of ordinary soldiers. At this moment of high excitement, everyone in Albemarle society was eager to participate in this grand show of honor and patriotism, the wealthy even more than the poor. The country was "afire," as Gilmer later recalled, but the widespread eagerness to participate led to social discrepancies. The body of officers and committeemen was barely distinguished from ordinary "soldiers." The average holdings of the soldiers filling out the company was fifteen slaves, twenty-seven cattle, and 932 acres, about the same numbers as the sixteen-to-twenty-slave median of officers and committee men. It was even more confusing when the possessions of some of the officers dipped as low as nine or even four slaves. How were officers and men to be distinguished socially? By the "Terms of Inlisting," every volunteer was to provide "Gun, shot-pouch, powder-horn," and "to appear on duty in a hunting shirt." Clad so much alike, they were little distinguished in appearance from one another. Gilmer solved the problem by addressing them all as "Gentlemen Soldiers," a contradiction in terms that he chose to overlook.[31]

The consequences of enlisting eminent planters as simple soldiers showed up when the companies marched. At the end of April 1775, companies like Gilmer's and Lewis's descended on Williamsburg to defend the colony in case Dunmore called in British troops. In a letter to Washington on April 29, Gilmer assured the colonel that the "Gentlemen Volunteers" of Albemarle "are truly alarmed, and highly incensed with the unjustifiable proceedings of Lord Dunmore." In July, they marched again. News came of Governor Dunmore's sending his wife away and then leaving Williamsburg himself. The hypersensitive colonists interpreted the move as a prelude to an invasion. Alert and eager, Albemarle's independent company rushed to the capital's defense.[32] On July 11–13, 1775, they marched to Waller's Grove just east of Williamsburg.

At last they saw action, but the troops' behavior in camp was disillusioning. These "gentlemen soldiers" were not easily disciplined. Gilmer marched with twenty-seven "chosen Riflemen" and was responsible for keeping order when they camped. Within a week, he wrote unhappily to Jefferson that "Capt. Scott our commander in chief, whose goodness and merit is great, fears to offend, and by that many members are rather disorderly." The company seemed more interested in setting a sumptuous table than in presenting a military face. "We appear rather invited to feast than fight. Anderson and Southall's entertain elegantly the first in the best manner by far." Two days after his arrival, Gilmer advised Charles Carter, soon to be a member of the assembly, that all must "become rigid Disciplinarians." What annoyed Gilmer most was the misbehavior of the presumed gentlemen in the company. "If the men of fortune can not submit to be bound by the same laws with the other soldiers, let them stay at home and complain." He apparently had suffered "censure and illiberal abuse" for his role as a leader. The "authors of infamous aspersions" were "actuated by malice" to "delude the populace, to raise factions," in short to undermine the popularity on which Gilmer's election to the office of lieutenant depended. Besides the natural unruliness that went with men away from home, the mobilization of troops opened up "divisions, disorders, and discentions amongst ourselves."[33]

The problem was not his alone. Less than a week after their arrival, the officers of all the companies resolved that "the many disorders that have arisen among the volunteers render it absolutely necessary that the Discipline may be kept up." In August the Virginia convention, which had taken on the responsibilities of the suspended assembly, reorganized the voluntary companies into "Minute Men," some of whom were paid. Instead of electing their own officers, the Minute Men were led by officers appointed by the elected county committees, thus relieving pressure on officers to please their men by moderating discipline.[34]

Gilmer's appointment to raise a company under the new Minute Men law was not entirely satisfying. The spring's excitement was wearing off. "We were once all fire, now most of us are become inanimate and indifferent." Typically for him, he dealt head-on with the objections he was meeting. He was aware of those, probably the Quakers in the county, whose consciences favored nonresistance. Others objected to war far from the home soil. Why should Virginia fight Massachusetts's battles? Many objected to the interruption of trade. "Wherewithal shall we be cloathed," they asked, "or where shall we get implements for carrying on manufactures?" Others were "alarmed at the imaginary want of salt."[35] How would they preserve their meat or salt their cattle when cessation of trade cut off their supply?

In this inventory of woes, Gilmer's complaints shed light on his ideas of social order. "The factious and dissatisfied," he said, trying to explain the lack of recruits, "say it is calculated to exempt the gentlemen and to throw the whole burthen on the poor." A "set of dissatisfied" men were saying "the men of Fortune should bear the whole weight of the contest." Those who could afford it should pay the costs. In defense of the present arrangements whereby all were taxed, Gilmer reminded his audience that "the men of fortune must unavoidably contribute more largely to the support of the Cause than those of small property."[36] His language revealed his sense of a bifurcated society: gentlemen and men of fortune versus the poor and those of small property.

Gilmer's problem was that the language of class only roughly fit Albemarle's blended spectrum of wealth. As Gilmer put it, "I should be glad if these that have persuaded themselves into this ill-grounded conceit, would first declare what they mean by the term Gentlemen and that of poor people." Class divisions were hard to define. Were people with five slaves the poor? Where did the Gentlemen begin? With nine slaves, or ten, or fifteen? Albemarle society lacked sharp delineations. The uncertainty led to disparate remedies. Some who were not officers "would enter the service if appointed officers." With the boundaries so blurred, many thought of themselves as officers rather than men. Some thought it better to disregard social class altogether. "Another set of dissatisfied persons are for no pay at all for officers, but all marching promiscuously and on equal footing as volunteers."[37] Without a class order defined in society itself, the distinctions of officers and men struck some as unnatural and unnecessary. Hierarchy may have been part of Albemarle's social thought, but a confused social reality in the middle ranks made actual distinctions elusive.

Dr. Gilmer hoped to heal these social rifts. He wanted to reinstate benevolent hierarchy in Albemarle. He saw benefits in the officers' superior salaries, one of the complaints he had to deal with. One reason for greater pay was democratic in spirit: "it is necessary that there should be a distinction in the pay to animate those in low rank to attain the highest posts by their great and good services." Other reasons for pay differences were more patriarchal. Everyone knew that "without some distinction there can be no subordination." Perhaps most telling were his appeals to hierarchical beneficence. "The distress of every soldier should deeply impress his officer's heart," and many distresses "require pecuniary assistance." The officers needed higher salaries because "It should be in the officer's power to do most of these kind offices, that his men may be wedded to him."[38]

Committed as he was to the merits of benevolent hierarchy, Gilmer wavered in his depiction of Albemarle. There was an obvious top and an obvious bottom in the county, but the steps in between were muddled. In the end, it was not wealth that made for good officers. "If they are really gentlemen, from their good behavior they will stand the best chance of raising the men and giving satisfaction." Not property, but character counted most. "If this matter is inquired into there will be found many commanders of small property." The committees who made the choices were less impressed by ownership than by ability. "Those who appoint require merit alone."[39]

Gilmer's vocabulary committed him to a hierarchy of gentlemen at the top and the poor below. He hoped for a social order led by men of fortune who were also kind and wise. But he struggled to map that formal structure onto the realities of Albemarle life. Jefferson belonged at the top; so did Charles Lewis and Gilmer himself. Such men were invariably the colonels and generals, the field officers in the military companies. But there were no fixed barriers to stop meritorious men of small property from claiming places as committee members and officers of companies. In the mélange of slave-owning farmers in the great middle of Virginia society, class lines broke down, re-formed, and broke down again.

The Trials of War

After the displays of military ardor in the summer of 1775, enthusiasm for the struggle with Britain faded rapidly. None of the county's farmers cared much for war or the sacrifices it visited upon them. Recruitment, as Gilmer learned, became an uphill battle. The costs of leaving their work were too high for farmers to pay willingly. Their lives were caught up in a schedule of cultivating, planting, weeding, harvesting, preserving, and marketing, on which their livelihoods depended. Any interruption could be devastating. As wartime conditions broke into their routines, farmers resisted. Self-sacrifice and patriotism were not the issue, nor resentment of the privileged. They stalled, protested, and refused because war disrupted their family economies.

The farm economy was vulnerable at many points. In the fall of 1775, as Gilmer noted, farmers worried that the Association's severance of trade with Britain and the West Indies would cut off the supply of salt. When animals were slaughtered in the late fall and winter, they were ordinarily cut to size and packed in salt before hanging to cure in the smokehouse. Jefferson calculated that it took a pound of salt to make bacon from ten pounds of pork. Without salt, the meat spoiled, and the staple of the family's diet for the coming year was lost. George Gilmer had noted in his 1775 recruiting speech that "there are amongst us that are already alarmed at the imaginary want of salt," and tried to placate the complainers with the assurance they could get by without it. Through 1776, the price skyrocketed from one shilling to fifteen shillings per bushel. Desperate, the Convention authorized projects to boil seawater.[40] Nothing met the need until a salt trade opened with the French in 1778.

War's most disastrous impact on the farm economy was the demand for men. Nothing hurt the household more than the removal of the workers who drove the domestic economy. The brief sallies to Williamsburg in the spring and summer of 1775 were one thing; long-term enlistments and removal to other colonies were another. Recruitment crippled the ability of the family to produce for its own subsistence, much less get a crop to market.

As the pressure for enlistments grew in 1776, perceived inequities came to the surface. The inhabitants of Lunenburg County petitioned the fifth Virginia Convention, which convened in May 1776, to revise an ordinance passed the previous December exempting overseers from the militia and the draft. "From this Indulgence many persons are become Overseers that Otherways wou'd not," the petitioners complained. "Many of your Petitioners are poor men with Families that are Incapable of Supporti[ng th] emselves without Our labour & Assistance and we look up[on] it to be extremely hard & no ways [*illegible*] that we Should be Obliged to leave our Farms [*illegible*] him that if ever we Shou'd return again Wou'd find our Wives & Children dispers'd up & down the Country abeggin, or at home aSlaving, and at the same time quite unable to help them to the Necessaries of life while the Overseers are aliving in ease & Affluence at the Expence of their Employers." Two hundred twenty-three men signed the petition. Their nightmare was to see their families turned to beggars or servants while the men in service could do nothing.[41]

Rather than forcibly tear men away from their families through a draft, the assembly preferred to elicit volunteers, allowing people to decide for themselves whether they could leave. Service in the local militias was compulsory for "all free male persons, hired servants, and apprentices, above the age of sixteen, and under fifty years," as it was considered only right that everyone defend his home county. But the Minute Men companies were voluntary, as were the companies enrolled for the Continental Army and the colony companies. The assembly preferred to entice men to enlist with bounties, usually ten dollars. As the quotas from Congress kept coming, the value of the bounties mounted. If the Congress offered a ten-dollar bounty, Virginia offered an additional ten to double the appeal. By 1780, the assembly was promising three hundred acres and a healthy slave age ten to thirty for those who enlisted for three years, appealing to the landless and slaveless who through military service might elevate themselves into a better life.[42]

The assembly held back on the draft, knowing it would impose hardships on the unlucky and perhaps damage the economic infrastructure that sustained life. They had to keep families producing while extracting the manpower required by war. Not until the British captured Philadelphia and drove Washington to Valley Forge in the winter of 1778 did the assembly at last take up what Edmund Pendleton, speaker of the Virginia House, called "the difficulty and Novelty of drafting men to recruit the Army."[43] In 1778 Congress asked for eight thousand men, and the assembly had to reconsider its options. The British had taken Philadelphia, and Washington's men were freezing at Valley Forge. For the first time, enemy troops threatened Virginia.

One possibility was to draft vagrants. They made up a class of people legally defined by a 1748 statute as "idle and disorderly persons, having no visible estates or employments, and who are unable to work." To rid himself of the title of vagrant a man had to prove that he had paid taxes.[44] Vagrants were imagined as men too lazy to work or unable to find work who had abandoned their families and drifted to other counties. Why not send these troublemakers off to fight? For a time, the legislature considered this group of unfortunates to be a natural source for the draft, but then it decided they were not competent or sufficiently trustworthy to serve as soldiers. They were shipped off instead to row the galleys that were part of the southern fleet.[45]

Instead of drafting vagrants, the assembly turned to single men without children. Their absence would least affect the families left at home. They were not fathers who bore direct responsibility for the wives and children spoken of in the Lunenburg petition. As Pendleton put it, "the young men are properest to go." The ordinance provided that the eligible young men were to be called together, examined for bodily ability, and then required to draw lots from a covered hat. Those who drew "clear" were free to return home; those who drew "service" were enrolled.[46]

Pendleton felt the assembly had done its best with the draft. "It is every way disagreeable," he wrote, "but being of absolute necessity, we must take a mode the least exceptionable." The draft still met resistance. Protests broke out all over the colony. Loudon County officials did not even try to draft men because of "the violent and riotous behavior of the People." Single men may not have had children, but many were older sons who significantly augmented the workforce of poorer families. Their labor before they struck out on their own was critical to the life plan that called for the increase of wealth at this point in the cycle to help launch the next generation. After one batch was drafted, Lund Washington wrote that the draft would have to be conducted again because "the men who were draughted cannot be found."[47] The vehemence of the complaints caused the assembly to back down. Pendleton wrote to George Washington, "Drafting in any Shape is so unpopular a measure, that our Assembly have laid it aside and depend for recruiting our Regiments upon high bounties only, which I fear will fail, as 'tis difficult to reach the Point of avarice now in fashion." One way or another, the assembly beguiled enough men to volunteer to meet roughly half of the congressional quotas.[48]

Persuading men to enlist was one step; keeping them in camp was another. Of the 3,500 soldiers that Virginia supposedly enlisted for continental service in 1778, only 1,242 reached Washington. The number of requests for furloughs embarrassed the officers, and if denied soldiers slipped away anyway. They could picture the wheat ready to harvest or tobacco ripe for cutting. The assembly appointed special agents to ferret out deserters, but it was hard when the populace was on the side of the defectors. Their "friends Secrete them and the Neighbours connive at it." Everyone understood the motives. The soldiers were not fleeing danger or giving up on the patriot cause or resisting the impositions of the government. They returned home to help their families make it through the agricultural year. An advertisement for deserters in the *Virginia Gazette* in 1776 took for granted that they had headed home.[49]

While hard on those who harbored deserters, the legislation specifically exempted from punishment "husband and wife, or of a child concealing a parent, or a widow her son."[50] The plight of families was apparent to everyone, and the legislature understood the injustice of punishing people who only sought to survive. The hope of returning home from time to time when their help was most needed was one reason recruits much preferred service in companies which remained in the colony. Some companies wrote a provision into their contracts that troops would not be marched out of the colony without the mutual consent of the soldiers and the governor. When attempts were made to violate these provisions, justices of the peace would come to the soldiers' defense to see that "they shall return to their Homes."[51]

Money

The state met the demands of war only through a series of unsatisfying compromises, none more so than in the matter of money. War brought to a head the colony's long suffering from want of sufficient currency. No problem caused more anguish in the decade after Independence than the lack of money. In the autonomous domestic economy, farmers could survive on the produce of their own hands. They could produce food, fuel, and even cloth for home consumption. As Edmund Pendleton put it, "we may furnish most of our own necessaries, if the wheel and the Loom be kept in brisk motion."[52] But farmers were also implicated in two other systems: the exchange economy, where debts were incurred and rents came due, and the public economy of taxes. Here bounteous production counted for nothing until it was exchanged for money. Debts and taxes for the most part had to be paid in currency, and the vicissitudes of war made that nearly impossible at times.

The problems began the minute war broke out. The Association's suspension of the tobacco and provisions trade in late 1775 hurt farmers, especially tenants who depended on trade for their rent money. In Loudon County, where the percentage of farm tenancy was especially high, the embargo on trade made it impossible to pay. Trade was the farmers' primary source of ready money. The squeeze at Christmas, when rents were due, drove people to desperation. "They say it is Cruel in the Land Holders to expect their Rents when there is not market for the produce of the Land." Debtors were caught in the same bind. They professed a willingness to meet their obligations when money was once more available, but until then had not the means to make payment. People high and low were affected. Lund Washington wrote to George Washington that "some of the Leadg men in Loudon" favored suspension of debt repayment until trade resumed.[53]

In the winter of 1776, Virginians began pressing for independence if only to rid the country of the regulations that prevented trade with other nations. They wanted an end to British rule so that they could start the flow of cash into the economy again. The instructions to delegates in the spring of 1776 frequently mentioned trade as one reason for moving quickly. James Cleaveland, a radical voice in Loudon County, urged immediate action. "Let us go and Fight the Battle at once, and not be Shilly Shally, in this way, until all the Poor, people are ruined." Only with independence could new markets be found, money acquired, rents paid, creditors satisfied, and taxes raised to pay for the war.[54] Although landlords like Lund Washington denounced the protesters, they understood. The protesters were never punished for withholding rent.[55]

After war began, money problems disappeared. Both the Continental Congress and the Virginia assembly paid for the war in the traditional fashion, by issuing paper currency. They followed the pattern of previous conflicts in paying for the sudden spike in expenditures with an issue of paper, then taxing these bills out of circulation in subsequent years. This method made the burden of war more bearable by stretching it out. In the interim, wartime expenditures released floods of currency into the economy, supplying all that farmers needed to pay their debts and taxes. Debtors enjoyed the benefits of paying off old debts with cheap money, much to the consternation of creditors like Jefferson, who felt he was cheated in the payment he received in a land sale.

The pressures on the money supply began again in 1780, when Congress sought to check the inevitable depreciation of the continental currency and urged the states to do the same. Congress pegged the value of its bills at 40:1 in Spanish silver dollars. Virginia currency was even more inflated—Jefferson estimated 1,000 to 1—but the assembly wavered on how to deal with the problem. Congress had recommended the currency be stripped of its status as legal tender, restricting its legal use to payment of taxes, and George Mason and Richard Henry Lee recommended that Virginia follow Congress's advice. Their proposal, however, went down to defeat because of the opposition of Governor Patrick Henry. Over the next year, the assembly waffled. Waiting for Henry to leave town, Mason and Lee persuaded the legislature to reverse itself and revoke the legal tender provision. In May 1781, however, the legislature reversed itself once more. As it met, the colony was in crisis; Cornwall had invaded Virginia, forcing the legislature to flee Richmond. The assembly had to issue money to pay for defense, and to uphold its value granted temporary legal tender status. But that was not to last either. In the fall of 1781, legal tender status was once more stripped away.[56]

The repeated reversals reflected the coming and going of the British, but also the state of mind of the delegates. They knew runaway inflation had to be stopped; excess currency had to be drained out of the economy. They also understood the pain and suffering deflation brought to their neighbors. For the next decade, the legislature was besieged by petitions for relief. Albemarle County submitted a petition dated November 3, 1787, pleading with the legislature to issue more currency. "We your Humble petitioners Sendeth these line to the Honourable House to Inform you of our Distressed Condition, which is coming on us daily for want of a circulating Medium among us; therefore we pray you to take it, under your Consideration and present our Request, which is this we pray . . . you to Emit as much paper money as will pay our Domestic Debt, and Said Money to be Lawfull Tender, in all debts, dues, and Demands, whatsoever (Except the Demands of Congress)." The petitioners understood creditors would suffer from inflation if money were issued, but it was "better for a few to Suffer a little than a majority of the State to become Servants to the Rest."[57] The impossibility of paying debts and taxes ground down everyone. One hundred seventy-five names appeared at the bottom of the petition, only seven of them by mark. In a society where probably a third of the population could not sign their names, the preponderance of signatures showed that the sufferers were not just the illiterate poor.[58]

If money could not be printed, the Albemarle petitioners pled, the county should at least require a fair evaluation of land. If the sheriff distrained their property—that is, seized and sold it at auction—people wanted a guaranteed fair price. "What heart can stand by and see his property that he has labour'd heard for, sell for one fourth of the value and in a few years perhaps not for over one Tenth of its Value, then power will naturly follow property, then God help the poor." The petitioners feared that eventually their property would fall into the hands of British merchants. Knowing the desperation of the farmers, the merchants could set prices where they pleased and acquire property in payment. To add to their worries, under an "Instaulment" bill under consideration, payment of British debts could be made in installments, but with interest added. The petitioners hated what they called "that Eating canker of six percent Interest." Between interest and land sold at unfairly low prices, the British might end up owning everything. "That Saying will soon come to pass, they have Taken Virginia without the force of a gun."[59]

The petitions to the assembly all told the same story. Some came from counties like Albemarle, numerous others from sheriffs who could not collect taxes and asked not to be held accountable. In 1786, eighteen county sheriffs petitioned for relief. They all said that money was not to be had, and not only by the lazy and incompetent. "Many of the most punctual, formerly, were now deficient for want of money." Besides being the victims of government's deflationary policies, farmers had had bad harvests in a rainy season and could not get a crop to market. In 1785, Sheriff Rhodes of Albemarle, one of twenty-five sheriffs asking for relief in that session, explained that he was "unable to collect taxes or sell property." Both "corn and money scarce," and "no bidders for property." Either people lacked the money to buy the land when the sheriff put it up for auction, or, more likely, they refused to bid for the land of a neighbor in distress. The Caroline sheriff reported that "the people unable to pay taxes, and when property is distrained upon no one will bid for it." Sheriff Waddy Thompson of Louisa County said that people actively "combined to prevent sales of property under execution."[60]

Another Louisa County sheriff, Thomas Johnson, ran into resistance of another kind. He had "distrained for the Taxes and sold the property so distrained, which, on account of the scarcity of specie and the poverty of the inhabitants went exceedingly low." Not to take this lying down, several people, whose property he had taken, came in the night and carried off their slaves, horses, and so forth, which he had in his possession, "not that they were opposed to the payment of Taxes, but could not suffer their property to sell for a trifle." They promised to pay when they sold their tobacco. One justice of the peace testified that land worth twenty shillings an acre was going for two.[61]

Faced with this prospect, planters in Louisa County threated to shoot the sheriff if he tried to distrain their property. In a few cases, they resorted to the same desperate violence as the rioters in the 1760s whose land titles along the colonial boundaries had been in jeopardy. Taking farm property cut to the bone. Loss of land and slaves could mortally wound the family economy, and farmers felt they had to fight in self-defense. Arthur Campbell, a radical justice, urged the court not to meet "or that the Sheriff desist from his purpose of collecting, as ruin, mobs, and anarchy must be the consequence if some-thing is not done to save the People."[62]

The bottom line was family. Children and wives would suffer if the law was enforced. As one sheriff explained, "the great scarcity of money, together with the late short crops, have put it out of the power of the people to pay, &c. They state also that many of the people will not be able to purchase the necessary supply of food for their families out of their last crop of tobacco." When drought followed by a hard winter had disrupted the family economy so badly families were forced to buy food, paying taxes was out of the question. One sheriff, under pressure to come up with the revenue he was responsible for collecting, pleaded "that the sale of his estate for ready money, considering the low price of property, would totally ruin him and his family."[63]

The Virginia assembly was well aware that tax collection was breaking down all along the seaboard and that violence threatened everywhere. Farmers in every colony suffered from currency problems. In Pennsylvania, farmers put up the same series of barriers to tax collection that were resorted to in Virginia: tax collectors frequently refused to exact taxes from families with no money, sympathetic justices refused to prosecute collectors and sheriffs for inaction, juries refused to convict, and neighbors refused to purchase distrained goods put up for auction. The neighbors would fill the space where the auction was held and stand silent when bids were called for. Terry Bouton found that in 1783, seventy-two sheriff's auctions in Westmoreland County, Pennsylvania, ended without anyone placing a bid. In 1786, when more than one thousand writs of foreclosure were issued, people stopped auctions at a rate of nearly six per week.[64]

There was little overt violence in Pennsylvania before 1787, but much was threatened. In Berks County, an observer warned "many People have not the money & if their Effects are sold it might drive them to desperate measures." From Dauphin County came the report that "People threaten to rise and oppose the Constables." After ratification of the Constitution, when enforcement measures were tightened, Pennsylvania farmers began creating barriers in roads. They felled logs, erected fences, or dug huge pits to prevent access to auctions or courthouses. Eventually their fears of dispossession through tax collection led to outright rebellion in 1794 and 1799, requiring federal troops to quash them.[65]

Agrarian unrest in the 1780s and 1790s recalled that of the 1760s. Earlier farmers had risen in protest because of the midcentury land crisis. The diminished supply of land and rising prices had driven farmers to tenuous areas where titles were shaky or their presence provoked Indian hostility. When Native Americans attacked or titles were challenged, farmers had put up stiff resistance, blocking enforcement of court orders by force or, in Pennsylvania, by marching on the capital. In the aftermath of Revolution, farm livelihoods were once more endangered. The shortage of currency put property in jeopardy. When farmers could not find money to pay debts or taxes, sheriffs distrained animals, crops, implements, and land. Families saw their livelihood being dismantled, and in desperation lashed out. Representative Edward Carrington gave Governor Edmund Randolph a detailed account of Shays's Rebellion in Massachusetts and warned that disaffection and rebellion were spreading. "The spirit of insurgency in Massachusetts has proceeded to a stage which renders the subversion of that Government an event too probable." And it would not stop there. "The troubles in Vermont, Connecticut, Rhode Island, and lately in New Hampshire" could spread to Virginia.[66]

Carrington's worried prediction, however, did not prove true. Mass violence never occurred in Virginia. The individual instances of resistance did not cohere into a movement like the Massachusetts rebellion. In the spring of 1787, citizens in Greenbrier County signed a statement of their grievances and vowed not to pay the unpopular "certificate tax" designed to siphon off war bonds from the economy. They sent their writing to other back counties, but it went nowhere. Rumors spread of plans to prevent the court from sitting, but no disturbances occurred. Many threats were uttered but none were put into action. Anger and discontent ran high without ever breaking out in rebellion.[67]

Rather than provoke mass resistance, the Virginia legislators bent in the storm. When they faced resistance, they revoked the unpopular certificate tax. The assembly did not issue more currency as the Albemarle petitioners desired—everyone understood the evils of rampant inflation—but it softened the blow. The most common expedient was to postpone the payment of taxes to permit payment over two crop cycles. For three years in succession after 1783, this respite was granted. In two years, 1781 and 1783, the legislature accepted commodity payment of taxes, a huge relief. Provisions were plentiful and were gladly offered in lieu of cash payments. But the most important compromise was administrative, not legislative. The legislature did not punish sheriffs when they failed to submit full tax returns. That meant the sheriffs could be lenient where circumstances required. The legislature acquiesced in the immense difference between taxes levied and taxes paid. Much as they lamented this breakdown, the legislature had no choice. Under a stricter policy, sheriffs would refuse to serve, and the hardships of families would be too much to bear.[68]

The occasional relief measures and the leniency in collection moderated tempers in Virginia.[69] The level of enmity was far lower than in Massachusetts. New England pamphlets were filled with anger and accusation. Merchants were accused of draining the economy of money, leaving the countryside with nothing with which to pay its debts. Speculators bought up paper money at low rates and profited fabulously when the legislature funded them at face value.[70] Farmers there felt someone was to blame for the financial ruin they faced. Little of that appears in the Virginia petitions. British creditors were blamed, but no one in Virginia. Conditions were the enemy, not a predatory interest group. Poor crops, poor markets, lack of currency hurt the farmers, they believed, not some clique of devious merchants and conniving speculators.

Virginians were held together by their encompassing agricultural economy. Delegates knew firsthand how currency shortages were hurting their neighbors, because many legislators suffered as well. Off and on, the assembly imposed severe measures to put currency on a stable, noninflationary basis, but they all knew the price ordinary farmers were paying. In 1783 Governor Henry was able to defeat a bill for higher taxes by oratory alone. He "drew a most affecting picture of the state of poverty and suffering in which the people of the upper counties had been left by the war. His delineations of their wants and wretchedness was so minute, so full of feeling, and withal so true, that he could scarcely fail to enlist on his side every sympathetic mind."[71]

The strongest movement for deflation in Virginia originated with James Madison, who felt helpless in the face of popular demands for easy money and forgiveness of taxes. Hard as he tried, Madison could not persuade the Virginia legislature to follow the Massachusetts example in fighting inflation. Norman Risjord has argued that political parties in Virginia began with Madison's campaign to bring easy money under control. He was the one to worry most about currency inflation and lax debt collection, because Virginia was among the worst offenders. Massachusetts suffered from insurrection, but Virginia failed to discipline its population, its officials, or its legislature in the critical matters of money supply and tax collection.[72]

The sloppy enforcement of the measures to curb inflation frustrated and appalled Madison. He was soon to lead the charge for a national government that could control fiscal affairs. Virginia disappointed him because the government was too pliable, too ready to yield to the appeals of suffering farmers. But the legislators understood what their neighbors were going through. They knew the impossibility of selling crops and the suffering that resulted from distraining property. The webs of exchange, especially the ones formed by the poor to extract a living from their limited resources, had woven rural society into an interactive network. The mighty knew their poorer neighbors because they relied on them for weaving, carpentry, and turkeys. That the exchange networks brought gentlemen face to face with the enterprising lower orders had consequences for politics. Despite the efforts of Madison and a few others to impose stricter monetary discipline, the legislators gave way, knowing the cost to their neighbors.

13. Learning Slavery

How Slaves Learned to Be Slaves and Whites to Become Masters

By the time of the Revolution, slavery had become a way of life in the American South, a distinctive culture shaped around plantation agriculture. Slavery evoked techniques of control, a set of postures, scripts for all occasions, an ethic, and measures of personal achievement. Slaves were something more than an economic expedient, a way to increase production. Owning slaves became an end in itself. They were a sign of status and competence. Mastery gave confidence and empowerment to those who dictated to other human beings, much as fine houses and fine clothing sustained the confidence of eminent northerners. Slaves were perhaps the chief mark of consequence in the South. For planters preparing for their children's future, it was as important to bequeath a slave as to bestow tools, clothing, and furniture. As part of growing up, white boys and girls had to learn mastery, and black boys and girls had to learn submission.

Southern Comfort

The cultural value of slavery became evident in a massive study of American wealth in 1774 on the eve of the Revolution. A team led by Alice Hanson Jones tabulated the wealth of individual households as recorded in probate records from a sample of counties across Britain's North American colonies. Jones was able to group the various forms of property named in the

Table 13.1 PHYSICAL WEALTH PER FREE CAPITA, 1774, IN POUNDS STERLING AND PERCENTAGE CONSUMER GOODS

	New England	Middle Colonies	South
Slaves, servants, land, and producer's capital	£33.7	£41.4	£87.2
Consumer goods	£4.5	£4.4	£5.3
Percentage consumer goods Of other wealth	13.4%	10.6%	6.0%

Source: Virginia estate inventories, 1774–75, in Alice Hanson Jones, *Wealth of a Nation to Be: The American Colonies on the Eve of Revolution* (New York: Columbia University Press, 1980).

inventories and make broad generalizations about wealth distribution in the three major sections: the South, the Middle Colonies, and New England. Her data confirmed the impression of the South's superior wealth in many forms: the workers they controlled, the land they owned, and the capital goods they possessed. One incongruity, however, emerged in Jones's study: the South outshone the other two sections in virtually every category of wealth except for consumer goods.

Southerners possessed over two and a half times as much producer wealth as New Englanders and more than twice as much as Middle Colony people. But measured by their consumer goods, southerners were relatively abstemious. Their consumer goods constituted only 6 percent of their other wealth, while in New England the number was more than 13 percent, and in the Middle Colonies more than 10 percent. Southerners were not fully employing their wealth to raise their standard of living. They lived somewhat better on the average, but owning twice as many resources as Middle Colony residents and two and a half as much as New Englanders did not result in a proportionately better lifestyle.

Consider Callam Bailey, whose estate inventory was returned in Albemarle County in 1787. Bailey had the fifth-most slaves, twelve, among the people who died in the decade between 1779 and 1788. Ranked in the upper third of the total population in wealth, he represents the comfortable middling slaveholder. At his death he owned "9 china plates & 1 ditto dish," a sign of aspiration, to be sure, but what accompanied the china in the family's household by way of furnishings?

1 tub and 1 looking glass
1 table 2 jugs and 3 bottles
1 d[oz] table spoons & 1 large ditto
1 pewter dish & 5 pewter plates
3 ditto basins ½d [oz] knives & forks
Sundry books 1 horn
Sundry china ware
2 awls 1 jug & nutmeg
2 drinking glasses 1 cupboard
Chest 1 tea kettle handle
1 blanket and rug
1 table 1 chest
8 seting chairs
3 table cloaths

Besides these items, Bailey owned three feather beds and bedsteads, a razor, and a pair of spectacles, but nothing of elegance beyond the china dishes. He owned a table and eight chairs, but his family when he died consisted of four sons and seven daughters. Where would they have sat for dinner when they were young and still at home? How many children slept in the two beds left for them after the parents claimed one? The Baileys had a teakettle but no teacups. They had the basics but nothing fine. The china dishes were only a touch of gentility in an otherwise drab interior.[1]

Bailey was typical of modest slaveholders of Albemarle County. The one luxury object small slaveholders were most likely to have was a looking glass. They did not have fine furniture or tableware. They had no carpets and clocks. They ate from pewter and wooden plates and dishes. Desks and cupboards, common in households with ten or more slaves, were rare below that level.

Based on the ads for property in the *Virginia Gazette*, Camille Wells has concluded that even well-off Virginians, those just below the stratospheric heights of the great planters, lived in one- or two-room houses with a loft above and perhaps an extension to the side or back. Between 1736 and 1780, 1,016 residences were mentioned in 838 for-sale notices in the *Gazette*, probably representing the better properties in the colony. Yet more than half of the ground dimensions of the houses were less than 576 square feet, or 24 by 24 feet, meaning the two main rooms were each 12 × 12. Only 9 dwellings in a thousand ads were described as 1,500 square feet or more, and only 47 of

Table 13.2 LUXURY OBJECTS IN ALBEMARLE COUNTY ESTATE INVENTORIES, 1779–88, BY NUMBER OF SLAVES IN HOUSEHOLD

Slaves in Household (Inventories)	1–4 (8)	5–9 (13)	10–20 (4)
Luxury Object	*Percentage with Object in Inventory*		
Mahogany, cherry, walnut tables and chairs	13	15	0
Ceramics	13	23	25
Linens	0	0	50
Looking glass	38	23	25
Carpet	0	0	0
Clock	0	0	0
Desk, cupboard	13	15	75

Source: Virginia County Court Records, *Will Book: Albemarle County, Virginia, 1752–1756, 1775–1783* (n.p.: Antient, 2002); Virginia County Court Records, *Will Book: Albemarle County, Virginia, 1785–1798* (n.p.: Antient, 2002).

the advertisements mentioned a second floor, suggesting that one story was the norm. Brick or stone was rarely mentioned. A housing survey of Halifax County in 1785 found that more than three-quarters of the inhabitants lived in one-room log or plank houses of less than 310 square feet.[2]

The *Gazette* ads were probably for the upper end of Virginia housing, save for the mansions of the extravagant elite, another category altogether. The little huts of the poorest people were not likely to be advertised. Virginia houses impressed travelers as shabby and cramped. On the eve of the Revolution, one visitor described the Virginia landscape: "Now & then a solitary farm house was to be seen, a narrow wood building, two stories high, with gable ends & a small portico over the central door. A cluster of small, miserable negro huts, a canoe & a brood of little negroes paddling in the mud completed the landscape." Two stories and houses for the slaves would have put the owner of these buildings toward the top of the scale, and travelers were not impressed.[3]

Where southern planters stood out among their fellow colonists on the eve of Revolution was in the large proportion of their wealth invested in labor. Estate inventories in New England in 1774 showed less than a pound invested in slaves and servants; the Middle Colony households averaged £1.8

on average. In the South the average value of their labor was £31.2 per household. In Virginia in 1774–75, the figures were even more stark. Among the smallest slaveholders, those with only one to five servants, estates on average were valued at £191; the value of their slaves was £91, nearly 48 percent of the total.[4]

How are we to understand this high investment in the productive capacity of slaves and yet so little inclination to raise the family's standard of living? Judging from how they deployed their resources, southerners measured their success by the ownership of slaves. Owning slaves in itself, apart from their use, had value. Slaves imparted worth in the South, much as central-passage houses with elegant scroll doorjambs did in the Connecticut Valley.[5] Mastery of other human beings represented competence and achievement as consequential as houses and furniture.

Callam Bailey left his estate to eleven children in 1787. The four boys all received land; four of the unmarried older girls received a horse and saddle. But each of the children, save one daughter, also received a slave. If maximization of productive capacity was the goal, the slaves would have been gathered into a workforce for one or two of his sons. Instead, Bailey bestowed a servant on each of his children, including his daughters. Bailey's girls were to have a horse to ride and a servant to command. A servant was part of proper demeanor. John Davis, who opened a school in sight of the Blue Ridge Mountains in Virginia at the end of the century, described two sisters arriving on a horse on the first day accompanied by a "running footman" who carried a basket of food.[6] Propriety and self-respect required a servant.

Charles Lewis, the wealthiest of the Albemarle County decedents in the 1780s, went even further than Bailey. Each of his six daughters received at least one girl named in the will: Albey daughter of Nan, Yaf daughter of Phoebe, Suck daughter of Judith, Lucy daughter of Phoebe, Mary daughter of Mulatto Lucy, Amy daughter of Mulatto Lucy, and Hanah daughter of Tamar. Then, having slaves to spare, Lewis went on to the next generation. Grandson Howell received "Negro boy Bob son of Cate," while granddaughter Sally was given "Negro girl Lucinda daughter of Patt." The same for all his progeny. Three boys were each given "a Negro boy between the ages of four and seven years," and four granddaughters "a Negro girl between the ages of four and seven years."[7] Lewis felt that every one of his descendants should have a girl or boy slave, perhaps first as playmate and eventually as servant. A slave marked the standing he hoped they would enjoy.

This mingling of slaves and white children was both congenial and cruel, for it inevitably led to a crisis. At some point in time, childhood ended. A French visitor to Virginia in the early nineteenth century called this passage "the time of transition from happy ignorance to painful knowledge."[8] The assignment of black children aged four to seven years to white children not much older suggests a question for southern farm history: How did white and black humans differentiate themselves? How did slave children learn to be slaves and white children learn to be masters?

Stories

Hints of how young slaves learned their roles can be found in the narratives collected from former slaves in the 1930s. Even though shaped by time and many retellings, the tales suggest the complexities of childhood relationships. In 1937, long after slavery had ended, ninety-six-year-old Mrs. Fannie Berry, born a Virginia slave in 1841, remembered her adventures with "young marser Tom," as recorded by an interviewer who tried to capture her colloquial speech. "He was my real marser too," she told the interviewer, "but I b'longed to Miss Sarah Ann, 'cause he couldn't own me till he was 21." For the time being they "used to play together all de time. Used to come down to de quarters early in de mornin' an' call neith de window, 'Fanny, git up, we gonna git bark.' " The children collected strips of bark in the woods to lay on the coals while clothes were being ironed. The bark kept the ashes off the iron when it was put in the fire to reheat.[9]

"Marse Tom an' me used to make a game of it. We'd go runnin' from tree to tree each tryin' to find de bigges' pieces of bark," Fannie remembered. The big pieces had the advantage of lasting a long time before burning away. Trouble began when Fannie spotted a big tree and put her arms around it to claim it as hers, taunting Tom by saying "I got de bigges', I got de bigges'." Not to be out done, Tom came running up and warned her away. That day he had brought a forbidden axe with him instead of the paring knife he was supposed to use. "Fanny take your han away fo' I cut it off," he threatened. "Go way, I saw it fust," Fannie said. "Git yo' own bark." Swinging the axe menacingly to scare off Fannie, Tom lost his grip and the axe came down on Fannie's finger. "Chip de end right off. Twas jus' hanging on by a little thread of skin, an' de blood come flyin' out." Terrified, Tom pled with Fannie, "Don't tell Missus, I give you all my sweet bread in de mornin'." Fannie agreed not to tell and then tended to her wounded finger. "I ketch holt to dat little piece dat's hangin' an' pulled it off an' throwed it in de bushes. Den I tore off piece my petticoat, an' wrapped all roun' it an' started for home." Tom followed carrying the bark, calling out "Member, Fanny, you promised you won't gonna tell."[10]

When they got to the yard, the petticoat bandage came off and the blood spurted again. Looking out the window, Sarah Ann saw the bleeding. "She come runnin' out, an' yellin', 'Chile, what you do?' " She washed off the finger, applied mustard, and tied it up tight again, asking all the time how it happened. True to her word, Fannie said nothing, but Sarah Ann guessed the truth. She took hold of Marse Tom and "give him a good whuppin'." "How I knowed dat," Fannie explained, "was cause I heard him cryin'. White folks never whupped white chillum in front of niggers, no matter what dey do." Through it all, Fannie said nothing about Tom, "an' show nough next mornin' he gimme his sweetbread."[11]

It is hard to tell what Fannie Berry knew as a child playing with Tom and what she added later after growing up in slavery. As a little girl, did she understand the complicated relationship of a playmate who was to be her master, but not quite yet? The story suggests that as a child she was sure enough of her friendship with Tom to take liberties with him. "I got de bigges', I got de bigges'," she gleefully shouts. When he demands the tree for himself, she does not meekly yield but boldly claims "I saw it fust." Just as telling, she promises to cover up his crime and keeps her promise. She was proud of her loyalty to Tom. Before she was a slave, Fannie was a playmate of a young white boy. For her, slavery emerged from friendship, which, for all the suffering she underwent, she never forgot. Thomas Jefferson had grown up with Jupiter, one of his father's slaves born the same year. In adulthood Jupiter served as Jefferson's body servant and later his coachman. Jupiter's son Philip was the friend of Thomas Jefferson Randolph, the president's grandson. Randolph referred to Phil as his "companion in childhood and friend through life."[12]

Judging from her respectful comments, Fannie was as close to her mistress as she was to Tom. One wonders what she means to convey by recounting Sarah Ann's binding of the wound. Throughout her long narrative, Fannie invariably speaks well of her mistress. Is Fannie trying to say she was valued? Sarah Ann cared that this little black girl had lost her fingertip, and the girl never forgot. At the time, she may not have understood why Tom was whipped out of view. She wouldn't have known that white owners never wanted slaves to see a white person subjected to the same punishment as blacks. Fannie was caught up in a swirl of affections, loyalties, and limits she could scarcely have understood at first.

And what did Tom learn? He had put himself at the mercy of Fannie's goodwill. That was not a wise course for an emerging master. What should he have done? One conclusion would be not to play with slaves. More distance was required, so as never to have to beg for a slave's favor. Five years later, Tom would not have begged for Fannie's mercy; he would have threatened to beat her if she betrayed him.

At another time, Tom showed Fannie some little sticks with yellow ends. He "drawed one cross a rock, an' it made a fire." She begged for one and put it in her hair. Later, on her own, she went into the barn to try it out. She struck it across a rock and "sho' nough it made a fire." She dropped it into some leaves in the barn and then ran away terrified. Hiding in the cornfield, she saw smoke and flames rolling out of the barn, and she "could hear it crackin'." She watched as the master formed a bucket chain to pass water from the well. Once the fire was under control, the master "called all de nigger chillum together an' tole em he gonna whup ev'y last one of 'em cause he knows one of dem don made dat fire. An' he whupped 'em too till he got tired, whilst I lay dere in de corn fiel' not darin' to raise my head. Never did whup me."[13]

By this time, whippings stood out in Fannie's mind. She had learned to respect those outbursts of the master's passion. She did not rush to protect the "chillum" as she had protected Tom. She stayed out of the firefighting scene and watched the master whipping the children until he tired, glad she was not one of them. She showed no regret or guilt for the trouble she had made for the others. She showed more concern for Tom than for the other slave children. What she remembered was that she had made a terrible mistake and yet escaped punishment.[14] As a child, self-preservation meant more to her than solidarity.

By slow and precarious steps, Fannie learned to act the part of a young slave. Somehow she found the courage to resist white lust. "I wuz one slave dat de poor white man had his match." When one tried to throw her down, she fought back. "We tusseled an' knocked over chairs an' when I got a grip

I scratched his face all to pieces." One wonders how her assailant told the tale, but Fannie had her story: "dar wuz no more bothering Fannie from him." She was not claiming that she and her sisters always won out. "Us colored women had to go through a plenty, I tell you."[15] But the stories she told about white advances were the ones in which the slave women fended off their attackers.

On big plantations, slaves often knew their parents. Men and women could find a spouse among the twenty or thirty people living in a quarter and maintain a modest family life. Cornelia Carney remembered her father as "de purties' black man you ever saw." John Jones Littleton "had a long thin nose like a white man, an' had de lovelies' white teef, an' hones' chile, de purties' mouf." He could make anything, Cornelia remembered, including a chest she owned. She refused to sell the chest to white folks because they treated her father "so mean. Ole Marsa Littleton used to beat father all de time. His back was a sight. It was scarred up an' brittled fum shoulder to shoulder."[16] The dispute between them was that John wanted to work with wood and the master wanted him in the fields.

After many whippings, John Littleton ran away and lived in the woods, slipping back on Saturday or Sunday when the master and mistress were in church. "Mama used to send John, my oldes' brother, out to de woods wid food fo' father, an' what he didn't git from us de Lawd provided." With her father were Gabriel his cousin and a man named Charlie. The master searched the woods without ever capturing the fugitives. "Niggers was too smart fo' white folks to git ketched. White folks was sharp too, but not sharp enough to git by ole Nat." Cornelia explained that "git by ole Nat " was a phrase folks used referring to Nat Turner. "De meanin' I git is dat de niggers could always out-smart de white folks."[17]

Limited as was her time with her beautiful father, Cornelia loved and admired him. He stood for something. She classed him with clever, rebellious blacks like Nat Turner, thus mingling black national history with local, personal history. The very absence of father John was turned into a sign of his smarts and his heroism. Her tale of a proud father—who stood up against the cruel master who had unjustly beaten him until his back was brittle—inspired and instructed her.

Black oral culture consisted of stories like these. They were the slaves' literature, an imaginative world they created to sustain their dignity and hope. This lore, kept alive by many retellings, instructed the rising generation about the nature of their plight and the possibilities of life under slavery. The stories probably conveyed more of life's truth than explicit admonitions from masters and parents. They illuminated a slave's ambiguous relationships to masters and mistresses, to other slaves, to their parents, and to themselves. The stories laid out possibilities, often in a way to give slaves hope and agency, while conveying the ambivalence and conflict in slave life. Learning took place whenever the stories were told.[18]

Monticello's "Roll of the Negroes"

Most of the stories about slavery in eighteenth-century Albemarle County were told by the slaves of Thomas Jefferson. They were written by people who worked close to him and remembered their experiences in the light of their master's eminence. The stories are warmhearted and admiring. They depict a strong, wise, powerful master. The storytellers showed no inclination to outwit their master or hold him at bay.

On the master's side, no stories are forthcoming. From Jefferson himself, we learn the statistics of slave management as recorded in his Farm Book and Memorandum Book. He occasionally commented on his slaves in his correspondence, but said almost nothing personal. In his extensive correspondence, he left no anecdotes. The death of his house servant Burwell in 1819 upset Jefferson, but he never spoke of his feelings for Jupiter, the slave who was born at Shadwell the same year as Jefferson and who later served as his valet and coachman. Jefferson attributed Jupiter's death to "an imprudent perseverance in journeying" when Jefferson wanted him to stay home. Jefferson said he was sorry to lose him but was miffed that "he leaves a void in my administration which I cannot fill up." Someone else would have to bottle the cider.[19]

Most of what we know about Jefferson's management of his slaves comes from his Farm Book. He made many entries from 1794 to 1796 after his resignation as secretary of state, and again after retirement from the presidency in 1809. Jefferson arrived at Monticello from Philadelphia on January 16, 1794, and wrote nothing for ten months. Then in December 1794, impressed perhaps with the complexity of running a plantation again, he turned to his instinctive method for gaining control—charting a plan. For the next two months, perhaps the high point of Jefferson's engagement with farming, he turned his thoughts into tables and calculations. He made lists and created charts, often estimating costs for every activity. At one point he set aside sixty-eight pages as a filing system for what he styled "Aphorisms, Observations, Facts in husbandry." He put headings on the pages and left space for information under seventeen categories from "Implements of husbandry & operations with them," to "Potash" and "Tenants." The Farm Book reveals the mind of a farmer with unusually strong rational impulses trying to bring his plantation into order.[20]

Judging by his record, Jefferson's highest priority was management of his large, valuable, and unwieldy workforce. Of all the things a rising planter had to learn, regulation of his slaves was the most challenging. The first entry in the Farm Book, dated November 1794, was a "Roll of the negroes." Keeping track of the people he owned was a big job, especially when births and deaths constantly altered the names on the list. The second entry in the Farm Book in 1794 was a "Register of births." He made similar lists in 1774, when he had inherited 135 slaves from his father-in-law and was beginning to take farming seriously. Many subsequent lists appear in the Farm Book, even after he had relinquished management of his farm to his son-in-law and grandson.[21]

In 1794 Jefferson owned 154 slaves, 105 of them at the adjoining Albemarle plantations of Monticello, Tufton, Shadwell, and Lego. The remainder were at Poplar Forest in Bedford County. The 64 slaves at Monticello were the single largest contingent. He knew all of them by name—Bagwell, Minerva, Ursula, Mary, Virginia, Judy, Austin. The names were not listed alphabetically but grouped by two categories, family and skill. In the left margins, he placed brackets around families, and in the right margin around skill groups. Eight families resided at Monticello, accounting for 34 of the 64 slaves. Four categories of skills were named, smiths, carpenters, carters, and spinners, and one was left unlabeled, nail makers. The first three were all men; the spinners were all women. The skills categories were not rigorous or exclusive. "Phill shoemaker" was bracketed with the carpenters.[22]

Once Jefferson had listed his slaves by families and skills, he began another series of lists accounting for supplies. Food, clothing, and bedding were the ongoing expenses of slavery, and Jefferson sought for control here as in everything else on the plantation. His first list recorded the distribution of blankets. He assumed a blanket was good for ten years and so headed each column with a ten-year period: 1792–1801, 1793–1802, 1794–1803. Betty Brown received a blanket for herself in 1792, and a year later another blanket for her two children, Wormeley Hughes and Burwell Colbert. Doll received her own blanket in 1792 and blankets for her children in 1794. Had Jefferson kept the lists up, he could have told, when a slave begged for another blanket, the date when the previous blanket had been issued.[23] No one could sell a blanket and then request another ahead of schedule.

Jefferson was even more careful with cloth. Rather than purchase ready-made clothing for his workers, he purchased cloth and thread for each slave and assigned slave tailors to cut and sew. To know how much to buy, he calculated that it took three "skaines" of thread to make a shirt and three to mend it. The same for a "suit of cloth." He made an attempt to scale the yards of cloth required according to age. A one-year-old's suit called for a yard of linen, a two-, three-, or four-year-old's two yards, and so on up to sixteen years, when six yards were required. Grown men or women needed seven yards, and very large people eight yards.[24] Jefferson drew a line through these calculations as if they were in some way unsatisfactory, but they accorded with his way of working.

Having determined just amounts for their winter clothing, Jefferson noted the cloth needed for each slave. John Hemings was allotted seven yards of linen and eight "half ells" of "knap." An ell was generally forty-five inches, so that eight half ells was roughly five yards. Knap or nap was a heavy woolen, probably for winter wear. With the fabric, John required six skeins of thread plus three more. Probably the six was the ration for making his "suit" and the three for mending, a slight change from Jefferson's earlier calculation. In this list, men generally required seven yards of linen, and eight of knap, adult women the same, teenagers five yards, and the children two or three. The adults needed shoes and stockings; the children neither. Monticello's slave children went barefoot and sockless even in winter.[25] In summer, another batch of cloth and thread was required.

The primary purpose of the lists was to calculate purchases. Jefferson had to know how much cloth to order. In December 1794, the month after he had made an accounting of his slaves, Jefferson sent off a bulk order to Fleming and McLanahan for 343 yards of knaps and halfthicks, five dozen stockings in four different sizes, and twenty-eight blankets. He ordered 514½ yards of "oznabrigs," the rough linen named for its origins in Osnabruck, Germany, and commonly used for slave clothing. He ordered thread by weight, four pounds of it. Earlier he had calculated that he could derive 100 to 130 skeins of thread from a pound.[26] He served as his own procurement officer, a necessary part of providing for his numerous workforce.

Jefferson had similar responsibilities for his slaves' food. Less accounting was necessary for provisions because of the standard weekly ration: one peck of cornmeal (two dry gallons), a half-pound of pork or pickled beef, and four salted fish. In 1797 Jefferson listed the names of slaves and their ration by groups, usually by family. Lucy received two rations because of her son Zach; Betty B three pecks because of children Melinda and Edwin; Jupiter four because of his wife Suck and their sons Philip and Johnny. Fifteen teenage nail makers formed another group.[27] A fish list follows the same pattern, though somewhat more roughly. Betty Brown and her two sons received eight fish rather than twelve because her children were young. Five hired enslaved men received six fish each. During the arduous harvest season all the workers received extra rations, fresh meat every day with peas.[28]

To provide sufficient food was in Jefferson's interest as well as his slaves'. To keep them working, he needed a well-stocked storehouse. In December 1794, when he was rationalizing the whole system, he calculated what he would need for all the consumers in his family economy. He counted the barrels of corn on hand at Monticello and Shadwell, 229½ and 256½, and then calculated his needs for the 120 persons at the two plantations, plus all the riding horses, broodmares, colts, mules, workhorses, oxen, and so on down the list of animals, to beeves and hogs. In a column opposite each type, he noted their needs: 1 peck of corn a week for each of the 120 persons; 1½ gallons a day in winter for each of eight riding horses and 1 gallon in summer. The hogs received a half-bushel a day, or 2 pecks, which was 4 dry gallons. All of the animals, save for riding horses and workhorses, were fed corn from December 15 to April 1; after that they foraged in the woods and at pasture. When everything was added up, Jefferson calculated that he would need 512 barrels of corn by November 15, 1795, and he had only 486 barrels on hand, putting him in the market for 26 additional barrels.[29]

Jefferson was unusual in writing down and preserving all of his calculations and plans for his plantation, but not unusual in his thinking. Every farmer with slaves had to keep track of them by name, note the births in his mind, figure out how to house them by family groups, provide cloth and thread for clothing, and supply them with food. Every young planter-to-be had to acquire the skills of a quartermaster to keep work in the fields and barns humming along.

The masters had to be ready to deal with breakdowns too. Slave populations were subject to epidemics and common diseases, as well as the perils of childbirth and aging. A sick slave was of no use to his master and commonly an expense. Jefferson spent from forty to sixty dollars a year on doctors to tend to his slaves. He limited their attendance to certain diseases: "pleurisies, or other highly inflammatory fevers, intermitting fevers, dysenteries, and venereal cases." As was common in his day, Jefferson doubted the doctors' efficacy. Except for the diseases he named, "they oftener do harm than good." Jefferson thought for most of the slaves' illnesses that "a dose of salts as soon as they are taken is salutary in almost all cases, and hurtful in none." "A lighter diet and kind attention restore them soonest." He forbade bleeding, a common remedy, but did inoculate a few slaves at Monticello against smallpox in the 1770s, a risky procedure. Beginning in 1801, after the arrival of Edward Jenner's procedure, all the slaves were vaccinated.[30]

Jefferson would have liked to achieve the same degree of efficiency in every aspect of his farm operations, including the management of work. In July 1795, while still at the peak of his interest in agriculture, he kept close notes on the harvest of a parcel of wheat near Monticello, reducing the entire operation to numbers: twelve workers cradled the seventy-three acres in two days, which he calculated as three acres a day for each worker. Oxcarts manned by three loaders plus a driver transported the sheaves from the field. Each loading took fifteen minutes, and carrying it a quarter of a mile and returning took another twenty-two minutes. Having broken down the process into its parts, Jefferson projected what should happen "were the harvest to go over again with the same force."

A treading floor should be laid down before harvest
A half dozen spare scythes should be mounted and a half dozen more made ready
The slave George with tools and a grindstone mounted should stand ready to mend cradles and grind scythes.
18. Cradlers should work constantly. Smith George, John, Davy, Lewis, Johnny, Isabel, Patrick, Isaac, Ned, Toby, James, Val. Bagwell Caesar Jerry Tim & Philip.
18. binders. Of the women & abler boys. Isabel. Jenny. Jenny. Doll. Molly. Amy. Minerva. Lucinda. Judy. Belinda. York. Burwell, Jamy, Barnaby. Davy. Patty. Lucy.
6. gatherers, to wit 5 smaller boys & 1 larger for a foreman. Wormely. Brown. Davy. John. Ben. Kit.

3. Loaders. Moses, Shepherd & Joe.
6. stackers. Squire. Abram. shoemkr. Phill, Essex, Goliah. Austin.
2. cooks. O. Betty & Fanny.
4. Carters. Tom. Phill. Frank. Martin.
8. would remain to keep half the ploughs a going. Rachael. Mary. Nanny. Sally. Thamar. Iris. Scilla. Phyllis

Jefferson named the slaves he would deploy to their various posts, suggesting that he did see them as individuals, but the aim, as with all who measure work in the interests of efficiency, was the creation of a human machine. Speaking of his plan, he observed that "in this way the whole machine would move in exact equilibrio, no part of the force could be lessened without retarding the whole, nor increased without a waste of force." His aim, as with his plow, was mathematical exactitude and machinelike efficiency. It was as far as he could carry rational agriculture in the human department. Sickness, recalcitrance, mistakes, and accidents all lay waiting to disrupt the plan. Yet Jefferson could not forgo his desire to achieve some measure of control, something more effective than his current harvesting program. While his nailery was in operation, he personally weighed the iron given to each worker in the morning and returned in the evening to weigh their nail production, hoping to prevent theft and to measure the productivity of each slave.[31]

In 1794 he saw more practical ways to extract labor from this workforce. The slaves, he knew, were a resource that must be employed to maximum advantage. How could little children, for example, be tended without keeping valuable female hands from the fields? "Build the Negro houses nearer together that the fewer nurses may serve & that the children may be more easily attended to by the super-annuated women." That put the old women to work and released the young females for the field. Old men and women, termed by Jefferson the "senile corps," could garden. "The negroes too old to be hired," he suggested to his steward in 1788, "could they not make a good profit by cultivating cotton?" The sick enjoyed some respite. "Invalids," he proposed, should be made to work "only when they shall be able," at such tasks as hauling dirt from a canal Jefferson was digging.[32]

There was also work for children. To help the old women, he wanted "children till 10. years old to serve as nurses." They could help the "super-annuated" with child care. From ten on, they could go on to more productive labor. "from 10. to 16. the boys make nails, the girls spin. at 16. go into the ground or learn trades." He was proud of a thirteen-year-old who "works well at the plough already." Jefferson was not alone in his thinking about child labor. In the 1780s, the Virginia assembly altered the tax list categories to take into account the economic worth of young slaves. In 1782 tax legislation simply called for the number of slaves without distinguishing their ages. That changed in 1784 to distinguish titheable slaves, the truly valuable adults, from those under sixteen. By 1788, there was column for "No of Negroes abo 16" and another for "no of Negros between 12 and 16," implying that by twelve, they could be put to work. By 1794, all slaves from twelve up were taxed the same. Children were part of the remunerative workforce.[33]

Discipline

All these schemes presumed the slaves would work when told. In 1794 Jefferson owned 154 slaves. How were they to be kept in order? They had every motive to steal and damage and worse. As Jefferson put it rather ominously, a slave must seek "the evanishment of the human race, or entail his own miserable condition on the endless generations proceeding from him." Every slave owner faced the same difficulty. Callam Bailey had to teach his sons and daughters the right techniques and attitudes before he bequeathed them slaves. Bailey seemed to be confident he had prepared his children when he gave to "Nancy and Phanny Baily one Negro woman named Jenny and her future increase."[34] By the time they were young adults, southern white children had learned to deal with black servants.

Jefferson avoided harsh punishment most of the time. One of his most talented slaves, Isaac Granger, said later, "Old Master very kind to servants." Madison Hemings, Jefferson's son by Sally Hemings, left the same impression. "About his own home he was the quietest of men. He was hardly ever known to get angry, though sometimes he was irritated when matters went wrong." Occasionally he did authorize a whipping of particularly fractious slaves, and he allowed his overseers to whip slaves as part of ordinary discipline. But it was not to his taste. The harshest punishment he regularly inflicted was to sell slaves. Workers who repeatedly ran away or were consistently troublesome could count on being disposed of. He sold more than a hundred slaves over the course of his life.[35]

Monticello was proof that whippings were not the only way to make slaves work. While traveling, Jefferson tipped slaves, and so did his guests.

Judging from their later accounts, servants remembered tips as well as they did whippings. Isaac related a story about a gift from Mrs. Wiley, a baker in Richmond, whom he helped while serving Jefferson in the state capital. She sometimes gave Isaac a loaf of bread or a cake and, when she later visited Monticello, gave him ninepence, remarking that "this is the boy that made fires for me." Jefferson did the same when he traveled. As a reward for their labors in the nailery, he gave the young workers an extra meat ration, with suits of red or blue for the best producers.[36]

Colonel Archibald Cary was a heavy tipper. As the grandfather of Jefferson's son-in-law Thomas Mann Randolph, Jr., Cary regularly visited Monticello. He owned more slaves than Jefferson and had his own ways of treating them. One was to tip liberally. Isaac remembered Cary giving five or six dollars to the house servants on his departure. He was demanding, too. Soon after his arrival he would inquire in the kitchen about the menu. If he was not pleased, he would insist that they cook his favorite. As he came up the long drive to Monticello, Cary expected the three gates to be opened, one a mile from the house, another three quarters of a mile, then the yard gate at the stable three hundred yards from the house. Cary would write when he was coming, and Jefferson sent Isaac to open the gates. If Isaac was not there in time, as soon as he got to the house, Cary would "look about for him and whip him with his horse-whip." Isaac said Cary gave him "more whippings than he has fingers and toes."[37] Jefferson apparently had to tolerate his guest's presumption. The whippings implied a white person had the right to mete out discipline to slaves under any circumstances.

Observant in all things, Thomas Jefferson understood the education of children in the management of slaves. In *Notes on the State of Virginia,* he recognized that children learned the arts of mastery by watching. "The parent storms, the child looks on, catches the lineaments of wrath, puts on the same airs in the circle of smaller slaves, gives a loose to his worst of passions, and thus nursed, educated, and daily exercised in tyranny, cannot but be stamped by it with odious peculiarities." Was Jefferson thinking of Cary when he wrote that "the whole commerce between master and slave is a perpetual exercise of the most boisterous passions, the most unremitting despotisms on the one part, and the degrading submissions on the other?" Or had he felt boisterous passions himself? One of his infrequent outbursts of anger was directed at Jupiter, his close companion from boyhood and coachman at Monticello. Jupiter objected to Jefferson letting a young slave take one of the carriage horses to run an errand and told his master so. Jefferson was thrown into a passion. He chastised Jupiter for using "so blunt a method of 'telling his mind.'" One biographer said that "never before or afterwards" was such a tone "witnessed at Monticello." For an instant Jefferson showed signs of rage below the calm exterior.[38]

Jefferson probably had witnessed "boisterous passions" in other households. His indictment of the "customs and manners" of a slave society has to be a commentary on his Albemarle neighbors. Nothing he had seen caused Jefferson to mitigate his disheartening judgment about "the lineaments of wrath." He would lead us to believe that Charles Lewis's bequest of a slave age four to seven to each of his grandchildren implied that they had learned from their parents how to put on "airs in the circle of smaller slaves." The arts of mastery, Jefferson seemed to say, required little explicit instruction. Children absorbed those manners with the air they breathed. Even little girls learned to be cruel at times.

Small Planters

The size of the slave workforce on each plantation made a big difference in slave family life. If the workers lived in the same quarters, husbands and wives could cobble together a much more conventional family order. The chances of finding a mate close to home were much better, and after a slave marriage, some big planters housed family groups so that they could cook and sleep together. Husband, wife, and children could raise chickens in the yard and tend vegetables in the little plots by their houses, and husbands could hunt and fish. Jefferson's sparse food allowances assumed that slaves would augment their diets with fresh food from their gardens and meat from the woods. On big plantations, moreover, slave children could look to their parents for guidance on how to live as a slave. After age sixteen, they worked alongside their mothers and fathers, making it more likely that they would grow up with memories of their parents. Cornelia Carney remembered her father's white teeth and beautiful mouth.[39]

In Albemarle County in 1792, about 23 percent of the slaves lived on plantations with more than twenty slaves, 20 percent on plantations with eleven to twenty slaves. The rest, 57 percent, were divided between small slaveholders with one to five slaves and slightly larger groups with six to ten slaves. The 32 percent who worked on farms with five or fewer slaves are the most difficult to recover. It is hard to know even where slaves slept on small farms. On larger plantations by the last quarter of the eighteenth century, barracks that housed a parcel of slaves were giving way to log cabins large enough for one or two families. At Monticello, the house servants' families were given earthen-floor cabins ranging from 12 by 14 feet to 12 by 20 feet. We can picture the slave quarters as small villages, like Mulberry Row at Monticello, where slave families worked at their trades, cooked, gathered at night to sing, and lived as families in their own cabins. The 12 × 14 cabin was the usual dwelling on middling plantations, too.[40]

On small farms, scarcely any evidence of living quarters survives. Households with only a slave or two probably housed them in work sheds or barns, with straw or old rags for a bed and little warmth and less privacy. An architectural survey of Halifax County in 1785 estimated that a third of all slaves dwelled in kitchens or outbuildings. The slaves occupying these make-do accommodations were probably the ones on small farms. If they lived in kitchens or stretched out between tools and stalls in outbuildings, where did they cook, eat, converse, rest, make love?[41]

The poverty of the sources limits our knowledge of slave lives on modest farms. Small farmers did not keep farm diaries or write their friends about plantation affairs, and the legal documents where slaves are mentioned are sparse. Slaves always appeared in tax lists, but only as numbers—how many "negroes over age 16" or "between 12 and 16." Wills give the slaves' names and specify the people to whom they were bequeathed, but without comment about how they were treated or where they lived. Probate inventories offer elusive clues to the slaves' material environment without saying which implements or pieces of furniture they used. To reconstruct the lives of small-farm slaves from this spare offering, we have to use our imaginations a bit more freely than usual.

The name of William Owens, a small Albemarle County planter, appeared on the 1782 tax list with four slaves. Owens was nearing the end of his life. In the eight years before he died in 1790, Owens set up his three sons, David, William, Jr., and Stewart, on their own farms in Albemarle. Meanwhile, three of Owens's daughters, Mary, Elizabeth, and Elenor, married, leaving only Jane at home to help in the household. No wife is mentioned in the will. By 1791, when William's will was probated, he had provided for his three sons and settled three daughters in marriage, a record to be proud of by eighteenth-century standards.[42] Strangely, no mention is made in the will of the five slaves named in the estate inventory. According to the tax lists for succeeding years, they remained with David. Everyone must have agreed they were his.[43] The three slave men named in the probate inventory, Simon, John, and Stephen, were probably three of the four slaves consistently numbered under David's name in the tax lists. Father William also had two female slaves to help in the house, perhaps under the direction of David's wife with Jane's assistance.

How did the Owens family employ their five slaves? The inventory points to a bevy of nonagricultural operations. William and his boys owned cattle or hogs, to be sure—"2 stock locks & 1 branding iron" evidenced that—but little to indicate crop production: no scythes, reaping hooks, sieves, casks, hogsheads, plows, hoes, carts, butter pots. The will does mention "Plantation" tools going to David, indicating that some of those items had passed to him before the appraisers came, but the inventory emphasizes what the will refers to as "carpenters tools and stilliards [steelyards]." William Owens owned fourteen "cut saws" (probably crosscut saws), three augers, three chisels, an axe, a gouge, a drawing knife, a claw hammer, a pair of maul rings, and three wedges.[44] The maul rings reinforced the heavy mallets used to drive wedges into logs. Together they suggest a lumbering operation, perhaps to split shingles and fence rails or make siding. The augers, the chisels, and the gouge would be useful in rough carpentry, perhaps raising slave cabins. The family may have made barrel staves, as the drawing knife suggests.

Inside the house, more making was going on: "1 cotton wheel, 1 flax ditto, 1 jack reel, 2 pr. Cotton and wool cards," and "1 loom and gear," plus the presence of a pair of "Taylors shears," suggest that the Owenses were running sheep, shearing them, carding the wool, spinning, and weaving—a lot of labor for the girls growing up, doubtless aided by the slave women Ann and Fanny.[45] The steelyards for weighing bulky objects suggest that they were trading in wool, too. They probably grew their own flax for spinning on the flax wheel. The box iron with two heaters smoothed the linen after it was woven. The Owens household was a small textile factory, handling the entire process from sheep and flax to finished wool and linen. The women held up their side of "manufacturing," as the will put it, to match the men's lumbering and carpentry.

The male slaves, Simon, John, and Stephen, may have managed the cattle and sheep and worked in the cornfields that were certainly under cultivation to provide basic food for the family. But they must also have been part of the work crews that felled and cut the logs. So many saws—fourteen of them—provide further evidence of a lumber operation. As William grew older, either Stephen or John held one end of the saw while David probably pulled the other. Many saws suggest many people working at once.

On large plantations, tradesman slaves were distinguished from those who worked the land. In small households like the Owenses', slaves were into everything. They were members of flexible work crews managed by the masters. Small owners had every incentive to enlarge the range of their slaves' skills. If they did not teach slaves to read and write, they certainly taught them to plow and fell trees, to cut grain and sift wheat, to card and spin. Like all farmers, slave farmers were people of many skills. How about their slaves? On large plantations like Monticello, there could be a division of labor between the skilled craftsmen and the people who worked in the ground. Jefferson favored the skilled people who worked under his direct command, while the field hands only saw the master sitting on his horse, watching as they hoed. That division of labor was not possible on small plantations. Male slaves learned all the male skills, and the females learned to spin, garden, and dairy. Over a lifetime, they would all develop a number of talents and come close to being coworkers rather than drudges.[46] Stephen's appraisal at seventy pounds, a good price, suggests that he was skilled.

Owens or one of the sons would always have been in charge of the work in the woods or on building projects, but the masters did not stand by and watch while the slaves labored. By the same token, William's wife and then the older girls probably sat at the spinning wheels alongside Fanny and Ann. Especially for labor that required two sets of hands, like moving logs or rails, slave and master worked together. Grain harvests required as much help as possible to mow, rake, shock, and thresh. A female slave would have been in the fields in that season along with all the men in the family. Slaughter of the hogs required someone to separate out the victim, hold the animal while it was bound, and carry away the cuts of meat to pack in salt. Slaves were part of a black-and-white work crew. Work can go on in silence for long spells until grunts or hand signals or words come into play to coordinate the action. Each worker has to have the other in mind to move the task along. A kind of camaraderie of work takes over, even if one worker is boss. In households with one or two male slaves and one or two female slaves, work wove ties across the master-slave divide.[47]

But at night, separation occurred. Philip Morgan, who studied slavery in Virginia for many years, judges it unlikely that masters would invite a slave into the house to sleep. Because the Owenses probably occupied a very small house themselves, the slaves probably slept in a shed, denied the comfort and warmth the Owens family enjoyed. Did they eat meals together? Probably not. Domestically, white and black were divided. Whatever degree of companionship developed through common work, it could not erase the bedrock realities of the relationship. Small-farm slaves had to learn to divide their feelings. Work brought slaves closer to their white masters, but the camaraderie of work ended once work stopped. Slave children had to learn to live within bounds. There had to be a gulf, a psychic space, a callus to protect them from the rebuff they met every night when they went "home" after work.[48]

Education

The history of education has little to say about slaves before 1865. No one thought to send them to school. Jefferson's Isaac Granger slept in the "out-chamber" fifty yards from Monticello where the young scholars from the neighborhood studied while going to school. He slept on the floor in a blanket and made the fire in the classroom each morning. That was the closest Isaac got to formal schooling. He did, however, learn a trade. Jefferson apprenticed him to a tinsmith in Philadelphia and later put him to work in the nailery. After Granger gained his freedom, he worked as a blacksmith. Like other masters, Jefferson picked out promising young slaves for training. The pattern was for the master to hire a skilled tradesmen to train the slaves, then let the slaves take over the skilled work to reduce labor costs.[49] Skilled slaves were essential to the workings of large plantations, and they were more valuable by 20 percent or more.[50]

By happenstance and inclination, slaves also picked up learning incidentally. Madison Hemings learned to read by "inducing the white children to teach me the letters." The slaves also taught each other. Isaac Granger learned to play the drum from a slave named Mat Henderson, who was courting Mary Hemings. Henderson would visit her in the kitchen at Monticello while Granger was working in the house. Mat had learned to beat the drum while his master played the fife on ceremonial occasions, and when Mat came to the kitchen, he brought the drum along. According to his memoir, "Isaac would beat on it and Mat larnt him how to beat." Fifty years later, he remembered the chance circumstances that put him in the path of a drum and a drummer as a significant moment. One can imagine a host of skills like trapping, weaving, and singing passed along by chance and imitation through the veins and arteries of communal life.[51] The slave community can be thought of as a learning order, disseminating information by example, observation, imitation, and the telling of stories.

It is less clear how well the slave community guided young slaves in their great life choices. One of the greatest was how much to seek the master's trust and how much to resist him. The slaves whose names come down in history from Jefferson's household were trust seekers: Madison Hemings, Isaac Granger, Israel Gillette Jefferson, Sally Hemings, George Granger, Ursula Granger, Jupiter, Mary Hemings. They were the ones to leave stories and their names in the record. For them, Jefferson's return home was "a great event," as Israel Jefferson, a house servant and carriage driver, remembered. They reaped the benefits of being faithful. "For when he came home many of them, especially the leading ones, were sure to receive presents from his hands." Less is said of the slaves who tried to escape or stood up to their overseers. At Monticello, they were quickly disposed of and drop out of sight. Elsewhere they were flogged as examples to their fellows. Slave backs were crusted with scars. Though the faithful slaves stand out in the historical record, in real life the rebels offered a stark alternative for young slaves finding their way in the precarious slave world.[52]

Most of Jefferson's trusted slaves came from the ranks of the skilled. Madison Hemings said, "It was his mechanics he seemed mostly to direct, and in their operations he took great interest." Once a slave had worked in the nailery and then gone on to carpentry or blacksmithing, he was in a position to win trust. George Granger was foremost among Jefferson's trusted slaves. In 1773 Jefferson purchased Ursula as a housekeeper for his wife Martha and bid for her husband George to keep the couple together. Ursula ran the kitchen, preserved meat, and washed and ironed clothes. Their son George learned blacksmithing and ran the nailery. Jefferson even granted him 2 percent of the revenue. When Jefferson was away, his son-in-law Thomas Mann Randolph managed Monticello. Randolph wrote that he left the nailery to George. "I am sure he could not stoop to my authority and I hope and believe he pushes your interests as well as I could."[53] Faithful service brought George his own domain.

The elder George's other son, Isaac Granger, tells the story of his father's courage and ingenuity during the British capture of Richmond. Jefferson, then governor, had hurriedly fled as the British under Benedict Arnold swept up the James in January 1781. According to Isaac, George remained behind to receive the British officer who hoped to surprise Jefferson. The office demanded the keys to the house and then asked "Whar is the silver?" George told him the silver had gone with Jefferson "to the mountains." Actually, George had hidden the silver in a bed tick and stashed it under a bed in the kitchen. The officers had to content themselves with raiding the wine cellar and meat house and commandeering Jefferson's stock of corn for their horses. Isaac said George "continued to sarve Mr. Jefferson and had forty pounds from Old Master and his wife." But the immediate reward was only part of George's compensation. He made himself a hero in Isaac's eyes. Isaac admired him for protecting his master, in a sense reversing their roles.[54]

George showed what Jefferson called "character," by which he meant loyalty and trustworthiness. Jefferson valued "character" above all other qualities. He refused to punish a slave who ran from one plantation to another because Jefferson trusted the man's character. It was always an issue. Whom could he trust among all the people doing his bidding? Who acted because he chose to act loyally? There was a kind of manhood and honor in bearing up under temptation. Jupiter drove Jefferson's horses the length of Virginia alone under the mantle of trust, doubtless gaining his master's approbation.[55]

But choosing to show one's honor and manhood by earning trust had its risks. Thomas Mann Randolph reported the case of a slave on another plantation who took the loyalty route and suffered by it. The "sensible, lively, and likely young mulatto man" had avoided "any misconduct." Despite the man's compliance, a new overseer concluded that "fear would be [a] safer security for good conduct than any determination to do right" and flogged the man for leaving his tools behind in the field. Horribly ashamed by the humiliation, the slave "hung himself 30 feet from the ground, in a tree near his Master's door, the same night." It was enough to turn Randolph against the "hideous monster" that was "our Southern system."[56]

No matter how loyal to his master, a trustworthy slave was always in danger of degradation. He could not be sure that some misstep would not destroy his master's confidence. A surer path to honor, though not to safety, lay at the other end of the spectrum, in saying no to masters. In September 1769 Jefferson placed an ad in the *Virginia Gazette* for Sandy, a slave in his mid-thirties who had run away—how far Jefferson could not say. He offered forty shillings for the runaway's recovery in Albemarle County, and ten pounds if he was captured in another colony. Sandy was a tradesman, the kind of slave

Jefferson valued most, a shoemaker and capable of rough carpentry. The problem was that "he is greatly addicted to drink, and when drunk is insolent and disorderly." However compliant on the surface, Sandy was resistant inside. Jefferson saw nothing honorable or admirable in this recalcitrance. In the ad, Jefferson called Sandy "artful and knavish." He may have appeared compliant while privately seething. Sandy took his shoemaking tools with him, doubtless betting that they could earn him an income as a free man. Unfortunately for him, he lost the wager. He was captured, returned to Jefferson, and sold away within three years to a neighbor for one hundred pounds.[57]

Did Sandy think of himself as daring and manly? The ad said "he swears much." Apparently, he was not willing to suppress his feelings all of the time, even within hearing of white ears. Just as important, how did the young slaves feel about Sandy when they heard he was gone and then when he was dragged back? Did they secretly admire him, or did they think him foolhardy to have risked his position as a trusted slave tradesman? Whom should they emulate? George or Sandy? The repercussions of resistance could be horrible. On most plantations, it meant a severe whipping or, with Jefferson, separation from friends and family by sale. Was Sandy admired for risking so much?

Slaves might not initially have had a language for describing the honor in Sandy's flight to freedom. But the Revolution helped. One slave later hanged for involvement in an insurrectionary plot was asked why he turned against his masters. He borrowed language he must have heard often during the past decade. "I have nothing more to offer than what General Washington would have had to offer, had he been taken by the British and put to trial by them. I have adventured my life in endeavouring to obtain the liberty of my countrymen."[58] Like religion later, revolutionary rhetoric gave slaves words to express their sufferings and anger.

For most slaves, the choice was rarely as stark as George versus Sandy. Compliance and resistance operated in a much narrower range. Slaves were mostly caught up in everyday labor—for the master during the day and for themselves at nightfall. They watched after children, hunted for possum and squirrels, tended their gardens, devised more comfortable beds, cared for the sick, and courted. For slaves absorbed in daily routines of survival, resistance may have taken more modest forms, such as the phenomenon the French traveler Count Constantine de Volney observed on his way to visit Jefferson. From a distance, he saw slaves in a field under the watch of an overseer plying a whip. To Volney it appeared that while the overseer was looking at them they worked at one pace, and as soon as he turned his attention elsewhere, the pace slowed.[59] The overseer's gaze was like a searchlight sweeping prison walls. When it fell upon the slaves, they heeded their duties. When the gaze moved on, they let down, spoke, or rested. Young slaves who never came near a radical choice between the paths of George and Sandy would have learned to feel the overseer's gaze upon them and to act accordingly. It was a modest gesture toward Sandy but still a form of resistance. Learning to sense when the overseer was looking and how to meet his expectations was a first step toward artful avoidance of the master's power.

Until the Revolution, most slaves steered a middle course between striving for trust and flaunting their independence. Young, single men were the ones who most often tried to flee.[60] Family men and women held back. During the Revolution, this sensible avoidance of conflict came to an end for some. Beginning with Lord Dunmore's invitation to join him as he left Virginia in 1775, slaves had opportunities to flee to the British lines. More than six thousand in Virginia and Maryland took the leap. Twenty-three of Jefferson's slaves left him (including three men and a boy from Monticello), sixteen of Washington's. They met a miserable fate. About two thousand followed the British out of the United States to Canada. The sick and dying were left behind in their sufferings, either to perish or to be returned to their masters. Jefferson eventually retrieved six of his slaves.[61]

Six thousand was a tiny fraction of the 210,000 slaves in Virginia when the Revolution began, but this time many fled in family groups, some with five or six children.[62] Their willingness to take the risk in wartime suggests that restive, single young men were not the only ones to contemplate escape. Families must have asked the question: Is now the time to go? Will the British king protect us? Will we find safety in the care of the British army? Thoughts of escape may have been brewing for years. How many others mulled possible escape plans, weighed the chances, listened carefully to reports of those who tried? In 1806 Jefferson was surprised that twenty-six-year-old Joe ran away "without the least word of difference with any body, & indeed having never in his life received a blow from any one." For twelve years he had worked at the blacksmith's trade, and then one night, he was gone. During the Revolution, Washington's farm manager reported "there is not a man of them, but would leave us, if they believ'd they coud make their escape."[63] Some left when news of the British army filtered into the quarters; most held fast; many must have imagined how they might play the part of Sandy.

The first thing slaves had to learn was how to deal with the master's ever-present power. What bodily posture, what words, what precautions, what preemptive actions best preserved one's dignity and avoided brutality? It required more than a knowledge of one's duties and the routines of labor. Masters and mistresses could be capricious. As Jefferson said, they gave way to their passions. Slaves had to be ready for anything. They necessarily became expert readers of emotions, especially on the spectrum of calm and wrath. Jefferson's trusted servants spoke appreciatively of his contained behavior. He was not easily ruffled, "the quietist of men," as Madison Hemings put it. Isaac Jefferson, who worked for Thomas Jefferson's daughter Martha, liked her because she was a "mighty peaceable woman: never holler for servant: make no fuss nor racket."[64] They commented because other slaves had to deal with masters who knew no bounds. Slaves were as alert to the turbulent passions as Jefferson was to evidence of loyalty. Masters watched eagle-eyed for signs of subversion; slaves grew hypersensitive to evidence of wrath.

Because slaves harbored thoughts of escape and feelings of resentment, they developed secret selves where lay buried their true feelings and seditious ideas. To stay out of trouble, slaves had to appear compliant and willing. When the British army was tempting slaves to leave, Robert Carter's slaves assured him "we all fully intend to serve you our master," yet thirty of them left when given a chance.[65] Many more than Sandy turned artful to conceal the "knavish" nature that Jefferson detected in his runaway. Slaves dug holes in the earthen floors of their cabins where they buried things they had purchased or stolen. They had to dig holes in their minds for hiding their resistant thoughts and angry feelings. Monticello slaves knew secret paths on the mountain for spiriting away slaves in trouble or getting away themselves to visit other quarters.[66] Secret paths wound through their own minds. They did not begin that way as children paddling in the mud near their huts or hunting for bark in the woods. It was the constant presence of the masters' power that formed the slaves' inner selves.

PART SIX

Approaching the Present

14. American Agriculture, 1800–1862

The family farm idea persisted unchanged through the eighteenth century. Despite setbacks and failures, families did not waver in their belief that farms offered a more dependable livelihood than any other employment. Everywhere it was thought that given adequate land, animals, and the cooperation of their neighbors in the local economy, a family could provision themselves and even prosper. Moreover, with the help of the children's labor, families could give the next generation a start on farms of their own. It always seemed possible that by migration or clever bargaining, beginning farmers could get a foothold. The plentitude of America was the guarantor of that promise.

Nothing in the eighteenth century disrupted this hopeful life plan, though there were obstacles. At midcentury, the progressive contraction of suitable nearby land and the breakdown of the old land distribution systems provoked a temporary crisis. Farmers were forced onto lands with precarious titles or exposure to Indian attack. For a generation or more, violence broke out at the pressure points. But the crisis passed. In the 1780s the new government began to regularize land distribution. By strenuous effort, aspiring farmers could make their way to available land. The system worked because the individual units, the families, were so intent on finding places for themselves. They had the energy and will to locate land and turn it into farms.

The self-provisioning mentality continued into the nineteenth century, even as the structure of the agricultural economy began to shift. Not long after 1800, new markets began to reshape the environment, gradually wearing away eighteenth-century practices. In 1790, when Washington was settling into the presidency, eighteen people lived in rural areas of the United States for every one person residing in a town. In 1860, at the time of Lincoln's election, there were only four rural inhabitants for each town dweller. By the later date, each American farmer had to produce food for roughly four and a half times as many people as his counterpart in 1790.[1] In those seventy years, the urban population multiplied more than thirty times, while the farm population grew less than sevenfold. By midcentury, American farmers had learned to produce vastly more food per capita than their colonial ancestors. The world around the family farm took a new shape.

Until 1790, global demand had determined what staple crops American farmers grew and how they prospered. Tobacco, rice, breadstuffs, indigo, flaxseed, ship masts, furs, and ship stuffs all made their way via the Atlantic to the West Indies and European markets. After 1790, the nation's own cities became the farmers' best markets—with far-reaching consequences. Under the stimulus of expanding urban demand, American farmers adopted better methods of cropping, put fertilizers to work, and invented machines to multiply each worker's efficiency. It took a strenuous effort on many fronts to meet the urban challenge, but farmers rose to the occasion. They fed the burgeoning city population and achieved unprecedented levels of prosperity themselves. The title to the agricultural historian Paul Gates's survey of the years from 1815 to 1860 is appropriate: *The Farmer's Age*.[2]

At the same time that expanding urban markets stimulated increased production, urban cultural values stimulated heightened consumption. In the first half of the nineteenth century, the national economy produced more and more desirable items that were beyond the powers of farmers to make for themselves. Books, stylish clothes, carpets, curtains, prints for the wall, walnut desks and cabinets, school tuitions, newspapers and magazines, flowers and shrubs for front yards, and eventually washing and sewing machines had to be purchased. Provisioning was more than a family could do on its own. Farmers had to increase their buying power in order to increase their purchasing power. There was no other way to meet expanding family needs. More elaborate consumption and improved production went together. The combination eventually transformed the farmer's world.

Urban Markets

As city markets expanded, farm crops brought in unprecedented returns. Hinton Rowan Helper, the eccentric antebellum critic of southern agriculture, claimed that hay was king of all crops in the United States, outranking cotton. Hay was essential for feeding carriage horses, dray horses, and stable nags in northern cities. The market was huge. Helper exaggerated, but Philadelphia did consume 20,561 tons of hay in 1845. Prices in New York ranged from eight to twenty dollars a ton. New York merchants shipped hay to New Orleans and obtained prices five dollars a ton more than the cost of purchase. Farmers estimated their profits at three to six dollars a ton above their costs.[3]

City markets also stimulated production of new crops. Products that had been of minor importance before became significant moneymakers. Farmers gave up staples like wheat in favor of crops that satisfied the expanding urban markets. It was not competition from western grain that reduced wheat production in the East but the better returns from products such as fresh milk and butter.[4] In the penumbra of the city, specialty products that once had a limited market mushroomed in value. Delaware had grown peaches almost since its settlement in the seventeenth century, but not until 1832 was a commercial orchard planted to take advantage of the Philadelphia market. The promise of high prices led to the multiplication of orchards, and with them a spike in rural wealth. Delaware farmers attained levels of prosperity never before experienced. Beginning in the 1840s, large, square, three-story "peach" mansions began to line the New Castle County highways. Peach money helped finance the Chesapeake and Delaware Canal on the county's southern boundary and a railroad down the spine of the state. By 1869, a million peach trees were within shipping distance of the railroad. Forty-one thousand railroad cars, each holding five hundred baskets, went to New York alone. Until refrigerated freight cars went on line after the Civil War to carry fruit from western and southern farms to cities in the Northeast, Delaware, because of its proximity, had an immense competitive advantage.

It was not to last. After a few decades of peach prosperity, wiry shoots appeared on the trees. The foliage turned yellow, and the fruit was spotted and tasteless. Two seasons after the trees were first afflicted with "the Yellows," they died. By the end of the century, the peach boom and its bonanza wealth faded. But not Delaware agriculture. Peach prosperity had built the railway, and farmers had only to search for new products to fill the boxcars headed for the city.[5]

Cities had the power to evoke new products. In 1797 Levi Dickinson, a Hadley, Massachusetts, farmer, began growing broomcorn and manufacturing brooms. He stripped the seeds from the stalks, bound the corn to a stick with twine, and peddled the brooms in the neighboring towns. At first he and his neighbors made only a few thousand brooms a year, but the market kept expanding. Corn brooms did a much better job of cleaning floors than the old twig broom. Twigs swept up clods and leaves, leaving silt behind; corn brooms swept the floors clean, a much desired condition in respectable households. By 1831, Dickinson and his neighbors were manufacturing several million brooms a year, and farmers in New York State even more. Brooms could be made in the winter, when farm work was less pressing, often by young men who had not left home. Meanwhile, farmers in the thin-soiled hill towns to the west of the Connecticut Valley were producing broom handles by the tens of thousands. Most of the brooms from the Connecticut Valley went to New York City to meet the rising standards of cleanliness in city households.[6]

The booming urban markets for a host of products put tremendous pressure on farmers to increase production. They had always welcomed opportunities to improve their income. Increased production promised a higher level of family security and prosperity. But how to squeeze more out of their farms? One natural course was to crop their fields continuously, rather than throwing them into long fallow. Departing from earlier practices, cropping every field every year was a quick way to increase production.

In the beginning of settlement, many American farmers, especially in the South, had adopted the shifting agriculture frequently practiced in places with an abundance of land. After clearing the trees, the colonists planted continuously for six or seven years until yields dropped, and then moved on. While fresh new fields were brought into production, the old fields grew up in bushes and saplings and gradually recovered their strength.[7] Probably animals grazed the fallow lands lightly in the summer, just as they grazed virgin wooded areas. After twenty years of this long fallow, the land recuperated and was ready for clearing and replanting.[8] Everywhere the landscape appeared more closed than open.[9] Gloria Main's description of seventeenth-century Maryland applied generally to the colonies: "The thick stands of trees alternated with abandoned and overgrown fields, all interspersed with small clearings and occasional wooden buildings, many of them quite ramshackle." The landscape appeared as patches of smooth space amid an enclosing roughness.[10]

As prices improved, it was natural to extract one more harvest from a field before throwing it into fallow, even though the farmer knew the land would suffer. Even a small harvest was better than none when prices were up. Instead of letting fields go back to weeds, bushes, and saplings, the land was kept open. One sign of the change in practice was the adoption of more permanent fencing than the ragged but portable rail fences that had sufficed for earlier farmers. With fields in active use for longer periods, a sturdy fence became a good investment. Stone fences came into their own in New England at the end of the eighteenth century, and in the Middle Colonies hedges enjoyed a season of popularity about the same time. As late as 1850, an estimated 79 percent of all rural fencing was still portable worm-rail, but after 1800 the new agriculture, coupled with the shortage of timber, made permanent and more respectable fences relevant to American farmers for the first time.[11] By the beginning of the nineteenth century, travelers' accounts and other kinds of evidence suggest that improving farmers in all the more settled portions of the United States were beginning to crop continuously on permanent fields, deserving of more stable fences.[12]

Continuous cropping, however, brought American farmers face to face with the nemesis of European agriculture: soil depletion. Yields per acre decreased. "Continual cropping will destroy the best soils," one agricultural writer commented. "There must be change or rest; it is preposterous to talk of not understanding the reason of land growing poorer, while the suicidal course adopted by many of our farmers is persisted in." Although sometimes depicted as oblivious to the anger, farmers did make efforts to restore fertility.[13] Timothy Dwight, ever the New England booster, reported in 1796 that "the cultivation of clover has become a considerable object, and the use of gypsum been widely extended." The entire aspect of the farm was improving. "Fences are in many instances better made. The quantity of labor is frequently confined to a smaller extent of ground, and farms in many places are assuming a neater and more thrifty aspect." In the village of Riverhead on Long Island, after yields declined markedly at the end of the eighteenth century, farmers began changing their ways. By 1820 they were carting and plowing in dung, spreading fish on the soil, and alternating clover and grass pastures with corn and potatoes.[14] The charges of ignorance and stubbornness that filled the agricultural handbooks and the correspondence between gentleman farmers seem now to have been beside the point. As farmers developed confidence in the new methods of restoring the soil, those methods were put into effect.[15]

John Walker of King and Queen County, Virginia

As change swept across American farmlands, the basic farm idea remained in place. Farmers were no more profit-seeking capitalist farmers in the nineteenth century than they had been in the eighteenth. They had always been responsive to markets; they had to be to survive. But the improvement in the markets did not lessen the commitment to family self-provisioning. Their first goal was to keep in balance with the world by minimizing debt. As they maximized market sales to make the most of nineteenth-century urban growth, farm families still produced all they could for themselves. They combined market production and home production without any radical change in their orientation.[16] Parents still felt a responsibility to set their children up on farms if possible.

John Walker (1785–1867) of King and Queen County in the Virginia Tidewater was an improving, market-oriented farmer in the antebellum years when urban demands for wheat were steadily rising. He marketed his wheat in Baltimore and Newport and purchased the latest farm equipment to improve the productivity of his slaves. Seizing upon an investment opportunity, he collected interest from railroad bonds. Yet Walker held on to his thrifty, self-provisioning ways. He grew all the food his family and workforce consumed and made everything he could within his household.

Walker worked land that an ancestor six generations earlier had patented in the 1650s. Thomas Walker received a ten-mile grant along the Mattaponi River, a tributary of the York River. As a gentleman, he was expected to provide military protection to the settlers along the river. Down to John, the heads of the family were men of eminence—majors in the militia, sheriffs, delegates to the House of Burgesses. Walker's father, Humphrey, lived in a grand style and entertained lavishly. His brother Thomas attended William and Mary and moved to Albemarle County, where he built a house he named Castle Hill. For a short time, he was Thomas Jefferson's guardian.[17]

John Walker remained on family land in King and Queen but lived in another world from his father and uncle. As a young man, he worked in the family mill in Walkerton on the Mattaponi. In 1817 he moved for a year to Tennessee, where he converted to Methodism, then returned to King and Queen. In 1824, age thirty-nine, he obtained five hundred acres of family land at Chatham Hill, which he worked with a dozen or so slaves. Compared with those of the preceding generations, his possessions were modest. They put him in the upper third of the county's planters, but he never held office in the militia, served as sheriff, or ran for election to the legislature. As a strict Methodist, he disdained dancing, though he had received lessons as a teenager.[18] He was a prosperous but plain farmer in the postplanter generation.

Walker attained his measure of prosperity by strict attention to detail. He kept an eye on the wheat markets and sent his crop to the ports where he could get the best price. Practicing continuous cropping like others of his generation, he bought Osage orange plants for permanent hedges and replaced rail fences with planks and cedar posts and woven wattle. To restore nutriments to the soil he went in for heavy manuring. He carted leaves from the woods to catch droppings in the barnyard—sixty or seventy cartloads of leaves at a time. Pens for sheep or cattle were set up on vegetable patches to manure the ground directly. He covered manured fields with lime to accelerate rotting.[19]

Walker tried to get the most from his workers as well as his land. He read *The Southern Planter* for advice on machinery and methods. He purchased patented plows like Cary's, with its moldboard that turned over the soil so as to bury the weeds. Washington and Jefferson designed their own plows; by Walker's time inventors patented their designs and sold them to the thousands of farmers seeking improvement. Walker purchased machines for threshing, shelling corn, and seeding, the brainchildren of ingenious mechanics responding to the demand. He was one of many farmers by the 1840s who practiced rational agriculture, leading to significant improvements in productivity. Between 1800 and 1840 the number of man hours to produce one hundred bushels of wheat dropped by more than a third, from 373 to 233.[20]

Yet for all his effort to maximize production for the market, Walker still was a self-provisioning farmer. He was just as zealous to produce for household consumption as he was to increase his market crops. He grew an acre of cotton for his slave women to spin into thread for slave clothing. At first he sent the thread to a weaver to make cloth, but later he purchased a loom and had his workers weave the fabric themselves. The women in his household produced "textiles from sheep to shawls and from cotton boll to shirt." As with textiles, Walker steadily moved shoemaking onto the farm. He constructed a vat, soaked hides and skins in lime, beat out bark for the tanning solution to make leather for slave brogans, then trained his slave Enock to curry and dress leather. In 1847 he planted sugar beets to save on purchase of molasses and sugar.[21] To save on medical bills, he practiced self-help botanical medicine, using herbs and natural substances. When he purchased a desk after twenty-three years of journal keeping without one, he cut down walnut trees on his own property and turned them into planks as part payment to the cabinetmaker. He carried on the tradition noted by a British visitor in 1765 who found the planters "living handsomely and plentifully, raising all they required, and depending for nothing on the Market."[22]

Walker could no more calculate return on investment in 1840 than Jefferson could in 1793 when he was answering Arthur Young's inquiries. Like most American farmers, Walker did not think that way. He divided his accounts into two parts. In one, he kept track of his cash returns. What did wheat sales bring in, plus interest on the railroad bonds, repayment of debts, and any other cash receipts? In the other account, he recorded expenditures, not just for capital goods like animals or equipment, but for shoes, a dress for his wife, Margaret, church contributions, medical fees—everything that required a cash outlay. Nothing he produced for consumption on his own farm, such as food for his slaves and his family or firewood or clothing he produced himself, entered into the accounts. His bookkeeping was more like national accounts in the modern world, with the household taking the place of the nation. The accounts measured the balance of trade: income versus outgo between the household and the world beyond. Production and consumption within the domestic economy went unrecorded.[23]

Like the accounts of eighteenth-century farmers, Walker's books aimed at a favorable balance of trade. Under this system, it only made sense to reduce every purchase from outside the household economy. In the first year of farm operation, Walker's only purchase was a pair of shoes. He tried every year to keep cash outlays to a minimum. Tanning his own leather eliminated the cost of shoes. Making his own cloth meant he could strike out the cost of paying a weaver. The more he could reduce payment for outside goods and services, the more likely he was to meet his goal of a balance of trade. Eventually he taught two slaves, Fuller and Croxton, to cobble shoes. Spinning and weaving in the household represented a huge saving. The women's economy made it possible for the whole system to work. Barter exchange also helped. If he paid a neighbor for services rendered with work of his own, or with corn or butter produced on his farm, no entry had to be made in the expenditures column. He paid his added harvest workers in bacon or grain. Walker kept careful track because barter exchanges involved real obligations, but they did not figure in his cash accounting.[24]

Most years he came out slightly in the red, spending more than he received, but an unfavorable balance did not mean he was growing poorer. The books were not a measure of his wealth. His total wealth measured in crops, land, animals, slaves, buildings, and implements might be growing every year, even while his cash balance showed a negative return. Most years he rented out his skilled slave Daniel for a substantial sum. Sometimes Walker entered Daniel's rent money in the income accounts; sometimes he did not, as if he did not mind coming out in the red. He let the accounts drive him to increase market production and reduce purchases.[25]

Walker adopted a more modern accounting system after 1850, when he purchased Locust Grove, a nearby family farm. He assigned different functions to the two properties. At Chatham Hill, his original farm, he concentrated on production for household consumption. At Locust Grove he focused on market crops and "bought" food from Chatham Hill. Locust Grove was run like a business. Walker kept separate books for each plantation and charged Locust Grove for the food it bought from Chatham Hill.[26] Here his accounts came closer to measuring business profit. Could Locust Grove come out ahead when it had to pay for the food its workers consumed?

It was as if Walker had two minds, a traditional mind that ran farms as southerners had done for generations, and a modern mind that could conceive of a farm as a business, offering a return on investment after expenses were deducted. Once he thought modern, he could calculate whether it was more profitable to put a slave to work on shoes or to keep him in the fields and buy shoes with profits from the market crop. He could follow the advice of Horatio Seymour for the farmer to "buy for money every article that he cannot produce cheaper than he could buy," counsel echoed in *The Southern Planter*.[27] That made sense from a capitalist perspective, but it required Walker to abandon the "national accounts" method of bookkeeping. He was a man in transition from one system to another.

The immediate incentive for purchasing Locust Grove was to provide a farm for his second son. Watson took over Chatham Hill when John Walker died, and his younger son, Melville, inherited Locust Grove. That completed Walker's responsibilities as a father-farmer. He had kept his family alive and working, including his twenty slaves, and accumulated the means to purchase a second farm for his second son. He did not look to the West for land as so many Virginians did in the antebellum years. Three of Walker's nephews migrated to Alabama, some owing him money for the slaves he sold them. None of them flourished. Walker commented that they expected to make money "by half bushels as some of them said," but failed "from dreadfull bad management."[28] Walker took his opportunities in King and Queen.

City and Country

Farms, whether in East or West, were not the only places to get a start. Nineteenth-century cities offered a multiplicity of opportunities. In the middle of the eighteenth century, a handful of the Lincoln children became cordwainers and carpenters in Philadelphia; after 1800, as cities burgeoned, a tide of rural people flooded city streets. Some farm children chose to seek their fortunes in urban places out of preference, like the ambitious Abraham Lincoln. Others out of necessity moved to wherever there was work. Not all went to the metropolises. Lincoln first went to New Salem. Little towns were sprouting all over the country, brought to life by a river, a mine, or a courthouse. In the Northeast, some mills employed entire families; others hired single young women. Every city had its army of clerks in the mercantile houses and retail stores. There were thousands of places in artisan shops, stables, and along the waterfront. Women found jobs as serving girls.

Few of these jobs were as stable as farming. City life was precarious. Little businesses came and went. Ice closed the ports in the winter, stifling trade. The ups and downs of the business cycle created and then extinguished jobs. The sick and the aged had trouble supporting themselves in a city. That the National Reform Association campaigned for cheap land for urban workers in the 1840s was one measure of the instability of urban employment. Real security could only be realized with agricultural property of one's own. The huge turnover in the urban population every decade suggests farm children might work for a time in the city and then flee back to the country when their employment failed. Mill jobs or casual labor in a city was no life plan. Most city jobs were an expedient until something more lasting could be found. A farm remained the ideal.

With all the back and forth between city and country in the nineteenth century, cities became a presence in farm thinking as never before.[29] Farmers went to market with their produce and came home with urban goods. Young men and women went to town to get work and meet their spouses. City and country also competed as ideals of good living. Culturally speaking, farms were at a disadvantage in the comparison. The farmer, it is true, was the beneficiary of the classical tradition of agrarian writing that exalted the simple virtues of rural life over the corruptions of the city, but the agricultural reformers, who monopolized the literature about farmers in the nineteenth century, often belittled rural ways. They credited only the improving farmers with rural virtues. Plain farmers practicing traditional agriculture were thought to be improvident and wasteful. American reformers, like their English counterparts, as often as not spoke of the ordinary farmer as lazy and slow-witted. Strickland thought of the mass of farmers as "ignorant, uneducated, poor, and indolent."[30] The vast agricultural press that came into being after 1819, ostensibly to aid the farmer, was not much more complimentary. The editors' efforts to defend farm life began with the assumption that it was under attack. "There is a belief in this country," one of them said, "that agriculture is a vulgar occupation." A farmer writing from Batavia, Illinois, said that the farmer's boasted independence consisted of "an absolute denial of most of the comforts and refinements of life, indispensably necessary to maintain a creditable station in society."[31]

The loss of children to the city made the cultural deprivation of farm life most painful. The editors rebuked the sons and daughters who left "in pursuit of some genteel mode of living" and who preferred "some more easy sedentary occupation with the fallacious idea of appearing genteel in the eyes of the world." But the press was ambivalent about polite life. Even as the editors deplored the lure of gentility, their pages instructed farmers in good manners: how to set a proper table with napkins and glasses, and how to eat with a fork. Farm journals offered recipes for such staples of elegant life as Beef Soup a la Française and an "excellent polish for mahogany." An essay entitled "Make Farm Life Attractive" acknowledged that children found farm work dull, monotonous, and totally lacking in mental stimulation and so left for the city to achieve a "certain means of refinement." The trouble was that "on the farm, very frequently are rooms without books, walls without pictures, manners without grace, clothes without fitness and grounds without shaping and decoration."[32] To hold their children, farmers had to introduce curtains, swept floors, carpets, and of course a parlor, plus a front yard with lawn, shrubs, and a picket fence. There had to be a realm set off from the animals, dirt, and sweat that were the farm's natural environment.

As those cultural pressures built up, enhanced income from sales to city markets found a ready use.[33] Genre painters from the period reveal interiors filled with items not to be found in an ordinary colonial household: a wide array of ceramics—vases, figurines, and pots—and a lot of fabric, some of it quite luxurious, even occasional rugs. The boots and shoes worn in the pictures appear to be stylish improvements on the work of the village cobbler. All in all, farmers do not appear to have limited their purchases to the bare necessities of life. Instead of going to the store to replace homemade with purchased goods, rural families actually added new things to their household inventories to adorn themselves and their houses. They did not give up self-provisioning as purchases increased, but enhanced their lives with things they had not enjoyed before. Along with the transition to improved farming practices, marked by opening land and continuous cropping, came the beginnings of rural consumerism. The smoothing, softening, and embellishing of the farmhouse was a rural rejoinder to the aspersions of boorishness, vulgarity, and coarseness that haunted the nineteenth-century American farmer.

The struggle for respectability gradually eroded self-provisioning. Even the most ingenious farmer could not produce teacups for himself. The long-avoided shops in town became an ever more frequent destination, even for thrifty farmers. The profits from selling peaches or brooms in urban markets went to purchase furniture or fabrics made in the city. Some of the expenditures went for carpets or mirrors that the farmer could not possibly make, but some of farm income was expended on cloth once left to farm women to produce. The incidence of looms in farm households decreased substantially in the first half of the nineteenth century, especially in the North. Southern household kept their looms to make crude cloth for their slaves. Jefferson had noted while writing *Notes on the State of Virginia* that Americans could not content themselves with homemade fabric. It was too "coarse, unsightly, and unpleasant."[34] Instead, they would take their crops to market and buy finer cloth. The annual value of home manufactures declined from $40 million in 1810 to $25 million in 1860.[35] Farmers had not given up on the idea of self-sufficiency. They still grew, processed, and preserved virtually all their own food and fuel. They made rough furniture and built their own fences. But little by little, they substituted factory goods for the work of their own hands.

Lincoln

The culmination of the "Farmer's Age" came in 1862. In a single year Congress passed three landmark pieces of legislation: the Homestead Act granted 160 acres from federal lands to any man or woman who headed a family or was over age twenty-one and who would live on the land for five years; the Morrill Act set aside 30,000 acres of public land for each senator and congressman to endow agricultural and mechanics arts colleges in each state; and a bill establishing a Department of Agriculture headed by a commissioner who would collect and disseminate useful information about farm practices.

The Homestead Act adopted the small farm as the predominant plan for disposing of the national domain. Designed to get farms into the hands of families who would work the land, the act implicitly endorsed the farm idea. The vast national domain, the nation's great treasure, was to be given to families on the assumption that with a 160-acre farm they could sustain themselves. Though speculators connived to acquire lands by hook or crook, the aim of the legislation was to preserve the land for families on modest farms. Applicants had to submit an affidavit "that such application is made for his or her exclusive use and benefit, and that said entry is made for the purpose of actual settlement and cultivation, and not either directly or indirectly for the use or benefit of any other person or persons whomsoever." Knowing that farmers themselves were among the most avid speculators, the law also specified "that no individual shall be permitted to acquire title to more than one quarter section under the provisions of this act." On the whole the act succeeded. Virtually all the farms in Illinois, Michigan, and Kansas in 1880 occupied less than 250 acres. Although the manipulation of claims under Homestead allowed a few big operators to consolidate spreads of many thousands of acres, the small farm dominated the midwestern landscape.[36]

The companion pieces to Homestead, the land-grant colleges and the Department of Agriculture, filled out the picture of farmers on the land. The legislation charged the department to diffuse "useful information on subjects connected with agriculture in the most general and comprehensive sense of that word." To assure that farmers' minds would be informed by science, the commissioner was to hire "chemists, botanists, entomologists, and others skilled in the natural sciences," and then "to teach such branches of learning as are related to agriculture and the mechanic arts." The law assumed that farming could be taught from books in a classroom, a dubious proposal a half century earlier. The farm mind was assuming a rational cast. Every farmer was to think like Jefferson or Washington seventy years earlier.[37]

These two impulses, to spread small farms across the nation and to stock them with informed, educated farmers, were summed up and given their point at the Wisconsin State Agricultural Society fair in September 1859 by Abraham Lincoln, then campaigning for the Republican Party presidential nomination. Ever the politician, Lincoln opened his address at the fair by saying "farmers, being the most numerous class, it follows that their interest is the largest interest. It also follows that that interest is most worthy of all to be cherished and cultivated."[38] He worried that many farmers fell short of their potential. He advocated what he called "thorough agriculture," by which he meant intensive rather than extensive farming. He lamented the drop in yields from fifty bushels of wheat per acre to as little as eight and called for manuring and good fencing to turn yields around. He wanted all farmers to become improving farmers. Lincoln believed that the way you farmed affected the way you thought. Thorough agriculture would invigorate the mind, improve the business of farming, and energize the farmer's own character.

A lot was at stake for Lincoln in the success of family farmers. They were his hope and his trump card in the national debate over labor. Southern thinkers had propounded the mud sill theory of labor, according to which every society required a laboring class. In the South, planters bought labor and forced it to work; in the North, capitalists also bought labor and paid it to work. Either way, someone had to do the dirty work at the muddy bottom of society. Labor under either system, the southerners argued, formed a permanent lower class.

Lincoln was trying to refute this dim view. He felt that it was untrue to the American reality. He acknowledged that "a few men own capital; and that few avoid labor themselves, and with their capital, hire, or buy, another few to labor for them." But that was not true for most of the population. Most farmers and independent artisans were neither capitalists nor permanent laborers. "A large majority belong to neither class—neither work for others, nor have others working for them. Even in all our slave States, except South Carolina, a majority of the whole people of all colors, are neither slaves nor workers."[39]

Lincoln's argument turned the farm idea into political ideology. He juxtaposed the realities of farm life, where families provisioned themselves and survived on their own labor, against the southern idea of labor exploitation. In Lincoln's view, family farmers stood alone, businesses unto themselves. "Men, with their families—wives, sons, and daughters—work for themselves on their farms, in their houses and in their shops, taking the whole product to themselves, and asking no favors of capital on the one hand, nor of hirelings or slaves on the other." These were the family farmers Jefferson admired. They were the ones to resist the crushing hand of slavery or capitalist exploitation. They lived in a system that for Lincoln as for Crèvecoeur made men whole. "This, say its advocates, is *free* labor—the just and generous, and prosperous system, which opens the way for all—gives hope to all, and energy, and progress, and improvement of condition to all." For Lincoln the principles of the Homestead Act, not yet enacted but under discussion, would perpetuate this system. Free land kept alive the hope that "the prudent, penniless beginner in the world" could buy tools or land and in time labor "on his own account" as both capitalist and laborer.[40] The farm idea was the nation's best hope. Family farmers and their brethren the independent artisans were the keystone of the Republic. They made democracy a social and economic as well as a political reality.

Lincoln was equally aware of the division into the educated versus the noneducated. Lincoln told his Wisconsin audience that "the old general rule was that *educated* people did not perform manual labor. They managed to eat their bread, leaving the toil of producing it to the uneducated."[41] The educated would include merchants and professionals—clergy, doctors, lawyers—who bought their food rather than growing it, as farmers did. As people whose work was mental, they were as widely separated from workers as capitalists.

Lincoln looked for ways to bridge this gap by combining education and work. "Free Labor insists on universal education," he argued. Agricultural colleges and the Department of Agriculture were instruments to achieve this end. Unlike earlier generations of plain farmers, Lincoln valued books about farming. He considered "the rudiments of science" useful to farmers: botany to deal with the vegetable world and chemistry with the analysis of soils and selection of manures. The "mechanical branches of Natural Philosophy" helped with implements and machinery. Education or "cultivated thought," as Lincoln termed it, was of particular value for "thorough" farming. "Careless, half performed, slovenly work" had no need for an educated farmer. Lincoln wanted every farmer rational and informed.[42]

Lincoln's speech wove together all the strands of his program for farmers and for the nation: free land to keep alive the hope of independence free of capitalist domination, education to dissolve the differences between hands and head, and thorough farming that turned slovenly farmers into mindful nurturers of the soil. Like so many other agrarians, Lincoln was part utopian, but his dreams for the nation were grounded in the realities of the great national domain and the subsequent legislation Congress provided in 1862. He pictured a new kind of farmer, an informed as well as independent farmer, spreading westward across the land.

Lincoln took pleasure in the thinking part of farming. "No other human occupation," he said confidently, "opens so wide a field for the profitable and agreeable combination of labor with cultivated thought, as agriculture." He saw it as a supremely cerebral occupation, requiring encyclopedic knowledge. "The mind, already trained to thought, in the country school, or higher school, cannot fail to find there an exhaustless source of profitable enjoyment. Every blade of grass is a study; and to produce two, where there was but one, is both a profit and a pleasure. And not grass alone; but soils, seeds, and seasons—hedges, ditches, and fences, draining, droughts, and irrigation—plowing, hoeing, and harrowing—reaping, mowing, and threshing—saving crops, pests of crops, diseases of crops, and what will prevent or cure them—implements, utensils, and machines, their relative merits, and [how] to improve them—hogs, horses, and cattle—sheep, goats, and poultry—trees, shrubs, fruits, plants, and flowers—the thousand things of which these are specimens—each a world of study within itself."[43] One marvels that a man capable of such praise for farm thinking should have abandoned the soil for a law office.

The Twentieth Century

Even in 1859 Lincoln could see that American prospects, though bright, were not limitless. Sometime the great American land bonanza would end. "Population must increase rapidly—more rapidly than in former times," he told his Wisconsin listeners, "and ere long the most valuable of all arts, will be the art of deriving a comfortable subsistence from the smallest area of soil." Independent farmers, Lincoln realized, would have to squeeze a living from ever shrinking patches of land, and his foresight proved accurate. The amount of land in farms in the United States tripled between 1850 and 1910 and then stopped growing.[44] The nation's geographical limits were reached. Lincoln spoke of this dim future in a sentence or two without dwelling on the consequences. What would happen to free labor when no more land was available? Would children be forced into cities to work as hirelings for capitalists? Would the nation be riven by class as the mud sill theorists thought? What was the prospect for democracy?

Until World War II, the farm idea continued to shape farm lives. Through the Great Depression farmers sought to provision themselves as far as possible, in the spirit if not to the extent of their eighteenth-century predecessors. The agrarian novelist and essayist Wendell Berry describes the remnants of self-provisioning in the Kentucky tobacco farm where he grew up in the 1930s:

> In my boyhood, Henry County, Kentucky, was not just a rural county, as it still is—it was a *farming* county. The farms were generally small. They were farmed by families who lived not only upon them, but within and *from* them. These families grew gardens. They produced their own meat, milk, and eggs. The farms were highly diversified. The main money crop was tobacco. But the farmers also grew corn, wheat, barley, oats, hay and sorghum. Cattle, hogs, and sheep were all characteristically raised on the same farms. There were small dairies, the milking more often than not done by hand. Those were the farm products that might have been considered major. But there were also minor products, and one of the most important characteristics of that old economy was the existence of markets for minor products. In those days a farm family could easily market its surplus cream, eggs, old hens, and frying chickens. The power for field work was still furnished mainly by horses and mules. There was still a prevalent pride in workmanship, and thrift was still a forceful social ideal. The pride of most people was still in their homes, and their homes looked like it.[45]

While the Berrys were marketing tobacco to distant markets, they still produced most of their own food and found local outlets for surplus cream, eggs, and old hens. As Berry puts it, they lived within and from their farms.

In 1948, two years away from his appointment as president of Yale University, A. Whitney Griswold, then professor of history, published a volume that marked a break with traditional practices. Griswold's focus was on politics. He contested the proposition that "farming as a family enterprise is the 'backbone of democracy.'" By then the national domain had been exhausted. No more land remained to homestead, and existing farms were floundering. He referred twice to Franklin Roosevelt's message to Congress on February 16, 1937, wherein the president had warned that "the American dream of the family-sized farm, owned by the family which operates it, has become more and more remote." Griswold's book, *Farming and Democracy*, asked whether democracy itself was in jeopardy because family farming was in decline. Family farmers were the Founders' trusted citizens who made democracy possible. If they disappeared, would democracy survive?[46]

Griswold cited statistics on the comparative disadvantages of farm life. Despite booming wartime prosperity, farmers still earned less than half the national average per capita income. Farmers were falling behind in "living standards and cultural opportunities—in housing, medical and health facilities, schools, and libraries." Griswold asked: How could such a deprived people serve as the foundation of democracy? Farmers were leaving the land and moving to cities; economic necessity left them no choice. If the foundation of democracy was shrinking, what would be the fate of the nation?[47]

In posing his political question, Griswold inadvertently marked a turning point in the agricultural history of the United States. He announced the demise of the farm idea. Not only was the supply of new land exhausted, the statistics made clear that a family with land could no longer sustain itself at a worthy level. Griswold said nothing about food or warmth. Families with land may have kept themselves alive as they always had done, but they were not thriving by the standards of the day. Farmers fell short in medical and health facilities, schools and libraries, cultural opportunities of all kinds. The farm idea as it had been pursued in the eighteenth century no longer worked. Families could not achieve the "comfortable subsistence" that Lincoln thought was possible. Griswold believed the only alternative now was to dismantle false dreams and find alternative lives for the farm population.[48]

Griswold sought to demythologize farming by arguing that democracy did not depend on a foundation of family farmers. They were not uniquely qualified to sustain popular government. "Farmers have been called the backbone of every form of government in the world, including fascism and communism," he pointed out.[49] Britain had allowed corporate farm factories to flourish yet was easily as democratic as France, where the government had been at pains to protect peasant holdings. The comparisons proved that democracy could flourish where small farms had disappeared.

Griswold realized that demythologizing the family farm would not be easy. "It is the daydream of city dwellers, the inspiration of poets and artists, the biographer's security for the youth of great men. It stands for democracy in its purest and most classic form. For millions of Americans it represents a better world, past but not quite lost, one to which they may still look for individual happiness or, maybe, national salvation."[50] This daydream had to be dispelled. Griswold marshaled every argument he could to break down what he called "the Jeffersonian Ideal." He repudiated the assertion of the president of the Farmers' Union that family farming was the "final stronghold" against tyranny and oppression. Family farmers as a body, Griswold believed, were now incapable of sustaining American democracy.

Yet despite his efforts to deflate agrarianism, Griswold did not want family farms to disappear. He did not favor the British model of efficient large-scale agriculture. Skeptical as he was about family farming, Griswold admitted that it "affords scope for a citizen to live and work more or less on his own terms, to develop the initiative and resourcefulness, the sense of responsibility and the self-respect that have always and everywhere been considered among the greatest assets of democracy." With all his reservations, Griswold still believed that family farming was "the outstanding form of individual economic enterprise." He was searching for realistic ways to preserve it.[51]

Griswold's practical proposals were no more inspiring than other fruitless attempts to defend family farming under the New Deal. Having lived through the mass agricultural migrations of the 1930s, Griswold knew that much of the farm population must move to the cities to avoid debilitating poverty: "We know that family farming cannot thrive on the terms of hillbillies and Okies." He believed that the right public policy could halt the decline, but the best he could come up with was a formula taken from the liberal economic orthodoxy of his decade: "full production" and "full employment" engineered by a democratic government. As he put it: "The lesson is plain in history. Family farming cannot save democracy. Only democracy can save the family farm."[52] Exactly how, he did not make clear.

Griswold's impassioned denunciation of the agrarian myth coupled with his plea for a more rational farm policy attest to the enduring force of the family farm idea in the American imagination. As late as the mid-twentieth century, family farming was still considered desirable for its effect on character. It was thought to instill virtue, as commerce and industry did not. Griswold the critic could not shake off his inbred sense that the family farm was the best training ground for a democratic people. He saw a moral dimension in the traditional farm idea. Farm life bred useful traits: independence, ingenuity, and industry. He regretted its decline.[53]

The waning of farming in Griswold's time turned into a rout in the next two decades. In the first half of the century, the farm population ranged between 30.5 million and 32.5 million. Between 1945 and 1960, 15 million of these people, nearly half of the farm population, left the farm. By the end of the twentieth century, only 5 million people still farmed, less than 2 percent of the population. Where there had been 6.8 million farms, by 2000 there were only 2 million. The average-sized farm grew from 175 acres to 487, as small farmers gave up and sold out. Sharecroppers and small farmers suffered most. The small family farm became a sideline for people earning their living in other ways. Nowadays almost half of all farms lose money each year.[54]

The farm idea as practiced in the eighteenth century is obsolete. Self-provisioning, the most basic principle of farm thinking, has been virtually abandoned. Farmers buy their food in grocery stores. In 1910 almost 90 percent of American farms reported raising chickens, more than 80 percent tended dairy cows, and more than 75 percent grew their own corn. By the early 1980s, 10 percent raised chickens, 15 percent tended dairy cows, and 32 percent grew corn.[55] Today, farmers do not come close to providing for themselves. People buy what they need rather than make for themselves.

The end of self-provisioning created a crisis in the Great Depression. What was to sustain people when jobs disappeared? In 1933 Congress passed the Subsistence Homestead Act to get people back onto farms in hopes that they could grow enough food to live on while working in nearby light industry.[56] But the act was not the answer for an urbanized population. Recognizing that the form of security that had served the nation for centuries was no longer adequate, Congress eventually wrote its own social security bill based on the recognition that most of the population did not have land to fall back on.

Farm parents nowadays are also unable to set up their children on farms of their own as eighteenth-century farmers tried to do. The costs are prohibitive. Most families can provide at best land for one child, and then only if debt has not eroded their ownership. Like other American families, farm families send their children to college, a relatively inexpensive way to secure their future livelihoods compared with purchase of a farm. Many farm children are delighted to leave. The endless toil is more than they can bear. One woman, writing in the 1930s, remembered the farm day. "Up at four o'clock in the morning to get berries picked and hoeing done before the heat of the day . . . washing milk bottles and heavy cans, milking, into the house at night—the dirty dishes of the hasty breakfast still on the table, often too tired to eat or do anything but drop into the unmade bed."[57] The hard work that once was considered inescapable now can be avoided by taking a city job. Children abandon farm life even when a farm is available to them.

But for all the changes, family farming has not disappeared. About the same percentage of the agricultural workforce now is made up of family members as in 1910.[58] Families still manage farms, and they still hope that one or two of the children will carry on the family business. The grandparents of Nancy and Terry Williams started farming in California in the 1930s and the 1950s. Both families survived the winnowing of the farm population after World War II and are still on the land. Nancy and Terry grow rice and walnuts on five hundred acres of prime farming land in Richvale, California, north of Sacramento. The Williamses' son Darin farms nearby. Nancy Williams's account of their relationship gives an idea of what family farming means today. "We farm 'with' Darin," she writes, "in that we both farm rice & walnuts, own some equipment together, utilize the same labor crew and shop, and make many decisions together. However, we each farm separate properties and make our own financial decisions independently of each other. There are as many different ways to split or share resources, responsibilities & revenue on a family farm as there are family farms."[59]

Nancy's writing about her other children reveals a hope that perhaps they will find their way back to farming as Darin did. The Williamses have two daughters, Rebecca and Jenny. "Jenny has a degree in ag business and is just finishing up a masters program at UCDavis in Economic Ag and Resource Management." She and her husband, Andy, an engineer, are spending three years in Uganda. But, Nancy adds, "coming back to farm with the family is something they might be interested in." Her other daughter, Becca, now a high school teacher in Seattle, "is not in farming but her heart is. She and her sister farmed a rice field together in 1997 and I know they both would like to be able to be involved more some day."[60]

The Williamses live in a different world from the one Crèvecoeur described in 1782, when he wrote that "we are all tillers of the earth, from

Nova Scotia to West Florida. We are a people of cultivators."[61] Crèvecoeur's America has disappeared. Only a small percentage of Americans till the earth, and those who do think differently from their forebears. They are businesspeople who calculate profit and run their fields like factories. They are scientific and rational. Self-provisioning means nothing to them.

Yet family is still interwoven with these complicated enterprises and will be so long as people want their children to farm. The Williamses farm in a big way with huge pieces of equipment, working immensely valuable land, but the appeal of farming is not the promise of high life. The Williamses live unostentatiously in a tiny agricultural town dominated by tall rice elevators. For them the promise of farm life is not material. Partly it is communal. The Williamses are closely involved with neighbors. The farmers in town regularly gather for breakfast after the first round of work in the morning to talk farming and ways to cooperate. Farming is also valued for instilling a down-to-earth, sensible, and real attitude toward life. Terry Williams could be a latter-day Joshua Hempstead, a person of steady, shrewd judgment, without pretense but highly effective. The Williamses believe that kind of life grows out of farming, and they want their children to have it.

Notes

1. The Farm Idea

1. J. Hector St. John de Crèvecoeur, *Letters from an American Farmer and Sketches of Eighteenth-Century America*, ed. Albert E. Stone (New York: Penguin, 1986), 67. "The mass of our citizens," the assistant secretary of the treasury Tench Coxe observed, are "cultivators (and what is happily for us in most instances the same thing) the independent proprietors of the soil." Tench Coxe, *A View of the United States of America, in a Series of Papers, Written at Various Times, between the Years 1787 and 1794* (New York: August M. Kelley, 1965 [orig. pub. Philadelphia: William Hall, 1794]), 13.
2. Allan Kulikoff, *From British Peasants to Colonial American Farmers* (Chapel Hill: University of North Carolina Press, 2000), 291. Thomas Weiss, "U.S. Labor Force Estimates and Economic Growth, 1800–1860," in *American Economic Growth and Standards of Living before the Civil War*, ed. Robert E. Gallman and John Joseph Wallis (Chicago: University of Chicago Press, 1992), 22, 68–69. I am indebted to David Hall for this perspective and much of the language.
3. Farm numbers were estimated by assuming that three-quarters of the 2,148,000 people in the thirteen colonies in 1770 were farmers and dividing by an average household size of five. *Historical Statistics of the United States: Colonial Times to 1970*, 2 vols. (Washington, D.C.: U.S. Department of Commerce, Bureau of the Census, 1975), 2: 1168. The population of Canada in the late 1770s after the Loyalist migrations was around 100,000.
4. After the first years of settlement, there never had been a shortage of food. This self-sufficiency was not to be taken for granted. Spanish America depended on the mother country for foodstuffs for more than half a century after conquest. J. H. Elliott, *Empires of the Atlantic World: Britain and Spain in America, 1492–1830* (New Haven: Yale University Press, 2006), 92. As late as the early seventeenth century, parts of Europe suffered from occasional starving times. Andrew B. Appleby, *Famine in Tudor and Stuart England* (Stanford: Stanford University Press, 1978).

5. Top ten exports from the British continental colonies in 1770, ranked by value in pounds:

Tobacco	906,638
Bread and flour	504,553
Fish, dried and pickled	397,945
Rice	340,693
Other grains (wheat, maize, oats)	176,086
Indigo	131,552
Staves and boards	120,237
Whale oil and fins	104,134
Furs	91,486
Horses, cattle, sheep, hogs	79,035

Source: *Historical Statistics of the United States: Colonial Times to 1970*, 2: 1183–84.

6. Jason Haven diary interleaved with *Astronomical Diary, or Almanack for the Year of our Lord Christ 1769*, by Nathaniel Ames, Boston, in Jason Haven Diary, 1769–1776, Haven Family Papers, vol. 2, Haven Family; Papers; 1747–1908, American Antiquarian Society, Worcester, Mass., on the page opposite "On the Manufacture of Silk."
7. Lorena S. Walsh, *Motives of Honor, Pleasure, and Profit: Plantation Management in the Colonial Chesapeake* (Chapel Hill: University of North Carolina Press, 2010), 19. Alice Hanson Jones, *American Colonial Wealth: Documents and Methods*, 3 vols., 2nd ed. (New York: Arno, 1977), 2: 1300–1400.
8. Dennis D. Moore, ed., *More Letters from the American Farmer: An Edition of the Essays in English Left Unpublished by Crèvecoeur* (Athens: University of Georgia Press, 1995), 62. Half of Connecticut carpenters and joiners had twenty or more acres of land. Jackson Turner Main, *Society and Economy in Colonial Connecticut* (Princeton: Princeton University Press, 1985), 25. Sixty percent of a sample of Chester County, Pennsylvania, tradesmen also farmed. Lucy Simler, "Tenancy in Colonial Pennsylvania: The Case of Chester County," *William and Mary Quarterly*, 3rd ser. 43, no. 4 (1986): 545. In Chester County at midcentury, 84.6 percent of artisan decedents owned livestock and 43.6 percent stored grain. Mary M. Schweitzer, *Custom and Contract: Household, Government, and the Economy in Colonial Pennsylvania* (New York: Columbia University Press, 1987), 63.
9. Jerome H. Wood, Jr., *Conestoga Crossroads: Lancaster, Pennsylvania, 1730–1790* (Harrisburg: Pennsylvania Historical and Museum Commission, 1979), 7, 9. Hamilton acted in keeping with William Penn's original plan for

Philadelphia, which foresaw plots of ten to a hundred acres for each resident. Even in the diminished version, each family was to have at least a half-acre, enough for "House, Garden, and small Orchard." Sylvia Doughty Fries, *The Urban Idea in Colonial America* (Philadelphia: Temple University Press, 1977), 88–90. Lancaster's 1773 tax list with entries for artisans showed 55 percent of them with a horse or a cow. William Henry Egle, ed., *Provincial Papers: Proprietary and State Tax Lists of the County of Lancaster for the Years 1771, 1772, 1773, 1777, and 1779* (n.p.: William Stanley Ray, 1898), 454–58. In Concord, Massachusetts, in 1771, six households owned more than £100 in "stock in Trade, Goods, Wares and Merchandize"; these were the town's storekeepers. Five of these six owned land ranging from five to twenty-nine acres, and four owned animals. Bettye Hobbs Pruitt, ed., *The Massachusetts Tax Valuation List of 1771* (Boston: G. K. Hall, 1978), 194–200.

10. Main, *Society and Economy*, 200. For a similar analysis, see John J. Waters, "Patrimony, Succession, and Social Stability: Guilford, Connecticut, in the Eighteenth Century," *Perspectives in American History* 10 (1976): 131–60. By the time men reached maturity, most of them owned land sufficient to farm. A study of estate inventories in the 1690s found that only 4 decedents ages forty to sixty in a sample of 119 owned no land and only 25 of them fewer than twenty-five acres. Main, *Society and Economy*, 13, 370, 377.

11. Harry J. Carman, ed., *American Husbandry* (1939; Port Washington, N.Y.: Kennikat, 1964), 124.

12. Average farm size varied widely from section to section. Except for the most intense rice-producing areas, average farm size in the South by the mid-eighteenth century was around 200 acres. In five Virginia counties at the time of the Revolution, from 52 percent to 59 percent of the plantations were between 100 and 300 acres. Going north, farm size diminished. Farms in Chester County, Pennsylvania, by the time of the Revolution averaged about 125 acres. Farms were smallest in New England. In Connecticut in the 1750s, half of the established farmers owned fewer than 120 acres; only 11.3 percent owned more than 200 acres, the average in the South. All those numbers were high by the standards of England, where the yeoman idea originated. A hundred-acre farm in England was considered so large as to require hired labor to work. James T. Lemon, *The Best Poor Man's Country: A Geographical Study of Early Southeastern Pennsylvania* (Baltimore: Johns Hopkins University Press, 1972), 89–91. Main, *Society and Economy*, 208. Leigh Shaw-Taylor, "The Rise of Agrarian Capitalism and the Decline of Family Farming in England," *Economic History Review*, 65, no. 1 (2012): 26–29.

13. Daniel Vickers, "Competency and Competition: Economic Culture in Early America," *William and Mary Quarterly*, 3rd ser. 47, no. 1 (1990): 4, defines competence as "comfortable independence."
14. David Minor, "Account Book for Farm Produce and Farm Wages, 1765–1773," Ms Montgom, number 154, p. 17 (quotation), 19–20, Columbia University Rare Book and Manuscript Library, New York.
15. Daniel Vickers, "Errors Expected: The Culture of Credit in Rural New England, 1750–1800," *Economic History Review* 63, no. 4 (2010): 1043.
16. Carman, *American Husbandry*, 7–8, 80–84, 136–47, 167–73, 227–33, 285–86, 292–300.
17. Moore, *More Letters*, 62.
18. *Hacendados* in New Spain followed the same practice. Alan Knight, *Mexico in the Colonial Era* (Cambridge: Cambridge University Press, 2002), 160.
19. John Demos, *Little Commonwealth: Family Life in Plymouth Colony* (New York: Oxford University Press, 1970).
20. National income for the colonial period is notoriously difficult to calculate. To estimate colonial income, Alice Hanson Jones accepted a ratio of 3.0 to 3.5 of wealth to annual income, arriving at these numbers by comparison to other nations and times. Jones estimated wealth per capita from data collected from estate inventories and then divided this number by these two ratios. Her low estimate was £10.7 per capita income in 1774, the date of her inventory sample. Of this amount, £1.7 came from exports, leaving £9.0 from the domestic economy. Assuming a nonfarm population of 25 percent and equal productivity from both segments of the population, three-quarters or £6.75 of the £9.0 can be attributed to nonexport farm production—food and provisions that were not shipped out. Perhaps one-quarter of the £6.75 was sold to nonfarm consumers, and three-quarters, or a little more than £5.0, was consumed within the household. Alice Hanson Jones, *Wealth of a Nation to Be: The American Colonies on the Eve of the Revolution* (New York: Columbia University Press, 1980), 61–65. Lorena Walsh found that nearly 45 percent of estimated total returns on a Maryland plantation from 1662 to 1672 was produced for subsistence. Walsh, *Motives of Honor, Pleasure, and Profit*, 162–63. Walsh found the ratio of wealth to income in the seventeenth-century Chesapeake to vary between 2.4 and 4.3. Ibid., 191. Lois Green Carr, Russell R. Menard, and Lorena S. Walsh, *Robert Cole's World: Agriculture and Society in Early Maryland* (Chapel Hill: University of North Carolina Press, 1991), 8. James Lemon estimated the Pennsylvania farmers sold between a third and a half of their production during peacetime. James T. Lemon,

"Household Consumption in Eighteenth-Century America and Its Relationship to Production and Trade: The Situation among Farmers in Southeastern Pennsylvania," *Agricultural History* 41, no. 1 (1967): 59–70. See also Lemon, *Best Poor Man's Country*, 180–81. Russian peasant economies at the beginning of the twentieth century varied between 39.6 and 87 percent production for home consumption. A. V. Chaianov, Daniel Thorner, Basile H. Kerblay, and R. E. F. Smith, *The Theory of the Peasant Economy* (Homewood, Ill.: R. D. Irwin, 1966), 123–24. For the high estimate of household consumption, see James A. Henretta, "Families and Farms: *Mentalite* in Pre-Industrial America," *William and Mary Quarterly*, 3rd ser. 35, no. 1 (1978): 17.

21. Lois Green Carr, "Diversification in the Colonial Chesapeake: Somerset County, Maryland, in Comparative Perspective," in *Colonial Chesapeake Society*, ed. Lois Green Carr, Philip D. Morgan, and Jean B. Russo (Chapel Hill: University of North Carolina Press, 1988), 342–88. Paul G. E. Clemens, *The Atlantic Economy and Colonial Maryland's Eastern Shore: From Tobacco to Grain* (Ithaca, N.Y.: Cornell University Press, 1980), chapter 6. Allan Kulikoff, *Tobacco and Slaves: The Development of Southern Cultures in the Chesapeake 1680–1800* (Chapel Hill: University of North Carolina Press, 1986), 99–104. Carville V. Earle, *The Evolution of a Tidewater Settlement System: All Hallow's Parish, Maryland, 1650–1783* (Chicago: University of Chicago, Department of Geography, 1975), 122–23. Walsh, *Motives of Honor, Pleasure, and Profit*, 249, 290, 339–40. Carr, Menard, and Walsh, *Robert Cole's World*, 81, 249.
22. For an example of a wealthy Connecticut farmer's trade with the store, see John Morgan, "General Account books of farm and household, 1754–1790." Ms Montgom, 130, Columbia University Rare Books and Manuscript Library. Morgan averaged eight to ten visits a year to the store. His most common purchases were rum and sugar. He settled his accounts with oats, wheat, and flaxseed.
23. William Byrd to the Earl of Orrery, July 5, 1726, quoted in Pierre Marambaud, *William Byrd of Westover, 1674–1744* (Charlottesville: University Press of Virginia, 1971), 146.
24. Moore, *More Letters*, 98.
25. Daniel Defoe, *The Life and Strange Surprising Adventures of Robinson Crusoe*, 4 vols. (Boston: Houghton Mifflin, 1908), 1: 96 (quotation), 109–12.
26. Moore, *More Letters*, 98.
27. This line of thought was developed by Henretta in "Families and Farms," 3–32.

28. Peter Laslett, *The World We Have Lost: England before the Industrial Age Further Explored* (New York: Scribner, 1984), 77–78.
29. David F. Weiman, "Families, Farms, and Rural Society in Pre-Industrial America," *Research in Economic History* 10 (1988), supplement.
30. For an elaboration of this theme, see Carolyn Merchant, *Ecological Revolutions: Nature, Gender, and Science in New England* (Chapel Hill: University of North Carolina Press, 1989), 172–74.
31. Daniel Scott Smith, "A Malthusian-Frontier Interpretation of United States Demographic History before c. 1815," in *Urbanization in the Americas: The Background in Comparative Perspective*, ed. Woodrow Borah, Jorge Hardoy, and Gilbert A. Stelter (Ottawa: History Division, National Museum of Man, 1980), 15–24. The theory of marketless subsistence farming was developed by the Soviet economist Alexander V. Chaianov. See Chaianov et al., *The Theory of the Peasant Economy*.
32. Mary Beth Norton, *Founding Mothers and Fathers: Gendered Power and the Forming of American Society* (New York: Knopf, 1996), 96–101, 294–99. Quotation on 106.
33. The most notable diaries were by two New Englanders, Matthew Patten of Bedford, New Hampshire, and Joshua Hempstead of New London, Connecticut. Farmer account books are scattered through the major depositories, especially in the Northeast. For an example of an account book arranged by individuals with an index of names in front, see John Morgan, "General Account Books of Farm and Household, 1754–1790."
34. Vickers, "Errors Expected," 1038. Matthew Patten, *The Diary of Matthew Patten of Bedford, N.H.: From Seventeen Hundred Fifty-Four to Seventeen Hundred Eighty-Eight* (Concord, N.H.: Rumford, 1903), 3. For another example of trading and provisioning from an early-nineteenth-century diary, see Vickers, "Competency and Competition."
35. Patten, *Diary*, 13 (March 19, 1755). A few weeks later, another son came close to death. Ibid., 13–14 (March 30–31, 1755).
36. Ibid., 5 (June 18, 19, July 1, 1754), 6 (July 29, 1754), 7 (Aug. 13, 1754), 8 (Sept. 16–17, 1754), 7 (Sept. 12, 13, 1754), 9 (Jan. 1, 1755), 10 (Jan. 8, 1755), 13 (Jan. 14, 1755).
37. Ibid., 8 (Nov. 30, 1754). "Sable" probably refers to martens, a near relative of the more valuable Russian sables.
38. Number of pelts for July 1754–June 1755 tabulated ibid., 10 (Jan. 17, 27, Feb. 10, 1755), 15 (May 12, 1755, April 16–17, 1755), 6 (July 26, 1754).
39. Ibid., 7 (Sept. 3, 1754), 8 (Sept. 21, Nov. 19, Dec. 2, 1754), 6 (Aug. 1, 1754).

40. Ibid., 8 (Sept. 20, Nov. 25, 1754).
41. Ibid., 6 (July 30, 1754). Benjamin Linkfield's indentures expired, and he married and leased land. Ibid., 14 (April 5, 1755), 15 (April 28, 1755), 16 (May 24, 1755). "Benjn Linkfield and my oxn workt at the highway with Willm Barnet." Ibid., 5 (July 1, 1754).
42. Ibid., 9 (Jan. 3, 4, 1755).
43. Ibid., 10 (Jan. 22, 1755), 7 (Sept. 6, 1754), 9 (Dec. 31, 1754).
44. For an elaboration of the exchange system in the Hudson Valley, see Martin Bruegel, "Uncertainty, Pluriactivity, and Neighborhood Exchange in the Rural Hudson Valley in the Late Eighteenth Century," *New York History* 77, no. 3 (1996): 245–72.
45. Tabulated from Patten, *Diary*, 5–17.
46. Ibid., 5 (July 1754), 14 (April 4, 1755), 16 (May 23, 1755). A week after buying the thread and some buckram, Patten brought five tailors into the house to make a fly-coat, a jacket, and a pair of breeches. Ibid., 14 (Sept. 9, 1754).
47. Daniel Vickers asks this question in "Errors Expected," 1033–34.
48. Ibid., 1056. For the continuation of neighborly exchanges, see R. Todd Welker, "Neighborhood Exchange and the Economic Culture of Rural California in the Late Nineteenth Century," *Agricultural History* 87, no. 3 (2013): 391–415.
49. John Murrin, "Self-Immolation: Schools of Historiography and the Coming of the American Revolution," paper delivered at the Columbia University Early American History seminar, Oct. 9, 2007, 29. For one family's effort to pass land down through the generations, see Christopher M. Jedrey, *The World of John Cleaveland: Family and Community in Eighteenth-Century New England* (New York: Norton, 1979), 6–8, 14–15, 58–94. On the importance of the lineal family, see Henretta, "Families and Farms," 3–32.
50. For a statistical description of these stages, see Schweitzer, *Custom and Contract*, 24–34.
51. For various aspects of this process, see Main, *Society and Economy*, 117, 375. Lee Soltow, *Patterns of Wealthholding in Wisconsin since 1850* (Madison: University of Wisconsin Press, 1971), 42, 46. Paul G. E. Clemens and Lucy Simler, "Rural Labor and the Farm Household in Chester County, Pennsylvania, 1750–1820," in *Work and Labor in Early America*, ed. Stephen Innes (Chapel Hill: University of North Carolina Press, 1988), 116–17. Sue Headlee, *The Political Economy of the Family Farm: The Agrarian Roots of American Capitalism* (New York: Praeger, 1991). Merchant, *Ecological Revolutions*, 185–90. Christopher Clark, "Economy and Culture: Opening Up the

Rural History of the Early American Northeast," *American Quarterly* 43, no. 2 (1991): 279–301. Barry Levy, *Quakers and the American Family: British Settlement in the Delaware Valley* (New York: Oxford University Press, 1988), 14, 125. Vickers, "Errors Expected," 1042.

52. Philip J. Greven, *Four Generations: Population, Land, and Family in Colonial Andover, Massachusetts* (Ithaca, N.Y.: Cornell University Press, 1970); Jean Butenhoff Lee, "Land and Labor: Parental Bequest Practices in Charles County, Maryland, 1732–1783," in Carr, Morgan, and Russo, *Colonial Chesapeake Society,* 306–41; Daniel Scott Smith, "Parental Power and Marriage Patterns: An Analysis of Historical Trends in Hingham, Massachusetts," *Journal of Marriage and the Family* 35, no. 3 (1973): 419–28; Jedrey, *The World of John Cleaveland*. For a poignant example of the tensions around the passage of property, see Laurel Thatcher Ulrich, *A Midwife's Tale: The Life of Martha Ballard Based on Her Diary, 1785–1812* (New York: Knopf, 1990), 278–84.

53. *Thomas's Massachusetts, Connecticut, Rhode-Island, Newhampshire & Vermont almanack, with an ephemeris, for the year of our Lord 1795: . . . Fitted to the latitude and longitude of the town of Boston, but will serve without essential variation for the adjacent states. . . .* (Worcester, Mass.: Isaiah Thomas, 1794), no pagination.

54. Virginia DeJohn Anderson, *New England's Generation: The Great Migration and the Formation of Society and Culture in the Seventeenth Century* (New York: Cambridge University Press, 1991), 160.

55. Holly Brewer, *By Birth or Consent: Children, Law, and the Anglo-American Revolution in Authority* (Chapel Hill: University of North Carolina Press, 2005). On the reproduction of society, see Merchant, *Ecological Revolutions,* 175.

56. On the difficulties of providing for children, see Merchant, *Ecological Revolutions,* 185–88. On the struggle to acquire land, see David Jaffee, *People of the Wachusett: Greater New England in History and Memory, 1630–1860* (Ithaca, N.Y.: Cornell University Press, 1999); Alan Taylor, *Liberty Men and Great Proprietors: The Revolutionary Settlement on the Maine Frontier, 1760–1820* (Chapel Hill: University of North Carolina Press, 1990). On families with moderate properties moving to new areas, see Patricia Tracy, "Re-considering Migration within Colonial New England," *Journal of Social History* 23, no. 1 (1989): 93–113.

57. Quoted in Greven, *Four Generations,* 170.

58. From 1690 to 1790, population in the British colonies multiplied eighteen-fold. *Historical Statistics,* 1: 8; 2: 1168.

59. Quoted in Robert E. Brown, *Middle-Class Democracy and the Revolution in Massachusetts, 1691–1780* (1955; New York: Harper and Row, 1969), 15.
60. Migration and expansion are given lucid treatment in Bernard Bailyn, *Voyagers to the West: A Passage in the Peopling of America on the Eve of the Revolution* (New York: Knopf, 1986), 7–20. See also the volumes in the Histories of the American Frontier series, including Jack M. Sosin, *The Revolutionary Frontier, 1763–1783* (New York: Holt, Rinehart and Winston, 1967); Douglas Edward Leach, *The Northern Colonial Frontier, 1607–1763* (New York: Holt, Rinehart and Winston, 1966); and W. Stitt Robinson, *The Southern Colonial Frontier, 1707–1763* (Albuquerque: University of New Mexico Press, 1979). For the pressure on land prices, see Kulikoff, *From British Peasants to Colonial American Farmers*, 127–35.
61. The word "conquest" comes from Tzvetan Todorov, *The Conquest of America: The Question of the Other*, trans. Richard Howard (New York: Harper and Row, 1984).
62. Francis Jennings, *The Invasion of America: Indians, Colonialism, and the Cant of Conquest* (Chapel Hill: University of North Carolina Press, 1975); Hans Koning, *The Conquest of America* (New York: Monthly Review Press, 1993).
63. Richard White, *The Middle Ground: Indians, Empires, and Republics in the Great Lakes Region, 1650–1815* (New York: Cambridge University Press, 1991); Alan Taylor, *The Divided Ground: Indians, Settlers, and the Northern Borderland of the American Revolution* (New York: Knopf, 2006).

2. *A Note on Sources*

1. I am indebted to Claudia Bushman for the conception of a migrating farm.
2. "Deeds and Maps. Auburn-Hardwick," Worcester County, Mass., Records, 1665–1954, Box 5, folder 1 [7?], American Antiquarian Society, Worcester, Mass.
3. Andro Linklater, *Measuring America: How the United States Was Shaped by the Greatest Land Sale in History* (New York: Penguin, 2003), 13–18, 21.
4. Ibid., 39.
5. Orange County Promissory Notes, N.D., 1773–1819, N.C. State Archives, Raleigh.
6. Promissory notes for Orange County are found in Orange County Civil Action Papers, No Date, 1771–1781, N.C. State Archives, Raleigh; and Orange County Promissory Notes, N.D., 1773–1819, N.C. State Archives, Raleigh.
7. Orange County Estates 1758–1785, N.C. State Archives, Raleigh, 251–53.

8. John Armstrong, filed in Orange County Wills, 1753–1937, Adams-Benton, N.C. State Archives, Raleigh.
9. Bettye Hobbs Pruitt, ed., *The Massachusetts Tax Valuation List of 1771* (Boston: G. K. Hall, 1978).
10. Bettye Hobbs Pruitt, "Self-Sufficiency and the Agricultural Economy of Eighteenth-Century Massachusetts," *William and Mary Quarterly*, 3rd ser. 41, no. 3 (1984): 333–64.
11. Michel Foucault, *Discipline and Punish: The Birth of the Prison*, trans. Alan Sheridan (New York: Pantheon, 1977).
12. Cori Field, "His Home Was His Castle," course paper, History Department, Columbia University, Feb. 24, 1993.
13. Pruitt, *Massachusetts Tax Valuation List*, xvii.
14. The values of farm properties on the valuation lists correspond closely with the values in estate inventories. Pruitt, "Self-Sufficiency and the Agricultural Economy," 336.
15. Joshua Hempstead in the course of his forty-eight-year diary mentioned ninety-six farms by the names of the owners. Patricia M. Schaefer, *A Useful Friend: A Companion to the Joshua Hempstead Diary, 1711–1758* (New London, Conn.: New London County Historical Society, 2008), 193–95.
16. Crèvecoeur judged a farm by the "Barn & Barnyard. . . . Indeed it is ye Criterion by which I allways Juge of a farmer's Prosperity." Dennis D. Moore, ed., *More Letters from the American Farmer: An Edition of the Essays in English Left Unpublished by Crèvecoeur* (Athens: University of Georgia Press, 1995), 61.

3. *The Nature of the South*

1. There were slaves in southern Pennsylvania, but only about 8 percent of the households in Lancaster County, Pennsylvania, for example, owned slaves, while it was close to 50 percent in most of Maryland and Virginia. Lancaster County slave ownership calculated from "Return of the Effective Supply Tax for the County of Lancaster, 1779," and "Returns and Assessments for the Fourteenth Eighteen-Penny Tax for the County of Lancaster, 1771," *Provincial Papers: Proprietary and State Tax Lists of the County of Lancaster for the Years 1771 1772, 1773, 1777, and 1779*, ed. William Henry Egle (n.p.: William Stanley Ray, 1898), 491–684, 3–166.
2. Philip D. Curtin, *The Rise and Fall of the Plantation Complex: Essays in Atlantic History* (Cambridge: Cambridge University Press, 1990), 7–11. J. H. Galloway, "The Mediterranean Sugar Industry," *Geographical Review* 67, no. 2 (1977): 26, 177–94. Curtin offers a definition of plantation that stresses that

the worker population was not self-sustaining and was large—averaging fifty to several hundred workers (11–13). By this definition few Chesapeake plantations would qualify. For the spread of planation agriculture, see Seymour Phillips, "The Outer World of the European Middle Ages," in *Implicit Understandings: Observing, Reporting, and Reflecting on the Encounters between Europeans and Other Peoples in the Early Modern Era*, ed. Stuart B. Schwartz (New York: Cambridge University Press, 1994), 23–63.

3. Richard S. Dunn, *Sugar and Slaves: The Rise of the Planter Class in the English West Indies, 1624–1713* (Chapel Hill: University of North Carolina Press, 1972), 60–62, 117–18. K. G. Davies, *The North Atlantic World in the Seventeenth Century: Europe and the World in the Age of Expansion* (Minneapolis: University of Minnesota Press, 1974), 181–82.
4. Quoted in Lois Green Carr, Russell R. Menard, and Lorena S. Walsh, *Robert Cole's World: Agriculture and Society in Early Maryland* (Chapel Hill: University of North Carolina Press, 1991), 160. John C. Coombs, "The Phases of Conversion: A New Chronology for the Rise of Slavery in Virginia," *William and Mary Quarterly*, 3rd ser. 68, no. 3 (2011): 332–60. The stated price for a twelve- to forty-year-old slave in Virginia, according to the 1672 charter of the Royal African Company, was eighteen pounds sterling. Ibid., 351.
5. Of seventeenth-century Maryland: "By century's end, enough 'responsible men' whose 'purses would endure it' were available to sustain a large-scale slave trade, in part because they had built farms that generated sufficient income to pay for blacks or that stood as collateral for a loan from an English merchant to buy them." Carr, Menard, and Walsh, *Robert Cole's World*, 160.
6. Russell R. Menard, "The Tobacco Industry in the Chesapeake Colonies, 1617–1730: An Interpretation," *Research in Economic History* 5 (1980): 111, 145–47, 156–61. Population figures in *Historical Statistics of the United States: Colonial Times to 1970* (Washington, D.C.: U.S. Department of Commerce, 1975), 1168.
7. Carole Shammas, *The Preindustrial Consumer in England and America* (Oxford: Clarendon, 1990), 79, 82. The mean annual number of servants arriving in Maryland from England from 1668 to 1680 was 310; in 1680 it dropped to 77. Russell R. Menard, "British Migration to the Chesapeake Colonies in the Seventeenth Century," in *Colonial Chesapeake Society*, ed. Lois Green Carr, Philip D. Morgan, and Jean B. Russo (Chapel Hill: University of North Carolina Press, 1988), 124. Total Bristol servant migrants dropped from 2,394 between 1670 and 1679 to 622 in the years from 1680 to 1686. Ibid.,

113. Coombs, "Phases of Conversion," 355. Ira Berlin, *Many Thousands Gone: The First Two Centuries of Slavery in North America* (Cambridge: Harvard University Press, 1998), 99–132. Lorena S. Walsh, *Motives of Honor, Pleasure, and Profit: Plantation Management in the Colonial Chesapeake, 1607–1763* (Chapel Hill: University of North Carolina Press, 2010), 21.

8. Dunn, *Sugar and Slaves*, 111–15. For the South Carolina–Barbados connection, see Jack P. Greene, "Colonial South Carolina and the Caribbean Connection," *South Carolina Historical Magazine* 88, no. 4 (1987): 192–210. Wesley Frank Craven, *The Southern Colonies in the Seventeenth Century, 1607–1689* ([Baton Rouge]: Louisiana State University Press, 1949), 341–42.

9. Kinloch Bull, "Barbadian Settlers in Early Carolina: Historiographical Notes," *South Carolina Historical Magazine* 96, no. 4 (1995): 338–39. Russell R. Menard, "Plantation Empire: How Sugar and Tobacco Planters Built Their Industries and Raised an Empire," *Agricultural History* 81, no. 3 (2007): 320–24. Berlin, *Many Thousands Gone*, 370. For an analysis of slave population growth in South Carolina, see Peter H. Wood, *Black Majority: Negroes in Colonial South Carolina: From 1670 through the Stono Rebellion* (New York: Knopf, 1974), 142–66. For the whole story of founding rice plantations in South Carolina, see ibid., 3–62, and Philip D. Morgan, *Slave Counterpoint: Black Culture in the Eighteenth-Century Chesapeake and Lowcountry* (Chapel Hill: University of North Carolina Press, 1998), 40–44.

10. For a bibliography on how this question has been addressed, see John J. McCusker and Russell R. Menard, *The Economy of British America, 1607–1789* (Chapel Hill: University of North Carolina Press, 1985), 238–43.

11. Josiah Child, *A Discourse about Trade* (London: A. Sowle, 1690), preface, 205–6. For the ideological significance of Child's Toryism, see Steve Pincus, "Rethinking Mercantilism: Political Economy, the British Empire, and the Atlantic World in the Seventeenth and Eighteenth Centuries," *William and Mary Quarterly*, 3rd ser. 69, no. 1 (2012): 17–20. The rough North-South division appears earlier in Carew Reynel[l], *The True English Interest* (London, 1674), 91. Thomas C. Barrow, *Trade and Empire: The British Customs Service in Colonial America, 1660–1675* (Cambridge: Harvard University Press, 1967), 4–12.

12. Charles D'avenant, *The Political and Commercial Works of that Celebrated Writer Charles D'avenant, LL.D*, 5 vols. (London: London, R. Horsfield, 1771), 2: 12–16, 17–21. Portion quoted first published in 1698.

13. Lewis Cecil Gray, *History of Agriculture in the Southern United States to 1860*, 2 vols. (1933; Clifton, N.J.: Carnegie Institution, 1973), 1: 284–85.

14. For sectional groupings in the Constitutional Convention of 1787: John Richard Alden, *The First South* (Baton Rouge: Louisiana State University Press, 1961), 9; Jack P. Greene, "The Constitution of 1787 and the Question of Southern Distinctiveness," in *Imperatives, Behaviors, and Identities: Essays in Early American Cultural History*, ed. Jack P. Greene (Charlottesville: University Press of Virginia, 1992), 331–35. On regionalization in this era, see Robert J. Gough, "The Myth of the 'Middle Colonies': An Analysis of Regionalization in Early America," *Pennsylvania Magazine of History and Biography* 107, no. 4 (1983): 393–419.
15. James Madison, *Notes of Debates in the Federal Convention of 1787 Reported by James Madison* (New York: Norton, 1966), 295. The concern about uniting the sections is discussed in Greene, "Constitution of 1787," 327–46; and Peter S. Onuf, "Federalism, Republicanism, and the Origins of American Sectionalism," in *All Over the Map: Rethinking American Regions*, ed. Edward L. Ayers, Patricia Nelson Limerick, Stephen Nissenbaum, and Peter S. Onuf (Baltimore: Johns Hopkins University Press, 1996), 11–37.
16. Not knowing what to do with Delaware, at one time Pennsylvania's "lower counties," another delegate earlier said there were six northern states above Pennsylvania and six southern states below. Mr. Dayton, in Madison, *Notes of the Debates*, July 10, 1787, 224. For examples of sectional configurations in the 1780s, see Joseph L. Davis, *Sectionalism in American Politics, 1774–1787* (Madison: University of Wisconsin Press, 1977), 7–15.
17. Madison probably had in mind comfort and health more than the consequences for the economy. Karen Ordahl Kupperman, "The Puzzle of the American Climate in the Early Colonial Period," *American Historical Review* 87, no. 5 (1982): 1262–89.
18. Ulrich Bonnell Phillips, *Life and Labor in the Old South* (New York: Little, Brown, 1929), 3. John Alden credited climate, soil, and crops. Alden, *The First South*, 14. See also Carl N. Degler, *Place over Time: The Continuity of Southern Distinctiveness* (Baton Rouge: Louisiana State University Press, 1977), 10–12.
19. Phillips, *Life and Labor in the Old South*, 3–4. A. Cash Koeniger proposes the 55 degree mean annual temperature as an outline for the South. "Climate and Southern Distinctiveness," *Journal of Southern History* 59, no. 1 (1988): 26. For climate maps of all the states, *Climates of the States: National Oceanic and Atmospheric Administration, Narrative Summaries, Tables, and Maps for Each State with Overview of State Climatologist Programs*, 2nd ed., 2 vols. (Detroit: Gale Research, 1980), 907 ff. For online resources, "Median/Mean Length

of Freeze-Free Period," National Climate Data Center, "Climate Atlas of the United States," http://webharvest.gov/peth04/20041030080846/http://lwf.ncdc.noaa.gov/oa/about/cdrom/climatls2/datadoc.html#SKIP1.

20. Charles B. Hunt, *Natural Regions of the United States and Canada* (San Francisco: W. H. Freeman, 1974), 122–23, 126, 134, 209, 235, 293–94 (quotation). According to Hunt, the acidic "weathering" of southern mountains occurred before the Wisconsin glaciation, under climatic conditions now unknown. At that time, all of the Appalachians were decomposing from rock into residual clays. Phillips, *Life and Labor in the Old South*, 5.

21. An early critic of the climate explanation argued that "a theory which makes the plantation depend upon something outside the processes of human interaction, that is, a theory which makes the plantation depend upon a fixed and static something like climate, is a theory which operates to justify an existing social order and the vested interests connected with that order." Edgar T. Thompson, "The Climatic Theory of the Plantation," *Agricultural History* 15, no. 1 (1941): 49–60. For an argument to take climate into account, see David Hackett Fischer, "Climate and History: Priorities for Research," *Journal of Interdisciplinary History* 10, no. 4 (1980): 821–30.

22. Daniel K. Richter, *The Ordeal of the Long-House: The Peoples of the Iroquois League in the Era of European Colonization* (Chapel Hill: University of North Carolina Press, 1992), 1–20. Carolyn Merchant, *Ecological Revolutions: Nature, Gender, and Science in New England* (Chapel Hill: University of North Carolina Press, 1989), 74–83. Charles C. Willoughby, "The Virginia Indians in the Seventeenth Century," *American Anthropologist*, n.s. 9, no. 1 (1907): 78–86. Philip Alexander Bruce, *Economic History of Virginia in the Seventeenth Century*, 2 vols. (1895; New York: Peter Smith, 1935), 1: 166.

23. George Arents, "The Seed from Which Virginia Grew," *William and Mary Quarterly*, 2nd ser. 19, no. 2 (1939): 125; Melvin Herndon, *Tobacco in Colonial Virginia: "The Sovereign Remedy"* (Williamsburg: Virginia 350th Anniversary Celebration Corporation, 1957), 19.

24. Dennis D. Moore, ed., *More Letters from the American Farmer: An Edition of the Essays in English Left Unpublished by Crèvecoeur* (Athens: University of Georgia Press, 1995), 44.

25. Gray, *History of Agriculture in the Southern United States*, 1: 235–37; Howard S. Russell, *A Long Deep Furrow: Three Centuries of Farming in New England*, abridged Mark Lapping (1976; Hanover, N.H.: University Press of New England, 1982), 74–76, 167–68.

26. Carr, Menard, and Walsh, *Robert Cole's World,* 37, 55–58. For a summary of the tobacco cycle, see T. H. Breen, *Tobacco Culture: The Mentality of the Great Tidewater Planters on the Eve of Revolution* (Princeton: Princeton University Press, 1985), 46–49. Gloria L. Main, *Tobacco Colony: Life in Early Maryland, 1650–1720* (Princeton: Princeton University Press, 1982), 31–36; Walsh, *Motives of Honor, Pleasure, and Profit,* 155–58.
27. Carr, Menard, and Walsh, *Robert Cole's World,* 55–65, 298 n. 23. See also Walsh, *Motives of Honor, Pleasure, and Profit,* 155–59.
28. Connecticut tobacco cultivation, begun in earnest after 1840, depended heavily on high prices. Christopher Clark, *The Roots of Rural Capitalism: Western Massachusetts, 1780–1860* (Ithaca, N.Y.: Cornell University Press, 1990), 295–96, 304.
29. For an economist's formulation, see Evsey D. Domar, "The Causes of Slavery or Serfdom: A Hypothesis," *Journal of Economic History* 30, no. 1 (1970): 18–32.
30. Daniel Vickers, "Working the Fields in a Developing Economy: Essex County, Massachusetts, 1630–1675," in *Work and Labor in Early America,* ed. Stephen Innes (Chapel Hill: University of North Carolina Press, 1988), 64. John Frederick Martin, *Profits in the Wilderness: Entrepreneurship and the Founding of New England Towns in the Seventeenth Century* (Chapel Hill: University of North Carolina Press, 1991), 32–33; Stephen Innes, *Labor in a New Land: Economy and Society in Seventeenth-Century Springfield* (Princeton: Princeton University Press, 1983). There were a few examples of agricultural slavery in this region. Isaac Royall, Jr., who had connections to Antigua, farmed with slaves along the Mystic River north of Boston, Massachusetts. Daniel R. Coquillette and Bruce A. Kimball, *On the Battlefield of Merit: Harvard Law School, the First Century* (Cambridge: Harvard University Press, 2015), 81–82.
31. Rupert P. Vance, *Human Geography of the South: A Study in Regional Resources and Human Adequacy,* 2nd ed. (1935; New York: Russell and Russell), 356–57.
32. Sung Bok Kim, *Landlord and Tenant in Colonial New York: Manorial Society, 1664–1775* (Chapel Hill: University of North Carolina Press, 1978), 212–13. Paul G. E. Clemens and Lucy Simler, "Rural Labor and the Farm Household in Chester County, Pennsylvania, 1750–1820," in Innes, *Work and Labor in Early America,* 106–43. James T. Lemon, *The Best Poor Man's Country: A Geographical Study of Early Southeastern Pennsylvania* (Baltimore: Johns Hopkins University Press, 1972), 94. Lucy Simler, "Tenancy in Colonial

Pennsylvania: The Case of Chester County," *William and Mary Quarterly*, 3rd ser. 43, no. 4 (1986): 558–59.

33. Dunn, *Sugar and Slaves*, 323–25. Lewis Gray propounds a similar line of reasoning in *History of Agriculture in the Southern United States*, 1: 473–75.

34. Simler, "Tenancy in Colonial Pennsylvania," 568; Harry J. Carman, ed., *American Husbandry* (1939; Port Washington, N.Y.: Kennikat, 1964), 121, 137, 141, 168, 171–73, 176. Jackson Turner Main, *Society and Economy in Colonial Connecticut* (Princeton: Princeton University Press, 1985), 82, 130, 177–79. Graham Russell Hodges, *Slavery and Freedom in the Rural North: African Americans in Monmouth County, New Jersey, 1665–1865* (Madison, Wis.: Madison House, 1997), esp. 47. Richard Shannon Moss, *Slavery on Long Island: A Study in Local Institutional and Early African-American Communal Life* (New York: Garland, 1993), 150–51. Russell, *Long Deep Furrow*, 111. Robert Fitts, "Inventing New England's Slave Paradise: Master/Slave Relations in 18th Century Narragansett, Rhode Island," Ph.D. diss., Brown University, 1995. A manor holder in east New Jersey in 1685 owned sixty to seventy slaves. In South Kingston, Rhode Island, in 1720 a third of the population were Indians and blacks. Percy Wells Bidwell and John I. Falconer, *History of Agriculture in the Northern United States, 1620–1860* (1925; New York: Peter Smith, 1941), 33, 118–19.

35. William J. Cooper, Jr., and Thomas E. Terrill, *The American South: A History* (New York: Knopf, 1990), 183, 185. Wheat prices in southern Europe rose rapidly in the 1760s and 1770s. The transition to wheat is analyzed in Paul G. E. Clemens, *The Atlantic Economy and Colonial Maryland's Eastern Shore: From Tobacco to Grain* (Ithaca, N.Y.: Cornell University Press, 1980).

36. Barbara Jeanne Fields, *Slavery and Freedom on the Middle Ground: Maryland during the Nineteenth Century* (New Haven: Yale University Press, 1985), 4–6, 10. John T. Schlotterbeck, "Plantation and Farm: Social and Economic Change in Orange and Greene Counties, Virginia, 1716 to 1860," Ph.D. diss., Johns Hopkins University, 1980, 187.

37. Clemens, *Atlantic Economy*, 194.

38. Clemens and Simler, "Rural Labor and the Farm Household," 144–88. Lucy Simler points out that "smallholders" with twenty acres of land helped meet the demand for seasonal labor and other services. They were part-time farmers, part-time laborers, part-time tradesmen. "Tenancy in Colonial Pennsylvania," 562–64.

39. Stephen Sargent Visher, *Climatic Atlas of the United States* (Cambridge: Harvard University Press, 1954), 1, 27. Vance, *Human Geography*, 359. As the

author of *American Husbandry* observed, "frosts come on with very little warning, and after a warm day"; 154; cf. 111, 117. C. F. Volney, *A View of the Soil and Climate of the United States of America,* trans. C. B. Brown (New York: Hafner, 1968), 109.

40. Brooke Hunter, "Rage for Grain: Flour Milling in the Mid-Atlantic, 1750–1815," Ph.D. diss., University of Delaware, 2002, 26–27, 33, 61.

41. Quoted in Lemon, *Best Poor Man's Country,* 85. Ideally a laborer could be turned to craft work in the off months, but such workers were expensive. Daniel Vickers, *Farmers and Fishermen: Two Centuries of Work in Essex County, Massachusetts, 1630–1850* (Chapel Hill: University of North Carolina Press, 1994), 51. Jean B. Russo, "Self-Sufficiency and Local Exchange: Free Craftsman in the Rural Chesapeake Economy," in Carr, Morgan, and Russo, *Colonial Chesapeake Society,* 408. Claudia L. Bushman, *In Old Virginia: Slavery, Farming, and Society in the Journal of John Walker* (Baltimore: Johns Hopkins University Press, 2002), 68–74.

42. Robin Blackburn, *The Making of New World Slavery: From the Baroque to the Modern, 1492–1800* (London: Verso, 1997), 476. For a discussion of winter work in Massachusetts, see Winifred Barr Rothenberg, *From Market-Places to a Market Economy: The Transformation of Rural Massachusetts, 1750–1850* (Chicago: University of Chicago Press, 1992), 188–98.

43. Breen, *Tobacco Culture,* 46–55. Robert C. Baron, *The Garden and Farm Books of Thomas Jefferson* (Golden, Colo.: Fulcrum, 1987), 275, 294. Feb. 26, 1760, "[February 1760]," Founders Online, National Archives (http://founders.archives.gov/documents/Washington/01-01-02-0005-0002, ver. 2014-02-12) [original source: *The Diaries of George Washington,* vol. 1, *11 March 1748–13 November 1765,* ed. Donald Jackson (Charlottesville: University Press of Virginia, 1976), 230–49].

44. *The Virginia and North Carolina Almanack for the Year 1802* (Petersburg, Va., 1802), January. Work slowed down during the winter, but not so far that there was nothing profitable for slaves to do. Walsh, *Motives of Honor, Pleasure, and Profit,* 159, 190–91. The author of *American Husbandry* reported that "negroes are employed in sawing and butting timber, threshing corn, clearing new land, and preparing for tobacco"; *American Husbandry,* 164, 189.

45. Clemens, *Atlantic Economy,* 184. For accounts of yearlong labor on southern farms, see Bushman, *In Old Virginia,* 24–40; Richard S. Dunn, "After Tobacco: The Slave Labour Pattern on a Large Chesapeake Grain-and-Livestock Plantation in the Early Nineteenth Century," in *The Early Modern*

Atlantic Economy, ed. John J. McCusker and Kenneth Morgan (Cambridge: Cambridge University Press, 2001). Lewis Gray understood year-round labor as essential to efficient slavery. Gray, *History of Agriculture in the Southern United States*, 1: 478–79. For annual work schedules in Pennsylvania, see Clemens and Simler, "Rural Labor," 118–19, 132–33.

46. Through efficient management of its labor, Mount Airy plantation in Virginia prospered as well after it turned to wheat as when it grew labor-heavy tobacco. Dunn, "After Tobacco." William Strickland, *Observations on the Agriculture of the United States of America* (London: W. Bulmer, 1801), 32, 34, published with *Journal of a Tour in the United States of America, 1794–95*, ed. Reverend J. E. Strickland (New York: New-York Historical Society, 1971).
47. Visher, *Climatic Atlas*, maps 164 and 171. The number of days below 43 degrees (when vigorous plant growth begins) was fewer than 50 in most of the South and between 50 and 100 in most of Virginia. From northern Maryland northward through Pennsylvania, the slow growth period averaged between 100 and 150 days. Ibid., map 909. *American Husbandry*, 197.
48. Visher, *Climatic Atlas*, maps 164, 171. For Maryland and Pennsylvania, ibid., maps 35, 37, 152, 193, 196, 206, 209.
49. Brian Donahue, *The Great Meadow: Farmers and the Land in Colonial Concord* (New Haven: Yale University Press, 2004). An average 125-acre farm in Pennsylvania, according to James Lemon, had 20 acres in hay, second only to 26 acres in corn. Lemon, *Best Poor Man's Country*, 152–53.
50. "From George Washington to John Sinclair, 11 December 1796," Founders Online, National Archives (http://founders.archives.gov/documents/Washington/99-01-02-00080, ver. 2014-02-12). *American Husbandry*, 42, 94–95. For comparison of cattle values in estate inventories, see Alice Hanson Jones, "Components of Private Wealth per Free Capita for the Thirteen Colonies, by Region, 1774," U.S. Bureau of Census, *Historical Statistics: Colonial Times to 1970* (Washington, D.C.: Government Printing Office, 1976), 1155–56.
51. The summer heat was an "enemy to the vegetation of grass." *American Husbandry*, 256, 319. Main, *Tobacco Colony*, 63–66. Virginia DeJohn Anderson, *Creatures of Empire: How Domestic Animals Transformed Early America* (New York: Oxford University Press, 2004). *American Husbandry*, 324.
52. Anderson, *Creatures of Empire*, 117–18, 154–55; Main, *Tobacco Colony*, 64. As open forage land decreased in the Chesapeake, more hay was required. For

hay production in midcentury, see Walsh, *Motives of Honor, Pleasure, and Profit*, 254, 336, 436, 444, 485, 529–30. Pennsylvania farmers also skimped on winter food for their animals. *American Husbandry*, 118, 119, 124–25.

53. Carr, Menard, and Walsh, *Robert Cole's World*, 36; Gray, *History of Agriculture in the Southern United States*, 1: 200–201; 2: 842–45. Barns are mentioned in descriptions of colonial Chesapeake farms, but none has been excavated in the scores of sites that have been investigated. Donald W. Linebaugh, " 'All the Annoyances and Inconveniences of the Country': Environmental Factors in the Development of Outbuildings in the Colonial Chesapeake," *Winterthur Portfolio* 29, no. 1 (1994): 1–18. In Virginia ads for farm properties at midcentury, only one in five mentioned a barn of any kind. Camille Wells, "The Planter's Prospect: Houses, Outbuildings, and Rural Landscapes in Eighteenth-Century Virginia," *Winterthur Portfolio* 28, no. 1 (1993): 1–31. The author of *American Husbandry* allowed for the construction of a barn in setting up in Pennsylvania, but not in Virginia. *American Husbandry*, 140, 168.

54. Most of the indentured servants who arrived in Pennsylvania between 1682 and 1686 went to the cities. Indentured servants were used in hemp production, which required processing after harvest to ret the hemp and extract the fibers. Lemon, *Best Poor Man's Country*, 215–16, 253 n. 23.

55. For a discussion of agrosystems in Europe, see Jan Bieleman, "Farming System Research as a Guideline in Agricultural History," in *Land Productivity and Agro-Systems in the North Sea Area (Middle Ages–20th Century): Elements for Comparison*, ed. Bas J. P. van Bavel and Eric Thoen (Turnhout: Brepols, 1999), 235–50.

56. For a summary of the debate on the role of climate, see James O. Breeden, "Disease as a Factor in Southern Distinctiveness," in *Disease and Distinctiveness in the American South*, ed. Todd L. Savitt and James Harvey Young (Knoxville: University of Tennessee Press, 1988), 1–28. For a caution against an overly sharp definition of the South, see Edward L. Ayers, "What We Talk about When We Talk about the South," in *All Over the Map: Rethinking American Regions*, ed. Edward L. Ayers et al. (Baltimore: Johns Hopkins University Press, 1996), 73.

57. Quoted in William M. Dabney and Marion Dargan, *William Henry Drayton and the American Revolution* (Albuquerque: University of New Mexico Press, 1962), 206.

58. Quoted in Davis, *Sectionalism in American Politics*, v. British writers used the terms more crisply too. John Fothergill, *Considerations Relative to the North American Colonies* (London: Henry Kent, 1765), 36–43.

59. Madison, *Notes of Debates*, 548; Jonathan Elliot, ed., *The Debates in the Several State Conventions on the Adoption of the Federal Constitution*, 5 vols. (Philadelphia: J. B. Lippincott; Washington, D.C.: Taylor and Maury, 1836–59), 4: 324.

4. Generation of Violence

1. Geoffrey Gilbert, *World Population: A Reference Handbook*, 2nd ed. (Santa Barbara, Calif.: ABC Clio, 2005), 9–10; Massimo Livi-Bacci, *A Concise History of World Population*, 3rd ed. (Malden, Mass.: Blackwell, 2001), 27, 58. For the causes of England's rapid growth, see E. A. Wrigley, "The Growth of Population in Eighteenth-Century England: A Conundrum Resolved," *Past and Present*, no. 98 (1983): 121–50. On population in the British colonies, U.S. Bureau of the Census, *Historical Statistics of the United States: Colonial Times to 1957*, 2 vols. (Washington, D.C.: Government Printing Office, 1960), 1: 8; 2: 1168.
2. Benjamin Franklin, *Observations Concerning the Increase of Mankind, Peopling of Countries* (Boston: S. Kneeland, 1755, rpt. Tarrytown, N.Y.: W. Abbatt, 1918), 4.
3. On Husband's father's slaveholding, see Mary Elinor Lazenby, *Herman Husband: A Story of His Life* (Washington, D.C.: Old Neighborhood, 1940), 11. For Husband's life, see in addition to Lazenby, Mark H. Jones, "Husband (or Husbands), Herman (or Hermon, Harmon)," in *Dictionary of North Carolina Biography*, vol. 3, ed. William S. Powell (Chapel Hill: University of North Carolina Press, 1988), 242–43. For migration from Pennsylvania, James T. Lemon, *The Best Poor Man's Country: A Geographical Study of Early Southeastern Pennsylvania* (Baltimore: Johns Hopkins University Press, 1972), 73–77.
4. *Historical Statistics of the United States*, 2: 756. James P. Whittenburg, "Planters, Merchants, and Lawyers: Social Change and the Origins of the North Carolina Regulation," *William and Mary Quarterly*, 3rd ser. 34, no. 2 (1977): 221–22.
5. A. Roger Ekirch, "'A New Government of Liberty': Hermon [*sic*] Husband's Vision of Backcountry North Carolina, 1755," *William and Mary Quarterly*, 3rd ser. 34, no. 4 (1977): 638.
6. Ibid., 639–40.
7. Ibid.
8. Ibid., 640.
9. Lorena S. Walsh, *Motives of Honor, Pleasure, and Profit: Plantation Management in the Colonial Chesapeake, 1607–1763* (Chapel Hill: University of North

Carolina Press, 2010), 111. Skilled craftsmen in Berkeley and Smith's Hundreds in the 1620s were promised fifteen to fifty acres of land at the end of their terms of service. The inclusion of land in freedom dues in the indenture varied according to the terms agreed upon. Ibid., 52, 109, 112.

10. The head right systems in all of the colonies are summarized in Marshall Harris, *Origin of the Land Tenure System in the United States* (Ames: Iowa State College Press, 1953), 194–236, and the New England township system on 273–88.

11. John J. McCusker and Russell R. Menard, *The Economy of British America, 1607–1789* (Chapel Hill: University of North Carolina Press, 1985), 248. Gloria L. Main, *Peoples of a Spacious Land: Families and Cultures in Colonial New England* (Cambridge: Harvard University Press, 2001), 60. For the effect on actual families in a single place, see Philip J. Greven, *Four Generations: Population, Land, and Family in Colonial Andover, Massachusetts* (Ithaca, N.Y.: Cornell University Press, 1970), 201. The extent of this population boom is now under question, as John McCusker has pointed out in "Colonial America's Mestizo Agriculture," in *The Economy of Early America: Historical Perspectives and New Directions,* ed. Cathy Matson (University Park: Pennsylvania State University Press, 2006), 117. He cites the conclusion of Jackson and Gloria Main on New England that there was no Malthusian crisis. "The Red Queen in New England?" *William and Mary Quarterly* 56, no. 1 (1999): 121–50. That the population was growing at a breathtaking pace is, of course, not in question.

12. John Murrin, "Self-Immolation: Schools of Historiography and the Coming of the American Revolution," paper delivered at the Columbia University Early American History seminar, Oct. 9, 2007, 30. Alan Taylor succinctly states the fundamental contradiction in *Liberty Men and Great Proprietors: The Revolutionary Settlement on the Maine Frontier, 1760–1820* (Chapel Hill: University of North Carolina Press, 1990), 9.

13. Robert J. Taylor, *Western Massachusetts in the Revolution* (Providence: Brown University Press, 1954; rpt. New York: Kraus Reprint, 1967), 4. David Jaffee eloquently relates the New England migration story in *People of the Wachusett: Greater New England in History and Memory, 1630–1860* (Ithaca, N.Y.: Cornell University Press, 1999), 170. Migration and expansion are given lucid treatments in the Histories of the American Frontier series, including Jack M. Sosin, *The Revolutionary Frontier, 1763–1783* (New York: Holt, Rinehart and Winston, 1967); Douglas Edward Leach, *The Northern Colonial Frontier, 1607–1763* (New York: Holt, Rinehart and Winston, 1966); and

W. Stitt Robinson, *The Southern Colonial Frontier, 1607–1763* (Albuquerque: University of New Mexico Press, 1979). The best overview is Bernard Bailyn, *Voyagers to the West: A Passage in the Peopling of America on the Eve of the Revolution* (New York: Knopf, 1986), 7–28.

14. Robert Gross, *The Minutemen and Their World* (New York: Hill and Wang, 1976), 79–82, 106–7, 177. Greven, *Four Generations*, 272–74. The consequences of failing fathers are developed by Honor Sachs in *Home Rule: Manhood and National Expansion on the Eighteenth-Century Kentucky Frontier* (New Haven: Yale University Press, 2015).
15. Allan Kulikoff, *From British Peasants to Colonial American Farmers* (Chapel Hill: University of North Carolina Press, 2000), 129–33. For an overall analysis of the crisis, see 127–35. For price increases of similar magnitude in other areas, see Carville V. Earle, *The Evolution of a Tidewater Settlement System: All Hallow's Parish, Maryland, 1650–1783* (Chicago: University of Chicago Department of Geography, 1975), 210; David B. Ryden and Russell R. Menard, "South Carolina's Colonial Land Market: An Analysis of Rural Property Sales, 1720–1775," *Social Science History* 29, no. 4 (2005): 617; Lemon, *Best Poor Man's Country*, 67, 69, 88; Lucy Simler, "Tenancy in Colonial Pennsylvania: The Case of Chester County," *William and Mary Quarterly*, 3rd ser. 43, no. 1 (1986): 560.
16. The prices of farm products rose rapidly under the stimulus of the wartime economy, but not sufficiently to facilitate land purchases. Gloria L. Main, "Gender, Work, and Wages in Colonial New England," *William and Mary Quarterly*, 3rd ser. 51, no. 1 (1994): 63.
17. Kulikoff, *From British Peasants to Colonial American Farmers*, 129–35; quotations at 129, 133, 135–36. See also Steven Sarson, "Landlessness and Tenancy in Early National Prince George's County, Maryland," *William and Mary Quarterly*, 3rd ser. 57, no. 3 (2000): 569–98, and Peter O. Wacker, *Land and People: A Cultural Geography of Preindustrial New Jersey Origins and Settlement Patterns* (New Brunswick, N.J.: Rutgers University Press, 1975), 138, 399–401.
18. Jaffee, *People of the Wachusett*, 112, 136; Gross, *Minutemen*, 80. Richard L. Bushman, *From Puritan to Yankee: Character and the Social Order in Connecticut, 1690–1765* (Cambridge: Harvard University Press, 1967), 75–76.
19. Ekirch, "'A New Government of Liberty,'" 641.
20. Ibid. Orange County, Registration of Deeds, County Court, 1752–93, North Carolina Department of Archives and History, Raleigh, N.C., 83, 95–99, 115, 109, 129, 144. Lazenby, *Herman Husband*, 25.

21. John Frederick Martin, *Profits in the Wilderness: Entrepreneurship and the Founding of New England Towns in the Seventeenth Century* (Chapel Hill: University of North Carolina Press, 1991), 31–36. Some proprietors offered bonuses to attract settlers (34).
22. On emergence of land companies, see Ray A. Billington, "The Origin of the Land Speculator as a Frontier Type," *Agricultural History* 19, no. 4 (1945): 204–12; Shaw Livermore, *Early American Land Companies: Their Influence on Corporate Development* (New York: Oxford University Press, 1939). Alan Taylor, *William Cooper's Town: Power and Persuasion on the Frontier of the Early American Republic* (New York: Knopf, 1995), 44–52. Shaw Livermore lists ten pre-Revolutionary land companies in *Early American Land Companies*, 74–132. For the melee of other land speculators, see Bailyn, *Voyagers to the West*, 364–400, 430–47, 475–81, 546–51, 573–637.
23. Eric Hinderaker tells a story of contested titles in the Ohio Valley in *Elusive Empires: Constructing Colonialism in the Ohio Valley, 1673–1800* (Cambridge: Cambridge University Press, 1997), 166–73. For the Transylvania company's title controversies and similar disputes, see Livermore, *Early American Land Companies*, 90–97.
24. Taylor, *William Cooper's Town*, 210–11, 74–79.
25. William Wyckoff elaborates the distinction between developer and speculator in *The Developer's Frontier: The Making of the Western New York Landscape* (New Haven: Yale University Press, 1988), 9–11.
26. Speculators competed with each other for tenants by easing the terms of entry on to the land. Peter C. Mancall, *Valley of Opportunity: Economic Culture along the Upper Susquehanna, 1700–1800* (Ithaca, N.Y.: Cornell University Press, 1991), 105–7; Sosin, *The Revolutionary Frontier*, 42–43; Jaffee, *People of the Wachusett*, 109–15, 129–39.
27. John R. Dunbar, ed., *The Paxton Papers* (The Hague: Martinus Nijhoff, 1957); and Alden T. Vaughan, "Frontier Banditti and the Indians: the Paxton Boys' Legacy, 1763–1775," *Pennsylvania History* 51, no. 1 (1984): 3. The news shocked the Philadelphia gentry but not the populace as a whole. Dunbar, *The Paxton Papers*, 48, 93, 113. C. Hale Sipe, *The Indian Wars of Pennsylvania . . . Tragedies of the Pennsylvania Frontier* (Harrisburg, Pa.: Telegraph, 1929), digs out stories from the colonial archives. See esp. 217–23.
28. David L. Preston, "Squatters, Indians, Proprietary Government, and Land in the Susquehanna Valley," in *Friends and Enemies in Penn's Woods: Indians, Colonists, and the Racial Construction of Pennsylvania*, ed. William A. Pencak

and Daniel K. Richter (University Park: Pennsylvania State University Press, 2004), 199.

29. William A. Russ, Jr., *How Pennsylvania Acquired Its Present Boundaries* (University Park: Pennsylvania Historical Association, Pennsylvania State University, 1966). A. Roger Ekirch, *"Poor Carolina": Politics and Society in Colonial North Carolina, 1729–1776* (Chapel Hill: University of North Carolina Press, 1981), 176. Marvin Lucian Skaggs, "North Carolina Boundary Disputes Involving Her Southern Line," *James Sprunt Historical Collections* 25 (1941).
30. For Maryland and Pennsylvania, see William H. Bayliff, *The Maryland-Pennsylvania and the Maryland-Delaware Boundaries,* 2nd ed. (Annapolis: Maryland Board of Natural Resources, 1959); Edwin Danson, *Drawing the Line: How Mason and Dixon Surveyed the Most Famous Border in America* (New York: Wiley, 2001).
31. Sosin, *The Revolutionary Frontier,* 57–60; Boyd Crumrine, "The Boundary Controversy between Pennsylvania and Virginia, 1748–1785," *Annals of the Carnegie Museum* 1 (1901–2): 505–24.
32. For the actions of "claims clubs" in Pennsylvania in the 1730s, see Lemon, *Best Poor Man's Country,* 57.
33. Richard P. McCormick, *New Jersey from Colony to State, 1609–1789* (Princeton: D. Van Nostrand, 1964), 17–20, 26–27, 33–37, 77–78. Brendan McConville, *These Daring Disturbers of the Public Peace; The Struggle for Property and Power in Early New Jersey* (Ithaca, N.Y.: Cornell University Press, 1999), 6, 137, 161; quotation at 63.
34. A compelling description of the New York–New England contest can be found in Patricia U. Bonomi, *A Factious People: Politics and Society in Colonial New York* (New York: Columbia University Press, 1971), 200–228. See also Irving Mark and Oscar Handlin, eds., "Land Cases in Colonial New York, 1765–1767, The King v. William Prendergast," *New York University Law Quarterly Review* 19, no. 1 (1942): 174–80, 189–90. On Prendergast's role in the Cortlandt manor riots, see Sung Bok Kim, *Landlord and Tenant in Colonial New York: Manorial Society, 1664–1775* (Chapel Hill: University of North Carolina Press, 1978), 381–96. For land titles as the issue in New York, ibid., 413–15.
35. Mark and Handlin, "Land Cases in Colonial New York," 183–84.
36. Brendan McConville argues for a radical idea of property rights among farmers in *These Daring Disturbers of the Public Peace.* McConville's protesters laid claim to land based on Indian titles, a conception of ownership

resulting from labor mixed with the soil, rather than from governmental or proprietary titles. Ownership arose from the bottom up, from people working the land, rather than from the top down.

37. Whittenburg, "Planters, Merchants, and Lawyers," 232.
38. Ibid., 237. John S. Bassett, "The Regulators of North Carolina (1765–1771)," in *Annual Report of the American Historical Association for the Year 1894* (Washington, D.C.: Government Printing Office, 1895), 191–92.
39. William S. Powell, James K. Huhta, and Thomas Farnham, *The Regulators in North Carolina: A Documentary History, 1759–1776* (Raleigh, N.C.: State Department of Archives and History, 1971), xxii–xxv. Ekirch, *"Poor Carolina,"* 165. Jones, "Husband (or Husbands)," 243. The fullest account is Bassett, "The Regulators of North Carolina (1765–1771)," 196–208.
40. Roger Ekirch summarizes the historiography as well as offering a republican interpretation in Ekirch, *"Poor Carolina,"* 165–68 and 164–202, esp. 166–68. James Whittenburg similarly analyzes the historiography in presenting his competition model. Whittenburg, "Planters, Merchants, and Lawyers," 215–38, esp. 217–20.
41. [Herman Husband], *An Impartial Relation of the First Rise and Cause of the Recent Differences, in Publick Affairs, In the Province of North-Carolina; and of the past Tumults and Riots that lately happened in that Province* (Printed for the Compiler, 1770). Rpt. in William K. Boyd, *Some Eighteenth Century Tracts Concerning North Carolina* (Raleigh, N.C.: Edwards and Broughton, 1927), 251–333. The Sims excerpts appear on 254–56.
42. George Sims, "An Address to the People of Granville County," in Boyd, *Some Eighteenth Century Tracts,* 189–90.
43. Herman Husband, *A Fan for Fanning and A Touchstone to Tryon, Containing an Impartial Account of the Rise and Progress of the so much talked of Regulation in North-Carolina* (Boston: Willam Vassell, 1771), 347–48.
44. The best description of Fanning's later career in Nova Scotia and Prince Edward Island is J. M. Bumsted, "Biography of Edmund Fanning," *Dictionary of Canadian Biography Online,* http://www.biographi.ca/en/bio/fanning_edmund_5E.html.
45. Robert C. Kenzer, *Kinship and Neighborhood in a Southern Community: Orange County, North Carolina, 1849–1881* (Knoxville: University of Tennessee Press, 1987), 53–54.
46. Ekirch, " 'A New Government of Liberty,' " 641–42.
47. Ibid.
48. Ibid., 642.

49. Ibid.
50. Gross, *Minutemen*, 106.
51. For a detailed account of the Holland Company purchase, see Wyckoff, *Developer's Frontier*, 16–18, 52–59. Malcolm J. Rohrbough, *The Land Office Business: The Settlement and Administration of American Public Lands, 1789–1837* (New York: Oxford University Press, 1968), 9–10.
52. Rohrbough, *The Land Office Business*, 25, 30–37 (quotation).
53. Ibid., 12–14, 18 (Findley quotation), 22–23, 30, 32–34, 38, 141–43, 234.
54. Lazenby, *Herman Husband*, 125, 127, 131, 141, 147–52, 157, 160–62, 169, 172–79.

5. Uncas and Joshua

1. Frances Manwaring Caulkins, *History of Norwich, Connecticut: From Its Possession by the Indians to the Year 1866* (Hartford, Conn.: The author, 1866), 585–86.
2. Ibid., 17, 28–29, 48–50.
3. *Uncas and Miantonomoh; A historical discourse, delivered at Norwich (Conn.), on the Fourth day of July, 1842, on the occasion of the erection of a monument to the memory of Uncas, the white man's friend, and first chief of the Mohegans* (New York: Dayton and Newman, 1842), 12, 18. Michal Leroy Oberg, *Uncas: First of the Mohegans* (Ithaca, N.Y.: Cornell University Press, 2003), 3 tells the story of the monument's erection.
4. Frances Manwaring Caulkins, *History of New London, Connecticut: from the first survey of the coast in 1612, to 1852* (New London, Conn.: The author, 1852), 44–45.
5. Ibid., 45–46. Connecticut disputed Massachusetts claims by referring to a shadowy Warwick Patent that added a grant from the king to the claim by conquest.
6. Oberg, *Uncas*, 117–18.
7. The Last Will of Robert Hemstid, Sept. 30, 1653, in *A Digest of the Early Connecticut Probate Records*, comp. Charles William Manwaring (Hartford, Conn.: R. S. Peck, 1904–6), 2: 126–27; "Hemstid, Joshua, New London. Will dated, 7 October, 1683," *Connecticut Probate Records*, 7: 76.
8. Joshua Hempstead, *The Diary of Joshua Hempstead: A Daily Record of Life in Colonial New London, Connecticut, 1711–1758* (New London, Conn.: New London County Historical Society, 1998), 126 (Nov. 15, 1722). The diary was first published as *Diary of Joshua Hempstead of New London, Connecticut, Covering a Period of Forty-Seven Years from September, 1711, to November 1758:*

Collections of the New London County Historical Society, vol. 1 (New London: New London County Historical Society, 1901).

9. John William De Forest, *History of the Indians of Connecticut from the Earliest Known Period to 1850* (Hartford, Conn.: W. J. Hammersley, 1853), 316.
10. Wendy B. St. Jean, "Inventing Guardianship: The Mohegan Indians and Their 'Protectors,' " *New England Quarterly* 72, no. 3 (1999): 364–66. Oberg, *Uncas*, 38–40, 47–48.
11. Oberg, *Uncas*, 57.
12. There are many accounts of Mason's destruction of the Mystic fort and its aftermath. Among the most recent and complete is Oberg, *Uncas*, 66–72.
13. Ibid., 83–84.
14. Capt. Charles Hervey Townshend, "The Hartford Treaty with the Narragansetts and the Fenwick Letters," *New England Historical and Genealogical Register* 46 (1892): 355–56. Oberg, *Uncas*, 84–85.
15. Oberg, *Uncas*, 81, 82, 89. David W. Conroy, "The Defense of Indian Land Rights: William Bollan and the Mohegan Case in 1743," *Proceedings of the American Antiquarian Society*, 103, pt. 2 (1993): 397–98.
16. Roger Williams described a similar stratagem which he thought "false and trecherous" but the Indians considered politic. Roger Williams, *A Key into the Language of America* (London: Gregory Dexter, 1643; rpt. Providence: John Miller, 1827), 132–33.
17. Miantonomi did not dream up this idea on the spot. The Pequots had contemplated such schemes before the Pequot War, and Miantonomi had proposed the same idea to the Montauks on Long Island in 1642. Jenny Hale Pulsipher, *Subjects unto the Same King: Indians, English, and the Contest for Authority in Colonial New England* (Philadelphia: University of Pennsylvania Press, 2005), 22, 26.
18. Oberg, *Uncas*, 102–7.
19. Ibid., 91–138, 102–7. Pulsipher, *Subject to the Same King*, 26–27.
20. J. Hammond Trumbull, ed., *Public Records of the Colony of Connecticut*, 15 vols. (Hartford, Conn., 1850–90), 1: 208, 251, 257, cited in St. Jean, "Inventing Guardianship," 372; Oberg, *Uncas*, 154.
21. For a strategy of grazing cattle as a basis for claiming ownership, see David J. Silverman, " 'We Chuse to be Bounded': Native American Animal Husbandry in Colonial New England," *William and Mary Quarterly*, 3rd ser. 60, no. 3 (2003): 511–48.
22. Williams, *A Key*, 167. St. Jean, "Inventing Guardianship," 374. Copies of deeds with Uncas's mark on them can be seen in Stone, *Uncas and Miantonomoh*, 200, 202.

23. St. Jean, "Inventing Guardianship," 374. An illuminating analysis of the displacement is ibid., 362–87.
24. Quoted in Oberg, *Uncas,* 79.
25. St. Jean, "Inventing Guardianship," 375–77.
26. Oberg, *Uncas,* 158; St. Jean, "Inventing Guardianship," 378.
27. St. Jean, "Inventing Guardianship," 380.
28. Stone, *Uncas,* 201.
29. St. Jean, "Inventing Guardianship," 382–83.
30. Ibid., 384–85.
31. De Forest, *History of the Indians,* 313–15, 317; Caulkins, *History of New London,* 267–68, 428.
32. Hempstead, *Diary,* 153 (Feb. 12, 1724/25), 394 (Oct. 17, 1742). Oberg, *Uncas,* 166–70.
33. I take my cue from Pierre Bourdieu, *The Field of Cultural Production: Essays on Art and Literature* (Cambridge: Polity, 1993), 30.
34. Stone, *Uncas,* 201. Caulkins, *History of Norwich,* 428. Melissa Jayne Fawcett, *The Lasting of the Mohegans* (Uncasville, Conn.: The Mohegan Tribe, 1995), tells the story from the viewpoint of the tribal historian.
35. Stone, *Uncas,* 13.
36. Hempstead genealogical information is from Hempstead, *Diary,* vi, vii.
37. Ibid., 57 (Aug. 5, 1716), 58 (Aug. 10, 11, 1716).
38. Ibid., 59 (Sept. 18, 1716), 234 (June 16, 1731), 61 (Nov. 16, 1716). The Tallmage connection can be traced on familysearch.org through Thomas Tallmage of Easthampton, born 1676/77, and Mary Bailey, married 1706.
39. Ibid., 43 (March 23, 1715), 57 (Aug. 9, 1716), 61 (Dec. 12, 1716), 88 (July 10, 1719), 457 (Aug. 21, 1746).
40. Ibid., 78 (Aug. 6, 1718), 98 (July 17, 1720).
41. Ibid., 209 (May 11–June 7, July 4, 9, 10, 1729).
42. Ibid., vi.
43. Ibid., 52–62 (Jan. 12, 1715/16–Dec. 31, 1716). For the July figures, ibid., 56–57 (July 2–30, 1716). Quotations ibid., 57 (July 14, 18, 1716).
44. Ibid., 57 (July 31, 1716), 57 (Aug. 1, 2, 4, 5, 6, 1716).
45. Ibid., 68 (July 24, 25, 26, 1717), 69 (Oct. 14, 1717). The diary entry is ambiguous. It says Hempstead paid Whitney "his whole Sixth part of £400." Whitney may have received all of the £400, in which case the sloop sold for £2,400, or a sixth of £400, about £67.
46. Ibid., 72 (Jan. 9, 1717/18), 55 (May 2, 3, 4, 1716).

47. Patricia M. Schaefer, *A Useful Friend: A Companion to the Joshua Hempstead Diary, 1711–1758* (New London, Conn.: New London County Historical Society, 2008), 75–77.
48. Ibid., 9. For the *Plainfield*'s completion, Hempstead, *Diary*, 63–64 (Jan. 14, 18, 30, 1716/17). On women as substitute husbands, see Laurel Thatcher Ulrich, *Good Wives: Image and Reality in the Lives of Women in Northern New England, 1650–1750* (New York: Knopf, 1982), 35–50.
49. For a sketch of Hempstead's occupations, see Schaefer, *A Useful Friend*, 57–66, 119–28.
50. Hempstead, *Diary*, 1–2 (Sept. 10–12, 18, 20, 21, 29, 1711), 4 (Nov. 10, 12, 13, 1711), 72 (Jan. 13, 1717/18).
51. On hay as the limiting factor in the expansion of food and especially meat production, see Brian Donahue, *The Great Meadow: Farmers and the Land in Colonial Concord* (New Haven: Yale University Press, 2004), esp. 206.
52. Hempstead, *Diary*, 24–27.
53. Oats: ibid., 22 (May 15, 1713), 25–26 (Aug. 4, 15, 1713); corn: ibid., 24 (June 20, 1713), 27 (Sept. 25, 30, 1713), 27–28 (Oct. 1, 2, 20, 1713).
54. Ibid., 22–23 (May 14, 21, 1713), 24 (June 20, 26, 1713), 27 (Sept. 25, 30, 1713), 27–28 (Oct. 1, 2, 20, 1713).
55. Ibid., 22 (April 22, 1713); watermelons: ibid., 26 (Aug. 31, 1713); peach and pear trees: ibid., 84 (Mar. 12, 1718/19), 119 (April 10, 1722), 167 (April 15, 21, 1726).
56. Ibid., 24 (June 16, 1713).
57. Ibid., 8 (March 12, 1711/12), 21 (March 12, 18, 1713), 28 (Oct. 30, 31, 1713).
58. Ibid., 23 (June 5, 1713), 64 (Feb. 27, 1716/17), 22 (May 16, 1713), 24 (June 23, 1713), 25 (July 17, 1713), 34 (May 14, 1714), 124 (Oct. 19, 1722).
59. Ibid., 23 (June 4, 1713), 42 (Feb. 4, 1714/15). A year later "Ebe Pierce workt here al day & yesterday. finish 1 gacket 2 pr breeches." Ibid., 69 (Oct. 9, 1717).
60. Schaefer, *A Useful Friend*, 127. "Cotton wool" sometime arrived in the cargoes Hempstead was party to: "fetched home my Share of ye Cotton wool yt came home in ye Samll about 8 or 9 lbs." Hempstead, *Diary*, 59 (Oct. 5, 1716).
61. Hempstead, *Diary*, 59 (Sept. 10, Oct. 2, 1716).
62. He was forever settling accounts with fellow townsmen from the multiple transactions he was party to. Ibid., 8 (March 1, 1711/12), 42–43 (March 10, 1714/15), 44 (May 4, 1715), 52 (Jan. 7, 1715/16), 72 (Jan. 9, 1717/18).
63. Hempstead's daughter Elizabeth, on the eve of her marriage and unbeknownst to him, ran up a bill of £30 at Clement Minor's store. Ibid., 289 (Aug. 8, 1735).

64. John Locke, *Two Treatises of Government*, ed. Peter Laslett, 2nd ed. (Cambridge: Cambridge University Press, 1988), 310–15.

6. Sons and Daughters

1. Daniel Vickers, *Farmers and Fishermen: Two Centuries of Work in Essex County, Massachusetts, 1630–1850* (Chapel Hill: University of North Carolina Press, 1994), 64–77, 245–46 (quotation).
2. Jackson Turner Main, *Society and Economy in Colonial Connecticut* (Princeton: Princeton University Press, 1985), 117.
3. By the summer of 1714, Hempstead had four boys with him in the field, ranging from Joshua, age fifteen; Nathaniel, thirteen; and Robert, eleven, down to Stephen, just eight and a half, who occasionally helped out. In October 1714: "I workt at ye vessel al day ye boys gathering Corn." While he finished the sloop in July 1716, they carried on the arduous hay harvest. He apparently had confidence in the younger boys. By the time Joshua was sixteen he was working beside his father day after day in the shipyard, speeding along the completion of a sloop and racking up billable hours, while Abigail and the younger boys kept the farm going. Joshua Hempstead, *The Diary of Joshua Hempstead: A Daily Record of Life in Colonial New London, Connecticut, 1711–1758* (New London, Conn.: New London County Historical Society, 1998), 38 (Oct. 7, 9, 1714), 56 (July 3, 1716), 37–38 (Aug. 31, Sept. 1, 3, 13, 20, 21, 22, 25, Oct. 4, 5, 11, 1714).
4. Ibid., 36 (July 24, 27, 1714), 37 (Aug. 5, 1714).
5. Ibid., 224 (Sept. 5, 1730).
6. Part of the story of the Stonington property is summarized in Patricia M. Schaefer, *A Useful Friend: A Companion to the Joshua Hempstead Diary, 1711–1758* (New London, Conn.: New London County Historical Society, 2008), 84–86. The court finally cleared the title on March 31, 1719. Hempstead, *Diary*, 85. I am grateful to Barry Levy for information on Hempstead's sheep operation.
7. Hempstead, *Diary*, 86–88 (April 4, 13–15, May 11, 14, 15, 30, 1719), 89 (June 1, 1719), 102 (Nov. 18, 1720), 108 (May 23, 1721), 112 (Aug. 21, 1721).
8. Ibid., 197 (June 6, 1728).
9. Ibid., 187 (Oct. 27, 1727).
10. Allegra di Bonaventura incorporates Adam Jackson's story into a study of slavery in eighteenth-century Connecticut in *For Adam's Sake: A Family Saga in Colonial New England* (New York: Liveright, 2013). Cf. R. W. Stevenson, "Two Lives, Long Entwined, Are Revealed," *New York Times*, July 14, 2002. Two-thirds of Connecticut households in Hempstead's wealth

class owned slaves, but on average fewer than two. Main, *Society and Economy*, 181.

11. Hempstead, *Diary*, 314 (April 2, 1737), 692 (Oct. 19, 1758). For Adam Jackson's story, also see Joanne Pope Melish, *Disowning Slavery: Gradual Emancipation and "Race" in New England, 1780–1860* (Ithaca, N.Y.: Cornell University Press, 1998), 21–23.
12. Quoted in Schaefer, *A Useful Friend*, 21.
13. Hempstead, *Diary*, 295–96 (Jan. 2, 23, 1735/36), 302 (July 7, 1736). Daniel Vickers found that from twenty-one on sons were generally allowed to work for themselves. Vickers, *Farmers and Fishermen*, 67–68.
14. For Hempstead's landholdings and will, see Schaefer, *A Useful Friend*, 75, 279–81.
15. Hempstead, *Diary*, vi, 291 (Sept. 20, 1735), 300–301 (May 30, June 10, 1736), 482 (Nov. 2, 1747), 545 (Oct. 25, 1750), 607 (Jan. 26, 1754).
16. Di Bonaventura, *For Adam's Sake*, 224–25, 228. http://longislandgenealogy.com/Ledyard/one.htm, accessed Jan. 15, 2009. http://freepages.genealogy.rootsweb.ancestry.com/~dav4is/ODTs/SALMON.shtml, accessed Sept. 28, 2009. familysearch.org, ancestral file, accessed Sept. 28, 2009.
17. Schaefer, *A Useful Friend*, 285.
18. Hempstead, *Diary*, 326 (Jan. 2, 1737/38). For the colony's eighteenth-century land sales, Richard L. Bushman, *From Puritan to Yankee: Character and the Social Order in Connecticut, 1690–1765* (Cambridge: Harvard University Press, 1967), 75–76.
19. Hempstead, *Diary*, 302–7 (Sept. 4–5, 1736).
20. Ibid., 5 (Dec. 5, 7, 1711).
21. Hempstead did use a scythe. Ibid., 24 (June 29, 1713).
22. The year before: "I took my two Gransons with me to Learn Joshua near 100 hills & Natt about half so much." Ibid., 274 (July 12, 1734), 286 (June 21, 1735).
23. Ibid., 6–7 (Jan. 17–29, 1712).
24. Ibid., 6–7.
25. Ibid., 4 (Nov. 24–26, 1711). For a young man who recorded prices in his diary, see Daniel Vickers, "Competency and Competition: Economic Culture in Early America," *William and Mary Quarterly*, 3rd ser. 47, no. 1 (1990): 5–6.
26. Mary Cooper, *The Diary of Mary Cooper: Life on a Long Island Farm, 1768–1773*, ed. Field Horne (n.p.: Oyster Bay Historical Society, 1981).
27. Ibid., iv–vi, 15 (July 13, 1769), 39 (Sept. 8, 1772). "This day 17 years since my dear son Isaac was born. Oh alas, a short lived blessing ended." Ibid., 66 (Sept. 1, 1773).

28. Ibid., iv–vi, 6 (Jan. 12–14, 1769).
29. Ibid., 20 (Oct. 1, 1769). After a Sabbath meeting in 1772, Simon "come in hellish anger and talked extreme ill to Ester." The next day he came to the house and took some of his clothes. "Ester cryed most of this night about what S.C. said." Ibid., 38 (Aug. 24, 1772).
30. Ibid., ix.
31. Ibid., 44 (Nov. 7, 9 [quotation], 1772), 52 (Feb. 27, 1773).
32. Ibid., on wheat: 1 (Oct. 5, 1768), 9 (March 10, 1769), 28 (March 9, 1771); 32 (May 10, 1771); on green herbs in the garden: 44 (Nov. 7, 1772), 42 (Oct. 24, 1772); on fruit: 25–26, 28 (July 9–10, 24–25, 1769), 35–36 (July 9, 22, 1772); on apples: 1 (Oct. 11–13, 1768), 41 (Oct. 5, 1772), 42 (Oct. 14, 1772), 43 (Nov. 3–6, 1772); on pickles: 13–14 (June 2, 4, 16, 1769), 43 (Nov. 2, 1772), 46 (Dec. 16, 1772), 67 (Sept. 17, 1773).
33. Ibid., 24 (Nov. 23, Dec. 2, 1769). Souse was head cheese.
34. Ibid., 25 (Dec. 8, 12, 1769), 46 (Dec. 23, 1772), 47 (Dec. 24, 1772), 32 (May 7, 1771), 37 (Aug. 15, 1772), 41 (Oct. 5, 1772), 23 (Nov. 7, 15, 1769), 5 (Dec. 24, 1768).
35. Ibid., 67 (Sept. 18, 1773), 16 (Aug. 1–2, 1769).
36. Ibid., 19 (Sept. 17, 1769), 16 (Aug. 26, 1769), 40 (Sept. 17, 1772), 19 (Sept. 25, 1769).
37. Ibid., 3 (Nov. 12, 17, 1768), 4 (Nov. 20, Dec. 23, 1768), 6 (Jan. 7, 1769), 31 (April 14, 1771).
38. Ibid., 44 (Nov. 24, 1772), 29–30 (March 19, 22, 24, 1771), 31 (April 21–22, 1771), 39 (Sept. 1, 1772).
39. On May 3, 1769: "The early songsters warbling their notes and all nature seems to smile, but a darke cloud hangs continuly over my soul and makes the days and nights pass heavily along." Ibid., 11 (May 3, 1769).
40. Ibid., 29 (March 15, 1771), 33 (June 7, 1771); cf. 37 (Aug. 9, 1772) 40 (Sept. 25, 1772).
41. Ibid., 7 (Feb. 3, 1769), 20 (Sept. 29–30, 1769), 23 (Nov. 14, 1769), 48 (Jan. 9, 1773), 67 (Sept. 8, 1773), 20–21 (Oct. 8, 12, 20, 1769), 2 (Nov. 1, 1768), 11 (April 26, 1769), 20 (Oct. 1, 1769), 14 (July 3, 1769).
42. Michal Leroy Oberg, *Uncas: First of the Mohegans* (Ithaca, N.Y.: Cornell University Press, 2003), 23. Kathleen Joan Bragdon, *Native People of Southern New England* (Norman: University of Oklahoma Press, 2009), 122.
43. Roger Williams, *A Key into the Language of America* (London: Gregory Dexter, 1643; rpt. Providence: John Miller, 1827), 92, 163, 185. For more on Indian hoes, see Bragdon, *Native People*, 109.

44. The timing and reasons for maize horticulture are summarized in Bragdon, *Native People*, 85–88.
45. For an incisive and illuminating description of the Mohegan economy and culture before the Puritans, see Oberg, *Uncas*, 16–33. A more extensive description is in Bragdon, *Native People*, chaps. 2–3.
46. Williams, *A Key*, 117, 207. Jenny Hale Pulsipher, *Subjects unto the Same King: Indians, English, and the Contest for Authority in Colonial New England* (Philadelphia: University of Pennsylvania Press, 2005), 25.
47. Quoted in Bragdon, *Native People*, 177.
48. Williams, *A Key*, 126.
49. Not that significant differences did not exist between neighboring Indian bodies. Williams observed that "the varietie of their Dialets and proper speech within thirtie or fortie miles of each other, is very great." Williams, *A Key*, 174. The book was written in 1643 after Williams had dealt with the Narragansetts and specifically Miantonomi for about eight years. John J. Tenissen and Evelyn J. Hinz, "Introduction," Williams, *A Key*, 18–20.
50. Ibid., 18–19.
51. Williams, *A Key*, 115–16, 74, 80.
52. Ibid., 111.
53. Ibid., 86, 59.
54. Ibid., 121. John William De Forest, *History of the Indians of Connecticut from the Earliest Known Period to 1850* (Hartford, Conn.: W. J. Hammersley, 1853), 31. Williams noted the capacity of large numbers of Indian men to sit in perfect stillness to hear speeches. Williams, *A Key*, 62.
55. Williams, *A Key*, 62, 63. For a discussion of oratory practices, see Bragdon, *Native People*, 173–74. Governance also required the sachem's sons to share their provisions with neighbors even if they lacked for themselves. Williams thought there was "more free entertainment and refreshing amongst these Barbarians, than amongst thousands that call themselves Christians." *A Key*, 36–37.
56. Williams, *A Key*, 202; Bragdon, *Native People*, 143–45.
57. De Forest, *History of the Indians*, 249–51. For another instance of required vengeance, see Oberg, *Uncas*, 100–101.

7. Farmers' Markets

1. Joshua Hempstead, *The Diary of Joshua Hempstead: A Daily Record of Life in Colonial New London, Connecticut, 1711–1758* (New London, Conn.: New London County Historical Society, 1998), 90 (Aug. 29, 1720), 95–96 (March 19, 21, 22, 26, 28; April 8, 1720), 98–99 (July 18, Aug. 6, 8, 1720).

2. Ibid., 99 (Aug. 25, 1720), 101 (Nov. 3, 1720).
3. Ibid., 540 (July 18, 1750), 446 (Jan. 10, 1745/46).
4. Ibid., 95 (March 17, 1719/20), 96 (April 8, 13, 15, 1720), 97 (May 4, 1720), 99 (Aug. 13, 1720), 104 (Dec. 24, 1720), 95 (March 3, 10, 12, 1719/20), 98 (June 17, 1720).
5. In August, Christopher received another five pounds of Barbados silver from Hempstead for the same purpose. Meanwhile, he purchased eighty-seven gallons of rum from Captain Manwaring that he shipped to Hartford on Mr. Arnold's boat to sell in the colony capital. Ibid., 95 (March 6, 8, 10, 18, 31, 1719/20), 100 (Sept. 15, 1720), 99 (Aug. 13, 1720), 98 (June 17, 1720).
6. Ibid., 545 (Nov. 3, 1750).
7. For a similar economy in Virginia's Shenandoah Valley, see Warren R. Hofstra, *The Planting of New Virginia: Settlement and Landscape in the Shenandoah Valley* (Baltimore: Johns Hopkins University Press, 2004), 197.
8. For a detailed explication of this process, see Susan Geib, " 'Changing Works': Agriculture and Society in Brookfield, Massachusetts, 1785–1820," Ph.D. diss., Boston University, 1981.
9. Hempstead, *Diary*, 96 (April 6, 18, 1720), 99 (Aug. 24, 1720), 101 (Oct. 10, 14, 1720), 102–3 (Dec. 5, 27, 1720).
10. Ibid., 96 (March 29, April 2, 5, 14, 1720), 97 (May 6, 7, 9, 10, June 2, 3, 1720), 98 (July 23, 1720), 99–100 (Aug. 17, 23, 27, 1720), 100 (Sept. 3, 7, 8, 1720), 103 (Dec. 6, 13, 1720).
11. Ibid., 542 (Aug. 23, 1750).
12. Ibid., 1 (Sept. 10, 1711), 2 (Oct. 10, 1711), 3 (Nov. 9, 1711), 15 (Oct. 9, 1712), 19 (Jan. 1, 1712/13), 34 (May 14, 1714).
13. Frances Manwaring Caulkins, *History of New London, Connecticut: from the first survey of the coast in 1612, to 1852* (New London, Conn.: The author, 1852), 337. Hempstead, *Diary*, 45 (May 11, 16, 1715), 73 (March 1, 1717/18), 109 (June 17, 1721), 86 (April 7, 9, 19, 1719), 86 (April 9, 1719), 125 (Nov. 6, 1722).
14. On the social relations of account books, see Daniel Vickers, "Errors Expected: The Culture of Credit in Rural New England, 1750–1800," *Economic History Review* 63, no. 4 (2010): 1032–57. For a similar web of obligations in nineteenth-century California, see R. Todd Welker, "Neighborhood Exchange and the Economic Culture of Rural California in the Late Nineteenth Century," *Agricultural History* 87, no. 3 (2013): 391–415.
15. For analysis of trust, see Niklas Luhmann, *Trust and Power*, ed. T. Burns and G. Poggi (Chichester: Wiley, 1979).

16. Craig Muldrew, *The Economy of Obligation: The Culture of Credit and Social Relations in Early Modern England* (New York: St. Martin's, 1998), 5.
17. Ibid., 6.
18. Richard L. Bushman, *From Puritan to Yankee: Character and the Social Order in Connecticut, 1690–1765* (Cambridge: Harvard University Press, 1967), 99–101.
19. Patricia M. Schaefer, *A Useful Friend: A Companion to the Joshua Hempstead Diary, 1711–1758* (New London, Conn.: New London County Historical Society, 2008), 10, 45.
20. For those who were honored with titles, see Hempstead *Diary*, 183 (May 25, 1727), 146 (Sept. 22, 1724). Hempstead's son Robert qualified to marry Mary the daughter of Benjamin Young, Esqr. of Southold, Long Island. Ibid., 157 (June 9, 1725).
21. Schaefer, *A Useful Friend*, 47–48, 68.
22. Hempstead, *Diary*, 36 (July 13–15, 20, 21, 1714).
23. Staughton George, Benjamin M. Nead, and Thomas McCamant, eds., *Charter to William Penn and Laws of the Province of Pennsylvania Passed between the Years 1682 and 1700* (Harrisburg, Pa.: Lane S. Hart, 1879), 280. In the early nineteenth century, state legislation exempted certain amounts of food and farm and household implements from auctions for the repayment of debt. The legislators wanted to protect basic family subsistence from the hurly-burly of the market, as if the two should be separated. Carolyn Merchant, *Ecological Revolutions: Nature, Gender, and Science in New England* (Chapel Hill: University of North Carolina Press, 1989), 178–79.
24. For a discussion of Chesapeake farm accounts, see Lorena S. Walsh, *Motives of Honor, Pleasure, and Profit: Plantation Management in the Colonial Chesapeake, 1607–1763* (Chapel Hill: University of North Carolina Press, 2010), 228–32.
25. On Fanning, Hempstead, *Diary*, 98 (July 22, 1720). The examples of probate items are from Hempstead's own 1759 inventory. CT State Library, State Archives, Record Group #004:095, Records of the New London Probate District, Probate Record Books, Will Book 1 Joshua Hempstead, 1759.
26. Harry J. Carman, ed., *American Husbandry* (1939; Port Washington, N.Y.: Kennikat, 1964), 162.
27. On stores in Ubanna, Virginia, Darrett B. and Anita H. Rutman, *A Place in Time: Middlesex County, Virginia, 1650–1750* (New York: Norton, 1984), 205–10, 226–31. Pennsylvania's export crop, wheat, did not serve this purpose as well. Tobacco receipts had value only so long as there was tobacco in the

warehouse; flour, which did not store well, had to be moved out quickly. Mary M. Schweitzer, *Custom and Contract: Household, Government, and the Economy in Colonial Pennsylvania* (New York: Columbia University Press, 1987), 122. Hempstead, *Diary*, 260 (Aug. 27, 1733), 286 (June 5, 1735), 315 (April 8, 1737).

28. Patricia Schaefer lists twelve shops in the index to *A Useful Friend*, 241, but five of these were blacksmith's shops, one was a joinery, one a barber shop, one a boatwright's shop, and one was in Hartford. Richard Shaw was probably one shopkeeper in Hempstead's orbit, though not named among the merchants in Caulkins, *History of New London*. Hempstead dealt goods with Shaw perhaps a dozen times over thirty years. Hempstead, *Diary*, 114 (Oct. 30, 1721), 157 (June 8, 1725), 158 (July 26, 1725), 542 (Aug. 24, 1750), 446 (Jan. 15, 1745/46), 465 (Jan. 12, 1746/47), 692 (Oct. 20, 1758). Hempstead had little to do with the New London Society for Trade and Commerce, which the Connecticut Assembly chartered in 1832 to open a direct trade with Great Britain. When the eighty merchants involved failed to raise the capital on their own, the Society issued bills of credit. The bills quickly lost their value, and to protect the innocent parties who fell victim, the Assembly agreed to redeem them with fifty thousand pounds' worth of Connecticut bills. Leslie V. Brock, *The Currency of the American Colonies, 1700–1764: A Study in Colonial Finance and Imperial Relations* (New York: Arno, 1975), 51–52. The collapse of the company and its depreciated bills did not affect Hempstead. He was not one of the "Society men," as he called them. He noted the meeting when the Society met to dissolve itself and attended the hearing of the Society's case before commissioners appointed to settle the company's affairs.

29. Patten went to the store forty-one times from July 1, 1773, through June 30, 1774. Matthew Patten, *The Diary of Matthew Patten of Bedford, N.H.: From Seventeen Hundred Fifty-Four to Seventeen Hundred Eighty-Eight* (Concord, N.H.: Rumford, 1903), 303–24.

30. On southern storekeeping, see Ann Smart Martin, *Buying into the World of Goods: Early Consumers in Backcountry Virginia* (Baltimore: Johns Hopkins University Press, 2008); Charles J. Farmer, *In the Absence of Towns: Settlement and Country Trade in Southside Virginia, 1730–1800* (Lanham, Md.: Rowman and Littlefield, 1993); Darrett B. and Anita Rutman, *A Place in Time: Middlesex, Virginia, 1650–1750* (New York: Norton, 1984), 205–11; Jacob Price, "Buchanan & Simpson, 1759–1763: A Different Kind of Glasgow Firm Trading to the Chesapeake," *William and Mary Quarterly*, 3rd ser. 40, no. 1 (1983): 3–41.

31. Winifred Barr Rothenberg, *From Market-Places to a Market Economy: The Transformation of Rural Massachusetts, 1750–1850* (Chicago: University of Chicago Press, 1992), 69–71. Rothenberg based her study on twenty-two pre-1765 farm account books. Judging from WorldCat and Baker Library (Harvard Business School) catalogues, New England general store accounts for this period came only from coastal areas. Not until the Revolution did general store accounts increase in frequency in inland towns. Southern planters, who were likewise nodes of economic activity, also kept accounts. Lorena Walsh worked with thirty-two of them for *Motives of Honor, Pleasure, and Profit*, 11–12.
32. Hempstead, *Diary*, 465 (Jan. 12, 1746/47), 234 (June 2, 1731). Jean B. Russo, "Self-Sufficiency and Local Exchange: Free Craftsmen in the Rural Chesapeake Economy," in *Colonial Chesapeake Society*, ed. Lois Green Carr, Philip D. Morgan, and Jean B. Russo (Chapel Hill: University of North Carolina Press, 1988), 400.
33. For the forms of social connection in seventeenth-century Maryland, see Lois Green Carr, Russell B. Menard, and Lorena S. Walsh, *Robert Cole's World: Agriculture and Society in Early Maryland* (Chapel Hill: University of North Carolina Press, 1991), 137–42, and Lorena S. Walsh, "Community Networks in the Early Chesapeake," in Carr, Morgan, and Russo, *Colonial Chesapeake Society*. For sources of pride, see T. H. Breen, *Tobacco Culture: The Mentality of the Great Tidewater Planters on the Eve of Revolution* (Princeton: Princeton University Press, 2001).
34. Hempstead, *Diary*, 95 (March 8, 1720).
35. Ibid., 140 (March 11, 1723/24), 190 (Dec. 1, 1727), 207 (March 19, 1729).
36. Ibid., 228 (Dec. 26, 1730).
37. Ibid., 226 (Oct. 26, 1730). For lesser sums, notes were used. Hempstead's notes in this decade ranged from £2 14s 7d to £24. For the legal distinctions between bonds, notes, and book debts, see Bruce H. Mann, *Republic of Debtors: Bankruptcy in the Age of American Independence* (Cambridge: Harvard University Press, 2002), 9–12.
38. Hempstead, *Diary*, 129 (March 27, 1723), 206 (March 5, 10, 1728/29). On November 26, 1730, as an example of mixing bonds and cash, Hempstead sold his land in Colchester to Stephen Gardner for £416 to be paid the next Christmas. Gardner paid £100 immediately and promised £100 in ten days secured by a bond. Presumably Hempstead's earlier £200 bond to Gardner was part of the payment. By December 26, 1730, the debt was paid in full. Ibid., 226–28 (Oct. 26, Nov. 26, Dec. 26, 1730).

39. Bettye Hobbs Pruitt, ed., *The Massachusetts Tax Valuation List of 1771* (Boston: G. K. Hall, 1978).
40. Ibid., 423–37.
41. On the 1771 tax valuation lists, fifty-four of seventy-two loan amounts in Springfield were rounded. Ibid., 422–36.
42. Ibid., 423–37 (emphasis added).
43. Deborah Rosen found that 16 percent of the mortgagees in the Crum Elbow District of Dutchess County, New York, were widows. Deborah A. Rosen, *Courts and Commerce: Gender, Law, and the Market Economy in Colonial New York* (Columbus: Ohio State University Press, 1997), 146.
44. In New York, larger loans, secured by mortgages, were predominantly granted by merchants to farmers. Rosen, *Courts and Commerce,* 44. Different forces were in play in the large towns. In Salem the median loan was five hundred pounds. Lending involved large-scale commercial ventures beyond the range of farmers and traders in most places.
45. Ibid.
46. The importance of character in merchant relations is discussed in Mann, *Republic of Debtors,* 7–8, and Sarah M. S. Pearsall, *Atlantic Families: Lives and Letters in the Later Eighteenth Century* (New York: Oxford University Press, 2008), 114–17, 141–42.
47. Bushman, *From Puritan to Yankee,* 297. Margaret Ellen Newell, *From Dependency to Independence: Economic Revolution in Colonial New England* (Ithaca, N.Y.: Cornell University Press, 1999).
48. Rosen, *Courts and Commerce,* 36, 43.
49. Ibid., 47–48. Mary Cooper, *The Diary of Mary Cooper: Life on a Long Island Farm, 1768–1773* (New York: Oyster Bay Historical Society, 1981), 18 (Aug. 23, 1769) (quotation), 30, 31, 33.

8. Crèvecoeur's Pennsylvania

1. Gay Wilson Allen and Roger Aselineau, *St. John de Crèvecoeur: The Life of an American Farmer* (New York: Viking, 1987), 7.
2. Biographical information can be found in Albert E. Stone's introduction to J. Hector St. John de Crèvecoeur, *Letters from an American Farmer and Sketches of Eighteenth-Century America,* ed. Albert E. Stone (New York: Penguin, 1986), 9–14, and in Allen and Aselineau, *Crèvecoeur.*
3. Allen and Aselineau, *Crèvecoeur,* 31.
4. Crèvecoeur, *Letters,* 67, 82–83.

5. Leo Marx, *The Machine in the Garden: Technology and the Pastoral Ideal in America* (New York: Oxford University Press, 1964), 109.
6. The unused essays have been published in their entirety in a critical edition: Dennis D. Moore, ed., *More Letters from the American Farmer: An Edition of the Essays in English Left Unpublished by Crèvecoeur* (Athens: University of Georgia Press, 1995). Moore tells the story of the discovery at pages xi–xii. Nineteen of the twenty-two essays were in Crèvecoeur's hand. Ibid., xix.
7. Ibid., 23–24.
8. Ibid., 24. Cf. another explicit comparison on page 115.
9. Ibid., 19, 22, 28, 66.
10. The total number of "negroes" would exceed the 421 specified in the tax list because women and children were not included, but the percentage of the population would still not exceed 3 percent, since the named household heads also had families. "Return of the Effective Supply Tax of Lancaster County for 1779," *Provincial Papers: Proprietary and State Tax Lists of the County of Lancaster for the Years 1771, 1772, 1773, 1777, and 1779*, ed. William Henry Egle (n.p.: William Stanley Ray, 1898), 491–684.
11. For a comparison with All Hallow's Parish, Maryland, see Mary M. Schweitzer, *Custom and Contract: Household, Government, and the Economy in Colonial Pennsylvania* (New York: Columbia University Press, 1987), 46.
12. Paul G. E. Clemens and Lucy Simler, "Rural Labor and the Farm Household in Chester County, Pennsylvania, 1750–1820," in *Work and Labor in Early America*, ed. Stephen Innes (Chapel Hill: University of North Carolina Press, 1988), 106–43. Lucy Simler, "Tenancy in Colonial Pennsylvania: The Case of Chester County," *William and Mary Quarterly*, 3rd ser. 43, no. 4 (1986): 542–69. Clemens and Simler, "Rural Labor," 116–17.
13. Egle, *Provincial Papers*, 491–684.
14. For pictures of extant Pennsylvania houses, see http://en.wikipedia.org/wiki/List_of_the_oldest_buildings_in_Pennsylvania. Accessed 1/26/2013. For a description of top-of-the-line Pennsylvania farmers, see the analysis of Caleb and George Brinton of Chester County in Clemens and Simler, "Rural Labor," 127–40.
15. Simler, "Tenancy in Colonial Pennsylvania," 551, 557. Robert Swierenga, "Quantitative Methods in Rural Landholding," *Journal of Interdisciplinary History* 13, no. 4 (1983): 787–808.
16. James T. Lemon, *The Best Poor Man's Country: A Geographical Study of Early Southeastern Pennsylvania* (Baltimore: Johns Hopkins University Press, 1972), 181. For an analysis of wheat culture in the Shenandoah Valley, see

Warren R. Hofstra, *The Planting of New Virginia: Settlement and Landscape in the Shenandoah Valley* (Baltimore: Johns Hopkins University Press, 2004), 274–311.

17. B. H. Slicher van Bath, *The Agrarian History of Western Europe A.D. 500–1850*, trans. Olive Ordish (London: E. Arnold, 1963), 195–206. Joan Thirsk, ed., *The Agrarian History of England and Wales*, vol. 4, *1500–1640* (London: Cambridge University Press, 1967), 575–77. On rising prices for grain, see Paul G. E. Clemens, *The Atlantic Economy and Colonial Maryland's Eastern Shore: From Tobacco to Grain* (Ithaca, N.Y.: Cornell University Press, 1980), 179–83.
18. Brooke Hunter, "Rage for Grain: Flour Milling in the Mid-Atlantic, 1750–1815," Ph.D. diss., University of Delaware, 2002, 26–27, 61. B. H. Slicher van Bath, "Eighteenth Century Agriculture on the Continent of Europe: Evolution or Revolution?" *Agricultural History* 43 (1969): 174–75.
19. Hunter, "Rage for Grain," 27–28, 62, 67. Brooke Hunter, "Wheat, War, and the American Economy in an Era of Revolutions," *William and Mary Quarterly*, 3rd ser. 62, no. 3 (2005): 508–9. On the increase of hay and meat production after 1750 as Philadelphia grew, see Schweitzer, *Custom and Contract*, 67–70.
20. Alice Hanson Jones, *Wealth of a Nation to Be: The American Colonies on the Eve of the Revolution* (New York: Columbia University Press, 1980), 96, cf. 98.
21. Hunter, "Rage for Grain," 42.
22. *Pennsylvania Gazette*, July 28, 1737, Aug. 4, 1737, April 3, 1761. Clemens and Simler, "Rural Labor," 123. Lemon, *Best Poor Man's Country*, 275 n. 164.
23. Moore, *More Letters*, 59–60. Lemon, *Best Poor Man's Country*, 165. Crèvecoeur, *Letters*, 95.
24. Bettye Hobbs Pruitt, ed., *Massachusetts Tax Valuation List of 1771* (Boston: G. K. Hall, 1978). Lemon, *Best Poor Man's Country*, 164, 270 n. 4. Pruitt, *Massachusetts Tax Valuation List*, 194–201. Egle, *Provincial Papers*, passim.
25. On the availability of wagons during wartime, see Stephenson Whitcomb Fletcher, *Pennsylvania Agriculture and Country Life, 1640–1840* (Harrisburg: Pennsylvania Historical and Museum Commission, 1950), 89.
26. Moore, *More Letters*, 59–60.
27. Lemon, *Best Poor Man's Country*, 165.
28. "Sketches, 1791"; and Board of the Philadelphia & Lancaster Turnpike, "To the Senate and House of Representatives of the State of Pennsylvania," Feb. 1, 1803, ms., Lancaster Historical Society, Lancaster, Penn.

29. Jerome Wood, *Conestoga Crossroads: Lancaster, Pennsylvania, 1730–1790* (Harrisburg: Pennsylvania Historical and Museum Commission, 1979), 6–11.
30. Wood, *Conestoga Crossroads,* 12.
31. Pruitt, *Massachusetts Tax Valuation List,* 422–36. The median tillage of property holders as a whole in Springfield was eleven acres. For Hartford, see James P. Walsh, *Connecticut Industry and the Revolution* (Hartford: American Revolution Bicentennial Commission of Connecticut, 1978), 34–35.
32. His imaginary immigrant Andrew sought land "as a shelter against old age, that whenever this period should come, his son, to whom he would give his land, would then maintain him, and thus live altogether." Moore, *More Letters,* 98.
33. Crèvecoeur, *Letters,* 92. Moore, *More Letters,* 94.
34. Moore, *More Letters,* 27, 29. Crèvecoeur, *Letters,* 83.
35. Better-off farmers would require costly slaves. To clear land, Crèvecoeur assumed a farmer would need a "Team a Negro" costing "[300 or 400] pounds." Moore, *More Letters,* 28–29.
36. Ibid., 27–28.
37. Ibid., 34, 38.
38. Ibid., 22, 39–41, 44–46.
39. Ibid., 40, 48.
40. Crèvecoeur, *Letters,* 82–83.
41. "Returns and Assessments," 243–48.
42. Ibid.
43. There were also patches of poverty in the county, places where townships or whole neighborhoods fell below the norm. The median tax assessment in Cocolico township was ten shillings, sixpence; in Elizabeth it was six shillings, and in Millerstown everyone was taxed four shillings or less. Ibid., 15–17, 113–14, 243–48.
44. Ibid., 55–58.
45. Crèvecoeur, *Letters,* 72, 76, 79.
46. John R. Dunbar, introduction to John R. Dunbar, ed., *The Paxton Papers* (The Hague: Martinus Nijhoff, 1957), 23; *A Serious Address to Such of the Inhabitants of Pennsylvania,* ibid., 94.
47. [Benjamin Franklin], *A Narrative of the Late Massacres, in Lancaster County, of a Number of Indians* (Philadelphia, 1764), ibid., 57–61; *A Serious Address,* 95. Letter of Edward Shippen to his son, Jan. 5, 1764, in Dunbar, *Paxton Papers,* 32. *An Historical Account* (Philadelphia: Anthony Armbruster, n.d.), ibid., 127–28.

48. [Franklin], *Narrative,* 60.
49. "Paxtons" was one of many terms employed at the time to refer to the frontier protesters. Sometimes it was Paxton Men, Men of Paxton, Paxton Boys, Paxton Volunteers, or Paxton Dogs. Dunbar, *Paxton Papers,* 155, 176, 177, 185.
50. In [Franklin], *A Narrative,* 61–62.
51. *A Declaration and Remonstrance of the distressed and bleeding Frontier Inhabitants* (Philadelphia, 1764), in Dunbar, *Paxton Papers,* 107–8; cf. "The Apology of the Paxton Volunteers addressed to the candid & impartial World," ibid., 190–201; [Franklin], *Narrative,* 63; *An Historical Account,* 129.
52. "Apology of the Paxton Volunteers," 185. *The Conduct of The Paxton-Men, Impartially represented* (Philadelphia: A. Steuart, 1764), in Dunbar, *Paxton Papers,* 270.
53. [Franklin], *Narrative,* 63. Crèvecoeur, *Letters,* 213.
54. *Conduct of The Paxton-Men,* 95; cf. Dunbar, Introduction, 295.
55. [Franklin], *Narrative,* 71.
56. "Apology of the Paxton Volunteers," 186. Dunbar, Introduction, 43. *An Historical Account,* 129.
57. *Declaration and Remonstrance,* 103, 108; cf. *Conduct of The Paxton-Men,* 293.
58. *Declaration and Remonstrance,* 104. John Elder to Richard Peters, Nov. 1755, *Pennsylvania Colonial Records,* 6: 704–5; Dunbar, Introduction, 10–11, 13.
59. Dunbar, Introduction, 17. Another burst of violence occurred in March 1765, when a band of Cumberland County residents known as the Black Boys intercepted a wagon train of goods intended for the Indian trade. Kevin Kenny, *Peaceable Kingdom Lost: The Paxton Boys and the Destruction of William Penn's Holy Experiment* (New York: Oxford University Press, 2009), 205–9.
60. "Apology of the Paxton Volunteers," 187–92. *Conduct of The Paxton-Men,* 274.
61. The Continental Congress settled the jurisdictional dispute in Pennsylvania's favor in 1782, but claimants with land titles from the two states battled on for decades.
62. Kevin Kenny tells the fascinating story of Lazarus Stewart in *Peaceable Kingdom,* 218–30. Quotations at 218, 222, 226, 227.
63. Paul B. Moyer, "'A Dangerous Combination of Villains': Pennsylvania's Wild Yankees and the Social Context of Agrarian Resistance in Early America," *Pennsylvania History* 73, no. 1 (2006): 40. Secure title to land was the aim of squatters all along the frontier. David L. Preston, "Squatters,

Indians, Proprietary Government, and Land in the Susquehanna Valley," in *Friends and Enemies in Penn's Woods: Indians, Colonists, and the Racial Construction of Pennsylvania,* ed. William A. Pencak and Daniel K. Richter (University Park: Pennsylvania State University Press, 2004), 197.

64. "Apology of the Paxton Volunteers," 204.
65. Moore, *More Letters,* 168–69, 172, 179–80.
66. Ibid., 183–84.
67. Ibid., 184–85.
68. Ibid., 186, 194, 198.
69. Ibid., 202–3.
70. Ibid., 203.

9. Revolution

1. J. Hector St. John de Crèvecoeur, *Letters from an American Farmer* (New York: Penguin, 1981), 203–4.
2. *Boston* (Massachusetts) *Evening Post,* April 28, 1766.
3. Smaller market towns such as Fredrick Town and Elk-Ridge, Maryland, were also involved. In September 1765, the inhabitants "diverted themselves with Carting, Whipping, Hanging, and Burning the Effigies of a Distributor of Stamps." *Maryland Gazette* (Annapolis), Sept. 5, 1765.
4. Pauline Maier, *From Resistance to Revolution: Colonial Radicals and the Development of American Opposition to Britain, 1765–1776* (New York: Knopf, 1972), 310–11.
5. John B. Frantz and William Pencak, "Introduction: Pennsylvania and Its Three Revolutions," in *Beyond Philadelphia: The American Revolution in the Pennsylvania Hinterland,* ed. John B. Frantz and William Pencak (University Park: Pennsylvania State University Press, 1998), xvi–xvii.
6. The whole story is told in Oscar Zeichner, *Connecticut's Years of Controversy, 1750–1776* (Chapel Hill: University of North Carolina Press, 1949). See also Richard L. Bushman, *From Puritan to Yankee: Character and the Social Order in Connecticut, 1690–1765* (Cambridge: Harvard University Press, 1967), 235–65, 284–85, and *Connecticut Gazette* (Hartford), Sept. 27, 1765, and *Boston* (Massachusetts) *Gazette,* Sept. 30, 1765.
7. Sung Bok Kim, *Landlord and Tenant in Colonial New York: Manorial Society, 1664–1775* (Chapel Hill: University of North Carolina Press, 1978), chapter 8 and 387–89. Edward Countryman, *A People in Revolution: The American Revolution and Political Society in New York, 1760–1790* (Baltimore: Johns Hopkins University Press, 1981), 46.

8. Robert J. Taylor, *Western Massachusetts in the Revolution* (1954; New York: Kraus Reprint, 1967), 55.
9. The editors of the Papers of John Adams could not substantiate that figure in town records. John Adams autobiography, part 1, "John Adams," through 1776, sheet 9 of 53 [electronic edition], *Adams Family Papers: An Electronic Archive,* Massachusetts Historical Society, 3, http://www.masshist.org/digitaladams/. Even if Adams's memory was accurate, the remaining two hundred towns in Massachusetts said nothing.
10. Normal turnover would account for six to ten changes in representation. Richard D. Brown, *Revolutionary Politics in Massachusetts: The Boston Committee of Correspondence and the Towns, 1772–1774* (Cambridge: Harvard University Press, 1970), 26–27. Although near Philadelphia, Chester County, Pennsylvania, with its heavy Quaker population, did nothing by way of protests until 1773, when eight thousand inhabitants forcibly prevented the landing of the *Polly* with a cargo of tea. Rosemary Warden, "Chester County," in Frantz and Pencak, *Beyond Philadelphia,* 5.
11. Leedstown Resolves available online at http://www.ragerlaw.com/leedstownresolutionspage.htm, accessed Nov. 5, 2013.
12. Edmund S. Morgan and Helen M. Morgan, *The Stamp Act Crisis: Prologue to Revolution,* rev. ed. (New York: Collier, 1963), 121–32 (quotation, 125). Marc Egnal, *Mighty Empire: The Origins of the American Revolution* (Ithaca, N.Y.: Cornell University Press, 1988), 218.
13. Paul E. Doutrich, "York County," in Frantz and Pencak, *Beyond Philadelphia,* 90–91.
14. Edmund S. Morgan, ed., *Prologue to Revolution: Sources and Documents on the Stamp Act Crisis, 1761–1766* (1959; New York: Norton, 1973), 36.
15. Morgan and Morgan, *Stamp Act Crisis,* 96–97.
16. Paul S. Boyer, "Borrowed Rhetoric: The Massachusetts Excise Controversy of 1754," *William and Mary Quarterly,* 3rd ser. 21, no. 3 (1964): 332.
17. Robert A. Becker, *Revolution, Reform, and the Politics of American Taxation, 1763–1783* (Baton Rouge: Louisiana State University Press, 1980), 59–61. Farmers spoke up when property taxes were in question. In the Stamp Act and the Townshend Duties controversy, rural interests were so slightly affected that the farm population scarcely stirred.
18. Peter Force, ed., *American Archives,* 4th ser., vols. 1–6 (Washington, D.C., 1833–46), 1: 235. *Gentlemen, By the last advice from London* (May 12, 1774).
19. John B. Linn and Wm. H. Egle, eds., *Pennsylvania Archives,* 2nd ser., vol. 13 (Harrisburg, Pa.: Clarence M. Busch, 1896), 271, 272, 273, 275, 277.

20. Frantz and Pencak, "Introduction," xx.
21. Warden, "Chester County," 5. Doutrich, "York County," 90–91. Francis S. Fox, *Sweet Land of Liberty: The Ordeal of the American Revolution in Northampton County, Pennsylvania* (University Park: Pennsylvania State University Press, 2000), 12. Charles Henry Lincoln, *The Revolutionary Movement in Pennsylvania, 1760–1776* (Philadelphia: University of Pennsylvania Press, 1901), 170. Merrill Jensen, *The Founding of a Nation: A History of the American Revolution, 1763–1776* (New York: Oxford University Press, 1968), 476.
22. *Virginia Gazette* (Williamsburg) (Purdie and Dixon), June 30, 1774. "Thomas Jefferson: Autobiography, 6 Jan.–29 July 1821, 6 January 1821," Founders Online, National Archives (http://founders.archives.gov/documents/Jefferson/98-01-02-1756, ver. 2016-03-28), accessed April 12, 2016.
23. Force, *American Archives,* 4th ser., 1: 307. Taylor, *Western Massachusetts,* 58, 62 (quotation), 63 (quotation), 75, 76. For the reaction to the Boston Port Bill in New England, see T. H. Breen, *American Insurgents, American Patriots: The Revolution of the People* (New York: Hill and Wang, 2010), 65–98. For a county that held back in 1774 and 1775, see Joseph S. Tiedemann, "Communities in the Midst of the American Revolution: Queens County, New York, 1774–1775," *Journal of Social History* 18, no. 1 (1984): 57–78. For a list of the localities which formulated resolves in 1774, see Jerrilyn Greene Marston, *King and Congress: The Transfer of Political Legitimacy, 1774–1776* (Princeton: Princeton University Press, 1987), 313–16.
24. Force, *American Archives,* 4th ser., 1: 434. Daniel Rupp, *History of the County of Lancaster to which is Prefixed a Brief Sketch of the Early History of Pennsylvania* (Lancaster, Pa.: Gilbert Hills, 1844), 377–78.
25. *Pennsylvania Archives,* 2nd ser., 13: 271.
26. Ibid., 13: 271–73, 275. Karen Guenther, "Berks County," in Frantz and Pencak, *Beyond Philadelphia,* 72.
27. *Pennsylvania Archives,* 2nd ser., 13: 272–73. Force, *American Archives,* 4th ser., 1: 331, 366, 369. *Virginia Gazette* (Purdie and Dixon), June 30, 1774.
28. Jack P. Greene, ed., *The Diary of Colonel Landon Carter of Sabine Hall, 1752–1778,* 2 vols. (Richmond: Virginia Historical Society, 1987), 817–18.
29. Force, *American Archives,* 4th ser., 1: 333. *Virginia Gazette* (Purdie and Dixon), May 26, 1774.
30. Force, *American Archives,* 4th ser., 1: 335–36.
31. For an elaboration of this argument, see Richard L. Bushman, *King and People in Provincial Massachusetts* (Chapel Hill: University of North Carolina Press, 1985).

32. Force, *American Archives,* 4th ser., 1: 434. *Virginia Gazette* (Purdie and Dixon), June 30, 1774, p. 2.
33. *Pennsylvania Archives,* 2nd ser., 13: 271–72.
34. Richard C. Knopf, ed., *Anthony Wayne: A Name in Arms* (Pittsburgh: University of Pittsburgh Press, 1960).
35. *Pennsylvania Archives,* 2nd ser., 14: 138–40, 13: 274, 258, 262, 267–68 (quotation).
36. Another example is James Smith of York County, an attorney and iron furnace operator, who took the lead in registering protests against Parliament. Doutrich, "York County," 90–91. The Cumberland committee consisted of attorneys, a university graduate, and an incumbent justice of the peace. Robert G. Crist, "Cumberland County," in Frantz and Pencak, *Beyond Philadelphia,* 119.
37. *Pennsylvania Archives,* 2nd ser., 14: 487–88. For this same transition in Maryland, see Jean B. Lee, "Lessons in Humility: The Revolutionary Transformation of the Governing Elite of Charles County, Maryland," in *The Transforming Hand of Revolution: Reconsidering the American Revolution as a Social Movement,* ed. Ronald Hoffman and Peter J. Albert (Charlottesville: University Press of Virginia, 1995), 99–102.
38. *Pennsylvania Archives,* 2nd ser., 13: 279. Force, *American Archives,* 4th ser., 1: 427.
39. The course of events can be followed in Lincoln, *Revolutionary Movement,* 17 ff., and in Merrill Jensen, *The Founding of a Nation,* 464–81.
40. *Pennsylvania Archives,* 2nd ser., 14: 67, 132–35, 244, 322, 493, 545, 563, 605.
41. Ibid., 2nd ser., 14: 605. "Declaration and Resolves of the First Continental Congress," in *Sources and Documents Illustrating the American Revolution, 1764–1788,* ed. Samuel Eliot Morison, 2nd ed. (New York: Oxford University Press, 1929), 124.
42. *Pennsylvania Archives,* 2nd ser., 14: 138–39, 322–23.
43. Ibid., 2nd ser., 14: 134.
44. Ibid., 2nd ser., 14: 135, 170, 244, 323, 606–7; 140, 141, 245–48.
45. Doutrich, "York County," 92, 93. Crist, "Cumberland County," 123.
46. "Congress recommends the formation of State Governments," in Morison, *Sources and Documents,* 148.
47. *Pennsylvania Archives,* 2nd ser., 14: 326. York County acknowledged that a legislative body dependent on the king was now "totally extinct," but nevertheless, for the time being "the Executive powers of Government ought to proceed in the usual channel . . . until a Government formed on the authority of the people only, takes place." Ibid., 2nd ser., 14: 560.
48. Doutrich, "York County," 95.

10. Family Mobility

1. Douglas Lamar Jones, "The Strolling Poor: Transiency in Eighteenth-Century Massachusetts," *Journal of Social History* 8, no. 3 (1975): 30. Michael Lee Nichols, "Origins of the Virginia Southside, 1703–1753: A Social and Economic Study," Ph.D. diss., College of William and Mary, 1972, 112–15. In Saint John Berkeley parish in South Carolina, 40 percent of slaveholders disappeared between 1762 and 1772. Philip D. Morgan, *Slave Counterpoint: Black Culture in the Eighteenth-Century Chesapeake and Lowcountry* (Chapel Hill: University of North Carolina Press, 1998), 520.
2. The interest in the Lincolns was great enough to justify the publication of two elaborate genealogies within twenty years of each other: J. Henry Lea and J. R. Hutchison, *The Ancestry of Abraham Lincoln* (Boston: Houghton Mifflin, 1909); and Waldo Lincoln, *History of the Lincoln Family: An Account of the Descendants of Samuel Lincoln of Hingham Massachusetts, 1637–1920* (Worcester, Mass.: Commonwealth, 1923). In addition, Marion Dexter Learned, professor of Germanic languages and literature at the University of Pennsylvania, published *Abraham Lincoln: An American Migration* to test the hopeful claim that the Lincolns were actually of German origin. In 1924 Ida Tarbell, the noted Progressive journalist, offered a colorful summary of the genealogical knowledge, *In the Footsteps of the Lincolns* (New York: Harper and Brothers, 1924). See also William E. Barton, *The Lineage of Lincoln* (Indianapolis: Bobbs-Merrill, 1929); and Louis A. Warren, *Lincoln's Parentage and Childhood* (New York: Century, 1926).
3. Lincoln, *History of the Lincoln Family*, 1–7.
4. Ibid., 23, 84, 86, 121, 127, 137, 152, 158.
5. Ibid., 43–53 (Mordecai), 53–57 (Abraham).
6. Ibid., 16, 17, 61–62.
7. Charles S. Boyer, *Early Forges and Furnaces in New Jersey* (Philadelphia: University of Pennsylvania Press, 1931), 212–16; Arthur C. Bining, *Pennsylvania Iron Manufactures in the Eighteenth Century* (1938; New York: Kelley, 1970). For a bibliography of the industry, see Lester J. Cappon et al., eds., *Atlas of Early American History: The Revolutionary Era, 1760–90* (Princeton: Princeton University Press, 1976), 105–6. Lincoln, *History of the Lincoln Family*, 45.
8. "Cranbury Brook," Wikipedia, https://en.wikipedia.org/wiki/Cranbury_Brook, accessed Dec. 20, 2013. Tarbell, *Footsteps of the Lincolns*, 32–34. Lea and Hutchison, *Ancestry of Abraham Lincoln*, 69. Lincoln, *History of the*

Lincoln Family, 46, 53–54, 57, 93. Tarbell, *Footsteps of the Lincolns,* 35–36.

9. Lincoln, *History of the Lincoln Family,* 50–53, 58–59, 92, 103, 109, 110–18.
10. Ibid., 54, 112–17.
11. Ibid., 100.
12. John W. Wayland, *The Lincolns in Virginia* (Staunton, Va.: McLure Printing Co. for the author, 1946), 43–44, 52, 65, 72, 103. Robert D. Mitchell, *Commercialism and Frontier: Perspectives on the Early Shenandoah Valley* (Charlottesville: University of Virginia Press, 1977), 77. Lincoln, *History of the Lincoln Family,* 93–96, 208.
13. Mitchell, *Commercialism and Frontier,* 86. Lincoln, *History of the Lincoln Family,* 96–97. Wayland, *Lincolns in Virginia,* 37–39.
14. Lincoln, *History of the Lincoln Family,* 89–90, 93, 97, 107, 193, 205, 208–9. Wayland, *Lincolns in Virginia,* 9, 68, 76–78, 84–85, 88–90, 107, 118–48.
15. Wayland, *Lincolns in Virginia,* 48–49. Lincoln, *History of the Lincoln Family,* 193–202.
16. Lincoln, *History of the Lincoln Family,* 193, 197–98.
17. Josiah did a little better in Indiana, where he moved sometime before 1815 and where he acquired 160 acres. He and his wife signed legal papers with marks rather than their signatures. Josiah's personal estate when he died was valued at $66.50. The estate inventory listed as the livestock one filly, one sheep, one cow. Ibid., 330–31.
18. Ibid., 328–29, 330–31, 335–38.
19. Ibid., 328–31, 337–38, 342, 469.
20. William Henry Herndon, *Herndon's Life of Lincoln: The History and Personal Recollections of Abraham Lincoln Originally Written by William H. Herndon and Jesse W. Weik* (1889; Cleveland: World, 1942, 1. Howells quoted in David Herbert Donald, *Lincoln* (New York: Simon and Schuster, 1995), 20.
21. Herndon, *Herndon's Life of Lincoln,* 2–3.
22. Ibid., 3.

11. Founding Farmers

1. The land was patented in 1735; Peter began building his house at Shadwell in 1737. Dumas Malone, *Jefferson and His Time,* vol. 1, *Jefferson the Virginian* (Boston: Little, Brown, 1948), 436.
2. For Jefferson's sketchy knowledge of his ancestry, see "Thomas Jefferson: Autobiography, 6 Jan.–29 July 1821, 6 January 1821," Founders Online, National Archives (http://founders.archives.gov/documents/

Jefferson/98-01-02-1756, ver. 2016-03-28), accessed April 12, 2016. Malone, *Jefferson the Virginian*, 6–7, 426.

3. Richard L. Morton, *Colonial Virginia*, vol. 1, *The Tidewater Period, 1607–1710* (Chapel Hill: University of North Carolina Press, 1960), 362, 539. Philip Alexander Bruce, *Economic History of Virginia in the Seventeenth Century* (1895; New York: Peter Smith, 1935), 526.
4. Malone, *Jefferson and His Time*, 1: 8–10.
5. Ibid., 10–11.
6. Bruce, *Economic History*, 527. Morton, *Colonial Virginia*, 1: 62–68.
7. Quotations from Morton, *Colonial Virginia*, 1: 421, 539–40.
8. Richard L. Morton, *Colonial Virginia*, vol. 2, *Westward Expansion and Prelude to Revolution, 1710–1763* (Chapel Hill: University of North Carolina Press, 1960), 477–81. John Hammond Moore, *Albemarle: Jefferson's County, 1727–1976* (Charlottesville: University Press of Virginia, 1976), 19, citing Edward Ayres, "Albemarle County, Virginia, 1744–1770: An Economic, Political, and Social Analysis," M.A. thesis, University of Virginia, 1968.
9. Malone, *Jefferson and His Time*, 1: 17–18, 436.
10. "Journals of the Council of Virginia in Executive Sessions, 1737–1763 (Continued)," *Virginia Magazine of History and Biography* 15, no. 2 (1907): 120–21, http://www.jstor.org/stable/4242865, accessed Jan. 28, 2013.
11. Harry J. Carman, ed., *American Husbandry* (1939; Port Washington, N.Y.: Kennikat, 1964), 169–70.
12. Bruce, *Economic History*, 1: 528–30.
13. Barbara McEwan, *Thomas Jefferson: Farmer* (Jefferson, N.C.: McFarland, 1991), 1–2.
14. Susan Kern, *The Jeffersons at Shadwell* (New Haven: Yale University Press, 2010), 261. Malone, *Jefferson and His Time*, 1: 3, 27, 31–33.
15. Jefferson kept track of the years when his Monticello well failed. Edwin Morris Betts, ed., *Thomas Jefferson's Garden Book, 1766–1824* (Philadelphia: American Philosophical Society, 1944), 629.
16. Alan Fusonie and Donna Jean Fusonie, *George Washington: Pioneer Farmer* (Mount Vernon, Va.: Mount Vernon Ladies Association, 1998), 10.
17. By the time he hired Edmund Bacon as his overseer in 1806, Jefferson was more conscientious about instructions. Hamilton W. Pierson, *Jefferson at Monticello: The Private Life of Thomas Jefferson, from Entirely New Sources* (New York: Scribner, 1862). The interest may not have lasted long. Madison Hemings said years later that in his retirement years Jefferson had "but little taste or care for agricultural pursuits." Quoted in Lucia Stanton, *"Those Who*

Labor for My Happiness": Slavery at Thomas Jefferson's Monticello (Charlottesville: University of Virginia Press, 2012), 94.

18. "The Memoirs of Madison Hemings," in Annette Gordon-Reed, *Thomas Jefferson and Sally Hemings* (Charlottesville: University Press of Virginia, 1997), 247. "From Thomas Jefferson to Thomas Mann Randolph, Jr., 11 July 1790," Founders Online, National Archives (http://founders.archives.gov/documents/Jefferson/01-17-02-0013, ver. 2013-12-27) [original source: *The Papers of Thomas Jefferson*, vol. 17, *6 July–3 November 1790*, ed. Julian P. Boyd (Princeton: Princeton University Press, 1965), 26]. McEwan, *Thomas Jefferson*, 198 n. 15.
19. For a facsimile of Jefferson's farm book, see Edwin Morris Betts, ed., *Thomas Jefferson's Farm Book* ([Princeton]: Princeton University Press, 1953), 1–178. An accessible transcription is in Robert C. Baron, ed., *The Garden and Farm Books of Thomas Jefferson* (Golden, Colo.: Fulcrum, 1987), 219–485, the version cited hereafter. The diaries are on pages 275–83, 292–94. An online version, based on the Baron transcription and sponsored by the Massachusetts Historical Society, is available at https://www.masshist.org/thomasjeffersonpapers/doc?id=farm_1&.
20. Douglas Southall Freeman, *George Washington: A Biography*, 6 vols. (New York: Scribner, 1948–57), 1: 15–23.
21. Ibid., 1: 29–35.
22. Ibid., 1: 29–47, 58, 73–74. On the Fairfax claim, see Morton, *Colonial Virginia*, 2: 545–48.
23. Freeman, *George Washington*, 1: 72–78.
24. Robert F. Dalzell, Jr., and Lee Baldwin Dalzell, *George Washington's Mount Vernon: At Home in Revolutionary America* (New York: Oxford University Press, 1998), 43–49. Fusonie and Fusonie, *George Washington*, 6–9. Diary entry: 21 May 1760, Founders Online, National Archives (http://founders.archives.gov/documents/Washington/01-01-02-0005-0005-0021, ver. 2014-02-12) [original source: *The Diaries of George Washington, 11 March 1748–13 November 1765*, ed. Donald Jackson (Charlottesville: University Press of Virginia, 1976), 1: 281–82]. Freeman, *George Washington*, 5: 53–54.
25. "From George Washington to William Pearce, 18 December 1793," Founders Online, National Archives (http://founders.archives.gov/documents/Washington/05-14-02-0356-0001, ver. 2014-02-12) [original source: *The Papers of George Washington*, Presidential Series, *1 September–31 December 1793*, ed. David R. Hoth (Charlottesville: University of Virginia Press, 2008), 14: 558–64].

26. Diary entry: 1 May 1760, Founders Online, National Archives (http://founders.archives.gov/documents/Washington/01-01-02-0005-0005-0001, ver. 2014-02-12) [original source: *Diaries of George Washington*, 1: 275].
27. Diary entry: July 8, 1785, Founders Online, National Archives (http://founders.archives.gov/documents/Washington/01-04-02-0002-0007, ver. 2014-02-12) [original source: *The Diaries of George Washington, 1 September 1784–30 June 1786*, ed. Donald Jackson and Dorothy Twohig (Charlottesville: University Press of Virginia, 1978), 4: 161–63].
28. Diary entry: 24 March 1760, Founders Online, National Archives (http://founders.archives.gov/documents/Washington/01-01-02-0005-0003-0024, ver. 2014-02-12) [original source: *Diaries of George Washington*, 1: 256].
29. "From George Washington to Anthony Whitting, 14 November 1792," Founders Online, National Archives (http://founders.archives.gov/documents/Washington/05-11-02-0217, ver. 2014-02-12) [original source: *Papers of George Washington*, 11: 388–89].
30. Diary entry: 12–13 April 1760, Founders Online, National Archives (http://founders.archives.gov/documents/Washington/01-01-02-0005-0004-0012, ver. 2014-02-12) [original source: *Diaries of George Washington*, 1: 266]. The association of practical farming and pragmatic thought is explored in Paul B. Thompson and Thomas C. Hilde, eds., *The Agrarian Roots of Pragmatism* (Nashville: Vanderbilt University Press, 2000).
31. "From George Washington to Anthony Whitting, 11 November 1792," Founders Online, National Archives (http://founders.archives.gov/documents/Washington/05-11-02-0206, ver. 2014-02-12) [original source: *Papers of George Washington*, 11: 370–76].
32. "George Washington to Anthony Whitting, 11 November 1792," Founders Online, National Archives (http://founders.archives.gov/documents/Washington/05-11-02-0206, ver. 2014-02-12) [original source: *Papers of George Washington*, 11: 370–76].
33. "George Washington to Arthur Young, 6 August 1786," Founders Online, National Archives (http://founders.archives.gov/documents/Washington/04-04-02-0185, ver. 2013-12-27) [original source: *Papers of George Washington*, Confederation Series, *2 April 1786–31 January 1787*, ed. W. W. Abbot (Charlottesville: University Press of Virginia, 1995), 4: 196–200].
34. See diary entry for April 21, 1786, "April 1786," Founders Online, National Archives (http://founders.archives.gov/documents/Washington/01-04-02-0003-0004, ver. 2013-12-27) [original source: *Diaries of George Washington*, 4: 315]. The correspondence with Young began after

Washington had asked George Fairfax to locate an English farmer who might take over the management of Washington's properties and introduce more enlightened English methods. Fairfax recommended a farmer named James Bloxham, whom Washington hired, though neither found the arrangement entirely satisfactory. Bloxham thought Washington's slaves "disagreeable." Wilbur Cortez Abbott, "James Bloxham, Farmer," Massachusetts Historical Society, *Proceedings*, 59: 177–203.

35. "To George Washington from Arthur Young, 17 January 1793," Founders Online, National Archives (http://founders.archives.gov/documents/Washington/05-12-02-0008, ver. 2013-12-27) [original source: *The Papers of George Washington*, Presidential Series, *16 January 1793–31 May 1793*, ed. Christine Sternberg Patrick and John C. Pinheiro (Charlottesville: University of Virginia Press, 2005), 12: 18–26, n. 10. *American Husbandry*, lv–lix. Young gave up on his American plans in 1793 after war broke out with France. "To George Washington from Arthur Young, 17 January 1793," Founders Online, National Archives (http://founders.archives.gov/documents/Washington/05-12-02-0008, ver. 2013-12-27) [original source: *Papers of George Washington*, 12: 18–26].
36. "To George Washington from Thomas Jefferson, 28 June 1793," Founders Online, National Archives (http://founders.archives.gov/documents/Washington/05-13-02-0109, ver. 2013-12-27) [original source: *The Papers of George Washington*, Presidential Series, *1 June–31 August 1793*, ed. Christine Sternberg Patrick (Charlottesville: University of Virginia Press, 2007), 13: 152–54].
37. "To George Washington from Arthur Young, 17 January 1793," Founders Online, National Archives (http://founders.archives.gov/documents/Washington/05-12-02-0008, ver. 2013-12-27) [original source: *Papers of George Washington*, 12: 18–26].
38. For a similar perspective, see Lorena S. Walsh, *Motives of Honor, Pleasure, and Profit: Plantation Management in the Colonial Chesapeake, 1607–1763* (Chapel Hill: University of North Carolina Press, 2010), 12–14.
39. "To George Washington from Arthur Young, 17 January 1793," Founders Online, National Archives (http://founders.archives.gov/documents/Washington/05-12-02-0008, ver. 2013-12-27) [original source: *Papers of George Washington*, 12: 18–26].
40. Jefferson was realistic in part of his report, admitting that "the husbandry is in general very slovenly. under such as it is. the lands of the first quality will produce 30 bushels of wheat to the acre when fresh, and being tended

alternately in wheat & Indian corn (the latter of which is a great exhauster) without ever being rested or manured they fall at length down to 8. or 10. bushels the acre. the soil of midling quality will yield 12 or 15 bushels of wheat the acre when fresh, & fall down to about 8." "To George Washington from Arthur Young, 18 January 1792," Founders Online, National Archives (http://founders.archives.gov/documents/Washington/05-09-02-0280, ver. 2013-12-27) [original source: *The Papers of George Washington*, Presidential Series, vol. 9, *23 September 1791–29 February 1792*, ed. Mark A. Mastromarino (Charlottesville: University Press of Virginia, 2000), 9: 471–81].

41. "From Thomas Jefferson to George Washington, 28 June 1793," Founders Online, National Archives (http://founders.archives.gov/documents/Jefferson/01-26-02-0360, ver. 2013-12-27) [original source: *The Papers of Thomas Jefferson*, vol. 26, *11 May–31 August 1793*, ed. John Catanzariti (Princeton: Princeton University Press, 1995), 26: 396–98].
42. Ibid.
43. "From George Washington to Anthony Whitting, 4 September 1791," Founders Online, National Archives (http://founders.archives.gov/documents/Washington/05-08-02-0344, ver. 2016-10-05) [original source: *The Papers of George Washington*, Presidential Series, vol. 8, *22 March 1791–22 September 1791*, ed. Mark A. Mastromarino (Charlottesville: University Press of Virginia, 1999), 487–89].
44. Diary entry: 24 March 1760, 22 May 1760, Founders Online, National Archives (http://founders.archives.gov/documents/Washington/01-01-02-0005-0003-0024, ver. 2014-02-12) [original source: *Diaries of George Washington*, 1: 256, 282–83]. Fusonie and Fusonie, *George Washington*, 23.
45. "From George Washington to Anthony Whitting, 4 September 1791," Founders Online, National Archives (http://founders.archives.gov/documents/Washington/05-08-02-0344, ver. 2014-02-12) [original source: *The Papers of George Washington*, Presidential Series, vol. 8, *22 March 1791–22 September 1791*, ed. Mark A. Mastromarino (Charlottesville: University Press of Virginia, 1999), 487–89].
46. Jefferson wrote his first note to Young on Aug. 3, 1791. "To George Washington from Arthur Young, 18 January 1792," Founders Online, National Archives (http://founders.archives.gov/documents/Washington/05-09-02-0280, ver. 2013-12-27) [original source: *Papers of George Washington*, 9: 471–81, n. 6].
47. Baron, *Garden and Farm Books*, 175–76. McEwan, *Thomas Jefferson*, 17.

48. Baron, *Garden and Farm Books,* 324–25, 329, 333. He organized this information into ten general categories and ninety-five subcategories filling seventy-one pages. Ibid., 306–76.
49. The plow that Washington invented had that disadvantage. "Tryd the new Plow brot. Yesterday, found she did good Work and run very true but heavy—rather too much so for two Horses, especially while the Gd. was moist." Diary entry: 11 April 1760, Founders Online, National Archives (http://founders.archives.gov/documents/Washington/01-01-02-0005-0004-0011, ver. 2014-02-12) [original source: *Diaries of George Washington,* 1: 265–66].
50. Jefferson to John Taylor, 29 Dec. 1794, Founders Online, National Archives (http://founders.archives.gov/documents/Jefferson/01-28-02-0172) [original source: *The Papers of Thomas Jefferson,* vol. 28, *1 January 1794–29 February 1796,* ed. John Catanzariti (Princeton: Princeton University Press, 2000), pp. 230–34.] For the story of the plow's invention, see Lucia Stanton, "Thomas Jefferson: Planter and Farmer," in *A Companion to Jefferson,* ed. Francis D. Cogliano (London: Blackwell, 2012), 253–70.
51. Diary entry: 26 March 1760, Founders Online, National Archives (http://founders.archives.gov/documents/Washington/01-01-02-0005-0003-0027, ver. 2014-02-12) [original source: *Diaries of George Washington,* 1: 257–58].
52. McEwan, *Thomas Jefferson,* 88.
53. Baron, *Garden and Farm Books,* 261.
54. Herbert E. Sloan, *Principle and Interest: Thomas Jefferson and the Problem of Debt* (New York: Oxford University Press, 1995), 18. "From Thomas Jefferson to William Jones, 5 January 1787," Founders Online, National Archives (http://founders.archives.gov/documents/Jefferson/01-11-02-0010, ver. 2014-02-12) [original source: *The Papers of Thomas Jefferson,* vol. 11, *1 January–6 August 1787,* ed. Julian P. Boyd (Princeton: Princeton University Press, 1955), 14–18].
55. Sloan, *Principle and Interest,* 14–15.
56. "From Thomas Jefferson to William Jones, 5 January 1787," Founders Online, National Archives (http://founders.archives.gov/documents/Jefferson/01-11-02-0010, ver. 2014-02-12) [original source: *Papers of Thomas Jefferson,* 11: 14–18]. Sloan, *Principle and Interest,* 16.
57. Freeman, *George Washington,* 3: 111. "From George Washington to Robert Cary & Company, 10 August 1764," Founders Online, National Archives (http://founders.archives.gov/documents/Washington/02-07-02-0200-0001, ver. 2014-02-12) [original source: *The Papers of George Washington,* Colonial Series,

1 January 1761–15 June 1767, ed. W. W. Abbot and Dorothy Twohig (Charlottesville: University Press of Virginia, 1990), 7: 323–26].

58. "From Thomas Jefferson to William Jones, 5 January 1787," Founders Online, National Archives (http://founders.archives.gov/documents/Jefferson/01-11-02-0010, ver. 2014-02-12) [original source: *Papers of Thomas Jefferson*, 11: 14–18].
59. Sloan, *Principle and Interest*, 18–20, 24.
60. "From Thomas Jefferson to John Dobson, 1 January 1792," Founders Online, National Archives (http://founders.archives.gov/documents/Jefferson/01-23-02-0002, ver. 2014-02-12) [original source: *The Papers of Thomas Jefferson*, vol. 23, *1 January–31 May 1792*, ed. Charles T. Cullen (Princeton: Princeton University Press, 1990), 4].
61. "From Thomas Jefferson to William Jones, 5 January 1787," Founders Online, National Archives (http://founders.archives.gov/documents/Jefferson/01-11-02-0010, ver. 2014-02-12) [original source: *Papers of Thomas Jefferson*, 11: 14–18]. Sloan, *Principle and Interest*, 20–21.
62. Quoted in Sloan, *Principle and Interest*, 30.
63. "From Thomas Jefferson to Mary Jefferson Eppes, 7 January 1798," *Founders Online*, National Archives, last modified Dec. 28, 2016 (http://founders.archives.gov/documents/Jefferson/01-30-02-0008) [original source: *The Papers of Thomas Jefferson*, vol. 30, *1 January 1798–31 January 1799*, ed. Barbara B. Oberg (Princeton: Princeton University Press, 2003), 14–16].
64. For the similar plight of Thomas Jones, see Walsh, *Motives of Honor, Pleasure, and Profit*, 471.
65. "Enclosure: Invoice to Robert Cary & Company, 1 May 1759," Founders Online, National Archives (http://founders.archives.gov/documents/Washington/02-06-02-0166-0002, ver. 2014-02-12) [original source: *The Papers of George Washington*, Colonial Series, *4 September 1758–26 December 1760*, ed. W. W. Abbot (Charlottesville: University Press of Virginia, 1988), 6: 317–18].
66. Freeman, *George Washington*, 3: 63. "From George Washington to Robert Cary & Company, 10 August 1764," Founders Online, National Archives (http://founders.archives.gov/documents/Washington/02-07-02-0200-0001, ver. 2014-02-12) [original source: *Papers of George Washington*, 7: 323–26].
67. Dalzell and Dalzell, *George Washington's Mount Vernon*, 56.
68. Cynthia A. Kierner, *Martha Jefferson Randolph, Daughter of Monticello: Her Life and Times* (Chapel Hill: University of North Carolina Press, 2012), 181.

69. The planters Lorena Walsh studied were taking measures to restore the soil rather than mindlessly exhausting plot after plot in their pursuit of maximum production. Only one suffered bankruptcy. *Motives of Honor, Pleasure, and Profit*, 7, 471.
70. William Byrd III, similarly over his head in debt, sponsored an auction with only modest results. William Byrd III, "Letters of the Byrd Family Continued," *Virginia Magazine of History and Biography* 38, no. 1 (1930): 59–60, http://www.jstor.org/stable/4244312, accessed Nov. 4, 2013. Kierner, *Martha Jefferson Randolph*, 197–98, 205, 246.
71. "George Washington's Last Will and Testament, 9 July 1799," Founders Online, National Archives (http://founders.archives.gov/documents/Washington/06-04-02-0404-0001, ver. 2014-02-12) [original source: *Papers of George Washington*, 4: 479–511].
72. Fusonie and Fusonie, *George Washington*, 6.
73. Gerald T. Dunne, "Bushrod Washington and the Mount Vernon Slaves," *Yearbook—the Supreme Court Historical Society* (1980). Robert and Lee Baldwin Dalzell, who have written most knowingly about Mount Vernon, conclude that Washington broke up his estate as a gesture toward equality. He freed his slaves and divided his land as an object lesson in democracy. Dalzell and Dalzell, *George Washington's Mount Vernon*, 220.
74. George Washington, Philadelphia, to the Earl of Buchan, Feb. 20, 1796, *The Writings of George Washington from the Original Manuscript Sources, 1745–1799*, ed. John C. Fitzpatrick (Washington, D.C.: Government Printing Office, 1931–44), 34: 471. For his advertisements for tenants, ibid., 34: 464–71. In 1787 Jefferson had unwillingly arrived at the same expedient, the best way to preserve the land as "the only sure provision for my children." He intended to lease both his land and his slaves. Thomas Jefferson to Nicholas Lewis, 29 July 1787, Founders Online, National Archives (http://founders.archives.gov/documents/Jefferson/01-11-02-0564) [original source: Boyd, *Jefferson Papers*, 11: 639–42.]
75. "From George Washington to William Strickland, 15 July 1797," Founders Online, National Archives (http://founders.archives.gov/documents/Washington/06-01-02-0214, ver. 2016-07-12) [original source: *The Papers of George Washington*, Retirement Series, vol. 1, *4 March 1797–30 December 1797*, ed. W. W. Abbot (Charlottesville: University Press of Virginia, 1998), 253–59].
76. Washington was not alone in wanting to disperse his slaves. In 1791 Robert Carter of Nomini Hall arranged to free all 509 of his slaves over a

twenty-two-year period. By 1810 there were 31,750 free blacks in Virginia. Michael A. McDonnell, *The Politics of War: Race, Class, and Conflict in Revolutionary Virginia* (Chapel Hill: University of North Carolina Press, 2007), 488–89.

12. *Jefferson's Neighbors*

1. Average per capita wealth of £262.1 in the South compared with £160.5 in New England and £179.6 in the Middle Colonies. Alice Hanson Jones, *Wealth of a Nation to Be: The American Colonies on the Eve of Revolution* (New York: Columbia University Press, 1980), 58.
2. Ibid., 173, 175, 176. King, a delegate to the Constitutional Convention, could say as if it were common knowledge that of the two sections "the Southern States are the richest." James Madison, *Notes of Debates in the Federal Convention of 1787 Reported by James Madison* (New York: Norton, 1969), 260.
3. Gloria L. Main, *Tobacco Colony: Life in Early Maryland, 1650–1720* (Princeton: Princeton University Press, 1982), 154. The value of consumer goods in the lower third of society in all three sections was virtually the same. Jones, *Wealth of a Nation to Be,* 163, 236, 241. Madison, *Notes of Debates,* 411. The second and third lowest deciles in Jones's table are treated as the lowest groups because the bottom decile in both sections had high negative worth. The figures for negative worth in both sections are so high that they seem to represent the insolvent estates of decedents with the ability to borrow significant sums rather than the estates of the indigent. The person to die with the largest negative worth in New England in 1774 was called "gentleman" in his estate papers. Jones, *Wealth of a Nation to Be,* 173, 241.
4. There were two levies, one on land and another on personal property. William Walter Hening, *The Statutes at Large: Being a Collection of All the Laws of Virginia from the First Session of the Legislature, in the Year 1619,* 18 vols. (Richmond: Samuel Pleasants, Jr., 1809–23), 10: 501.
5. Jefferson's tax came to £70 12s 6d. Albemarle County, Virginia, 1782–1799, Personal Property Tax Lists, CD (Williamston, Mich.: Binns Genealogy, 2008), 1782, p. 7. Hereafter Albemarle County Tax Lists. Carter's tax was 128£, 31s, 6d. Ibid., 22. Robert Carter Nicholas taxes ibid., 19.
6. Ibid., 16, 18, 20. Slaves who were exempt because of "age or infirmity" were not taxed. Hening, *Statutes,* 10: 504. S. Edward Ayres, "Albemarle County, Virginia 1744–1770: An Economic, Political, and Social Analysis," M.S. thesis, University of Virginia, 1968, 58, 59. Only 8 percent owned more than

a thousand acres. The division into thirds calculated from Albemarle County Tax Lists, 1782.

7. Fred Shelley, ed., "The Journal of Ebenezer Howard in Virginia, 1777," *Virginia Magazine of History and Biography* 62, no. 4 (1954): 414.
8. In Tidewater and Southside counties, there were more artisans and professionals who did no farming. Alice Hanson Jones, *American Colonial Wealth: Documents and Methods*, 3 vols., 2nd ed. (New York: Arno, 1977), 2: 1300–1400.
9. Animal ownership calculated from Albemarle County Tax Lists, 1782. George Gilmer, "Papers, Military and Political, 1775–1778," *Miscellaneous Papers, 1672–1865, Collections of the Virginia Historical Society, New Series* (Richmond: By the Society, 1887), 6: 87.
10. Virginia estate inventories, 1774–75, in Jones, *American Colonial Wealth*, 2: 1300–1400.
11. Virginia County Court Records, *Will Book: Albemarle County, Virginia, 1752–1756, 1775–1783* (n.p.: Antient, 2002), 62–63, 65, 78, 91. Hereafter *Albemarle Virginia Will Book*.
12. Ibid., 62–63.
13. This was the probate inventory for his holdings in Fredericksville parish. Another inventory was prepared for his quarter in St. Anne. Ibid., 50–53, 76–77, 79–82.
14. Ibid., 49.
15. Anna L. Hawley, "The Meaning of Absence: Household Inventories in Surry County, Virginia, 1690–1715," in *Early American Inventories: The Dublin Seminar for New England Folklife Annual Proceedings, 1987*, ed. Peter Benes and Jane Montague Benes (Boston: Boston University, 1989), 23–31.
16. Ibid., 23–31; Lois Green Carr and Lorena S. Walsh, "Inventories and the Analysis of Wealth and Consumption Patterns in St. Mary's County, Maryland, 1658–1777," *Historical Methods* 13 (1980): 81–104. Harold B. Gill, Jr., and George M. Curtis III, "Virginia's Colonial Probate Policies and the Preconditions for Economic History," *Virginia Magazine of History and Biography* 87, no. 1 (1979): 68–73.
17. The great need for slave clothing persuaded Jefferson in 1812 to set up spinning machines of his own. He managed one hundred spindles in 1813. Lucia Stanton, "Thomas Jefferson: Planter and Farmer," in *A Companion to Thomas Jefferson*, ed. Francis D. Cogliano (London: Blackwell, 2012), 265.
18. *Virginia Gazette* (Williamsburg), Nov. 15, 1769, 2. Women's economic role continued to enlarge in the next century. Joan Jensen, *Loosening the Bonds:*

Mid-Atlantic Farm Women, 1750–1850 (New Haven: Yale University Press, 1986).

19. "To George Washington from Lund Washington, 18 March 1778," Founders Online, National Archives (http://founders.archives.gov/documents/Washington/03-14-02-0193, ver. 2014-10-23) [original source: *The Papers of George Washington, Revolutionary War Series, 1 March 1778–30 April 1778,* ed. David R. Hoth (Charlottesville: University of Virginia Press, 2004), 14: 220–22].
20. *Virginia Gazette* (Williamsburg), Nov. 8, 1776.
21. Michael A. McDonnell, *The Politics of War: Race, Class, and Conflict in Revolutionary Virginia* (Chapel Hill: University of North Carolina Press, 2007), 516. Isaac Jefferson, *Memoirs of a Monticello Slave As Dictated to Charles Campbell in the 1840's by Isaac, one of Thomas Jefferson's Slaves* (Charlottesville: University of Virginia Press, 1951), 49.
22. In July 1775, Albemarle was one of fifteen counties charged to raise a company of "expert rifle-men." Those who provided a rifle were paid twenty shillings a year for its use. Hening, *Statutes,* 9: 12–13.
23. James A. Bear, Jr., and Lucia C. Stanton, eds. *Jefferson's Memorandum Books: Accounts, with Legal Records and Miscellany, 1767–1826,* 2 vols. (Princeton: Princeton University Press, 1997), 1: 516, 519–20, 523.
24. Ibid., 1: 68, 515, 2: 1049. Albemarle County Tax Lists, 1782.
25. *Jefferson's Memorandum Books,* 1: 523. Albemarle County Tax Lists, 1782, 23. Hamilton W. Pierson, *Jefferson at Monticello: The Private Life of Thomas Jefferson, from Entirely New Sources* (New York: Scribner, 1862), 83. Albemarle County Tax Lists, 1792, 1792B.
26. *Jefferson's Memorandum Books,* 515–23.
27. Bettye Hobbs Pruitt, "Self-Sufficiency and the Agricultural Economy of Eighteenth-Century Massachusetts," *William and Mary Quarterly,* 3rd ser. 41, no. 3 (1984): 333–64.
28. "George Gilmer," Thomas Jefferson Encyclopedia, Thomas Jefferson Monticello website, http://www.monticello.org/site/research-and-collections/george-gilmer, accessed April 24, 2015.
29. Gilmer, "Papers," 75–76. John E. Selby, *The Revolution in Virginia, 1775–1783* (Williamsburg, Va.: Colonial Williamsburg Foundation, 1988), 1–3.
30. Gilmer, "Papers," 80. Mary M. Sullivan, "The Gentry and the Association in Albemarle County, 1774–1775," *Papers of the Albemarle County Historical Society,* 23 (1964–65): 40–44.
31. McDonnell, *Politics of War,* 46. Sullivan, "The Gentry," 40–44. Gilmer, "Papers," 77, 82.

32. Gilmer, "Papers," 80, 89. Selby, *Revolution*, 45–49.
33. Gilmer, "Papers," 91, 101, 118, 127.
34. Ibid., 91–92. Selby, *Revolution*, 51–52.
35. Gilmer, "Papers," 103, 118, 119, 125.
36. Ibid., 122, 123.
37. Ibid., 123, 126.
38. Ibid., 126–27.
39. Ibid., 124.
40. Robert C. Baron, *The Garden and Farm Books of Thomas Jefferson* (Golden, Colo.: Fulcrum, 1987), 328. Gilmer, "Papers," 119. Selby, *Revolution*, 165–66. Salt was a major trade item in country stores. Ann Smart Martin, *Buying into a World of Good: Early Consumers in Backcountry Virginia* (Baltimore: Johns Hopkins University Press, 2008), 83.
41. Hening, *Statutes*, 9: 10. Robert L. Scribner and Brent Tarter, eds., *Revolutionary Virginia: The Road to Independence: The Time for Decision, 1776* ([Charlottesville]: University Press of Virginia, 1981), 6: 475. In May 1776, the exemption of overseers was revoked in two eastern shore counties. Hening, *Statutes*, 9: 139.
42. Hening, *Statutes*, 9: 27. McDonnell, *Politics of War*, 257, 304. Selby, *Revolution*, 254.
43. Pendleton to William Woodford, Caroline, Jan. 31, 1778, David John Mays, ed., *The Letters and Papers of Edmund Pendleton, 1734–1803* (Charlottesville: University Press of Virginia, 1967), 1: 246.
44. Pendleton to William Woodford, Williamsburg, Nov. 29, 1777, ibid., 1: 239. Hening, *Statutes*, 6: 29. One object of the legislation was to require vagrants to return to their home counties for welfare rather than putting the burden on the parish where they had moved. Hening, *Statutes*, 6: 29–31.
45. Hening, *Statutes*, 9: 216–17.
46. Pendleton to William Woodford, Nov. 29, 1777, *Letters*, 1: 239. Hening, *Statutes*, 9: 341.
47. Pendleton to William Woodford, Nov. 29, 1777, *Letters*, 1: 239. Selby, *Revolution*, 136. "To George Washington from Lund Washington, 18 March 1778," Founders Online, National Archives (http://founders.archives.gov/documents/Washington/03-14-02-0193, ver. 2014-10-23) [original source: *Papers of George Washington*, 14: 222].
48. Pendleton to George Washington, Caroline, Virginia, Dec. 22, 1778, *Letters*, 1: 276–77. Selby, *Revolution*, 136.
49. Selby, *Revolution*, 127, 136. Pendleton to Woodford, Williamsburg, Nov. 29, 1777, *Letters*, 1: 238–39. *Virginia Gazette* (Williamsburg), Nov. 8, 1776.

50. Hening, *Statutes*, 9: 344.
51. Quoted in McDonnell, *Politics of War*, 248, 291, 302.
52. Pendleton to William Woodford, Caroline, Oct. 9, 1778, *Letters*, 1: 273.
53. Quoted in McDonnell, *Politics of War*, 189, 191.
54. "To George Washington from Lund Washington, 29 February 1776," Founders Online, National Archives (http://founders.archives.gov/documents/Washington/03-03-02-0286, ver. 2014-10-23) [original source: *The Papers of George Washington*, Revolutionary War Series, *1 January 1776–31 March 1776*, ed. Philander D. Chase (Charlottesville: University Press of Virginia, 1988), 3: 397–98]. Scribner and Tarter, *Revolutionary Virginia*, 448; McDonnell, *Politics of War*, 193, 205–06.
55. In Charles County, Maryland, debt litigation virtually ceased in September 1775 as the Continental Association went into effect. Jean B. Lee, "Lessons in Humility: The Revolutionary Transformation of the Governing Elite of Charles County, Maryland," in *The Transforming Hand of Revolution: Reconsidering the American Revolution as a Social Movement*, ed. Ronald Hoffman and Peter J. Albert (Charlottesville: University Press of Virginia, 1995), 99.
56. Norman K. Risjord, *Chesapeake Politics, 1781–1800* (New York: Columbia University Press, 1978), 97–98.
57. Inhabitants, Albemarle County Petition, Nov. 3, 1787. Virginia Legislative Petitions, Library of Virginia, Virginia Memory LiVi, digital collections, http://digitool1.lva.lib.va.us:8881/R/T7CFG1RBMNIPXSNX3YYHM1KDJ8BYIPKLT8HFG4HC83V3V485GK-01963?func=results-jump-full&set_entry=000012&set_number=047411&base=GEN01-ARC01, accessed April 27, 2015. Hereafter, Albemarle County Petition.
58. Lee, "Lessons in Humility," 93–94.
59. Inhabitants, Albemarle County Petition.
60. William Palmer, ed., *Calendar of Virginia State Papers and Other Manuscripts from January 1, 1785, to July 2, 1789* (Richmond: R. U. Derr, 1884), 4: 221–22, 270, 377, 943.
61. Ibid., 4: 82.
62. Ibid., 4: 82, 93, 124.
63. Ibid., 4: 111, 119, 499; cf. 4: 530.
64. Terry Bouton, "A Road Closed: Rural Insurgency in Post-Independence Pennsylvania," *Journal of American History* 87, no. 3 (2000): 855–56.
65. Ibid., 866–67, 874–75.
66. Edward Carrington to Governor Edmund Patrick, Dec. 7, 1786, *Calendar of Virginia State Papers*, 4: 195.

67. Woody Holton, *Unruly Americans and the Origins of the Constitution* (New York: Hill and Wang, 2007), 11–12.
68. Risjord, *Chesapeake Politics*, 102–4, 149–53. McDonnell, *Politics of War*, 496, 500, 516. For similar practices in Maryland, see Lee, "Lessons in Humility," 102.
69. For an argument that Virginia taxes per capita were considerably lower than in Massachusetts, see H. James Henderson, "Taxation and Political Culture: Massachusetts and Virginia, 1760–1800," *William and Mary Quarterly*, 3rd ser. 47, no. 1 (1990): 90–114.
70. Leonard L. Richards, *Shays's Rebellion: The American Revolution's Final Battle* (Philadelphia: University of Pennsylvania Press, 2002), 74–88. Daniel P. Satzmary, *Shays' Rebellion: The Making of an Agrarian Insurrection* (Amherst: University of Massachusetts Press, 1980), 19–44.
71. William Wirt Henry, *Patrick Henry: Life, Correspondence, and Speeches* (New York: Scribner, 1891), 2: 213.
72. Risjord, *Chesapeake Politics*, 132. Holton in *Unruly Americans* propounds the persuasive thesis that the money crisis of the 1780s motivated the move toward a new federal constitution.

13. Learning Slavery

1. Virginia County Court Records, *Will Book: Albemarle County, Virginia, 1785–1798* (n.p.: Antient, 2002), 17–18. Hereafter *Albemarle Virginia Will Book*.
2. Camille Wells, "The Planter's Prospect: Houses, Outbuildings, and Rural Landscapes in Eighteenth-Century Virginia," *Winterthur Portfolio* 28, no. 1 (1993): 3, 6. Information on one-room cabins is summarized in Mechal Sobel, *The World They Made Together: Black and White Values in Eighteenth-Century Virginia* (Princeton: Princeton University Press, 1987), 104.
3. From John Harvey Darrell, "Diary of John Harvey Darrell: Voyage to America," *Bermuda Historical Quarterly* 5 (1948): 142–49, quoted in Alan Taylor, *The Internal Enemy: Slavery and War in Virginia, 1772–1832* (New York: Norton, 2013), 18. Wells, "The Planter's Prospect," 5–6. On the mean houses of ordinary farmers, see Sobel, *The World They Made Together*, 103–19. The anthropologist Alison Bell has found that Virginia planters continued to live below their means to the end the eighteenth century. Alison Bell, "Emulation and Empowerment: Material, Social, and Economic Dynamics in Eighteenth- and Nineteenth-Century Virginia," *International Journal of Historical Archaeology* 6, no. 4 (2002): 268–69.

4. Alice Hanson Jones, *American Colonial Wealth: Documents and Methods,* 3 vols., 2nd ed. (New York: Arno, 1977), 2: 97, and estate inventories, 2: 1300–1400.
5. Kevin M. Sweeney, "Mansion People: Kinship, Class, and Architecture in Western Massachusetts in the Mid Eighteenth Century," *Winterthur Portfolio* 19, no. 4 (1984): 231–55.
6. *Albemarle Virginia Will Book,* 19–20. John Davis, *Travels of Four Years and a Half in the United States of America During 1798, 1799, 1800, 1801, and 1802* (New York: Henry Holt, 1909), 397.
7. Virginia County Court Records, *Will Book: Albemarle County, Virginia, 1752–1756, 1775–1783* (n.p.: Antient, 2002), 76, 400. Hereafter *Albemarle Virginia Will Book.* In plantation culture, slaves were as vital to a daughter's position in the world as a son's. Jean Butenhoff Lee, "Land and Labor: Parental Bequest Practices in Charles County, Maryland, 1732–1783," in *Colonial Chesapeake Society,* ed. Lois Green Carr, Philip D. Morgan, and Jean B. Russo (Chapel Hill: University of North Carolina Press, 1988), 334–35. I am grateful to Lucia Stanton for identifying the names in the record.
8. *Letters from Virginia* (Baltimore, 1816), 100. My thanks to Alan Taylor for this reference. The author was probably George Tucker, cousin of the more famous St. George Tucker and a resident of Albemarle County.
9. Charles L. Perdue, Jr., Thomas E. Barden, and Robert K. Phillips, eds. *Weevils in the Wheat: Interviews with Virginia Ex-Slaves* (Charlottesville: University Press of Virginia, 1976), 47.
10. Ibid., 47.
11. Ibid., 47–48.
12. Lucia Stanton, *"Those Who Labor for My Happiness": Slavery at Thomas Jefferson's Monticello* (Charlottesville: University of Virginia Press, 2012), 110.
13. Perdue, Barden, and Phillips, *Weevils,* 48.
14. Ibid., 48.
15. Ibid., 36.
16. Ibid., 66.
17. Ibid., 67.
18. For black oral culture and the collecting of slave stories, see Lisa Francavilla, "Ellen Randolph Coolidge's 'Virginia Legends' and 'Negro Stories': Antebellum Tales from Monticello," *Massachusetts Historical Review* 17 (2015): 99–152.
19. For Burwell, Ellen W. Randolph (Coolidge) to Martha Jefferson Randolph, Poplar Forest, July 28, 1819, in "Jefferson Quotes and Family Letters,"

Monticello website, http://tjrs.monticello.org/letter/823, accessed March 9, 2017. "From Thomas Jefferson to Thomas Mann Randolph, 4 February 1800," Founders Online, National Archives (http://founders.archives.gov/documents/Jefferson/01-31-02-0304, ver. 2016-12-28) [original source: *The Papers of Thomas Jefferson,* vol. 31, *1 February 1799–31 May 1800,* ed. Barbara B. Oberg (Princeton: Princeton University Press, 2004), 359–61]. On Jupiter, see Stanton, *"Those Who Labor,"* 107–11.

20. Edwin Morris Betts, ed., *Thomas Jefferson's Farm Book* ([Princeton]: Princeton University Press, 1953), contains a facsimile of the Farm Book. Robert C. Baron, ed., *The Garden and Farm Books of Thomas Jefferson* (Golden, Colo.: Fulcrum, 1987), transcribes both books. Diary and tables in Baron, *Garden and Farm Books,* 244–305, aphorisms, 306–73.
21. Baron, *Garden and Farm Books,* 223–24, 244–48.
22. For Jefferson's slaves in 1773–74, see Mary Beth Norton, Herbert G. Gutman, and Ira Berlin, "The Afro-American Family in the Age of Revolution," in *Slavery and Freedom in the Age of the American Revolution,* ed. Ira Berlin and Ronald Hoffman (Charlottesville: University Press of Virginia, 1983), 184. Baron, *Garden and Farm Books,* 244–45.
23. Baron, *Garden and Farm Books,* 258–59.
24. Ibid., 262.
25. Ibid., 266–67; cf. 286–87, 295–97.
26. Ibid., 262, 268.
27. Stanton, *"Those Who Labor,"* 114. Baron, *Garden and Farm Books,* 288–89.
28. Baron, *Garden and Farm Books,* 279, 290–91.
29. Ibid., 272.
30. Stanton, *"Those Who Labor,"* 158–59. "List of Inoculations, 7 August 1801–17 September 1801," Founders Online,National Archives (http://founders.archives.gov/documents/Jefferson/01-35-02-0029, ver. 2016-12-28) [original source: *The Papers of Thomas Jefferson,* vol. 35, *1 August–30 November 1801,* ed. Barbara B. Oberg (Princeton: Princeton University Press, 2008), 34–35.
31. Baron, *Garden and Farm Books,* 278–79. Stanton, *"Those Who Labor,"* 9–10, 128.
32. Stanton, *"Those Who Labor,"* 11–12.
33. Baron, *Garden and Farm Books,* 327. Stanton, *"Those Who Labor,"* 144. Tax lists for 1782, 1788, 1788, Albemarle County, Virginia 1782–1799 Personal Property, Virginia County Tax Lists, scanned microfilm images, Binn's Genealogy, CDR 000467; William Waller Hening, *Hening's Statutes at*

Large, transcribed for the internet by Freddie L. Spradlin, 12: 336 http://vagenweb.org/hening/, accessed Feb. 18, 2015.

34. Thomas Jefferson, *Notes on the State of Virginia,* ed. William Peden (Chapel Hill: University of North Carolina Press, 1954), 163. *Albemarle Virginia Will Book,* 20.
35. Isaac Jefferson, *Memoirs of a Monticello Slave As Dictated to Charles Campbell in the 1840's by Isaac, One of Thomas Jefferson's Slaves* (Charlottesville: University Press of Virginia, 1951), 30. Madison Hemings, "The Memoirs of Madison Hemings," in Annette Gordon-Reed, *Thomas Jefferson and Sally Hemings: An American Controversy* (Charlottesville: University Press of Virginia, 1997), 247. Stanton, *"Those Who Labor,"* 13–15, 105. For a severe picture of punishment at Monticello, see Henry Wiencek, *Master of the Mountain: Thomas Jefferson and His Slaves* (New York: Farrar, Straus and Giroux, 2012).
36. Jefferson, *Memoirs,* 14. Stanton, *"Those Who Labor,"* 13.
37. Jefferson, *Memoirs,* 35. Stanton, *"Those Who Labor,"* 119.
38. Jefferson, *Notes,* 162. Henry S. Randall, *The Life of Thomas Jefferson* (Philadelphia, 1865), 3: 510, quoted in Stanton, *"Those Who Labor,"* 112.
39. Slave family life is worked out in Philip D. Morgan, *Slave Counterpoint: Black Culture in the Eighteenth-Century Chesapeake & Low Country* (Chapel Hill: University of North Carolina Press, 1998), chap. 9.
40. Ibid., 104–6. Stanton, *"Those Who Labor,"* 125; Betts, *Thomas Jefferson's Farm Book,* 6. William M. Kelso, "Mulberry Row: Slave Life at Thomas Jefferson's Monticello," *Archaeology* 39, no. 5 (1986): 3–34. Sobel, *The World They Made Together,* 105–10, 112, 117.
41. Morgan, *Slave Counterpoint,* 107–8, 144. Morgan and others rely on the unpublished work of Michael Nichols, "Building the Virginia Southside: A Note on Architecture and Society in the Eighteenth-Century," ms., 1982, Colonial Williamsburg. For slave housing generally, see Sobel, *The World They Made Together,* 100–126.
42. William, Jr., was already listed independently in the 1782 tax list, though with no slaves and only four head of cattle and two horses. "Albemarle County, Virginia 1782–1799 Personal Property."
43. *Albemarle County Will Book,* 88–89.
44. Ibid., 88–90.
45. Ibid., 89–90.
46. Connecticut slaves joined in the labor of their white masters. Allegra di Bonaventura, *For Adam's Sake: A Family Saga in Colonial New England* (New York: Liveright, 2013), 289–302.

47. Jefferson thought slave owners would not work alongside their slaves. "For in a warm climate, no man will labour for himself who can make another labour for him." Jefferson, *Notes*, 163. It is hard to believe that was true in households with grown sons and few slaves.
48. Morgan, *Slave Counterpoint*, 108. For a discussion of this division within the self, see Gerald W. Mullin, *Flight and Rebellion: Slave Resistance in Eighteenth-Century Virginia* (New York: Oxford University Press, 1972), 121–23.
49. Jefferson, *Memoirs*, 32–33, 42. Stanton, *"Those Who Labor,"* 31–33, 34, 42, 99, 118, 146, 155–57, 159, 161, 164–65. Sobel, *The World They Made Together*, 48–50.
50. Jack McLaughlin, *Jefferson and Monticello: The Biography of a Builder* (New York: Henry Holt, 1988), 102–4. Jefferson, *Memoirs*, 33–34. Hamilton W. Pierson, *Jefferson at Monticello: The Private Life of Thomas Jefferson, from Entirely New Sources* (New York: Scribner, 1862), 68–109.
51. Hemings, "Memoirs," 247. Jefferson, *Memoirs*, 16, 21. Sobel, *The World They Made Together*, 40.
52. Israel Jefferson, The Memoirs of Israel Jefferson. http://www.pbs.org/wgbh/pages/frontline/shows/jefferson/cron/1873israel.html, accessed July 10, 2017. Sobel, *The World They Made Together*, 41.
53. Hemings, "Memoirs," 247. Stanton, *"Those Who Labor,"* 11, 117–19.
54. Jefferson, *Memoirs*, 19–20. Similar tales were told of slave heroism when the British took over Monticello in 1781. Stanton, *"Those Who Labor,"* 133–34.
55. Stanton, *"Those Who Labor,"* 14, 16.
56. Ibid., 83. Alan Taylor, *The Internal Enemy: Slavery and War in Virginia, 1772–1832* (New York: Norton, 2013), 82–83.
57. Stanton, *"Those Who Labor,"* 151. "Advertisement for a Runaway Slave, 7 September 1769," Founders Online, National Archives (http://founders.archives.gov/documents/Jefferson/01-01-02-0021, ver. 2014-12-01) [original source: *The Papers of Thomas Jefferson*, vol. 1, *1760–1776*, ed. Julian P. Boyd (Princeton: Princeton University Press, 1950), 33].
58. Taylor, *Internal Enemy*, 85.
59. Stanton, *"Those Who Labor,"* 125.
60. For stories of slaves running away from the Jefferson family, see Stanton, *"Those Who Labor,"* 139, 141, 147.
61. Cassandra Pybus, "Jefferson's Faulty Math: The Question of Slave Defections in the American Revolution," *William and Mary Quarterly*, 3rd ser. 62, no. 2 (2005): 245–46, 258, 261; Taylor, *Internal Enemy*, 27.

62. Pybus, "Jefferson's Faulty Math," 249, 251–52. Cassandra Pybus, *Epic Journeys of Freedom: Runaway Slaves of the American Revolution and Their Global Quest for Liberty* (Boston: Beacon, 2006), 30–31.
63. Thomas Jefferson, Monticello, to Joseph Daugherty, July 31, 1806, in Betts, *Thomas Jefferson's Farm Book,* 22. "To George Washington from Lund Washington, 3 December 1775," Founders Online, National Archives (http://founders.archives.gov/documents/Washington/03-02-02-0434, ver. 2014-12-01) [original source: *The Papers of George Washington,* Revolutionary War Series, *16 September 1775–31 December* 1775, ed. Philander D. Chase (Charlottesville: University Press of Virginia, 1987), 2: 482].
64. Hemings, "Memoirs," 247. Jefferson, *Memoirs,* 38.
65. Taylor, *Internal Enemy,* 25.
66. Ibid., 25. William M. Kelso, *Kingsmill Plantations, 1619–1800: Archaeology of Country Life in Colonial Virginia* (Orlando, Fla.: Academic Press, 1984), 104–5, 191, 201. For the literature on house pits, Morgan, *Slave Counterpoint,* 116. Stanton, *"Those Who Labor,"* 117.

14. American Agriculture, 1800–1862

1. TableAa36-92—Population, by region and urban—rural residence: 1790–1990, *Historical Statistics of the United States—Millennial Edition,* https://hsus-cambridge-org.ezproxy.cul.columbia.edu/HSUSWeb/table/seriesnext.do, accessed Feb. 23, 2015.
2. Paul W. Gates, *The Farmer's Age: Agriculture, 1815–1860* (New York: Holt, Rinehart and Winston, 1960).
3. Ibid., 251–53.
4. Jeremy Atack, Fred Bateman, and William N. Parker, "The Farm, the Farmer, and the Market," in *The Cambridge Economic History of the United States,* ed. Stanley L. Engerman and Robert E. Gallman, 3 vols. (Cambridge: Cambridge University Press, 2000), 2: 249. Joan M. Jensen, *Loosening the Bonds: Mid-Atlantic Farm Women, 1750–1850* (New Haven: Yale University Press, 1986).
5. Carol E. Hoffecker, *Delaware: A Bicentennial History* (New York: Norton, 1977), 45–48.
6. Gregory H. Nobles, "Commerce and Community: A Case Study of the Rural Broommaking Business in Antebellum Massachusetts," *Journal of the Early Republic* 4, no. 3 (1984): 187–208.
7. Later reformers thought the practice primitive and reprehensible. Samuel Deane, *The New-England Farmer; or Georgical Dictionary,* 3rd ed. (Boston,

1822), 130. For a description of long fallow in New England, see Carolyn Merchant, *Ecological Revolutions: Nature, Gender, and Science in New England* (Chapel Hill: University of North Carolina Press, 1989), 157–63.

8. The American system was not classic shifting agriculture with villages that moved as the fields migrated through the forest. D. B. Grigg, *The Agricultural Systems of the World: An Evolutionary Approach* (Cambridge: Cambridge University Press, 1974), 57–60, 72–73.

9. On corn as well as tobacco depleting the soil, see W[illiam] Strickland, *Observations on the Agriculture of the United States of America* (London, 1801), 49–50. "An Account of the Present State and Government of Virginia [1696]," Massachusetts Historical Society, *Collections for the Year 1798*, 5 (Boston, 1835), 127. Brian Donahue believes Concord farmers must have manured their land to keep it in heart rather than going to fallow. The evidence is a bit thin, but he argues that the town's corn crops could not have continued without soil restoration. *The Great Meadow: Farmers and the Land in Colonial Concord* (New Haven: Yale University Press, 2004), 10–20. On the other hand, Jared Eliot, advocating reforms in the middle of the eighteenth century, said earlier farmers had "depended upon the natural Fertility of the Ground, which served their purpose very well, and when they had worn out one piece they cleared another." Jared Eliot, *Essays upon Field Husbandry in New England and Other Papers, 1748–1762*, ed. Harry J. Carman and Rexford G. Tugwell (New York: Columbia University Press, 1934), 29.

10. Gloria L. Main, *Tobacco Colony: Life in Early Maryland, 1650–1720* (Princeton: Princeton University Press, 1982), 43–44. Clarence H. Danhof, *Change in Agriculture: The Northern United States, 1820–1870* (Cambridge: Harvard University Press, 1969), 252.

11. Paul G. Bourcier, " 'In Excellent Order': The Gentleman Farmer Views His Fences, 1790–1860," *Agricultural History* 58, no. 4 (1984): 546–64. Martin L. Primack, "Farm Fencing in the Nineteenth Century," *Journal of Economic History* 29, no. 2 (1969). Clarence H. Danhof, "The Fencing Problem in the Eighteen-Fifties," *Agricultural History* 18, no. 4 (1944): 169.

12. By the middle of the century the median of cleared land in fifty-eight Worcester County towns was 62 to 63 percent. Judging from land usage in urban areas along the coast, 80 to 85 percent was maximum usage. Land-usage figures tabulated from "Massachusetts Valuation Returns for Worcester Co, 1781–1860," compiled by the research staff at Old Sturbridge

Village, Massachusetts, and available in the Old Sturbridge Village Research Library.

13. *Delaware Register* (Dover), 2 (Oct. 1838): 201. For a dimmer view of soil recovery, Strickland, *Observations on the Agriculture,* 43; Danhof, *Change in Agriculture,* 254.
14. Timothy Dwight, *Travels in New England and New York,* ed. Barbara Miller Solomon, 4 vols. (1823; Cambridge: Belknap Press of Harvard University Press, 1969), 1: 77. Richard A. Wines, "The Nineteenth-Century Agricultural Transition in an Eastern Long Island Community," *Agricultural History* 55, no. 1 (1981): 53–56.
15. Kathleen Bruce, "Virginia Agricultural Decline to 1860: A Fallacy," *Agricultural History* 6, no. 1 (1932): 3–13.
16. For another example of self-provisioning through neighborly exchange, see Mary Babson Fuhrer, *A Crisis of Community: The Trials and Transformation of a New England Town, 1815–1848* (Chapel Hill: University of North Carolina Press, 2014), 24–26.
17. Claudia L. Bushman, *In Old Virginia: Slavery, Farming, and Society in the Journal of John Walker* (Baltimore: Johns Hopkins University Press, 2002), 13, 18.
18. Ibid., 1–3, 20, 42.
19. Ibid., 33, 184.
20. Ibid., 30–31. *Historical Statistics,* 1: 449. Cf. Atack, Bateman, and Parker, "Farm, Farmer, and Market," 2: 258–63, 269.
21. Bushman, *In Old Virginia,* 4–6, 32, 48. A progressive Iowa corn-and-hogs farmer in the 1860s constructed a lye leach in his barnyard for making soap, grew sorghum for molasses, and sent wool from his sheep to a carding mill to prepare rovings for his wife to spin and dye with sumac and red-oak bark dyes. Allan G. Bogue, *From Prairie to Corn Belt: Farming on the Illinois and Iowa Prairies in the Nineteenth Century* (Chicago: University of Chicago Press, 1963), 278–79.
22. Bushman, *In Old Virginia,* xiv, 14 (quotation), 26, 31.
23. Ibid., 63–64.
24. Ibid., 64–65, 67.
25. Ibid., 63.
26. Ibid., 183–84.
27. Ibid., 51. Quotation from Atack, Bateman, and Parker, "Farm, Farmer, and Market," 2: 247.
28. Bushman, *In Old Virginia,* 173–76, 187.

29. The classic account of city and country in the United States is William Cronon, *Nature's Metropolis: Chicago and the Great West* (New York: Norton, 1991).
30. On eighteenth-century agrarianism, see Chester E. Eisinger, "The Farmer in the Eighteenth-Century Almanac," *Agricultural History* 28, no. 3 (1954): 110. Strickland, *Observations on Agriculture,* 55.
31. Quoted in Richard H. Abbott, "The Agricultural Press Views the Yeoman: 1819–1859," *Agricultural History* 42, no. 1 (1968): 37–38.
32. Samuel Deane, *New England Farmer; or, Georgical Dictionary* (Worcester, Mass.: Isaiah Thomas, 1790), 1. Gilbert C. Fite, "The Historical Development of Agricultural Fundamentalism in the Nineteenth Century Agricultural Press," *Journal of Farm Economics* 44, no. 5 (1962): 1206–7. E. G. Storke, ed., *The Family and Householder's Guide* (Auburn, N.Y., 1859), 31, quoting from *The American Agriculturalist, A Consolidation of Buel's Cultivator and Genesee Farmer, Designed to Improve the Soil and the Mind* (Albany, 1840), 93. *The Genesee Farmer* (Rochester, N.Y.), 15 (1854): 160, 16 (1855): 158, 279.
33. On the profitability of farms in the mid-nineteenth century, see Atack, Bateman, and Parker, "Farm, Farmer, and Market," 2: 276–77.
34. Thomas Jefferson, *Notes on the State of Virginia* (1785; New York: Harper and Row, 1964), 156.
35. Rolla Milton Tryon, *Household Manufactures in the United States, 1640–1860* (Chicago: University of Chicago Press, 1917), 166, 308–9.
36. George P. Sanger, ed., *The Statutes at Large, Treaties, and Proclamations of the United States of America* (Boston: Little, Brown, 1863), 12: 392–93. Jeremy Atack, "Northern Agriculture," in Engerman and Gallman, *Cambridge Economic History,* 2: 301, 304–7.
37. *Statutes at Large,* 12: 387–88, 503–4. For the writings of an advocate of educated farmers, see Mary Turner Carriel, *The Life of Jonathan Baldwin Turner* (Urbana: University of Illinois Press, 1911).
38. Abraham Lincoln, *The Collected Works of Abraham Lincoln,* ed. Roy P. Basler, Marion Dolores Pratt, and Lloyd A. Dunlap, 9 vols. (New Brunswick, N.J.: Rutgers University Press, 1953–55), 3: 473.
39. Ibid., 3: 478.
40. Ibid., 3: 478–79. For the view that independence was less important to Lincoln than personal advancement, see G. S. Borritt, *Lincoln and the Economics of the American Dream* ([Memphis, Tenn.]: Memphis State University Press, 1978), 185–86, 188. Borritt believes the Wisconsin speech was an outlier in Lincoln's economic thought. For an elaboration of Lincoln's

ideology, see Eric Foner, *Free Soil, Free Labor, Free Men: The Ideology of the Republican Party before the Civil War* (New York: Oxford University Press, 1970), 11–39.

41. Lincoln, *Collected Works,* 3: 479.
42. Ibid., 3: 480–81.
43. Ibid., 3: 480.
44. Ibid., 3: 481. Figure Da-C, https://hsus-cambridge-org.ezproxy.cul.columbia.edu/HSUSWeb/search/searchessaypath.do?id=Da.ESS.02.
45. Wendell Berry, *The Unsettling of America: Culture and Agriculture* (San Francisco: Sierra Club Books, 1977), 39–40.
46. A. Whitney Griswold, *Farming and Democracy* (New York: Harcourt, Brace, 1948), 15.
47. Ibid., viii.
48. Griswold's book was a sequel to Theodore Roosevelt's *Report of the Country Life Commission* (1909); Roosevelt wrote that democracy did rely on a thriving farm population but one that had to be improved. For the context, see Scott J. Peters and Paul A. Morgan, "The Country Life Commission: Reconsidering a Milestone in American Agricultural History," *Agricultural History* 78, no. 3 (2004): 289–316; and Kevin Lowe, *Baptized with the Soil: Christian Agrarians and the Crusade for Rural America* (New York: Oxford University Press, 1916).
49. Griswold, *Farming and Democracy,* 180.
50. Ibid., 36.
51. Ibid., 203, 206–7, 209–10.
52. Ibid., 204, 214.
53. For a recent critique of the agrarian ideal in Griswold's spirit, see Melissa Walker, "Contemporary Agrarianism: A Reality Check," *Agricultural History* 86, no. 1 (2012): 1–25.
54. Alan L. Olmstead and Paul W. Rhodes, "Farms and Farm Structure," *Historical Statistics Millennial Edition Online,* https://hsus-cambridge-org.ezproxy.cul.columbia.edu/HSUSWeb/toc/showEssayPath.do?id=Da.ESS.02.
55. Ibid.
56. David B. Danbom, "Romantic Agrarianism in Twentieth-Century America," *Agricultural History* 65, no. 4 (1991): 6–8.
57. Quoted ibid., 4–5.
58. Olmstead and Rhodes, "Farms and Farm Structure," Table Da612–14 and Figure Da-E.

59. Nancy Williams to Richard Bushman, June 1, 2015, in author's possession.
60. Ibid., Nancy Williams to Richard Bushman, Aug. 11, 2016, in author's possession.
61. J. Hector St. John de Crèvecoeur, *Letters from an American Farmer and Sketches of Eighteenth-Century America*, ed. Albert E. Stone (New York: Penguin, 1986), 67.

Index